PLANT

PLANT

—

EXPLORING THE BOTANICAL WORLD

Φ

Phaidon Press Limited
Regent's Wharf
All Saints Street
London N1 9PA

Phaidon Press Inc.
65 Bleecker Street
New York, NY 10012

phaidon.com

First published 2016
Reprinted 2017, 2018, 2019
© 2016 Phaidon Press Limited

ISBN 978 0 7148 7148 6

Commissioning Editor: Victoria Clarke
Project Editor: Rosie Pickles
Production Controller: Amanda Mackie
Cover Design: Julia Hasting
Interior Design: Hans Stofregen
Layout: Mónica Oliveira

Printed in China

Arrangement
The artworks in this book have been arranged in pairs
to highlight interesting comparisons and contrasts based
loosely on their subject, age, purpose, origin or appearance.
This organizational system is not definitive and many other
arrangements would have been possible. A chronological
survey of botanical art can be found in the timeline at the back.

Dimensions
Dimensions are listed by height then width. Digital images
have variable dimensions, unless the artist has chosen to
make prints of a specific size. Where differences in dimensions
exist between sources, measurements listed refer to the
illustrated version.

Titles and Plant Names
Many of the artworks in this book have been given titles
that may not necessarily reflect the contemporary Latin name
for the plant. In these instances, the correct scientific name
for the plant is included in the text.

DEPICTING THE NATURAL WORLD: THE ART OF BOTANY

Drawing and painting flowers is one of our earliest instincts as very young children. Whether it's their colour, their shape or our in-built understanding of their transience, something about plants tempts us to try to replicate them on paper almost as soon as we can pick up a crayon or brush.

An awareness of plants seems to be hard-wired in the human brain, reflecting perhaps the central role wild plants played as food for early hunter-gatherers, or perhaps their aesthetic beauty, which has been lauded by poets, scholars and artists for millennia. Plants were one of the first subjects to be painted by early artists, after animals and humans themselves. The earliest known recognizable images of plants were created some 5,000 years ago in the Fertile Crescent of the eastern Mediterranean. Other early cultures depicted plants in rock paintings, friezes and frescoes from South Africa to Australia, from China and Central Asia to the Middle East, Egypt and the Mediterranean islands of Bronze Age Greece.

From the beginning, some of these depictions were merely aesthetic. Most, however, were intended to depict particular plants so as to make them recognizable to the viewer. This led rapidly to close observation of (and a concentration on) the details that distinguish plants from one another, a characteristic that underpins the enduring value of plant illustration in scientific study, where it is still used to identify and classify specimens. From the nineteenth century until today, countless artists have been enthralled not only by plants but also by the discipline of botanical art and the study of plants.

At the heart of all botanical art is the intention to document a plant's appearance: to immortalize it by reproducing its essential characteristics. The ways in which artists set out to achieve this common purpose, however, has varied widely in both form and approach. Hasty sketches made in the field, meticulously stippled and hand-coloured engravings, oil paintings and watercolours, paper découpage, glass models, iron or Plexiglass sculptures, impressions 'nature printed' from plants, high-resolution electron-scanning microscopy and photography: the varied forms of botanical art over the centuries have echoed the variety of art in general. *Plant: Exploring the Botanical World* reflects this wide variety of media and investigates the broad range of motivations that have stimulated botanical art throughout history. Often, these motivations are practical. Pictures are more effective than words at helping a viewer to identify a plant, and diagrams or drawings served as 'shopping lists' for apothecaries mixing early cures for illness or disease. At times, as with the case of poisonous plants, accurate identification of a plant can be literally a matter of life or death. Other motivations are more scientific. Since the eighteenth century,

plants have been classified largely according to a system introduced by the Swedish botanist Carl Linnaeus that depends on accurate observation of their reproductive organs. The accurate illustration of new species, therefore, became of paramount importance in deciding how to classify them (and what to name them). Botanical illustrators have also been prompted by commerce, whether to record the characteristics of useful plants that might be introduced to a new region during the colonial age or to illustrate seed catalogues to tempt amateur gardeners from the mid-nineteenth century onwards.

The most enduring motivation behind botanical art, perhaps despite its scientific origins, has been aesthetic. Flowers, in particular, have been constantly reproduced in botanical art because of their beauty or dramatic spectacle. This was as true of the ancient frescoes of lilies that decorate a bedroom wall in Thera, Greece, as it is of the beautiful flower albums painted in the early seventeenth century for the delectation of wealthy Europeans.

Many themes recur in botanical art across the centuries. The ancient Egyptian attempt some 3,500 years ago to record all the plants of the recently captured Syria was echoed centuries later by European efforts to record the flora of their global colonies. The painted illustrations that accompanied early medieval herbals – manuscripts of natural remedies – as aids to identifying species have their contemporary parallels in field guides to, say, wild flowers or monographs on one particular group of related plants. The scientific plates of the eighteenth century, in which plants were 'dissected' and their details magnified and itemized to enable accurate classification, are the forerunners of electron-scanned microscopic images that reveal the cellular structure within the tiniest parts of plants.

Rather than arranging this vast array of the world's botanical knowledge chronologically or thematically, however, contrasting or complementary images have been paired in this book in a way that not only highlights the uniqueness of individual artworks and artists, but also reinforces some of the features they share. Two images of orchids, for example, present Darwin's initial sketch of one species with a dramatic twentieth-century photograph of another, later named in association with his work (see pp.58 and 59). Some of the earliest observations of plants through a microscope are paired with the latest three-dimensional images generated by electron-scanning microscopes (see p.52). Images of the same plant at different points in history or as represented by different cultures are juxtaposed – European and Japanese irises, for example (see pp.120 and 121) – or those that bring together plants with contrasting characteristics, such as a sunflower with a night-blooming cactus (see pp.128 and 129).

THE ORIGINS OF BOTANICAL ART

The changing purposes of botanical art reflect the changing role of plants in human life. Early peoples saw plants as gifts of the gods, and thus they were closely associated with ritual and religion. The crowns of olive leaves awarded to victors at the Olympic Games in ancient Greece show how plants were already developing symbolic associations suggested by their natural qualities. Myths grew up around them to explain, for example, how the narcissus was created from a youth who stared at his own beauty in a reflecting pool until he turned into a flower, or the hyacinth from a man who was tragically killed attempting to catch Apollo's discus.

The correct identification of plants was necessary not only for efficacious ritual but also for effective healing: the gods gave plants special powers that could be unlocked by shamans, priests or witches. With the development of writing and the spread of papyrus and other writing materials, however, the knowledge of herbal cures was written down as part of a systematic development of medicine in the classical world. In southern Europe the great treatises of the fathers of botany – Theophrastus of Eresos, Pliny the Elder and Dioscorides – codified knowledge about the properties of plants. More than a millennium later, the works of these natural philosophers served as the basis of the texts of medieval medicinal herbals. *De Materia Medica*, written by Dioscorides in the first century BC, was probably illustrated by the artist and physician Crateuas, making it one of the earliest known illustrated books on medicinal plants.

After the fall of Rome in AD 476, Europe entered the period that was later known – somewhat unfairly – as the Dark Ages, when the preservation of knowledge was largely limited to the scriptoria of cathedrals and monasteries. The Greek and Roman classics were passed on mainly through scholars in the Islamic world, where plant illustration was commonly used for medicinal instruction. Early natural-history paintings of flowers and birds were produced by artists in Persia (Iran), Mesopotamia and India from the first century AD onwards. The medicinal and culinary use of plants remained very important to the Islamic world, and was recorded by scholars such as the twelfth-century Andalusian physician Abu Ja'far al-Ghafiqi (see pp.268 and 269).

Such scholars often repeated earlier herbals while adding their own remedies for particular physical ailments. Their work fused realistic folk cures with fabulous ingredients, such as unicorn horn, but the illustrations had a simple purpose: to enable the user to identify correctly which plant to use in which cure. All the illustration was done by hand, often copying prototypes from earlier herbals, which in some cases gradually became less and less like the originals until they were almost unidentifiable, even with the accompanying written descriptions.

In medieval Europe, meanwhile, flowers had developed a complex religious symbolism, often representing purity or similar Christian values. They formed the backgrounds to tapestries and other luxury artworks commissioned by wealthy nobles. A related symbolism is evident in the paintings of the Renaissance, which started in about 1350. With the general growth of knowledge – prompted in part by the rediscovery of classical learning through Islamic texts – and the emergence of figurative art coupled with the development of perspective, plants became widely studied. In the version of Leonardo da Vinci's *Virgin of the Rocks* (c.1483–86) in the Louvre, for example, the foreground is full of botanically accurate flowers: an iris, symbolizing hope; Jacob's ladder, *Polemonium*, symbolizing the desire to ascend to Heaven; and stars of Bethlehem, *Ornithogalum*, which are symbols of purity and atonement. (The flowers in a second version of the painting, in the National Gallery in London, are so unconvincing that experts believe they are not by Leonardo at all.)

A WIDER BOTANICAL WORLD

The invention of printing with movable type in the mid-fifteenth century allowed a wider circulation of herbals; they were often accompanied by illustrations, some of which were coloured by hand. Many early printed herbals were still based on classical prototypes reintroduced from the Islamic world, but there was also a new impulse to observe and record plants from life. The European world was growing larger, so herbalists were increasingly faced with plants for which there were no existing illustrations to copy. The great Italian trade republics such as Venice and Genoa had extensive contacts with the Islamic Ottoman Empire and became a route by which new species could enter Europe. Ogier Ghiselin de Busbecq, for example, the Austrian ambassador at the Ottoman court in the mid-sixteenth century, sent tulips home, and other popular flowering bulbs followed a similar route. So thrilling were these new arrivals at a time when Europe's wealth was growing that in the early seventeenth century the tulip caused the first stock-market bubble. Dutch investors rushed to invest in the bulbs, paying several times the average yearly salary for a single bulb before 'Tulipomania' ended as suddenly as it began (see p.112). The crash ruined thousands.

Meanwhile, navigators from Portugal had sailed around the southern tip of Africa to establish a sea route to India and Asia. Again, the tropics provided flora unknown to Europeans, but one of the key impulses behind these voyages of discovery was to challenge the Islamic monopoly on the valuable trade in spices from the islands of what is now Indonesia. In 1492 Christopher Columbus crossed the Atlantic on behalf of Spain and reached the Americas – only a couple of years later, he brought the first pineapple to Europe – and he was followed by Portuguese sailors who reached Brazil, which they named after its valuable brazilwood.

The influx of medicinal, decorative and food plants during this Age of Discovery from the fifteenth to the eighteenth century astounded Europeans, and botanical artists were at the forefront of the dissemination of the new information. The first known illustration of a South American pineapple was sketched by the Spanish explorer Gonzalo Fernández de Oviedo y Valdés in 1547 (see p.152). The arrival of new plants in Europe prompted the works of the great herbalists of the sixteenth and seventeenth centuries, including such pioneers as Otto Brunfels, Hieronymus Bock, Rembert Dodoens, Charles de l'Ecluse (Carolus Clusius), Matthias de l'Obel and Leonhart Fuchs. They accurately observed and described new plants alongside the older ones, obliging their illustrators to achieve new levels of accuracy (aided by improved methods of reproduction, such as engraving).

THE AGE OF REASON

The so-called Age of Reason, which broadly encompasses the sixteenth to the eighteenth century, introduced a new spirit of scientific enquiry in Europe and North America. Wealthy 'natural philosophers', as botanists and other scientists were known, collected unusual plants in their gardens or in 'cabinets of curiosity'. The interest extended to the highest levels of society – the monarchs of France, for example, paid great attention to their royal gardens – and many such wealthy patrons employed artists to make a permanent record of their botanical treasures. The celebrated French plant illustrator

Pierre-Joseph Redouté was the official flower painter to both Queen Marie Antoinette and, after he survived the French Revolution in 1789, Napoleon Bonaparte's empress Joséphine (see p.170).

Meanwhile, the focus of botanical research gradually shifted from herb gardens dedicated to purely medicinal plants to more comprehensive botanic gardens – of which the first opened in Padua, Italy, in the sixteenth century – dedicated to studying plants in general. The invention of the compound microscope in the Netherlands in the 1620s and its rapid improvement allowed botanists to study previously invisible details of plants. The study of botany became its own scientific discipline, separate for the first time from the study of medicine. Herbals became less common, replaced by books known as flora and florilegia, which concentrated not on the medical properties of plants but on their classification and – sometimes exclusively – on their beauty.

The emergence of flora (collections of all the plants of a particular region) coincided with a growth of nationalism as the modern nation-states of Europe began to take shape. Cataloguing the local flora became an expression of national pride. As European states conquered new regions, flora became a way to record local plants, particularly those hitherto unknown, those of great beauty and those that might have a practical use. The term florilegium, meanwhile, means 'gathering of flowers', and originally referred to a literary anthology. By the sixteenth century it had reverted to a literal meaning: there had been a market since the Dutch bulb craze for true-to-life depictions of beautiful flowers, particularly exotics, which were gathered into albums based, for example, on a species, a region, a particular garden – virtually anything – without necessarily having a unifying theme.

CLASSIFYING PLANTS

The need to identify and classify new imports encouraged the development of a systematic approach to botany. An increasing understanding of the means of reproduction of flowers – the 'male' stamen produces pollen, which is carried on the wind or by insects, birds or other pollinators and deposited on the 'female' stigma of another plant – also led botanists and others to pay closer attention to the parts of flowers and become aware of the potential of artificial cross-breeding. In this fast-changing world, where new information was accumulated constantly, accurate botanical illustration became essential to botanists such as John Ray, Joseph Pitton de Tournefort and Carl Linnaeus, who were attempting to develop a new system of taxonomy – classification – that would encompass all living plants.

Linnaeus introduced a system of classification in the early eighteenth century by showing that plants' sexual organs – the number and arrangement of the female pistils and male stamens – could be used to show close or distant relationships among flowering plants. This led to his monumental publication *Species Plantarum* in 1753, in which he classified some 6,000 plants in this way and introduced in his binomial system a simpler 'shorthand' method of naming them. This system had been used by earlier botanists but became standard throughout the work of Linnaeus and others after 1753, giving each plant (and animal) a genus name and a species name, both in Latin.

Plant-hunting now became global in scale. Linnaeus sent seventeen of his own pupils or 'disciples', such as Carl Peter Thunberg (see p.136), to collect plants from around the world (a few never returned), while botanists and botanical artists became frequent passengers on European voyages of discovery. The naturalist Joseph Banks sailed to Australia on the *Endeavour* with James Cook between 1768 and 1771, for example, accompanied by the talented botanical artist Sydney Parkinson (who died on the return voyage; see p.311). For centuries important botanical records were made by artists sent by governments, universities and the increasing number of botanic gardens to accompany scientific expeditions. Meanwhile, Asian flora was also being recorded by other pioneers, from Jesuit missionaries to officials of the great trading companies – in particular the British and Dutch East India Companies – and American flora by a series of colonial British plant-hunters, before the American Revolution of 1775–83. New forms of botanical art emerged from the collaboration between European botanists and native artists, particularly in the so-called Company School in British India.

Some parts of the world remained beyond the reach of Europe's eager botanists. China was almost entirely isolated, so the enormous richness of its flora stayed largely out of reach to the West. China has its own long history of botanical illustration, however. Song Dynasty artists from the tenth to the thirteenth century depicted many medicinal and decorative plants, as well as plants that had auspicious symbolic value. The knowledge of the uses of plants increased during successive dynasties, and woodblock prints of plants were produced to illustrate pharmacopoeia (medicinal manuals). As China's prosperity increased, the noble and scholarly classes of the eighteenth century became fascinated by all things Western, culminating in the extremely lifelike and accurate portrayal of plants blending traditional Chinese and European styles.

China's neighbour Japan also barred foreigners for centuries before being forced by the Americans to open up to the world in the mid-nineteenth century. Japan has a rich and exciting heritage of botanical art represented by naturalistic watercolours and gilded screens painted with images of plants. In Europe, a new craze known as 'Japonisme' followed the eastern country's opening to Western trade after 1853, and the Impressionist artists in France produced woodblock prints depicting Japanese plants. In Japan itself artists climbed on the Western bandwagon, producing many naturalistic plant illustrations, also from woodblock prints. European botanists, meanwhile, rushed to incorporate new species from East Asia into their classification system.

THE NINETEENTH CENTURY

Botanical art took on a new importance around the middle of the nineteenth century for two reasons. The first was technological: in the late 1830s French printers began using chromolithographs, in which oil-based paints created from designs etched into stone lifelike coloured images that could be reproduced widely and cheaply (all prints had previously had to be coloured by hand). Meanwhile, experiments with light-sensitive chemicals led to the development of early photography, both through the direct exposure of objects on to light-sensitive paper and, from 1839, through the use of a camera lens. The introduction of daguerreotypes by Nicéphore Niépce and Louis Daguerre, as well as photograms and calotypes invented by such pioneers as William Henry Fox Talbot and Anna Atkins, faithfully reproduced the physical appearance of plants. Such images aided botanists in their detailed examination of the anatomy of plants, which was itself part of a larger effort to understand both their cellular structure and also why particular plants grew in particular places (the forerunner of what is today called ecology).

The second reason for the renewed importance of botanical illustration came from Charles Darwin and Alfred Russel

Wallace's theory of evolution, which was outlined in *On the Origin of Species* in 1859. Observations of adaptations in nature – from the shapes of birds' beaks to the curious structure of orchids – led Darwin and other contemporary naturalists to describe an ongoing process by which plants evolve to attract pollinators. An unusual flower shape, scent or colour was no longer simply a novelty, he maintained, but part of an intricate series of adaptations to guarantee the survival of the species. Evolution has produced a range of plant forms, such as trees, shrubs, herbaceous plants, climbers and aquatics. Plants that produce bulbs and succulent stems evolved to withstand long periods of drought in dry regions; other plants have become adapted to being eaten by humans and other animals, so that their seeds can be eaten and distributed.

Some primitive plants have evolved to remain similar to their ancestors in life form and structure. Flowerless mosses and liverworts that reproduce by means of pollen-like spores probably existed on Earth more than 430 million years ago. The ferns, cycads and conifers first appeared more than 360 million years ago, and flowering plants emerged more than 130 million years ago, at the same time as the evolution of their insect pollinators. They form the great majority of all plants depicted by botanical artists. In the case of palms, bamboos and grasses the flowers are not obvious, having adapted to wind pollination without the need for showy, insect-attracting petals. In the highly modified orchids, on the other hand, complex floral adaptations attract very specific insect pollinators, even to the extent of replicating the female pheromones of certain insects in order to to attract a male insect as pollinator.

ART AND SCIENCE

Pictorial rendition based on observation of the external parts of a plant makes up only part of the story. The dissection of plant organs under a microscope was and still is a critical part of how a botanist can identify one plant from another. A good and accurate botanical drawing or painting, including diagnostic details of significant floral or vegetative parts, can make identification instant to the observer. Dissecting microscopes have brought the external features of plants such as hairs and glands readily to the naked eye. High-level microscopes have revealed the fascinating shapes of the internal make-up of plants, and of hitherto unknown structures such as pollen grains (see p.204). X-rays reveal the hidden veining on the inside of flower petals and leaves (see pp.258 and 284), while colour-enhanced micrograph scans of the simple and club-shaped glandular hairs on a tomato leaf open our eyes to yet another aspect of plant life.

Despite Linnaeus's introduction of a standard binomial system, the naming of plants remained somewhat in disarray until rules were formulated by which the names could be standardized. It was possible for one botanist to name a plant 'x' and another to call the same plant 'y'. In 1867, at a conference in Paris, the Swiss botanist Alphonse de Candolle laid out many of the 'rules' for naming plants that are still used today. The adoption of the rule whereby the earliest published botanical name is the correct one came later, however, and the International Code of Nomenclature that is today recognized worldwide is tweaked and updated every five years.

Botanical art remains crucial to this ongoing process. Every plant must have a type specimen, on which a name is based and to which all later collections can be compared, to ensure its identity and therefore the long-term stability of its name. If there is no 'type' specimen – a sample preserved in a recognized herbarium of dried plants – a botanical illustration can serve instead.

MODERN DEVELOPMENTS

The twentieth century brought a broadening of the types and creators of botanical art. Advances in photography, in particular, attracted practitioners from fields such as fashion and advertising – Irving Penn (see p.201) and Inez van Lamsweerde and Vinoodh Matadin (see p.141), for example – while other artists, such as Stella Ross-Craig, Margaret Stones and Pandora Sellars, sought to replicate the faithfulness of photography while using the detailed approach of earlier botanical illustration to provide more scientific information than a photograph could convey. Meanwhile, the influence of abstract and surrealist art was reflected in portraits of plants that embraced unusual framing or simplistic, distorted shapes, such as those produced by the American photographer Imogen Cunningham (see p.198).

Today, although diploma courses now train botanical artists as specialist professionals, fresh eyes continue to redefine our ideas of what constitutes 'botanical art'. Nick Knight's photographs of dried, pressed plants have been colour-enhanced to 'bring them back to life' (see p.241). Close-up photographs create depictions of flowers or parts of flowers that are very precise – but can be unrecognizable even as plants, let alone as specific species. These new ways of depicting the real world are balanced by new messages that can be conveyed through the auspices of botanical art. Alberto Baraya's *Herbario de plantas artificiales* (*Herbarium of Artificial Plants*), for example, is a collection of plastic flowers presented as a parody of colonial exploitation (see p.243). The American artist E. V. Day, meanwhile, uses wire frames to magnify and distort lily leaves until they resemble a Buddhist mandala, a microcosm of the universe (see p.193). Such explorations take the concept of botanical art to an almost mystical dimension (although one that is nothing like as mysterious as the fantasy botanical artwork that accompanies the fifteenth-century Voynich manuscript, which is written in a script that has never been deciphered despite the labour of many academics).

Botanical art remains at heart, however, concerned with the process of identification and preservation that has long been its central purpose. In May 2016 scientists at the Royal Botanic Gardens at Kew published the first study of the status of world flora. They estimated that 369,400 flowering plants were known to science, of which a fifth were in danger of extinction from habitat loss, climate change and other factors. Yet they also noted that plants continue to be discovered at a remarkable rate, mainly in China, Brazil and Australia: 2,034 in 2015 alone, including ninety new species of *Begonia* and one of the humble onion. With discovery continuing at such a rate, botanical art – whether in the form of illustrations or as digital images on tablets and smartphones – remains an essential global conduit for our shifting knowledge of the natural world and a platform for things to come.

Dr James Compton
Botanist and plant collector

Rosa centifolia: Rosier à cent feuilles, 1820
Hand-coloured stipple engraving, 23 × 32 cm / 9 × 12¾ in
Lindley Library, Royal Horticultural Society, London

Les roses, the series of plates by the renowned botanical artist Pierre-Joseph Redouté in which this cabbage rose appeared, was published during an epochal time in French history. On 2 December 1804 Napoleon Bonaparte crowned his wife, Joséphine, Empress of the French in Paris. Four months later Joséphine made Redouté 'plant painter of her Majesty', with a yearly salary of 18,000 francs, then a huge sum. At the time the publication

of the *Jardin de la Malmaison*, about Joséphine's garden near Paris, was approaching completion. It was lavishly illustrated, with colour-printed stipple engravings based on watercolours by Redouté and descriptions by Étienne-Pierre Ventenat. *Les roses* used the same technique of stipple engraving, this time with descriptions by Claude-Antoine Thory. In this case the association with Joséphine was indirect: she had died in 1814 at Malmaison, and

the roses documented by Redouté came from various gardens in and near Paris. One, in Saint-Denis, had been owned by Jacques-Louis Descemet, previously a supplier to Joséphine, who cultivated the cabbage rose shown here. When this illustration appeared in the nineteenth installment of *Les roses* in Paris in July 1820, Descemet had already gone bankrupt due to the plundering of his garden by British troops.

MACOTO MURAYAMA

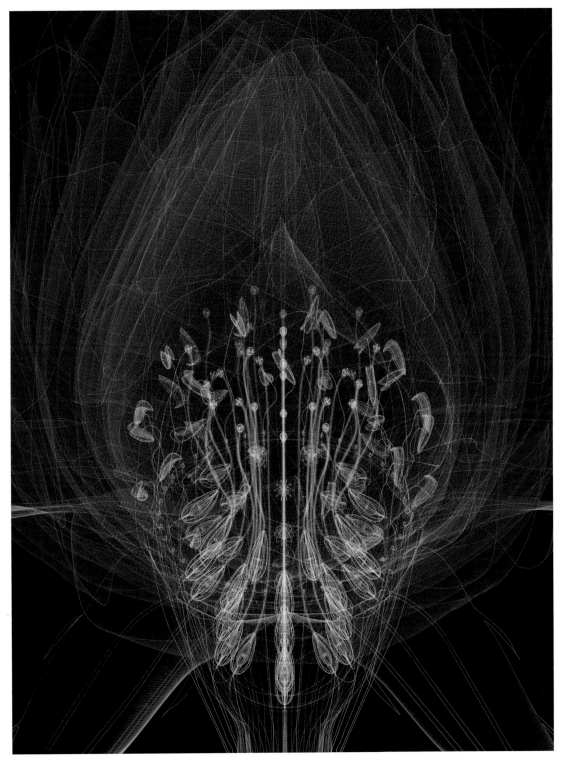

Rose III, 2008
Digital C-print, 56 × 45.7 cm / 22 × 18 in
Private collection

This 3D rendering of a rose brings together botany and architecture. The two forms have long been associated – the capitals of ancient Greek columns were carved with acanthus leaves – but the contemporary Japanese architect-turned-artist Macoto Murayama takes his fascination with plants into a luminous digital world. He uses software to render hand-drawn anatomical studies of dissected plants and flower organs with mathematical exactness,

like engineering blueprints for an alien world. Extending the conventions of architectural drawing, Murayama fuses multiple elevations and plans in a single image, often with dimensional information and labelling. The diaphanous linear mesh of the rendering program describes unfolding clusters of petals wrapped around stamens and anthers, giving the viewer X-ray vision. The ability to ascribe colour to individual parts allows Muryama to combine

technological analysis and romantic artistry. In *Rose III*, the flower takes on a balletic swirl in which the tulle-like petals enmesh the fragile organs within. The artist has exploited the potential for animation by making a film in which flowers are projected on to the gallery floor, with buds swelling and blooming as they entwine themselves to form a pastoral tapestry.

ERNST HAECKEL

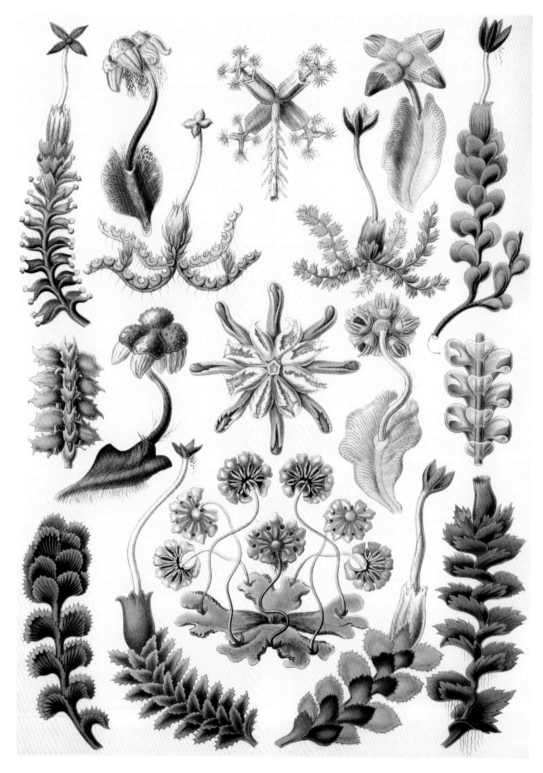

Liverworts (*Hepaticae*), from *Kunstformen der Natur*, 1899
Chromolithograph, 35.7 × 28 cm / 14 × 11 in
Bodleian Library, Oxford

The careful symmetry and balanced tonal palette of this arrangement of liverworts immediately signals that the German zoologist Ernst Haeckel was interested in decorative as well as botanical concerns. Taken from his book *Art Forms in Nature* (*Kunstformen der Natur*), the plate is intended to demonstrate the value of natural forms for ornamental design. Most of the plates in fact portrayed the marine invertebrates that were Haeckel's main area of interest. He was a zoologist who dedicated much of his career to gathering evidence to support Charles Darwin's theory of evolution by studying organisms within their environment – a study still known by the name Haeckel invented for it, ecology. Although he was criticized for exaggerating illustrations to support his arguments, he was a talented botanical illustrator. Despite the decorative arrangement, this plate still conveys important information about liverworts, simple plants that can be distinguished from mosses because the leaves lack midribs and are not arranged spirally. Haeckel's plate shows both major types of liverwort: leafy (with opposite ranks of usually two-lobed leaves) and thalloid (forming a thick mass without leaves). The arrangement depicts species from both above and below (as at bottom left and bottom right).

ERICH J. GESKE

Maidenhair spleenwort (*Asplenium trichomanes*), from *National Geographic*, 1925
Colour lithograph, 17.5 × 22.5 cm / 6¾ x 5 in
National Geographic, Washington, DC

This painting, which accompanied an article entitled 'Ferns as a Hobby' in *National Geographic* magazine in 1925, depicts the maidenhair spleenwort, *Asplenium trichomanes*, with its fronds spread in a rosette and a detail of a pinna. Described by the caption as the 'daintiest of North American ferns', the plant is also widespread. The American artist Erich J. Geske painted the fern at a slightly reduced scale, and the pinna with young sori shown above magnified twenty times. A section of notes on the plates – by either Geske or the article's author, William R. Maxon of the United States National Herbarium – emphasized the 'beautiful color contrast afforded by its dark clear-green pinnae and shining, purplish brown, threadlike stalks'. Geske is a shadowy figure, known for two picture essays in *National Geographic* in 1921 and 1925, on grasses and ferns respectively. He contributed eight plates of grasses to an article he wrote with W.J. Showalter, and sixteen plates of ferns to Maxon's article. They were described as paintings, but the medium was not specified further. They all made use of black backgrounds, rather in the manner of eighteenth-century German cabinet pictures, although whether Geske was aware of that tradition is not clear.

FERDINAND BAUER

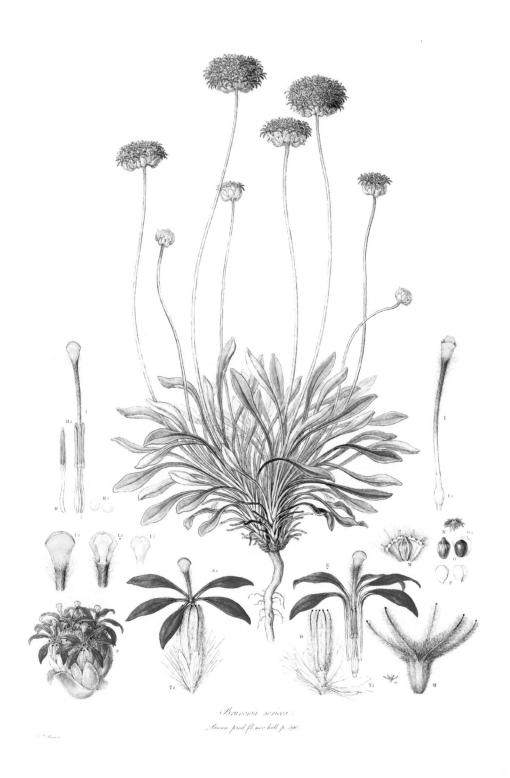

Blue pincushion (*Brunonia australis*), 1814
Hand-coloured copper engraving, 46.5 × 30.5 cm / 18¼ x 12 in
Natural History Museum, London

This hand-coloured engraving of the Australian blue pincushion (*Brunonia australis*) by the early nineteenth-century Austrian artist Ferdinand Bauer – brother of the equally celebrated botanical painter Franz Bauer (see opposite) – is clear evidence of the idea that progress in science often means paying more attention to detail and as a consequence gaining a better understanding of a fact. Bauer, who accompanied the English sailor Matthew Flinders as artist in the exploration of the Australian coast in 1801 and 1802, made four illustrations of the plant. In August 1802 he prepared a pencil outline drawing showing the plant in the wild in what is now Queensland. Later, he produced in London a line drawing that was published in the *Transactions of the Linnean Society* in 1811. This was followed by an undated watercolour prepared for the Admiralty. Bauer also engraved a copper plate for his *Illustrationes plantarum Novae Hollandiae* and had prints made that he coloured with his own hand in 1814. Compared to the original line drawing, the later versions show how Bauer's new study of the plant has increased his understanding: in the watercolour he added the fruit, seed and embryo; for the copper engraving, he adds another advance: two enlarged pollen grains.

FRANZ BAUER

Bird of paradise (*Strelitzia reginae*), c.1818
Watercolour on paper, 52.7 × 35.7 cm / 20¾ × 14 in
Natural History Museum, London

Many common ornamental plants occur naturally only in small areas. One of them is the spectacular bird of paradise (*Strelitzia reginae*), which is indigenous to a small region in the Eastern Cape Province of South Africa. Francis Masson, Kew Gardens' first plant-hunter, is reported to have been the first to bring this eye-catching plant into cultivation in Britain. The first illustration of it was published by the botanist and engraver John Miller in 1777; eleven years later

Daniel MacKenzie produced a copper engraving based on a drawing by James Sowerby (see p.256), who had documented a specimen cultivated in the garden of Sir Joseph Banks at Spring Grove in Isleworth, now west London. The former carried the name *Strelitzia reginae*, which is a dedication to the British queen Charlotte, who was born Princess of Mecklenburg-Strelitz. When Franz Bauer published his monograph *Strelitzia depicta* in 1817, illustrating

S. reginae and what later became known as *S. nicolai*, the Queen's life was approaching its end. Bauer's illustrations were considered to be of such superior quality that no text was printed except for that on the title page. The exceedingly rare slim, large-format volume contains only eleven lithographs, hand-coloured by Bauer. They are regarded by many as the first botanical illustrations produced using this new printing technique.

Gardenia volkensii subsp. *spatulifolia*, from *Trees of Central Africa*, 1956
Watercolour on paper, 25.2 × 17.5 cm / 9¾ × 6¾ in
Royal Botanic Gardens, Kew, London

The South African artist Olive Coates Palgrave included details of the dissected flower and ripe fruit in her watercolour of the small tree *Gardenia volkensii* subsp. *spatulifolia*. She began painting a series of watercolours of the trees of central Africa on pleasant excursions into the bush in the 1920s, little thinking that it would turn into a serious project and occupy her for the next twenty-eight years. Palgrave was born in South Africa in 1889, but her family moved to Southern Rhodesia (now Zimbabwe) in 1900 to join her father, who had left five years earlier. Her school botany teacher, Bertha Stoneman, had encouraged her love of plants, and when Palgrave's three children were small, she mosquito-proofed the pram and took them on plant-finding excursions; later they enjoyed catching butterflies and helping her to cut the specimens. Her bold but graceful watercolours included details of the leaves, flowers, fruit and seeds and were beautifully arranged. Palgrave's son Keith, who studied botany at university, provided a descriptive text for each of her 110 paintings, and they were published as *Trees of Central Africa* in 1956. The book became an essential guide, and the theme was continued by Keith and his wife, Meg Coates Palgrave, in a succession of books that reused Olive's pictures.

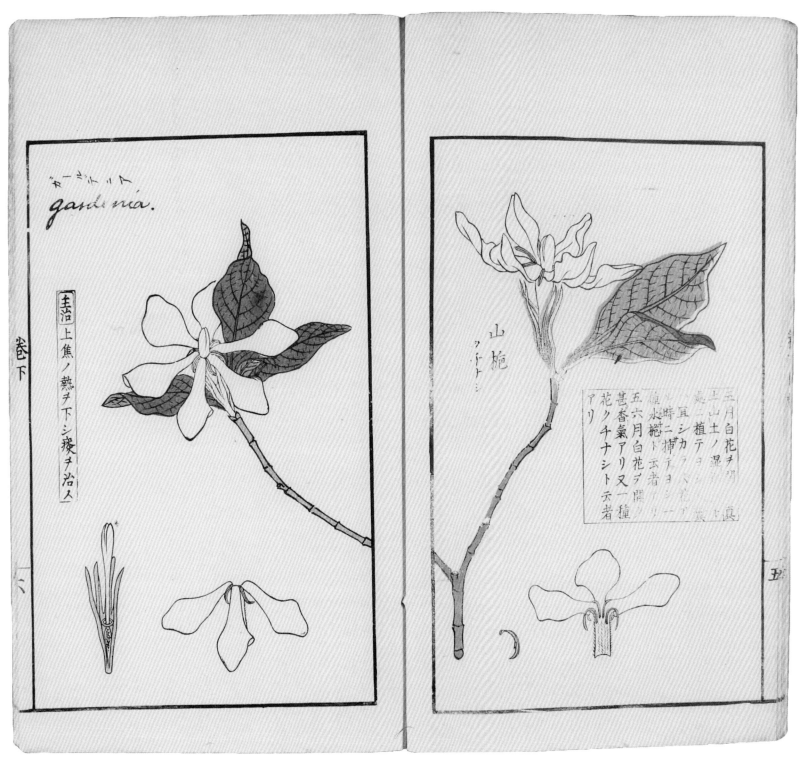

Gardenia jasminoides, from *Sōmoku kajitsu shashin zufu*, 1842
Colour woodblock print, 75 × 47.8 cm / 29½ × 18¾ in
Waseda University Library, Tokyo

This delicate woodblock of a gardenia offered Europeans a rare glimpse of Japanese botanical illustration near the end of a period of more than 200 years when foreigners – beyond those associated with the Dutch trading post at Nagasaki – were barred from Japan. When the country's military rulers assigned the artist Kawahara Keiga to document goods arriving at Nagasaki, they did not intend to begin a two-way exchange, but Kawahara also produced hundreds of drawings of Japanese plants for Philipp Franz von Siebold, an agent for the Dutch East India Company. Siebold later used them as the basis for the illustrations in his *Flora Japonica* (1835–70). Kawahara published seventy-six of his original drawings as *Keiga Shashin sō* (1836), including details of flowers and fruits, as required by Siebold. Kawahara's book, however, was not organized by Linnaean classes, and the commentary was based on ancient Chinese *materia medica*. The Japanese word *shashin* – which now means photograph – originally meant to copy or imitate truth, so Kawahara's title was the equivalent of early modern European botanists and artists claiming that their illustrations were 'drawn from life'. This illustration comes from a later edition printed as *Sōmoku kajitsu shashin zufu* (*Illustrations of Plants and Fruits*).

ANONYMOUS

Capparis spinosa (Capparidaceae), 1848–50
Watercolour, pencil and ink on paper, 27.3 × 38.3 cm / 10¾ × 15¼ in
Royal Botanic Garden Edinburgh

Long purple stamens rise in delicate clumps from the flowers of *Capparis spinosa* (in the family *Capparidaceae*) in this nineteenth-century watercolour drawing. The young flowers of this shrubby perennial are familiar in the kitchen as strongly flavoured capers, they open at night and fade by midday, or earlier in hot weather. The plant grows from Spain eastwards to the drier parts of India, where this example was painted by an artist trained by the East India

Company. It comes from a series of paintings of specimens cultivated in the botanic garden at Dapuri, near Poona (now Pune), Bombay (now Mumbai), most of which were made under the instruction of Alexander Gibson between 1827 and the 1840s. A Company surgeon and trained botanist, Gibson became director of the garden in 1838. Some of the illustrations show native Indian plants, but many are of exotic plants introduced to India for

ornamental or economic use, either culinary or medicinal. The names of the artists are not recorded, but the style of this image is more sophisticated than some of the earlier Company School paintings from Calcutta, with more natural shading and the careful disposition of the leaves to show both faces.

neg◊stil_03, 2015
C-print, 29.4 × 22.4 cm / 11½ × 9 in
Private collection

There is little realistic about this chromogenic print by the German photographer Thomas Ruff – and yet it is a precise depiction of what are probably three separate stems of European heliotrope (*Heliotropium europaeum*) created by combining positive and negative imagery. By digitally manipulating sepia-toned albumen prints, Ruff lends the plant a solid, almost three-dimensional effect that contrasts with its otherworldly background. This image is the result of Ruff's exploration of a technique known as the 'photogram', a camera-less photographic method that originated with the pioneer photographers of the mid-nineteenth century and which was employed by photographers such as the surrealist Man Ray (see p.320) in the early twentieth century. The technique continues to appeal to contemporary photographers seeking to recapture a more direct relationship between objects and their representation. Using this technique, an image is created by placing an object on light-sensitive paper and exposing it to light, thus removing the involvement of a lens. The result is a negative shadow image that produces a ghostly, translucent effect. Thomas Ruff, who studied and later taught at the Kunstakademie in Düsseldorf, has covered a wide variety of subjects from portraits to studies of buildings, the night sky and nudes.

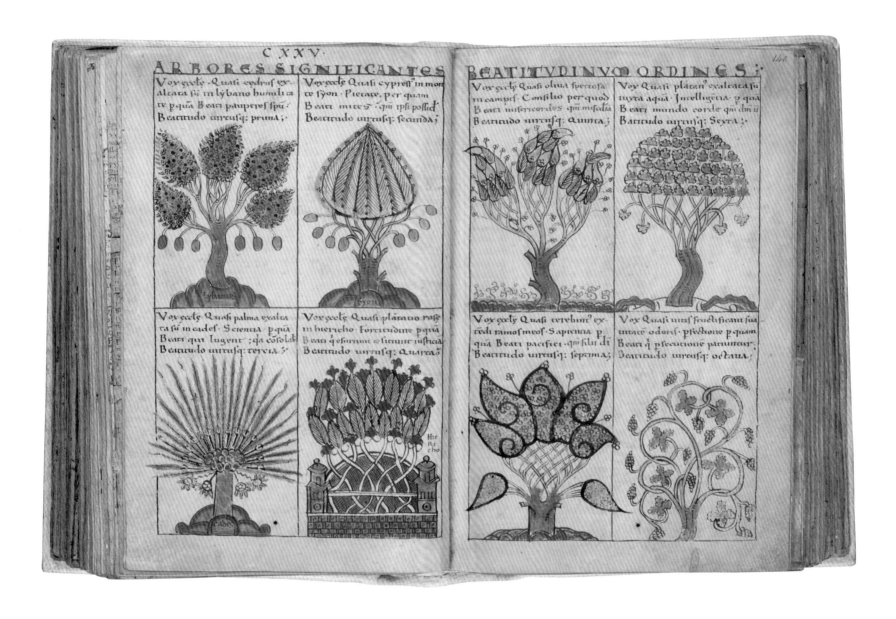

Pages from *Liber Floridus*, c.1121
Ink and colour on parchment, 32.7 × 23.9 cm / 12¾ × 9½ in
Ghent University Library, Belgium

The eight plants depicted on these pages from an early twelfth-century encyclopedia may be stylized, but they are easily identifiable. At top left a cedar is perched on Mount Lebanon; beneath it is a palm. Next to the cedar, a cypress on Mount Syon has cones dangling from its branches (like those on the cedar and the dates on the palm). Beneath it a red rose is trained over the walls of Jericho. Next an olive tree sports tiny olives, and beneath it a terebinth (turpen- tine tree) is identifiable by the curving galls on its leaves. At top right, water gushes from the roots of an oriental plane, as folklore ordained, while below it a grapevine twirls its branches. Ecclesiasticus 24 mentions all these trees and the rose of Jericho (not actually a rose), and Lambert's text links them to the Beatitudes from Christ's Sermon on the Mount. The encyclopedia was written by Lambert, the Benedictine abbot of Saint-Omer in northern France, who between 1090 and 1121 compiled historical chronicles, astronomy, a bestiary, maps, theology and music into what he named *Liber Floridus*, a 'book of flowers', suggesting that readers, like bees, might 'fly thither for the sweetness of its heavenly potions'.

PIA ÖSTLUND

Oak leaf (*Quercus robur*), 2013
Nature print à la poupée, 18 × 26.5 cm / 7 × 10½ in
Private collection

The Swedish-born printmaker Pia Östlund's oak leaf has the feel of a herbarium specimen that almost invites the viewer to feel its texture. Östlund, who moved to London in 1997 to study graphic design, created the image using a method known as nature printing. In its earliest form, in the fifteenth century, botanists would simply apply ink to a leaf or plant and press it on to paper to leave an exact impression, known as an *ectypa*. In 1853 a more refined process was patented by the Austrian Alois Auer. It involved pressing a plant into a sheet of lead to make an imprint, which was then copied on to a copper intaglio printing plate and printed *à la poupée* – a laborious method of hand-colouring the plate to produce greater tonal subtlety. Östlund came across the technique while working at Chelsea Physic Garden in London, where she found a copy of *Ferns of Great Britain and Ireland* by Thomas Moore, published in 1855 with nature prints by Henry Bradbury (see p.300). Not only did Östlund decide to revive the lost technique, but also she received an MA from the University of Reading in 2013 for her thesis *The Subjective Nature of Nature Printing*, a history of the medium from 1852 to 1860.

Trees, from *The I'nen Garden*, mid-17th century
Ink, colour and gold on paper, 154 × 357.8 cm / 60¾ × 140¾ in
Freer Gallery of Art, Smithsonian Institution, Washington, DC

Almost unnoticed on the extreme right panel of this six-fold Japanese screen is the red seal known as I'nen seals, that gives this double-screen work its name, *The I'nen Garden*. On this screen, against a background of gold leaf the artist has portrayed at least eight varieties of tree with contrasting shapes and colours of leaves and needles, including Japanese fir (*Abies firma*), Japanese black pine (*Pinus thunbergii*), umbrella pine (*Sciadopitys verticillata*) and *Magnolia*

kobus. Dating from the Edo period of the seventeenth century, the screen signalled a new departure in Japanese art. The Rimpa style, begun by Hon'ami Kōetsu, took natural subjects, such as flowers, trees and birds, and set them against a plain gold-leaf background. This painting was probably created by another Rimpa pioneer, Tawaraya Sōtatsu, or his studio, at a time when the Japanese were becoming increasingly interested in all aspects of botany,

from *ikebana* flower-arranging to the classification of plants and the study of imported exotics. The paintings were bought by a new class of warriors and merchants who wanted to acquire the cultural trappings of the royal court. Using revolutionary designs and painting techniques such as *tarashikomi* ('dripping in'), where paint was dropped on to a wet background, Sōtatsu and his studio created these new paintings for the new classes.

ALFRED RUSSEL WALLACE

Sugar Palm from Celebes, 1854–61
Pen and ink and pencil on paper, 10.2 × 8.9 cm / 4 × 3½ in
Natural History Museum, London

This ink sketch shows the huge feathery leaves, the disintegrating fibrous leaf stalks and the pendulous bunches of fruit (in pencil) of a sugar palm (*Arenga pinnata*) on the island of Celebes (now Sulawesi in Indonesia). The plant's sap was harvested for its sugar and fermented into palm wine and vinegar, while its fibre was used to make rope and for roofing. This sketch by the natural philosopher Alfred Russel Wallace was later engraved and enhanced by Walter Hood Fitch (see p.267) for publication in Wallace's *The Malay Archipelago* (1869), the record of an eight-year trip to Southeast Asia funded by the Royal Geographical Society. Wallace, who had previously visited Brazil as a freelance 'collector' with the entomologist Henry Walter Bates, based his narrative and illustrations on eight books of notes and sketches he kept during the trip. Visiting the island of Ternate in eastern Indonesia in 1858, Wallace wrote 'On the Tendency of Varieties to Depart Indefinitely from the Original Type', a similar theory of evolution to that for which Charles Darwin (see p.58) became renowned: indeed, the two men's essays on the subject were both read out at the same meeting of the Linnean Society of London on 1 July 1858.

Anapodophyllum canadense, from
The Natural History of Carolina, Florida and the Bahama Islands, 1731
Lithograph, 26.2 × 35.2 cm / 10¼ × 3¾ in
Missouri Botanical Garden, St Louis

This odd arrangement – a branch with wide leaves and attractive white flowers placed on top of a turtle dove – is typical of the illustrations the English naturalist Mark Catesby drew for his landmark *Natural History of Carolina, Florida and the Bahama Islands*, the first published natural history of North America and the first book of natural history to have folio-sized colour plates. Catesby often combined animals and plants in a more naturalistic way, but here he painted the branch as if it had been picked for a vase (he was not able to paint the fruit, which resembles a large yellow or reddish plum and is mildly poisonous). Catesby named the plant *Anapodophyllon canadense morini*, or Canadian duck's-foot leaf, after its deeply lobed leaves, but it has since been renamed *Podophyllum peltatum*. Recognized locally as an important medicinal plant since the early seventeenth century, it gained international recognition after Catesby sent it to Carl Linnaeus (see p.63). Catesby explored widely in Virginia, Carolina and the Caribbean, making drawings in the field and later turning them into watercolours. On his return to England he learned to etch in order to prepare the plates for his magnum opus, which took more than twenty years to complete.

MARIA MONINCKX

Aloe africana arborescens (*Aloe commixta*), from *Moninckx Atlas*, c.1700–2
Watercolour on paper, 58.5 × 42.5 cm / 23 × 16¾ in
University of Amsterdam

This lifelike watercolour of a flowering branch of the South African succulent plant *Aloe commixta* was one of 101 watercolours painted by the early eighteenth-century Dutch artist Maria Moninckx. It was produced for the nine-volume *Moninckx Atlas*, a record of 420 new and interesting plants being cultivated in Amsterdam. The atlas was conceived by Joan Huydecoper II, a director of the Dutch East India Company, and his botanist colleague Jan

Commelin, who in 1682 founded the Amsterdam Hortus Medicus, which soon became the city's Hortus Botanicus. Since the garden lacked a herbarium, unlike its rival Hortus Botanicus in Leiden, the pair commissioned the father-and-daughter artists Jan and Maria Moninckx to paint the plants arriving from the Cape and other Dutch colonies. While Jan Moninckx painted most of the 273 sheets between 1686 and 1709, Maria also contributed, as did Alida Withoos and

Johanna Merian, the eldest daughter of the renowned artist Maria Sibylla Merian (see p.207). *Aloe commixta* was one of the first plants to be listed in the Dutch East India Company's Cape Town garden, set up to provide fresh food for sailors on the Spice Islands route. The species is endemic to the Cape peninsula, but is now very rare in the wild.

LESLIE CAROL BERGE

Female Cones of *Encephalartos ferox*, 1998
Watercolour and pencil on paper, 70 × 51 cm / 27½ × 20¼ in
Shirley Sherwood Collection, London

The white background lends an abstract quality to this watercolour of the holly-leaved cycad, *Encephalartos ferox*, which the contemporary American artist Leslie Carol Berge pares down to the bright red female cones and a dramatic fan of foliage. The cycads form an ancient family of primitive plants. Fossils in Triassic rocks – from the age of the dinosaurs – suggest that cycads were once universal, but they have declined over millions of years and are now found only in Africa and Asia, with a few species in Australia. That might be because of their system of reproduction: male and female cones usually occur on separate plants, so wind or the odd beetle is essential for successful pollination. The cones vary dramatically, from these female ones resembling outsized raspberries to large pineapple-like cones and small seeds that sit on the periphery of the leafy stems. Cycad leaves are usually stiff and unfurl in the same way as those of the equally ancient ferns. Berge has specialized in painting the cycad family since a trip to the Kirstenbosch National Botanical Garden on the slopes of Table Mountain in Cape Town, South Africa. The plants are so rare in South Africa that cycad theft has become common, and some specimens are even microchipped to make them less attractive to thieves.

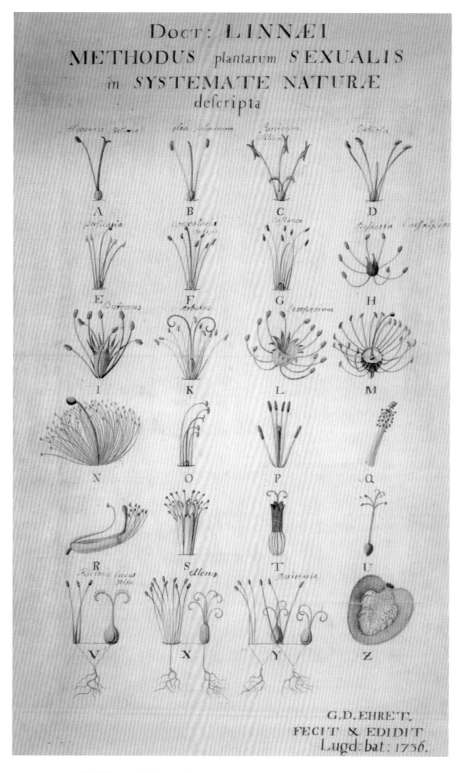

Carl Linnaeus's *Systema Naturae*, 1736, from *Genera Plantarum*, 1737
Watercolour, 33.5 × 20.7 cm / 13 × 8 in
Natural History Museum, London

This watercolour from 1736 by Georg Dionysius Ehret is the original version of one of the most iconic of all botanical images. It was the first graphic representation of the sexual system of plant classification that had been devised by the great Swedish botanist Carl Linnaeus. Ehret and Linnaeus had met recently in Holland, where the wealthy Anglo-Dutch banker George Clifford commissioned them to catalogue the rare plants in his garden (published as *Hortus Cliffortianus* in 1737, see p.63). Linnaeus had realized that flowers are actually the generative parts of flowering plants, and created a simple system for sorting plants according to the number and arrangement of their sexual organs (stamens and pistils). Linnaeus' twenty-four categories – illustrated here by Ehret – turned out to be too simple to have lasting value but his system of naming plants and animals is still in use today and has provided the world with what became, in effect, a universal scientific language. At the time, however, it enabled botanists to name and classify the mass of new plants arriving in Europe from voyages of exploration. Ehret published the illustration without Linnaeus's permission – Linneaus was furious and they fell out, but they later made up.

Plate from *Tabulae Phytographicae*, 1795
Hand-coloured engraving, 20 × 32.7 cm / 7¾ × 12¾ in
Lindley Library, Royal Horticultural Society, London

This group portrait of twelve genera of plants – represented in each case by a view of the flower and leaf, and in some cases also by fruits – was a revelation when it was created in the late eighteenth century by the Swiss botanist Johannes Gessner. The top row shows (from left to right): *Crocus*, *Colchicum*, *Sternbergia*, *Xyris*, *Aphyllanthes* and *Eriocaulon*; the middle row shows *Ixia*, *Gladiolus*, *Antholyza* (now included in *Babiana* and elsewhere), *Commelina* and

Sisyrinchium; the bottom row shows *Iris*. Gessner grouped the genera this way because they all belonged to the same class, *Triandria*, or plants with three anthers, in the classification system devised by Carl Linnaeus (see opposite). Gessner conceived the idea of a set of composite illustrations showing morphological variations within each of Linnaeus's families. On receiving the first plates in 1763, Linnaeus reported that they left him thunderstruck. Gess-

ner did not live to complete his series, however, and the incomplete work was published posthumously. Linnaeus's system of classification is now a distant memory – these plants are now distributed among six different families – but Gessner's idea of group portraits became a useful tool for botanists in the following century, with systems of classification based on less arbitrary criteria.

Knapweed (*Centaurea nigra*) and cornflower (*Centaurea cyanus*), 1689
Watercolour on paper, 38 cm × 24 cm / 15 × 9½ in
Royal Society, London

Richard Waller's watercolour of knapweed (left) and cornflower (right) appears contemporary, like meticulously observed dried specimens on a herbarium sheet: they would not look out of place in a modern botanical field guide. In fact, the painting is more than 320 years old. Waller, who was for many years secretary of the Royal Society in London, was far ahead of his time. He painted this plate in 1689 as part of a set of sixty-five images of common meadow and hedgerow plants. The paintings were never published, however: had they been, the little-known Waller might have taken his place among the most influential of scientific artists for his determination to render the natural world with the utmost accuracy. He went to the extent of teaching himself to engrave and of producing colour charts – like the Pantone charts used today – to ensure that his illustrations were lifelike.

The watercolours were probably created to illustrate *Historia Plantarum*, a three-volume work published by the British naturalist John Ray between 1686 and 1704, and intended to provide a systematic record of the natural world. It is possible that high printing costs ultimately prevented Waller's illustrations from being included in Ray's greatest work.

STELLA ROSS-CRAIG

Helichrysum cameroonense, 1930, from *Flora of West Tropical Africa*, 1931–6
Ink on paper, 30.3 × 19 cm / 12 × 7½ in
Royal Botanic Gardens, Kew, London

Stella Ross-Craig, was initiated from an early age into the discipline of plant science by her botanist father, and took evening classes in botany while she attended art college. In 1929, she became an illustrator at Kew and submitted her first illustration to the editor of *Curtis's Botanical Magazine*; over the next fifty years she went on to produce a further 300 plates for the magazine. She remained chief botanical artist at Kew until 1958. Ross-Craig's skill in line-work is most effectively demonstrated in publications such as *Drawings of British Plants*, *Flora of Tropical East Africa*, and *Flora of West Tropical Africa*, from which this illustration is taken. *Helichrysum cameroonense* is found only in Cameroon; the name *Helichrysum* comes from the ancient Greek, helix meaning 'spiral' and khrusos 'gold', denoting its crown of aromatic lemon-yellow flowers. Ross-Craig presents the various sections and magnifications required for scientific illustration, using clear composition and minimal shading to present an undiminished specimen. When living plants were unavailable, Ross-Craig would employ dried, pressed, specimens, restoring them to life with her pencil.

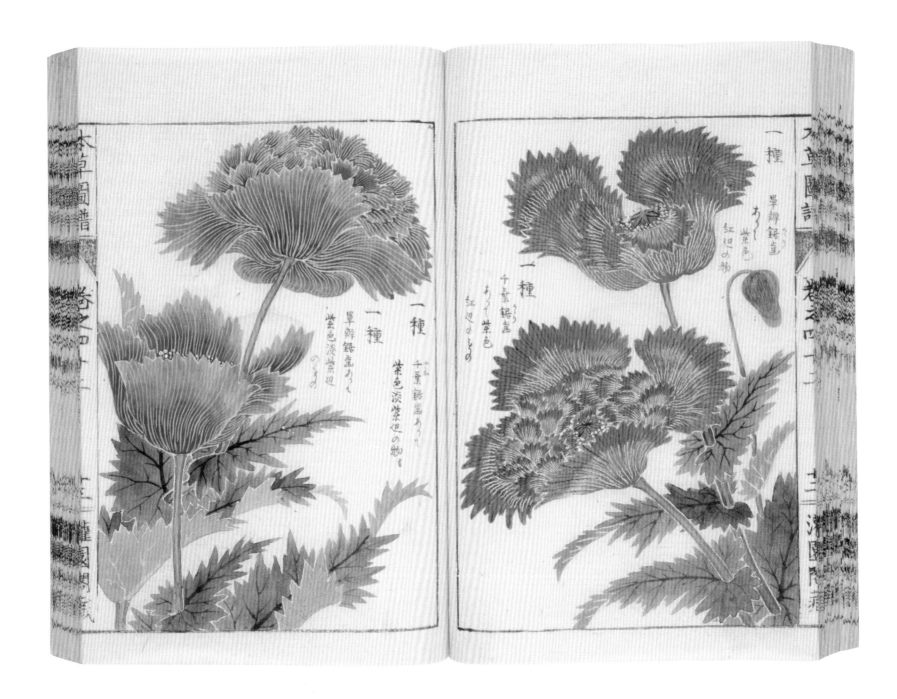

Papaver somniferum, from *Honzō Zufu*, 1920–2
Woodblock print and manuscript on paper, 26 × 33 cm / 10¼ × 13 in
The National Diet Library, Tokyo

This illustration of an opium poppy (*Papaver somniferum*) is heavily stylized. The blue colour is exaggerated – opium poppy flowers are white, pink or mauve – but the leaves are recognizably those of this species. The illustration comes from the most famous Japanese encyclopaedia of plants, the *Honzō zufu* (*Illustrated Manual of Medical Plants*), compiled by Iwasaki Tsunemasa (also called Iwasaki Kan'en) and published in ninety-six parts between 1828 and 1854. Although Japan was officially closed to foreign visitors until 1853, foreign books and other products were admitted, and some of the illustrations in the *Honzō zufu* were copied from Johann Weinmann's *Phytanthoza Icono-graphia* (1737–45); the idea of compiling the manual in the first place may have been stimulated by studying the German botanist's work. The original edition was uncoloured, but between 1920 and 1922 a new edition took advantage of Western-based printing technology to print all the illustrations in colour. (It may have been the first time the entire work was printed, for some of the later parts of the original edition circulated in manuscript only.) It is from this 1920s edition that this image is taken. The exaggerated colouring may therefore have been made for decorative rather than descriptive reasons.

Heart Flowers, 2011
Acrylic on canvas, 162 × 130.3 × 6 cm / 63¾ × 51¼ × 2½ in
Private collection

The dots of this black-and-white painting of unidentified flowers are somewhat reminiscent of Australian Aboriginal paintings of plants and animals, but in fact it was created by Japan's foremost female artist, Yayoi Kusama. Its sombre atmosphere reflects the circumstances of its creation in 2011; that March, northeastern Japan was rocked by a powerful earthquake and tsunami, which wrought devastation across a wide area and killed more than 15,000 people. Kusama's image is thus a form of memorial. She has been creating pointillist pictures for almost seven decades, usually in bright primary colours. Painting with repeated dots that form larger patterns is her way of dealing with the visual and aural hallucinations that have afflicted her since childhood: since 1975 she has chosen to live in a psychiatric hospital. She sees her art as therapy: 'I have been grappling with art as a therapy for my disease, but I suppose I would not be able to know how people would evaluate my art until after I die. I create art for the healing of all mankind.' Prolific and popular, Kusama was the subject of a touring art retrospective that made her the most seen artist of 2014, with over two million visitors drawn to her bright canvases, dotty installations and phallic compositions.

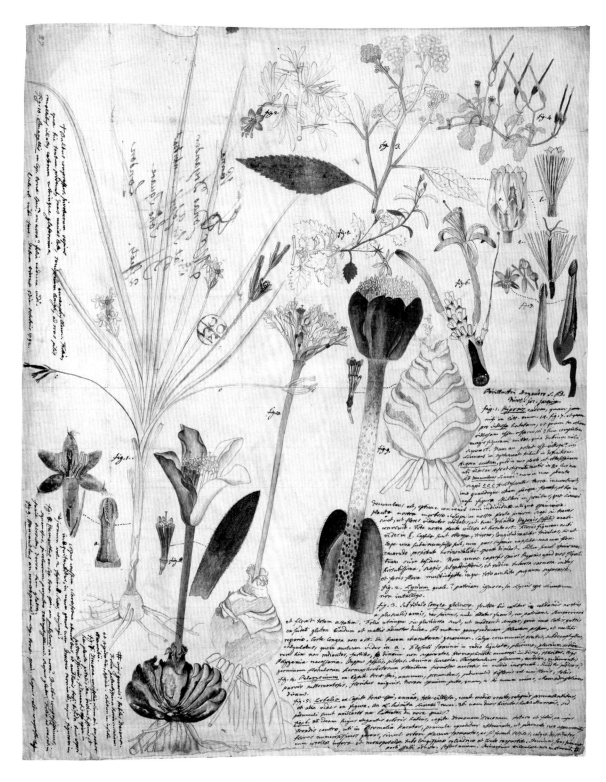

Various flowering plants, 1792
Pen and ink and watercolour on paper, 24 × 19.5 cm / 9½ x 7½ in
Natural History Museum, London

This letter carries illustrations in watercolour documenting ten plant species, including three species of the blood flower in the lower centre of the page: *Haemanthus amarylloides*, *H. coccineus* and *H. pubescens*. Dated 5 October 1792, it was sent by Nikolaus Joseph von Jacquin, a professor of botany and director of the botanic garden of Vienna University, to the Swedish botanist Jonas Dryander, librarian to the famous naturalist Sir Joseph Banks in London, and is a reminder that communication between botanists historically took many forms. Across Europe, naturalists were joined by networks of correspondence by which they exchanged not only letters, books and journals but also plant specimens, either living material such as cuttings, bulbs, fruits and seeds, or preserved material such as herbarium specimens. In addition, botanists commonly sent drawings, watercolours or prints of plants to colleagues for information or inquiry. Although it has been claimed that the illustrations shown are by Jacquin, they are probably by Johannes Scharf. Close analysis reveals that the three images of *Haemanthus* species are copies of the watercolours, now lost, that were used to prepare the copper engravings of Jacquin's famous flower book *Plantarum rariorum horti caesarei Schoenbrunnensis descriptiones et icones* (1797–1804).

Haemanthus nortieri, 2002
Ink and watercolour on paper, 30.5 × 53.5 cm / 12 × 21 in
Shirley Sherwood Collection, London

This bulb of the rare paintbrush lily *Haemanthus nortieri*, a relative of the amaryllis, had flowered only twice in twenty years when it was painted by the renowned contemporary South African botanical artist Vicki Thomas in 2002. On the left, three drawings show how the subterranean bulb (far right) produces a single red flowering stem, from the apex of which emanates a paintbrush of white flowers. To the right are two stages of the independently emerging single paddle-shaped leaf. Being sticky, it accumulates grit from the sandy soil, probably as an evolutionary defence against foragers. Thomas notes that the plant was collected in the Nardouw Mountains in the Western Cape of South Africa and grown at Kirstenbosch National Botanical Garden, where she painted it for the journal *Flowering Plants of Africa*. The paintbrush lily was first described by Linnaeus (see p.63) in 1753 and all twenty-two species are all native to southern Africa. The first to be described, by Linnaeus in 1753, had blood-red flowers, giving rise to the alternative common name of blood lily. Most species flower every year and produce attractive red, white or pink flowers followed by equally attractive berry-like fruits, which can be red, pink, orange or white. This species was only described in 1937.

Saxifraga stolonifera, 1775
Collage of coloured papers, with bodycolour and watercolour, and a leaf sample,
on black ink background, 27.5 × 18.1 cm / 10¾ × 7¾ in
British Museum, London

At first glance, this illustration of strawberry saxifrage so closely resembles a watercolour that it is hard to tell that it is in fact découpage – an arrangement of paper cut-outs on black ink. Mary Delany, a clergyman's wife who turned to découpage after her eyesight began to fail, shows the marbled leaves with their russet undersides and the inflorescence of irregular, white, star-shaped flowers. She also attaches a label with the plant's Chinese name:

'Lao – hu – er, Old – Tiger's – Ear'. The strawberry saxifrage had been very recently introduced to the West from Asia, so was still a real novelty: it was first described by William Curtis only in 1774. In Japan it had been used as a herbal remedy but it became a popular garden plant, thanks to its distinctive flowers. Mary Delany's second husband, the Irish clergyman Dr Patrick Delany, was interested in botany and gardening, while Mary honed

her artistic skill at their home in Dublin. After her husband's death in 1768, Mary spent much of her time at Bulstrode Park in Buckinghamshire with her friend the Dowager Duchess of Portland; there she met the naturalists Sir Joseph Banks and Daniel Solander. In spite of her fading eyesight, after 1771 Delany created more than 1,700 paper cut-outs in ten albums.

PHILIPP OTTO RUNGE

Hop plant (*Humulus lupulus*), c.1800
Collage on paper, 33.5 × 18.5 cm / 13¼ × 7¼ in
Hamburger Kunsthalle, Hamburg

This shoot of hop leaves captures the essence of the plant in a way that is reminiscent of early nature prints and photograms, but its lifelike quality is even more astonishing when one realizes that it is in fact a silhouette cut from a single sheet of paper. The German Romantic artist Philipp Otto Runge, who is better known for his paintings, shows not only the palmate lobes of the leaves with their serrated edges, but also – an incredible feat to achieve with nothing but scissors and scalpels – the tendrils, arranged to form loops. Silhouette portraits of people, made by cutting black paper into shapes, were a long-established tradition by the start of the nineteenth century, but Runge adapted this tradition by using white paper and cutting it into the shapes of plants. While he laboured on his more heavy-weight canvases, which combined scrupulous accuracy of natural depiction with allegorical meaning, he regarded his exercises in paper-cutting as a means of learning to depict what he described in a letter to a friend in 1809 as the 'architectonic shape and strength' of plants. More than 200 of his silhouettes depicting plants survive, most of them cut from white paper.

Mangosteen plant (*Garcinia mangostana*): fruiting branch and halved fruit, 1876
Photograph, 21.4 × 27.3 cm / 8½ × 10¾ in
Wellcome Library, London

Even for those who have never tasted the intensely sweet mangosteen (*Garcinia mangostana*), this photograph is tantalizing. An open fruit looks ready for the viewer to pick up and squeeze out the white flesh (the fruit itself is a rich purple colour), while more fruits hang invitingly above. The Scottish photographer Charles Scowen, or one of his assistants, arranged and photographed this image in Ceylon (now Sri Lanka) in 1876. The still-life quality of the image reflects the tendency of many early photographers to emulate the pictorial conventions of painting, but the photograph also echoes the scientific approach of botanical illustrators. Having arrived in Ceylon in about 1873, Scowen set up a studio in Kandy, the second city, close to the Royal Botanical Gardens at Peradeniya – at the time, with the island under British rule, an offshoot of Kew Gardens in London. The studio was known for its still lifes of tropical fruits, as well as for photographs taken in the botanic garden. The mangosteen, in Scowan's day an exotic rarity outside the tropics, remains unfamiliar to many, being confined largely to its Southeast Asian homeland: its peel is easily bruised, preventing its large-scale export.

ÁLVARO EVANDRO XAVIER NUNES

Annona crassifolia

ALVARO NUNES 2003

Araticum do cerrado (*Annona crassiflora*), 2003
Watercolour on paper, 37.8 × 53.7 cm / 14¾ × 21¼ in
Shirley Sherwood Collection, London

In this study of *Annona crassiflora*, a Brazilian relative of the custard apple, the Brazilian artist Álvaro Evandro Xavier Nunes shows the fruit in its entirety, as well as its constituent parts: seeds (top right); the development of its buds; and a cross section revealing the flesh. As this careful analysis of the different stages of the custard apple's development reflects, Nunes trained and practised as an architect, leading to an abiding interest in the structure

of plants. This relative of the custard apple, known as *araticum do cerrado* or *marolo* in Brazil, is a member of the Annonaceae, or soursop, family, which also includes the deciduous pawpaw of North America. *A. crassiflora* grows across the tropics and is notable not just for its distinctive pulpy fruit, with their large seeds, but also for its fragrant flowers. Nunes, who began studying botany in the late 1980s, often travels to remote parts of Brazil in search of

subjects. He spends up to eight months in the Amazon and Pantanal or on the Brazilian savannah, finding and drawing the fruits of native trees. In many ways, his career echoes that of the pioneering botanical artist Margaret Mee (see p.41), whose illustrations of plants painted on expeditions into the Brazilian Amazon brought the diversity of the rainforest to the fore in the 1950s and 1960s.

ANTON KERNER VON MARILAUN

Schmaroßende Balanophoreen: 1. Lophophytum mirabile, aus Brasilien. — 2. Sarcophyte sanguinea, vom Kap der Guten Hoffnung. Vgl. Text, S. 179—182.

Lophophytum mirabile and Sarcophyte sanguinea, from *Pflanzenleben*, 1887–91
Wood engraving, 12.9 × 13 cm / 5 × 5 in
Peter H. Raven Library, Missouri Botanical Garden, St Louis

This still-life arrangement of tubers reveals several stages in the growth of a secretive subterranean truffle-like existence that might otherwise go unnoticed in the deep litter of the forest floor. Only the eruption of the flowering spike betrays the existence of the little-known and even less understood parasitic plants *Lophophytum mirabile* from Brazil and *Sarcophyte sanguinea* from East Africa. After germinating near the root of a host tree, the seedling produces a sucker-like structure, or haustorium, which penetrates the host root and connects to the internal vascular system, from which the parasite gains its nutrition. The tuber then develops, enlarging gradually until it envelops the host root. Eventually it reaches maturity and a flowering shoot emerges. Both plants have proved impossible to cultivate, so this plate is a reminder of the enduring value of botanical art as a communicator of information and a springboard for exploration. It was created by the Austrian botanist Anton Kerner von Marilaun, who, after studying medicine and natural history, was appointed professor of botany at the Polytechnic Institute at Buda, Hungary, in 1858, becoming professor of natural history at Innsbruck University, Austria, in 1860. He relinquished that position in 1878 to become curator of the Vienna Botanical Garden and a professor of botany in the city.

Gustavia pulchra, 1979
Watercolour on paper, 65.4 × 47.6 cm / 25¾ × 18¾ in
Royal Botanic Gardens, Kew, London

This painting contrasts with conventional botanical illustration which isolates its subject in white space. Here, the white flowers of *Gustavia pulchra* are depicted in their habitat, the *igapó* or sunken forest of the Brazilian Amazon, with towering trees, a blue-headed hummingbird and the shadowy forest itself. The British artist who painted the scene, Margaret Mee, recalled: 'Leonardo, my Tariana Indian pilot … was steering skillfully through the stormy

waters … when I caught sight of the gleaming white flowers. The white flowers of this *Gustavia*, a relative of the brazil nut, are fragrant and ephemeral. There was no time to lose, for the wind was battering the delicate petals as I drew, seated on the deck of my little boat. Will the exquisite beauty of this species save it from extinction?' Such concerns were typical of Mee, who first travelled to Brazil in 1952 to care for an ailing sister but became

fascinated by the Amazonian flora and remained for thirty-five years. Mee repeatedly travelled to the Amazon, collecting specimens and making detailed sketches of the plants she found – four were later named in her honour – before depicting them often in situ, as here. Her skill in painting and her environmental campaigning make her an enduring influence on contemporary botanical illustrators, ecologists and conservationists.

勢川移種
今生葛西
漬塩收食
性味最齊

Radish (*Raphanus sp.*): root and leaves, 18th century
Watercolour, 21.8 × 30.3 cm/ 8½ × 11¾ in
Wellcome Library, London

The unknown Japanese watercolourist who painted this radish plant (*Raphanus sp.*) some time in the eighteenth century allowed his creative tendencies to take over in the dramatic flourish of the purple-grey leaves, where he outlines the vague shape in blended washes and inks to give the merest suggestion of veins. The darker colours draw the eye to the heart of the plant, where the stems meet the root. This image comes from a watercolour album of Japanese herbs and vegetables, and is annotated with Chinese script outlining the plant's medicinal use (Japan's *kampo* tradition of medicine is based on traditional Chinese remedies). The sulphur compounds that make the radish taste hot are said to be useful in treating stomach complaints, colds and coughs, and to stimulate digestion. The radish probably originated in Southeast Asia, but it has been widely cultivated in India, China and Central Asia (large radishes are usually referred to as *daikon* in Japan and *mooli* in India). The large white, mild radish known in Japan as *sakurajima* was in fact bred in China, but has been widely cultivated in Japan, especially on Kyushu Island. Radishes are common in Japanese cuisine, where they accompany virtually every meal, including breakfast.

ASUKA HISHIKI

Wasabi (*Eutrema japonicum*), 2011
Watercolour on paper, 37.5 × 54 cm / 14¾ × 21¼ in
Private collection

Like most Japanese people, contemporary artist Asuka Hishiki had seen only trimmed, knobbly stems of wasabi (*Eutrema japonicum*) in their markets – it is used to make a pungent condiment that is widely used in Japanese cooking. So she was astonished by the plant's enormous root system, which develops to anchor it to the rocky stream beds where it grows. In Hishiki's watercolour, the sturdy stem with its dark leaf scars like doleful eyes leans slightly above a labyrinth of roots reaching towards the edges of the paper. The artist's virtuososity permits the viewer to share in her wonder and to see the homely green vegetable as something sublime. The painting also echoes a tradition of the monstrous and grotesque in Japanese art. Hishiki's tomato portraits can also be compared to the portraits of citrus in Giovanni Battista Ferrari's baroque botanical masterpiece *Hesperides*. Although wasabi has been of great cultural importance to the Japanese for more than a thousand years, it is rarely illustrated. One of the most important early Japanese botanical works – the monumental early nineteenth-century *Honzō zufu*, with illustrations of more than 2,000 plants (see p.32) – includes a depiction of wasabi that barely shows its roots.

43

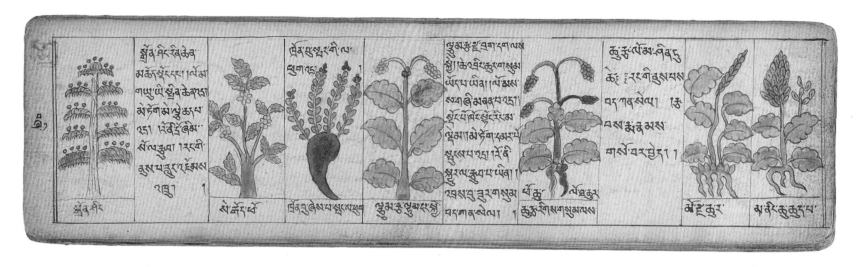

A Selection of Substances Used for the Production of Medicine
Based on the Teaching of the Four Tantras, 19th century
Ink and watercolour on paper, each 8.5 × 31 cm / 3¼ × 12¼ in
Wellcome Library, London

These fourteen plants and trees and two animals – one of which may be a yak – appear on two sheets of a Tibetan work on *materia medica*, describing the use of natural substances for medicinal purposes. The work is based on the Four Tantras: four books comprising 156 chapters containing the basic texts of medicine said to have been handed down by Buddha himself to be studied by all Tibetan physicians. The Four Tantras are considered to be a divine work. Writings on *Materia Medica* typically collected over centuries and reaching back to ancient times. Here, the text – its title translates as *A Selection of Substances Used for the Production of Medicine Based on the Teaching of the Four Tantras* – discusses how parts of plants or animals are to be applied in various remedies. The work is undated but may have been produced in the nineteenth century: experts see a similarity between these images and those in nineteenth-century Tibetan wood engravings of medical works that were available in Mongolia at the time. This text was made in the traditional manner, unbound, the loose sheets of thick paper stacked and held between two boards to act as covers and then wrapped in a piece of cloth.

Wild Emmer Wheat (*Triticum × dicoccoides*), 1352–1336 BC
Limestone carving, 23 × 52 × 4 cm / 9 × 20½ × 1¾ in
Metropolitan Museum of Art, New York

This relief of remarkably lifelike ears of wheat – they are 'bearded', with spiky bristles called awns – was carved in ancient Egypt during the reign of the pharaoh Akhenaten, from 1352 to 1336 BC. It shows emmer wheat, originally domesticated by the Egyptians at least 7,000 years earlier and similar to a wild wheat that still grows in northern Palestine and southern Syria today. The wild wheat differs from the cultivated one in that its ears shatter as soon as it ripens: the earliest farmers selected plants in which the ears remained intact, making the crop easier to harvest. Akhenaten was one of the most controversial of all Egypt's pharaohs. He forced his people to abandon their traditional gods to worship only the Aten, or sun god, and encouraged far more naturalistic styles of painting and sculpture – as here – than the established stylized images. He built a new capital city – El Amarna – whose inhabitants used emmer wheat for both making bread and brewing beer (which was more frequently made from barley or from a mixture of the two cereals). On Akhenaten's death, his religion was overthrown and his capital abandoned; he was replaced by a son destined to become far more famous than his father: Tutankhamun.

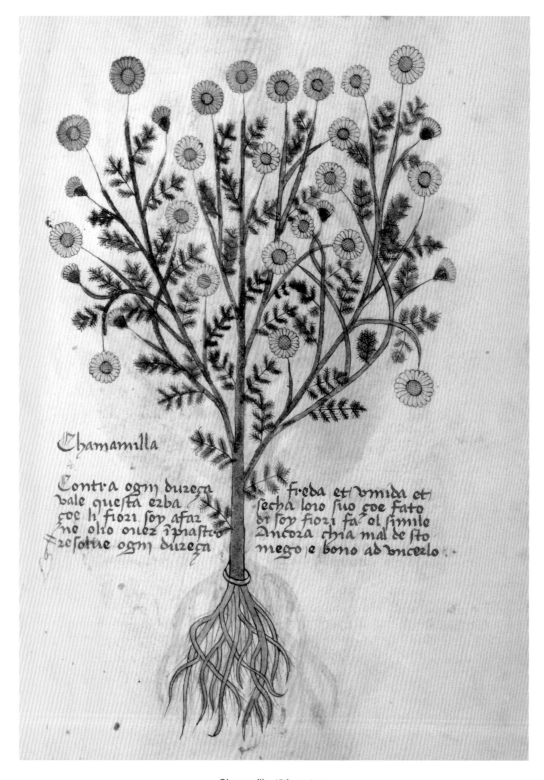

Chamamilla, 15th century
Ink and watercolour on paper, 29.1 × 20.5 cm / 11½ ×8 in
Biblioteca del Castello del Buonconsiglio
Monumenti e Collezioni Provinciali, Trento

This depiction of a chamomile plant from fifteenth-century Italy is highly stylized. The tiny flowers are blushed with golden colour, and the flat stalks arranged like the branches of a candelabra. There is little surprising in treating the plant as a rare treasure: in herbals such as this, produced in Trento, references to folklore and magic reflected both a sense of wonder at the remarkable powers of plants and people's utter dependence on plant products. The distinctive feature of chamomile (a name that encompasses several different plant species) is the smell of apple when its leaves are crushed (its name derives from the Greek for ground-apple). It was planted in medieval gardens, and possibly also on common land, where it would release its scent. The leaves taste bitter, so only the flowers were used to flavour beers for sweetness and infusions to cure everything from nightmares to intestinal disorders, inflammation and fevers. Members of the daisy family with pungent leaves, such as chamomile and tansy, were important insect repellants. From the time when chamomile was laid in the tombs of the pharaohs, daisy-like flowers were also linked to the gods and resurrection. The concept was originally practical, since mummification ointments included pungent insect-repellant plant extracts, which helped preserve the body and soul for everlasting life.

Creeping Buttercup, 2002
Etching on paper, 39 × 55 cm / 15½ × 21¾ in
Tate, London

The time it took the contemporary British artist Michael Landy to complete this life-sized etching of the creeping buttercup (*Ranunculus repens*) is reflected by the various stages of flowers it depicts, from fully open to past their prime, slipping into decay. The drawing – the composition of which underlines the plant's ability to spread and multiply – comes from Landy's portfolio *Nourishment*, a collection of plants he found growing in the hostile environment of inner London streets. Landy, who potted the plants up for detailed study in his studio, is best known for large-scale installations of overlooked subjects. Botanical artists have never shown much interest in the perceived status of plants, and Landy lavishes as much attention on a 'weed' – considered a menace by gardeners – as on any rose. *Ranunculus repens* is a true primitive plant, with the fewest known ancestors. Its flower parts are actually modified leaves: variations cause potential stamens to become additional petals instead. This fascinated Charles Darwin, who was captivated by swathes of golden-flowered creeping buttercup near his new home, Down House, in 1842. The variants of double, sometimes triple, flowers piqued his interest: double flowers are sterile, or partially so, and Darwin wondered whether this was a cause or effect of the variation of this tenacious plant.

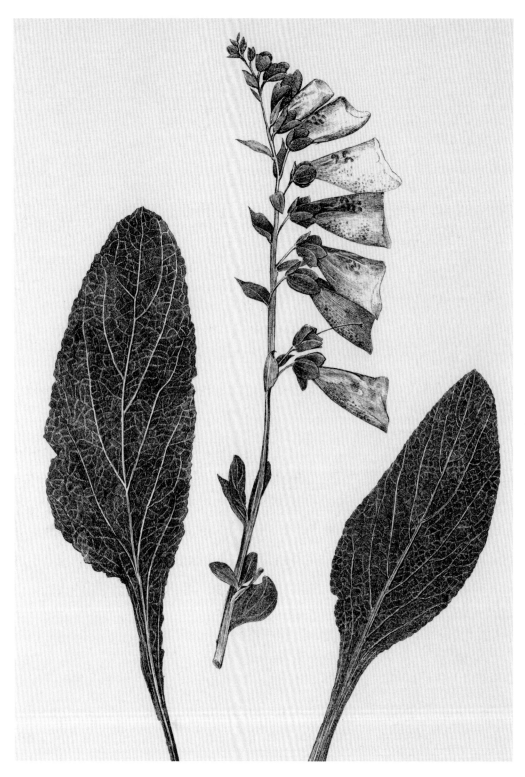

Foxglove (*Digitalis purpurea*), from *Textbook of Forensic Medicine and Toxicology*, 1895
Graphite on paper, 20 × 13cm / 7¾ x 5 in
Middle Temple Library, London

This engraving of a harmless-looking foxglove plant belies its inclusion in a book on the diagnosis and effects of poisonous and other life-threatening substances, the two-volume *Textbook of Forensic Medicine and Toxicology* (1895) by the pioneering English pathologist Arthur Pearson Luff. This illustration appeared in the first volume, along with other well-known poisonous plants, including poppy, henbane, belladonna, hemlock, monkshood and Christmas rose. The illustration shows the top part of the foxglove inflorescence, with its attractive speckled 'glove-like' flowers, and two of the large, felted leaves. Its purpose is to enable students to recognize the living plant. Luff wrote the book when he was lecturer in pathology and forensic medicine at St Mary's Hospital in Paddington, London – a post he held until 1908 – as an illustrated textbook for students interested in medico-legal cases. He describes the symptoms of foxglove poisoning, its treatment, fatal dose limit and fatal period, and the chemical tests used in order to identify the presence of digitoxin, the active ingredient. During his career, Luff gave evidence as an expert witness in several high-profile crime cases, including that of Dr Hawley Harvey Crippen, who was found guilty of murdering his wife and executed in 1910.

Foxglove (*Digitalis purpurea*), 1998
X-ray photograph, 35.6 × 43.2 cm / 14 × 17 in
Private collection

The striking composition of this X-ray turns delicate fox-glove flowers into a diaphanously clad miniature *corps de ballet* swaying in unison. Placing the stem horizontally across the upper part of the image enhances the pendant qualities of the flowers. Comparing Steven N. Meyers's image with early floral radiographs, such as those of Charles Rémy (see p.284), underlines the advances made in X-ray technology. Just over a century after the discovery of X-rays, they remain a relatively unexplored form of botanical art. Meyers came to photography through medicine, having studied radiological technology in the early 1970s and worked for more than thirty years in diagnostic medicine. At the same time, he developed an interest in camera-based photography, always printing his own work. Curiosity prompted him to experiment with taking X-rays of flowers and other objects, but he did not pursue radiography seriously until the late 1990s. He has become a specialist in this form of botanical art, and counts this one among his 100 favourites of the thousands of images he has created. Meyers believes most X-ray floral images fail because of weak composition, since without a lens, composition can only be achieved by arranging the subject carefully. Even so, full details remain invisible until after exposure.

JOHN NORTHCOTE NASH

Solanum dulcamara (woody nightshade),
from *Poisonous Plants: Deadly, Dangerous and Suspect*, 1927
Wood engraving, 16.2 × 12.9 cm / 6¼ × 5 in
Museum of New Zealand Te Papa Tongarewa, Wellington

The rich black background and dynamic composition of John Nash's wood engraving of woody nightshade (also known as bittersweet nightshade) justifies his description of himself as an 'artist-plantsman', although he was never trained. (John was the younger brother of the celebrated World War I artist Paul Nash). Nash was best known for painting the plants growing in and around his garden, rather than for engraving, since he preferred to work direct from life. However these studies show his skill as draughtsman and botanist and were used to illustrate *Poisonous Plants: Deadly, Dangerous and Suspect*. The book contained plant descriptions by W. Dallimore who, as the title implies, divided the plants into three categories with the common buttercup in the 'suspect' group. Woody Nightshade is 'deadly', but there are very few recorded deaths associated with it as the red berries taste so bitter. Despite his lack of training, John Nash taught at the Ruskin School of Art in Oxford from 1922 until 1927, and later at the Royal College of Art in London. He was awarded the CBE in 1964 and in 1967 became the first living painter to be given a retrospective exhibition at the Royal Academy of Arts in London. This engraving was gifted by the art dealer and collector, Sir Rex De Charembac Nan Kivell (1898-1977) to the Museum of New Zealand in 1951.

GEORGIA O'KEEFFE

Jimson Weed/White Flower No. 1, 1932
Oil on canvas, 121.9 × 101.6 cm / 48 × 40 in
Crystal Bridges Museum of American Art, Bentonville, Arkansas

The huge white flower fills nearly the whole canvas in this painting of jimson weed, *Datura stramonium*, a favourite flower of the renowned American artist Georgia O'Keeffe. O'Keeffe's painting – the most expensive work ever by a female artist when it sold at auction in 2014 for over $44 million (£28m) – was one of a number she made of the same subject. As in her other close-up flower paintings, here O'Keeffe combines an awareness of abstract form with a precise observation of detail and the use of bold colours and shapes (she always denied Freudian interpretations that found coded representation of genitalia in her images of flowers such as irises). Jimson weed grew in O'Keeffe's back garden in Santa Fe, New Mexico, which she visited frequently from the late 1920s before moving there permanently in 1946. The many names of this member of the nightshade family – including devil's ladder, devil's trumpet and mad apple – point to its traditional use as a powerful narcotic. The name 'Jimson' is a corruption of Jamestown, the town in Virginia where, in 1676, British troops ate the leaves in a salad. According to contemporary accounts, they became distracted, giggling and pawing at one another, and had to be locked up to prevent them from harming themselves.

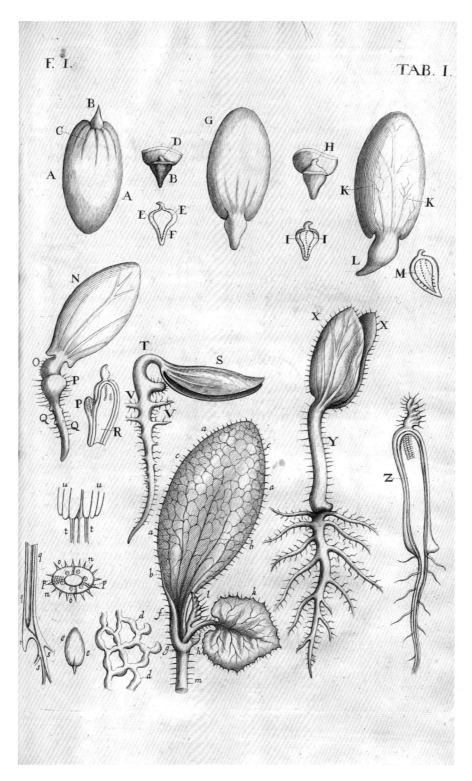

Seed Germination, 1675, from *Anatome plantarum*, 1679
Engraving, 27.5 × 18.3 cm / 10¾ × 7¼ in
Lilly Library, Indiana University, Bloomington

This carefully drawn illustration from the seventeenth century is of a cucurbit seed, probably a squash or melon, shown in the various stages of germination. The Italian biologist and physician Marcello Malpighi, who drew the originals, refers to the illustration simply as 'Ab ovis igitur *Cucurbitae* exordium capiemus ...' ['We begin with the "eggs" of a squash ...']. With the help of a microscope, Malpighi – who is often hailed as the father of embryology and microscopic anatomy – shows the root or radicle emerging from the seed embryo, then the emergence of the seed leaf or cotyledon and finally the first true leaf. At the time the drawings were made, the compound microscope had come into circulation only recently, following its invention by the Dutch in the early years of the seventeenth century, and natural historians in different parts of Europe were eagerly discovering the previously unseen world in nature. Malpighi in Bologna, Antonie van Leeuwenhoek in Delft and Robert Hooke (see p.214) and Nehemiah Grew (see p.160) in England used the new device to investigate animal and plant anatomy. This engraving by the Englishman Robert White is from the second part of Malpighi's *Anatome Plantarum* (1679), published by the Royal Society in London.

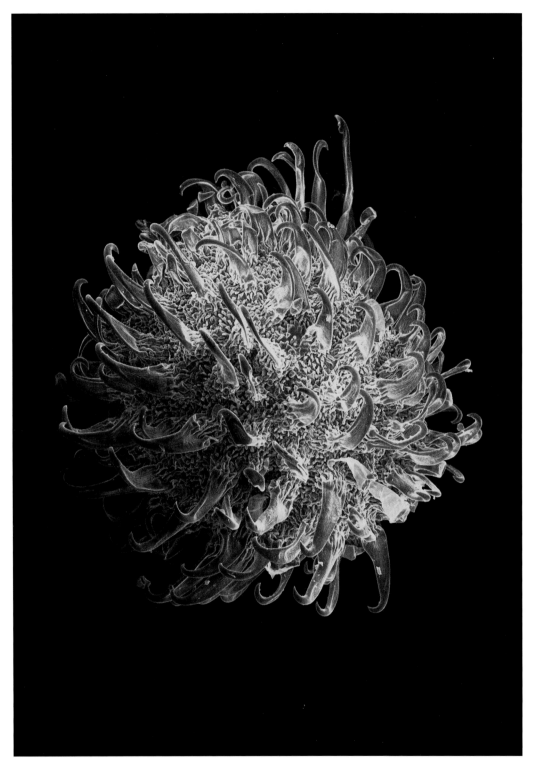

Plant Seed, 2001
Silver gelatin print, 50 × 40 cm / 19¾ × 15¾ in
Private collection

This remarkable image might at first glance suggest a heavenly object floating in space, but in fact it comes from the microcosmos, the term used to describe the world at microscopic level. This is a single seed that has been scanned with an electron microscope and enlarged many times over by the German photographer Claudia Fährenkemper, who magnifies her subjects by anything from 30 to 3,000 times their natural size. Since its invention in 1931, the electron microscope has developed rapidly to allow greater magnification, and its technical possibilities have been embraced eagerly not only by scientists but also by photographers, particularly in Germany. It works by assembling an image from a series of thin cross sections, thus allowing a revealing three-dimensional effect to be generated, as here, where the image reveals the tiny hook-like structures that help the seed to become fixed when it falls to the ground. Fährenkemper's images of plants and insects have a surreal quality, sometimes appearing alien to the everyday world, but they can also be seen as belonging squarely in an established German photographic tradition of formal monumentality – as achieved influentially by Fährenkemper's celebrated tutor, Bernd Becher, in the twentieth century.

JOHANN NEANDER

Tobacco plant (*Nicotiana tabacum*), from *Tabacologia*, 1622
Engraving, 12.5 × 17 cm / 4¾ × 6¾ in
Middle Temple Library, London

The tobacco plant is well known today, but when the German philosopher and physician Johann Neander published his monograph *Tabacologia* in 1622, this copper engraving was the first glimpse for many Europeans of the source of the leaves that had been smoked in Europe since the 1550s. Neander's copper engraving shows the long-tubed, trumpet-shaped flowers and broad leaves, together with a somewhat stylized peacock butterfly. The exposed roots offer a worm's-eye view of the whole plant. At the time, tobacco was highly controversial. In 1605 King James I of England himself had written a diatribe against it, while supporters such as Neander extolled its health-giving properties. If there was confusion about the effects of tobacco, it was also the subject of botanical confusion. Neander believed that there were both male and female species of tobacco; his legend in Latin reads 'I bring you this male species; nowhere on Earth is found anything more excellent than this herb; hence it is called panacea.' On the following page is a plant with narrower leaves, identified as female (it was possibly a different species, such as *N. longiflora*). Originally from Bremen, Neander enrolled in 1616 in the University of Leiden, where he published his treatise explaining the extraction of tobacco's active ingredient, nicotine.

Tab. 375.

Cinchona officinalis. L.

Quinine bark tree (*Cinchona officinalis*), 1796
Hand-coloured copperplate engraving
Natural History Museum, London

This modest-looking plate from 1796 records one of the most influential trees in world history: *Cinchona officinalis* from South America, also known as quinine bark tree or Jesuit's bark tree. Here, the German illustrator and pharmacist Johannes Zorn shows the tree's tubular pink flowers somewhat larger than life size, but the fruits, split to reveal small seeds, and the flat, two-dimensional leaves are accurately portrayed. The tree is famed, however, for its bark, which was ground by indigenous Peruvians as an antidote to malaria; by adding sweetened water to the ground bark, they also produced the first tonic water. In 1632 the Jesuit Barnabé de Cobo brought the tree to Europe, where it was later named by Linnaeus after the wife of Luis, Count of Chinchòn, Viceroy of Peru, who was said to have been cured of malaria by the ground bark in 1638. The bark's active ingredient – quinine – was isolated by French scientists in 1817. The discovery enabled much European exploration and colonization of malarial regions of Africa and Asia later in the nineteenth century. Zorn was passionate about the plants of South America, which he included as here in his influential *Icones plantarum medicinalium*, published in six volumes from 1779 to 1790.

MARY EMILY EATON

BRITTON AND ROSE, VOL. III

PLATE X

M. E. Eaton del.

A Hoen & Co

1. Flowering plant of *Echinopsis aurea*.
2. Flowering plant of *Copiapoa coquimbana*.
3. Flowering plant of *Lophophora williamsii*.
4. Flowering plant of same.
   (All natural size.)

Echinopsis aurea, *Copiapoa coquimbana* and *Lophophora williamsii*,
from *The Cactaceae: Descriptions and Illustrations of Plants of the Cactus Family*, 1919–23
Lithograph, 11 × 14 cm / 4¼ × 5½ in
LuEsther T. Mertz Library, New York Botanical Garden

This plate by the British botanical artist Mary Emily Eaton shows her skill in using light and shade to give distinctive depth to three species of cacti that flowered at the New York Botanical Garden in May 1916: the spiky, yellow-flowered *Echinopsis aurea* from Argentina (top left) and *Copiapoa coquimbana* from Chile (bottom), and a spineless, pinkish-blossomed *Lophophora williamsii* from Mexico and Texas (top and middle right); commonly known as peyote, this last one is well-known for its psychoactive properties. Eaton turned her passion for botanical painting into a long and distinguished career. After training at the Taunton School of Art in Somerset and the Royal College of Art in London she painted Royal Worcester porcelain before being offered in 1914 a job as a plant illustrator at the New York Botanical Garden. She remained at the garden until 1932, painting plants for its army of scientific staff and for the horticultural journal *Addisonia*. This drawing comes from volume three of *The Cactaceae*, an epic monograph of the cactus family published between 1919 and 1923 by the American botanists Nathaniel Lord Britton and Joseph Nelson Rose. The illustrations for this immense work earned Eaton international renown.

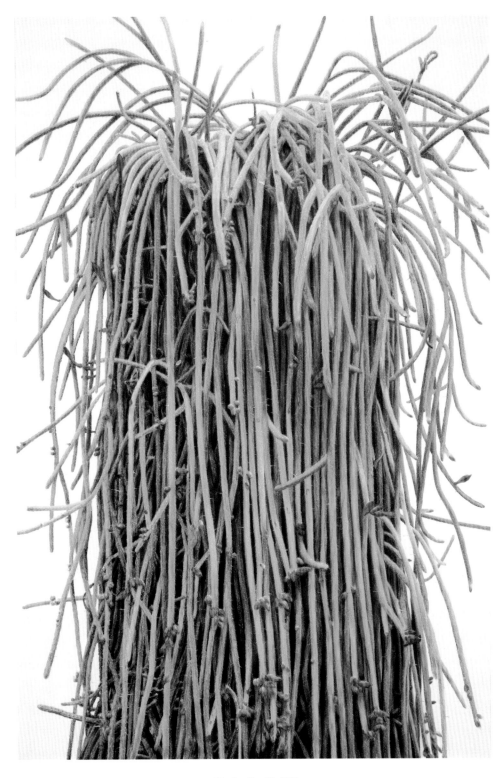

Cactus No. 59, 2011
Oil on canvas, 259 × 170 cm / 102 × 67 in
Private collection

In this highly enlarged, hyper-realistic painting, the red mistletoe cactus *Rhipsalis hoelleri* is deliberately made unfamiliar, revealing an alien and unsettling beauty that reflects the fascination these succulents exercise on the imagination through their varied and unusual forms and their adaptation to extreme conditions. This particular cactus is an endangered Brazilian species, which is threatened with extinction. The exaggerated scale is reminiscent of the intense scrutiny of flowers by Georgia O'Keeffe (see p.51), and, as with her work, has been interpreted in terms of sex and desire. A native of Seoul, South Korea, Lee Kwang-Ho has developed his practice out of similarly detailed portraits of human subjects that pay minute attention to the texture of clothes and skin, and his cactus paintings are just as much an articulation of personality and presence. He works from photographs using a variety of painstaking brushwork techniques to render these images. Lee's hyper-realistic style sets up multiple layers of illusion, seeming at once to deny the lengthy process of painting and to present the subject as it truly is in a moment, and yet magnified to lend it a frozen monumentality. But his depiction also points to a deeper reality, a reminder that we share the natural world with living things that are utterly different from us.

Orchid, 'Port Desire, C. Darwin esq.' (*Gavilea patagonica*), 1833
Graphite on paper, 15.2 × 11 cm / 6 × 4½ in
Royal Botanic Gardens, Kew, London

This drawing of an orchid is less important for what it shows than for the identity of the artist: Charles Darwin, who signed it next to the location where he drew it, Port Desire, now Puerto Deseado in the Patagonian south of Argentina. Darwin was there at Christmas 1833, during his voyage as the naturalist on HMS *Beagle* (1831–6). Christmas is summer in Patagonia and the flowering season of the *Gavilea* terrestrial orchids, whose 30-centimetre-high (12-inch) white inflorescences spring from the turfy grassland. Darwin's life sketch shows the six green streaked floral segments, the sexual organs on the column and below them the labellum (the name *G. patagonica* was first used in 1956, so is a later addition). The drawing itself was pinned to one of Darwin's orchid specimens, which was probably sent to his mentor John Stevens Henslow in Cambridge, who sent it on to Joseph Dalton Hooker (see p.248) at the Royal Botanic Gardens, Kew. There it remained in obscurity before its exciting recent discovery by Kew orchidologist Philip Cribb. Darwin's evolutionary writings are now legendary, and this little sketch will surely have played a part in his book *On the Various Contrivances by which British and Foreign Orchids are Fertilised by Insects* (1862).

ROBERT CLARK

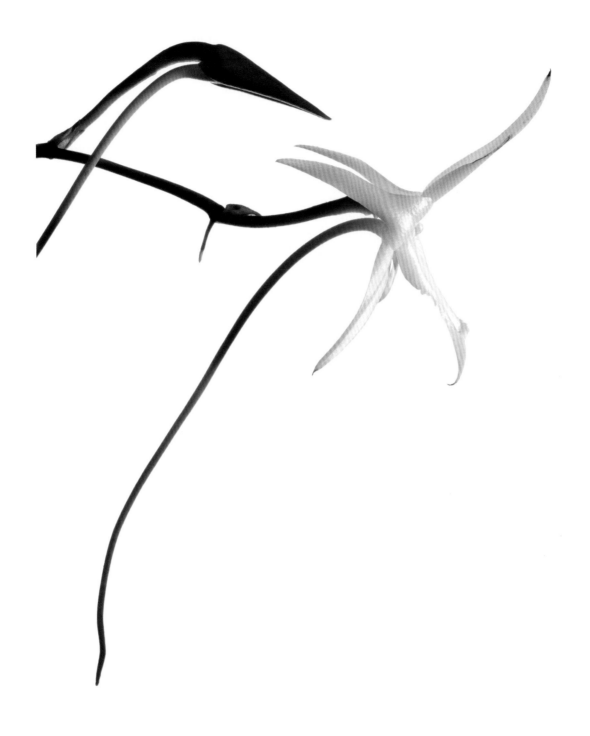

Darwin's Orchid, 2003
Slide film, dimensions variable
Private collection

This remarkable construction looks less like a flower than some kind of engineering feat. By choosing to highlight the unique shape of the star of the Bethlehem orchid, *Angraecum sesquipedale*, the American photographer Robert Clark links the flower to its role in the theory of evolution. The flower, discovered in eastern Madagascar by the French botanist Louis-Marie Aubert du Petit-Thouars, is also known as Darwin's orchid. When the famous naturalist

Charles Darwin was sent a specimen of the flower in 1862, he noticed that the nectar would be produced at the base of the long flower spur. He predicted that the long spur must have evolved alongside a pollinating insect that had a proboscis of similar length – but at the time, no such pollinator was known. In a letter to Joseph Dalton Hooker (see p.348), Darwin wrote: 'I have just received ... the astounding *Angraecum sesquipedalia* [*sic*] with a nectary

a foot long. Good heavens what insect can suck it.' It was not until forty-one years after Darwin wrote the letter – after the naturalist's death – that the insect he had predicted was indeed discovered, a subspecies of an African hawkmoth named *Xanthopan morganii praedicta*. Clark, whose work includes more than forty stories for *National Geographic*, is fascinated by evolution – as his choice of subject here demonstrates.

Geranium phaeum, 1905–9
Chinese white, pencil and watercolour on paper, 31.6 × 19.1 cm / 12½ × 7½in
Natural History Museum, London

The dark purple petals of *Geranium phaeum* spread like a fan across the centre of this cross section through the flower painted early in the twentieth century by the British botanist and educator Arthur Harry Church. Working at the University of Oxford, he evolved a distinctive style of illustration that still seems fresh and modern more than a century later, combining simple, bold forms with great detail of a plant's hidden inner structure, as in the filaments, anthers and pistil seen here. This illustration – one of many Church drew, often to use with his students – shows a true or wild geranium, a frost-hardy meadow or woodland plant from the northern hemisphere, rather than the bright red, frost-tender summer bedding or window-box plants that originated in South Africa and which are more accurately *Pelargonium*. Church's work failed to attract much attention from botanical journals, despite his reputation as 'one of the ablest and most original botanists' of the time. He set out to illustrate the hundred best flowers by season, partly to support his research into plant form and evolution; when he died in 1937 he left hundreds of watercolours illustrating types of flower mechanism. Some 773 of these are now held by the Natural History Museum in London.

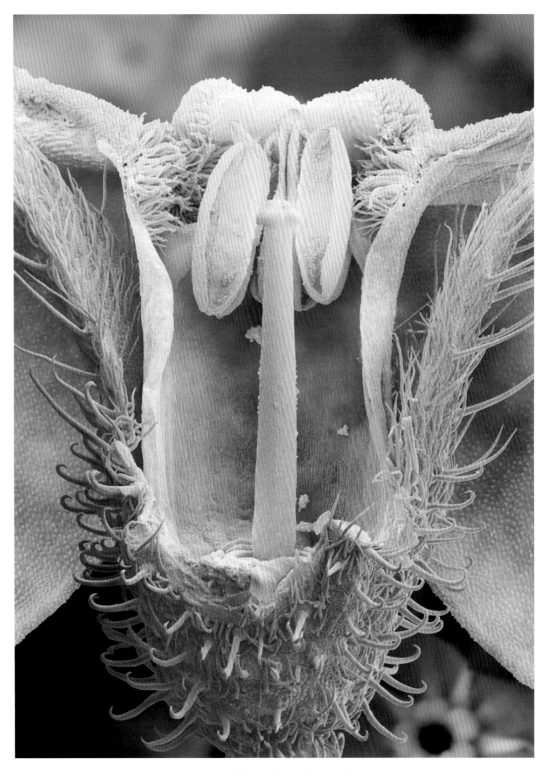

Forget-me-not flower (*Myosotis arvensis*), 2007
Coloured scanning electron micrograph (SEM)
dimensions variable

Recalling the delicacy and pastel tones of a scientific illustration from a century ago, this cross section revealing the sexual organs of a forget-me-not (*Myosotis arvensis*) was in fact produced by some of the latest technology in botanical illustration: the scanning electron microscope (SEM). For more than twenty years Andrew Syred has been using the SEM to create images of the microscopic world magnified up to 2,500 times, from the scales on a butterfly's wing to a gecko's foot and an individual grain of pollen. The SEM produces only black-and-white images, however, and they are then painstakingly coloured on the computer by Syred's partner, Cheryl Power. The forget-me-not, a genus containing more than 2,000 species, has a rich symbolic history that belies its humble appearance: it has customarily been seen as a symbol of lasting love and remembrance. In Newfoundland, Canada, it is worn to remember the dead of the world wars. To produce this SEM image, the sample was carefully dried – to prevent it being damaged in the vacuum where scanning takes place – and the outer petals removed before it was spattered with a layer of gold to help conduct electrons. However, the drying process and the vacuum create an inevitable distortion in the sample, making this a painfully laborious process with a high wastage rate.

Hemionitis crispa media obtusifolia, 1696
Hand-coloured copperplate engraving, 25.6 × 39.1 cm / 10 × 15¼ in
Private collection

Although this late seventeenth-century coloured engraving is clearly a more-or-less accurate botanical illustration of a fern – now identified as the hart's-tongue fern, *Asplenium scolopendrium* – its fronds form only part of a larger scene, complete with classical costumes and picturesque ruins. The illustration comes from a series of remarkable engravings of plants published in Leiden and Utrecht in the Netherlands to accompany a text by Abraham Munting, who also provided the specimens to be drawn. The artist depicted the plants against decorative landscape backgrounds: sometimes the plants were in ornamental vases or urns, as here, and sometimes they simply floated in the air. The lavish landscape settings were drawn by Jan Goeree, and Joseph Mulder carried out the engraving; the artist who drew the plants is unknown. The plates were first collected in 1696 under the title *Nauwkeurige beschryving der aardgewassen*, and were republished in 1702 as *Phytographia curiosa*. The unusual positioning of the plants in space and in defiance of perspective (notice how huge the plant appears – its fronds are seldom more than 60 centimetres/23 inches long – in comparison with the tiny people) was immediately widely imitated by other botanical illustrators, most notably Johann Christoph Volkamer in his *Nürnbergische Hesperides* (see p.273).

CARL LINNAEUS

'Papaperis oriental', from *Herbarium Cliffortianum*, 1737
Dried flower on paper, 41.8 × 25.1 cm / 16½ × 9¾ in
Naturalis Biodiversity Center, Leiden

An elaborate – but undersized – urn seems to support this dried *Papaver orientale*, the Oriental poppy, whose vivid colours have faded over 300 years. The cartouche has space for the name of the sample to be written in, so the paper was probably ready-printed for specimens to be mounted. What makes this specimen special is the identity of the man who catalogued it: Carl Linnaeus, now acknowledged as one of history's greatest taxonomists.

In the 1730s the young Swede travelled to the Netherlands, where his erudition and new ideas earned him an introduction to George Clifford, a rich banker and director of the Dutch East India Company. Clifford employed Linnaeus to be superintendent of his extensive garden of rare and exotic plants at his es tate, Hartekamp, near Haarlem and Leiden. He also commissioned an enormous and diverse catalogue of his outdoor and hothouse flowers, and the

Herbarium Cliffortianum, a collection of more than 3,000 dried specimens like this one. Exposure to Clifford's collection undoubtably helped Linnaeus to develop his binomial method of classifying and naming to all the plants then known to Western science.

ELIZABETH BLACKWELL

Dandelion (*Dens Leonis, Taraxacum officinale*), from *A Curious Herbal*, 1737–9
Hand-coloured engraving
British Library, London

This vibrant image of the common dandelion is the first plate in Elizabeth Blackwell's *A Curious Herbal*, a publication with a dramatic backstory. Blackwell was born in Aberdeen and trained as an artist before secretly marrying her cousin Alexander Blackwell, a physician. When a series of professional misadventures led Alexander to debtor's prison in London, Elizabeth rented a flat next to Chelsea Physic Garden and, to raise money for her husband's release, began drawing plants from the apothecaries' garden. She published the plates in weekly instalments over two years, with engraved notes on the plants' medicinal uses and various names (the text draws heavily from the *Botanicum officinale* of 1722 by Joseph Miller, who worked at the Physic Garden). The complete *Curious Herbal* contains 500 illustrations in two volumes, for which Blackwell drew, cut and coloured the engravings. It was later republished with 115 additional plates as *Herbarium Blackwellianum*. Blackwell was able to pay her husband's debts and release him from prison, but he later met with further troubles in Sweden, and was executed. Here, Blackwell numbers the flower (1), root (2) and seeds (3) of the dandelion, and a cross-section of the root (bottom right), which was widely used as a diuretic. The leaves, she adds in the accompanying text, were popular in salads.

Mericarp, 2008
Painted marine aluminium and galvanized steel, 301 × 171 × 140 cm / 118½ × 67½ × 55 in
Private collection

At 3 metres (10 feet) tall, this oversized dandelion (*Taraxacum officinale*) towers above viewers, giving an insect's-eye view that alters our perception of scale and space and highlights the remarkable attributes of this most 'ordinary' of plants. For one thing, the scale demonstrates the aptness of the flower's common name, from the French *dent de lion* or 'lion's tooth', derived from its jagged leaves: the aluminium and steel clearly define the saw-like quality of the signature leaf shape. The single seed head above the plant's central rosette underlines another common name: old-man's clock. Children still blow the clock heads to 'tell the time', the hour being given by the number of breaths needed to disperse the aerodynamically efficient seeds. Dandelion leaves have long been used in folk medicine as a laxative and diuretic; rich in potassium, with a distinctive peppery taste, they are also used in salads, to make the traditional French dish *pissenlit au lard* and to fill teatime sandwiches. The British artist Paul Morrison first exhibited *Mericarp*, which refers to the term for the dandelion parachutes alongside other representations of plants he created in different media, and at various sizes and scales. The artist is best known for his bold black-and-white landscape paintings, wall drawings, animations and sculpture.

PIETER CASTEELS III

April, from *Twelve Months of Flowers*, 1730
Hand-coloured engraving, 46.8 × 29 cm / 18½ × 11½ in
Private collection

It might not look like it, but this cornucopia of flowers is an illustration from the first ever illustrated commercial nursery catalogue, and was produced by the Flemish painter Pieter Casteels III in 1730. Casteels painted twelve floral bouquets, showing the plants that flowered or fruited in each month of the year. As in this plate for April, Casteels numbered each plant and listed their names in a key on the urn that held the bouquet. Although each urn holds as many as thirty to forty plants, every species is easily identifiable. In total Casteels illustrated more than 400 plants, which were engraved for Robert Furber's catalogues by Henry Fletcher and were offered for sale by subscription, either coloured or uncoloured according to price. Furber started his Kensington Nursery in 1710 on 2 hectares (5 acres) of land near what is now Kensington Square in west London. During the late seventeenth and eighteenth centuries, the nurseries around the capital city were becoming increasingly like botanical gardens as their proprietors propagated and sold the new plants that were constantly arriving from far-flung parts of the world. Furber grew rare plants, specializing in those from the then-fashionable wild lands of North America.

Vaughan's International Pansies, 1899
Chromolithograph, 26.7 × 20.3 cm / 10½ × 8 in
National Agricultural Library, Bettsville, Maryland

A dozen pansies, with colours ranging from the deepest purple and blue-black to vibrant yellow and startling white, crowd the cover of this catalogue from 1899 for Vaughan's Seed Store in New York City. A panel of text reminds readers that these images of Vaughan's award-winning 'International Pansies' are only a foretaste of what the seeds might produce in their own gardens. Who could resist? In the late nineteenth century American seed companies were among the pioneers who rushed to make use of the new, cheaper techniques of colour printing, such as chromolithography, that had recently been invented (this was also the great age of early mail-order catalogues). As business expanded after the Civil War (1861–5), trade catalogues with mass-produced, boldly coloured illustrations were one way to gain an advantage in an increasingly competitive market. Vaughan's Seed Store opened in Chicago, Illinois, in 1876 after customers asked the nurseryman John Charles Vaughan to start supplying seeds as well as plants. The company expanded, opening a branch in New York and issuing dedicated annual catalogues that listed and illustrated the extensive range of seeds Vaughan's offered. Colour was generally reserved for the cover, while the interior featured black-and-white lithographs.

PIERRE VALET

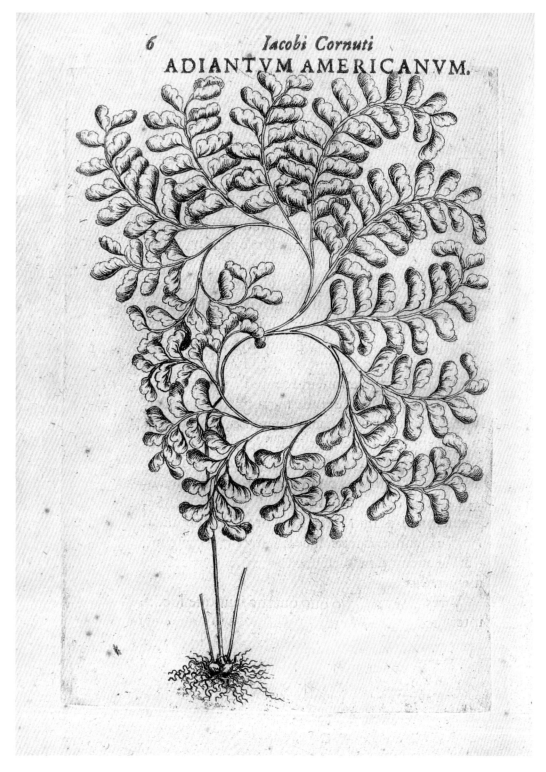

Adiantum americanum, from *Canadensium Plantarum aliarúmque nondum editarum Historia*, 1635
Engraving, plate 19.2 × 13.3 cm / 7½ × 5¼ in
John Carter Brown Library, Brown University, Providence, Rhode Island

The French botanical artist Pierre Valet – who engraved this American maidenhair fern, which is probably *Adiantum pedatum*, in 1635 for Jacques-Philippe Cornut's record of plants in French territory in North America, published that year – was also an embroidery designer, a fact that might explain the rhythmic arrangement of the plant's fronds. The first flora of Canada and one of the earliest illustrated books about North American plants, Cornut's work described and illustrated more than thirty species for the first time, along with five South African bulbs then being grown in Paris. In a separate section Cornut also created the first Flora of plants growing in and around Paris, a work that is considered pioneering in plant ecology. Cornut himself – a medical doctor – never visited North America, and depended instead on plant specimens from the botanists Vespasien Robin and his father, Jean Robin, who supervised the gardens of King Henry IV and the garden of the Faculty of Medicine in Paris, and from the Morin family, who owned several nurseries in the city. Valet produced several books of his own, including *Le Jardin du roi très chrétien Henri IV* (1608), which is said by many to be the first great florilegium. The great taxonomist Carl Linnaeus cited Cornut's book in his own survey of the plants of the world, *Species Plantarum* (1763).

ERNESTINE EBERHARDT ZAUMSEIL

Branches and Vines Quilt, c.1875
Cotton, silk and wool, 223.5 × 218.4 cm / 88 × 86 in
Metropolitan Museum of Art, New York

Among identifiable local flora from rural Illinois, such as oriental bittersweet, grapevine, maple and dogwood, this hand-stitched quilt from about 1875 is a document of nineteenth-century America. Created by a recent German immigrant, Ernestine Zaumseil, it tells a story of pioneer women, westward migration and life after the devastating Civil War (1861–5). Making quilts was a popular pastime for women in America from the seventeenth century: the quilts were used as bedspreads, wall hangings or draught excluders. They could be both a social activity – neighbours gathered for quilting 'bees' – and evidence of a woman's domestic skill and frugality. Most quilts were made from fabric remnants, particularly as the country recovered from the economic devastation of the war. Zaumseil settled in rural Illinois, where she spent many hours making this quilt, inspired in equal measure by history and nature. The leaves and vines in her 'Tree of Life' pattern are so realistic that they were almost certainly traced from living leaves and vines on to the fabric in early summer, when the trees were in full bloom. The idea of a Tree of Life came from early cotton from India, printed with *palampores*, designs of fantastical fruits and flowers growing on highly stylized trees.

Wisteria and Bee, c.1910
Ink and colour on paper, 34.3 × 18.8 cm / 13½ x 7½ in
Arthur M. Sackler Gallery, Smithsonian Institution, Washington, DC

The subtlety of the single long, pendulous raceme of Japanese wisteria hanging from a leafy bower, the hovering bee and the twisted, fading wisteria (*W. floribunda*) stem set against a pale-grey background mark this woodblock as belonging to the *shin-hanga* ('new prints') movement of Japanese printmaking. Such prints were designed to appeal to a Western audience by reflecting a romanticized image of Japan in the early part of the twentieth century. Ohara, who was part of the movement between 1910 and 1940, specialized in portraying birds, animals and plants in naturalistic settings (*kacho-e*), in what might best be described as 'printed paintings'. The process relied on different expertise for each stage – wood-carving, printing and publishing – and each stage was typically undertaken by a different expert. The prints themselves were regarded as modernized versions of the traditional *ukiyo-e* ('Floating World') woodblocks, with softer colouring, deeper space and more naturalistic light and subjects. The artist was born Ohara Matao, but rather confusingly his name changed at various stages of his life and with his different publishers. This print of wisteria and a bee was published by Daikokuya in Tokyo about 1910, and was signed and sealed Kōson.

Flowers of the Jade Vine (*Strongylodon macrobotrys*), 2015
Photograph, dimensions variable
Private collection

The translucent blue-green flowers of the jade vine trace sinuous arabesques in this close-up photograph by the South African botanist and photographer Brian Schrire, an expert on members of the pea family, *Leguminosae*, at Kew Gardens in London. Dangling and clustered from a central strap-like stem, the individual flowers of the vine have upturned, pointed petals. The jade vine, *Strongylodon macrobotrys*, is a remarkable member of the pea family native to rainforests on the islands of Luzon, Mindoro and Catanduanes in the Philippines. The woody climber can reach up to 18 metres (60 feet) in length and is best known for its hanging clusters of luminous blue-green flowers. The flowers have evolved to be pollinated by bats that feed while clinging upside-down, lapping up the copious sweet nectar. During this process pollen is dusted on to the bat's head and may be transferred to another flower, thus achieving pollination. The jade vine was unknown in the West until it was found by an American expedition to the forests of Luzon in 1854. Today it is threatened in the wild, mainly through deforestation, but it is not difficult to cultivate, and examples can be seen at Kew and elsewhere.

ANNIE FARRER

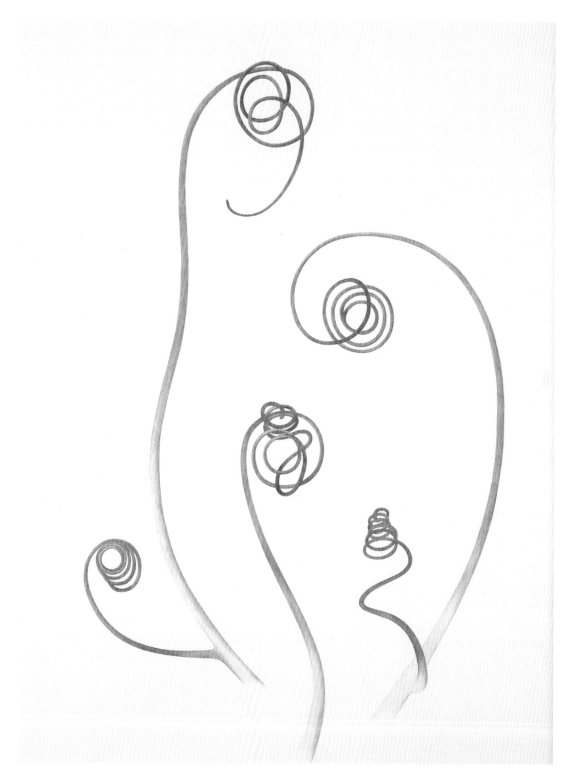

Courgette Tendrils II, 2002
Watercolour on paper, 28.5 × 40 cm / 11¼ × 15¾ in
Shirley Sherwood Collection, London

Set against a white background and without any vegetables and leaves to help identification, delicate green shoots twirl and dance on the page. Despite being almost photographic in its precision, this watercolour by the self-taught Australian-born artist Annie Farrer has an abstract quality that makes the accurate identification of the tendrils as belonging to the courgette genus (*Cucurbita*) almost impossible, instead emphasizing their colour gradations and sculptural quality. The graceful result belies the many hours of work it takes Farrer to draw in such detail, and forces the viewer to examine the plant anew, as she explains: 'My intention is to draw to your attention things that you may not have noticed.' Farrer was brought up in Yorkshire, and her interest in botany grew thanks to a famous relative, the early twentieth-century plant collector and 'father of rock gardening' Reginald Farrer, who introduced many new, exotic plants into Western gardens following his travels in China and Burma. While Annie Farrer illustrates anything from Himalayan flowers to Bolivian grasses, her preference is for painting the parts of plants that other people throw away: 'My interest isn't in portraying pretty flowers ... Bamboos, tangles of grass and moss are what I like.'

Bottle Gourd (*Lagenaria siceraria*), 2011
Copperplate etching on paper, 15.2 × 22.9 cm / 6 × 9 in
Private collection

The large, ruffled white flowers of the bottle gourd vine open at night, when the female flowers may be pollinated by a cucumber beetle, like the one pictured on a petal at the heart of this delicate copperplate etching by the American artist Bobbi Angell. Native to Africa and Asia, *Lagenaria* is a vigorous pantropical annual cultivated by ancient civilizations, and produces fruit of remarkably varied size and shape. As the fruit matures, it becomes woody and hollow. It has been used for many purposes, from making simple water dippers and bowls to fashioning musical instruments and elaborately carved and decorated objects. Even though the growing season is too short for the fruit to mature in her garden in Vermont, Angell grows bottle gourds for their broad, velvety leaves and large flowers. Her pen-and-ink illustrations for scientific journals and floras, and her drawings for seed catalogues, the *New York Times*'s gardening column and popular books make Angell one of the most recognized and admired contemporary botanical illustrators. For the last few years Angell has been etching her drawings on copper plates, echoing the early days of botanical book illustration.

BEATRIX POTTER

Study of Narcissus Flowers, c.1895
Pen and ink and watercolour on paper, 28 × 15 cm / 11 × 6 in
Victoria and Albert Museum, London

This delicate watercolour study of the *polyanthus narcissus* (*Narcissus tazetta*) displays a keen eye for detail and was clearly made from life, being faithful to the subject rather than simply decorative, with its twisted leaves and rather jumbled and artlessly arranged flowers. The artist, Helen Beatrix Potter, is most famous for the children's books she wrote and illustrated, including her familiar classic *The Tale of Peter Rabbit* (1901). Less well-known is that she produced many other illustrations, especially still-life studies. Her father, Rupert Potter, was a talented photographer who encouraged his daughter to develop her artistic talent. Largely self-taught at first, she went on to take drawing lessons and also studied at the National Art Training School in South Kensington. She developed her own style, studying nature closely and faithfully reproducing what she saw. The famous Pre-Raphaelite artist Sir John Everett Millais told her: 'Plenty of people can draw, but you have observation.' Potter often visited the nearby museums in Kensington to deepen her knowledge of biology, and at the Victoria and Albert Museum (V&A) she studied drawings, prints and costumes. It is fitting, then, that the V&A holds the world's largest collection of her drawings, manuscripts, photographs and correspondence, in the Beatrix Potter Showcase.

GERTRUDE JEKYLL

Campanula formanekiana, c.1860–90
Pencil and ink on paper, 13.6 × 18.1 cm / 5½ × 7 in
Lindley Library, Royal Horticultural Society, London

This delicate pen-and-ink drawing of the Macedonian harebell (*Campanula formanekiana*), is remarkable not so much for its artistic merit as for the identity of the artist. The Englishwoman Gertrude Jekyll, one of the most influential garden designers and writers of the early twentieth century, created more than 400 gardens in the United Kingdom, continental Europe and the United States, and published more than 1,000 articles and 13 books. Jekyll was a talented painter, who had studied at the South Kensington School of Art (now the Royal College of Art), and she frequently both drew and painted flowers, sometimes tracing her images in order to transfer them to embroidery. When her eyesight began to deteriorate in her forties, ending any possible career as an artist, she briefly used a camera to try to capture her images before turning to designing gardens. She became known for her 'painterly' approach, which combines colours in a somewhat impressionistic style. In particular she gave prominence to borders of hardy flowers, emphasizing the colours and textures of the various species and cultivars selected. In 1889 Jekyll met the architect Edwin Lutyens, with whom she formed a celebrated creative partnership, and together they designed houses and gardens in southeast England.

Six plates, from *Nature's Selfprinting: a Series of Useful and Ornamental Plates of the South Indian Flora*, 1861
Coloured ink on paper, each 32 × 41.5 cm / 12¾ × 16½ in
Basel Mission Archives

These six cultivated Indian plants represent a wide variety of foliage types, but all have been portrayed in exemplary detail by coating the leaves with paint and pressing them on to the paper. The Swiss printer Johann Jakob Hunziker arrived in the southwestern Indian port city of Mangalore (now Mangaluru) in the state of Karnataka in 1857 to work for the Basel Mission Press. He became fascinated by the plants growing near his workplace, and produced a series of nature prints of specimens gathered by himself and his colleagues and published in two volumes in English as *Nature's Selfprinting* (1862). This selection includes three native plants and three cultivated by local people. The native trees are the curry leaf tree (*Murraya koenigii*) and 'Uppalige mara' (*Macaranga peltata*), both of which are widely used in South Asian cooking, with the Indian blackwood or rosewood (*Dalbergia latifolia*). The cultivated plants are the grapevine, the South American sweet-sop and 'Villaitipippala', the Mexican poinsettia. Hunziker learned the local Kannada language and during 1859 collected plants in Mysore, Bangalore and Dharwad while visiting other missionaries. He was not a botanist, and so grouped his prints not along Linnaean lines but rather under headings such as 'Jungle Plants' or 'Nilgiri Ferns'.

JACOB VAN MEURS

Sykomous, 'Kalet', Tamarind, Balsam and Baobab,
from *Naukeurige Beschrijvinge der Afrikaenesche gewesten*, 1668
Engraving, 21 × 31 cm / 8¼ × 12¼ in
Middle Temple Library, London

The exaggeratedly large fruits and odd shapes of the five African trees and shrubs in this curious engraving by the Dutchman Jacob van Meurs – from left to right, sycamore, 'kalet', tamarind, balsam and baobab – are easily explained. Neither Van Meurs nor Olfert Dapper, the author whose *New Description of Africa* (*Naukeurige Beschrijvinge der Afrikaenesche gewesten*) the plate illustrated, had ever been to Africa or seen the plants. Dapper, a physician from Amsterdam, instead relied on earlier writers as well as Dutch traders and missionaries to provide him with sketches and information. However, for Van Meurs – from 1660 until his death in 1680 Europe's principal publisher and engraver of books and maps of foreign lands – Dapper's treatise was very attractive. The sycamore fig, *Ficus sycomorus*, was sacred to the Egyptians and symbolized regeneration, eternity and strength. 'Kalet' resembles the coffee plant (*Coffea arabica*), with rather peculiar flower clusters, while *Tamarindus indica* is an important source of food. Balsam – *Commiphora gileadensis* – is the source of the prized balm of Gilead, a fragrant medicinal resin similar to myrrh, and mentioned in the Bible. The tree Van Meurs labels as baobab is not the famed tree with swollen trunk but Sodom's apple, *Calotropis procera*, a poisonous plant in the milkweed family.

CHIKUSAI KATO

Asian pear (*Pyrus pyrifolia*), 1878
Tempera and paper on pear wood, 34 × 24 cm / 13½ × 9½ in, including frame
Royal Botanic Gardens, Kew, London

Botanical illustrations appear on a wide variety of surfaces: papyrus, parchment, metal, wood, silk and paper. This delicate tempera painting of the flower, leaves and fruit of the Asian pear (*Pyrus pyrifolia*) was painted, appropriately enough, on wood from the tree itself. It is one of a series made in 1878 by Chikusai Kato, who affixed the red impression of his seal to the reverse of a considerable number of woodblocks, each of which carried a botanical illustration

of the respective plant plus a paper panel with its scientific and Japanese name. The blocks were framed with the bark of the respective trees, with cylindrical slices from branches in the four corners. No fewer than 152 such woodblocks are kept in the Botanisches Museum in Berlin and twenty-six in the Economic Botany Collection of the Royal Botanic Gardens at Kew; a few more pieces are in other collections. It is plausible to assume that the purpose of

these woodblocks was mainly educational: Chikusai Kato was the first plant illustrator attached to the new Koishikawa Botanical Garden of Tokyo University, where botany was taught following Western methods. By contrast, very little is known about how this collection arrived in either Berlin or Kew.

CHARLES JONES

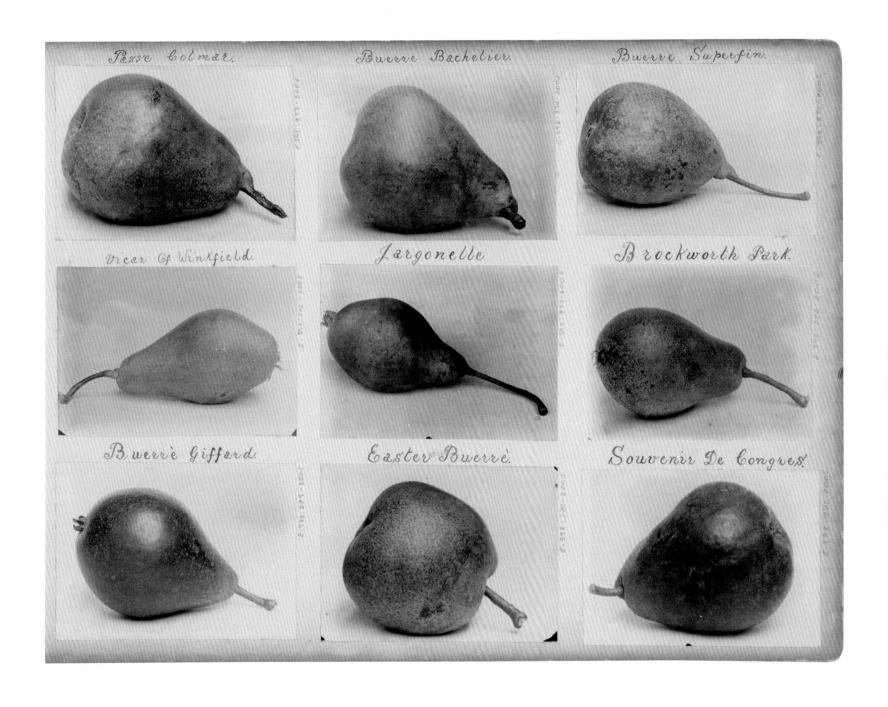

Passe Colmar.
Buerre Bachelier.
Buerre Superfin.
Vicar Of Winkfield.
Jargonelle
Brockworth Park.
Buerrè Giffard.
Easter Buerrè.
Souvenir De Congres

Photographs of pears, c.1901–20
Gelatin silver prints in album, each 7.5 × 10.5 cm / 3 × 4¼ in
Victoria and Albert Museum, London

These masterly photographs of nine cultivars of pear were seen by relatively few contemporaries of the photographer, Charles Jones, a gardener who in the early decades of the twentieth century worked at various country estates in England. Jones's work was never exhibited in his lifetime and its existence was largely unknown, even to his family. It remained undiscovered for more than twenty years after his death, until 1981, when a suitcase full of his photographs was discovered at Bermondsey Antiques Market in London. Since then, Jones's work has attained its rightful place in the history of botanical art. In this example, the composition of the images, all photographed in profile, highlights the variety of fruit size, shape and stalk length. Jones began taking photographs to record the fruit he grew, but as his mastery increased, he also worked for others who shared his desire to document horticultural developments. As a master gardener and superb photographic technician, Jones knew both how to produce and how to capture the beauty of a wide range of plants. Artistic composition, isolation of subjects and presentation against neutral backgrounds elevates his work from ordinary plant images to remarkable portraits that look consistently contemporary in their approach.

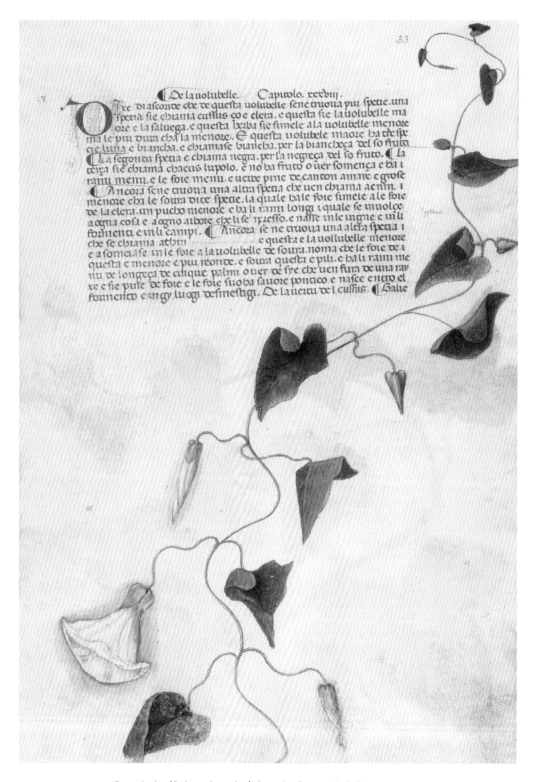

Convolvulus (*Calystegia sepium*), from the Carrara Herbal, c.1390–1403
Ink and colour on parchment, 35 cm × 24 cm / 13¾ × 9½ in
British Library, London

The artist who painted this delicate convolvulus (*Calystegia sepium*) – traditionally known as bindweed, trumpetweed or devil's garter – in the Italian city-state of Padua at the turn of the fifteenth century caused a revolution in the illustration of herbals. Earlier herbals tended to show diagrammatic identification guides, boxed in by the accompanying words. This illustrator, however, used the whole page to display individual plants to maximum advantage, as with these downward-pointing flowers, which are shadowed to stand out against the vellum, and the stem twining upwards to exert its stranglehold on surrounding plants. His vines and vegetables sprout vigorously, while herbs have a fragile intensity. The Carrara Herbal was created under the patronage of Francesco Carrara the Younger, ruler of Padua, at a time when the city was famous for its university and medical faculty. The herbal can be dated precisely, because when Carrara was deposed by the Venetians in 1403, work was abandoned with only fifty illustrations completed. Although convolvulus was thought of as a weed, its beauty meant that it was allowed to grow on garden arbours, and its flowers were compared to little bells. Since they fade as the day advances, this was the original morning glory, long before the name was transferred to the plant's blue counterpart in America.

YOSHIHIRO SUDA

Morning Glory, 2014
Painted wood, dimensions variable
Private collection

This delicate image of morning glory (*Ipomoea tricolor*) captures the creased, fragile texture of the petals of what in real life are ephemeral flowers, each lasting for only about a day: but in this version by the contemporary Japanese artist Yoshihiro Suda, the petals are carved from wood. Suda uses traditional tools to produce precise replicas of living plants that have an almost photographic realism. So meticulously worked and delicately painted are the sculptures that it is hard not to be fooled into thinking that they are real flowers. Growing up in the Japanese countryside, Suda was fascinated by the beautiful natural scenery, which he began to sketch. Later, after he had moved to Tokyo, he became aware of the contrast between the city and the countryside, between the artificial and the natural. He began by re-creating tiny weeds that he saw growing in the city streets, using wood to give them permanence, before moving on to other flowers. Suda sets out to make the viewer think about the boundaries between what is real and what is illusory: his creations are carefully placed in exhibitions where they are often in danger of being overlooked – then causing surprise when their true nature becomes apparent.

Plants Found in New Holland, from *A Continuation of A Voyage to New-Holland*, 1709
Copperplate engraving, 11.7 × 19.7 cm / 4¾ × 7¾ in
Royal Society, London

It is not known who drew these plants from New Holland (Australia) near the start of the eighteenth century, but the artist did an accurate if imperfect job of illustrating *Centropogon* sp. (1), the seaweed *Cystoseira trinodis* (2) and the Western Australian shrubs *Hannafordia quadrivalvis* (3) and *Solanum orbiculatum* (4). It is likely that he drew them from dried specimens brought back to England by the renowned navigator William Dampier from a voyage to Western Australia in 1699: the fish and animals drawn on board ship by the unknown expedition artist were far cruder (even if the plant artist mistakenly attributes the South American native *Centropogon* to Australia). The plate illustrated Dampier's account of his voyage, *A Voyage to New-Holland, &c. in the Year 1699*, which included some of the earliest accounts of the little-known southern oceans. This and Dampier's other books were immensely popular, particu- larly among sailors, who followed his routes in the absence of detailed charts. Dampier was the first to study the plants of the coast of Western Australia, collecting and preserving not only the species shown here but also the spectacular red-and-black Sturt's desert pea, now named *Swainsona formosa*; he is also remembered in the endemic Australian genus *Dampiera*.

MARIE RYDER

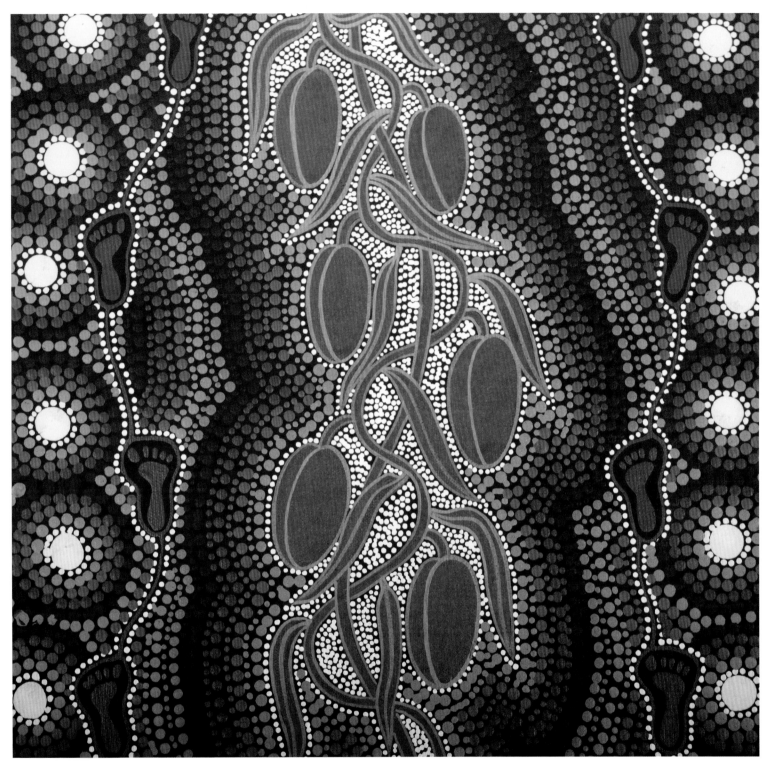

Bush Bananas, c.1997–2003
Acrylic on canvas, 32 × 32 cm / 12¾ × 12¾ in
Private collection

The aboriginal Australian artist Marie Ryder draws on traditional dot painting in this celebration of the bush banana, whose ability to thrive in arid areas makes it an important part of the diet of the Eastern Arrernte Aboriginal people of Central Australia. By placing the plant at the centre of her image, Ryder highlights this importance: it is almost a totem. The footprints on either side of the plant represent the spiritual journey known as walkabout, in which Aboriginal people visit places where they feel a strong connection to the land. The dot-painted background uses traditional browns and yellows to symbolize the soil and the sun, respectively, in one of a series of paintings Ryder calls 'Bush Tucker Dreamings'. The twining stems of the bush banana – named *Marsdenia australis* after the East India Company official William Marsden – contain an edible milky sap, while its greenish-yellow flowers are sucked for nectar. The large, avocado-like fruit are packed with yellow-brown seeds that taste similar to fresh peas. The fruit are eaten raw, or cooked in the hot ash around a fire. Flowers and fruit are collected soon after rainfall, before they deteriorate in the heat of the southern hemisphere summer.

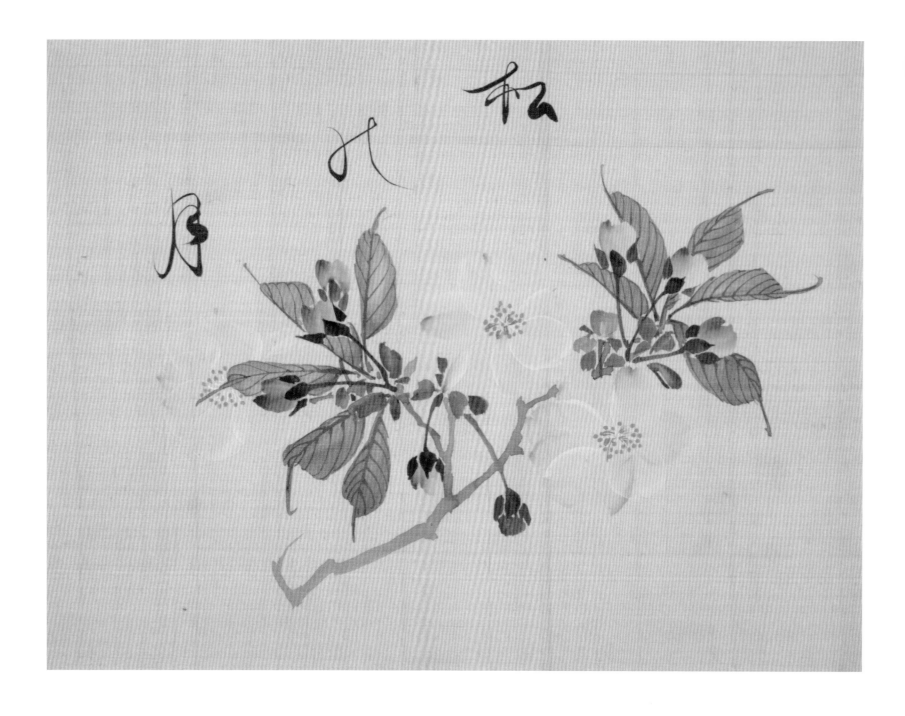

Cherry blossom (*Prunus serrulata*), from *Ōka-fu*, c.1830–53
Watercolour on silk, 29.6 × 35.3 cm / 11¾ × 14 in
National Diet Library, Tokyo

This striking illustration by the early nineteenth-century Japanese artist and physician Sakamoto Kōnen celebrates one of the most important elements of Japanese culture: cherry blossom. The white flowers are painted so sparingly as to appear translucent, with the background silk showing through the delicate petals, while the various tones of red give the buds an abstract quality. It comes from *Ōka-fu* (*A Sketchbook of Cherry Blossoms*), a lavish catalogue of twenty-nine cultivars of cherry, showing clearly the details of bud, leaf and fully opened flowers. The blossom of flowering cherry trees (*sakura*) plays an important role in Japanese history and culture. The massed blooms symbolize clouds and the short-lived flowers mirror the ephemeral nature of life. Cherry trees in flower recur constantly in Japanese art from earliest times, and each spring many people travel to witness the annual displays of cherry blossom, which are usually at their best in April. Most Japanese flowering cherries are cultivars of *Prunus serrulata*, a native of Japan, Korea and China. The timing of peak flowering varies a little from year to year, and websites give precise details to coordinate viewing opportunities in the annual celebration known as *hanami*.

Orange blossom (*Citrus sinensis*), 18th century
Gouache on paper, 27.5 × 19.5 cm / 10¾ × 7¾ in
Private collection

So subtle are the colours in this depiction of the white flowers of orange blossom that it might appear more like an early black-and-white photograph than an eighteenth-century painting. The almost black background throws the white flowers, the butterfly and the ladybird into dramatic relief. The orange tree and other citrus fruits were extremely fashionable at the time (they were cultivated under glass for their delicious scent). The German artist

Barbara Regina Dietzsch occupied a kind of middle ground between botanical illustration and still life, with careful, meticulous detail allied to a richness of texture and balance of composition. One of the Nuremberg School, the roots of which lay in the Dutch still-life painters of the seventeenth century, Dietzsch was the oldest of seven artist children of Johann Israel Dietzsch. Although she did not as a rule illustrate natural-history works, her plants were impres-

sive enough that engravings of her works were used in the celebrated *Hortus nitidissimis* by the great patron of the Nuremberg School, the naturalist Christoph Jacob Trew. Overall, the feeling of this particular image resembles that of the work of Dietzsch's older contemporary Maria Sibylla Merian (see p.207).

KARL BLOSSFELDT

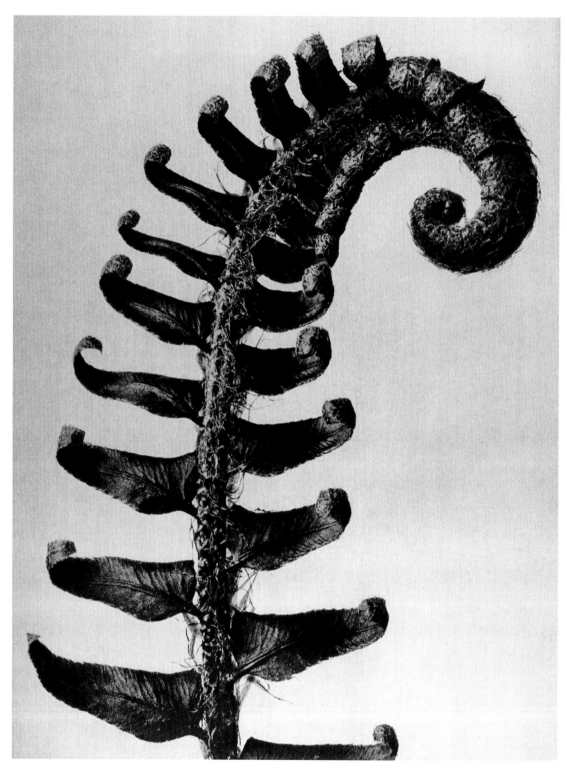

Polystichum acrostichoides, from *Urformen der Kunst*, 1928
Photograph, 20.3 × 25.4 cm / 8 × 10 in
Private collection

The uncurling leaf of an American Christmas Fern, *Polystichum acrostichoides*, takes on the solidity of a carving in this image by the German photographer Karl Blossfeldt. As an apprentice ironworker, Blossfeldt made casts of botanical specimens to be reproduced in metal. After he taught himself photography and built his own camera, his interest in plant structure led him to pioneer plant photography as an art form. As an art professor in Berlin from 1898 until 1930 Blossfeldt demonstrated how plant structure and symmetry had been copied in classical architecture and could be used as patterns for industrial design. His photographic work became popular after the publication of *Urformen der Kunst* (1928), known in English as *Art Forms in Nature*. Blossfeldt concentrated on young leaves and buds, flowers and seed heads, strikingly lit and printed with high contrast in black and white, and sometimes greatly enlarged with remarkable depth of focus. He was particularly interested in plants with strong surface textures, complex flower heads, or uncurling fronds showing spirals that obey the Fibonacci sequence. Exhibitions of his photographs in the 1970s brought Blossfeldt's work back to public attention.

STEPHANIE BERNI

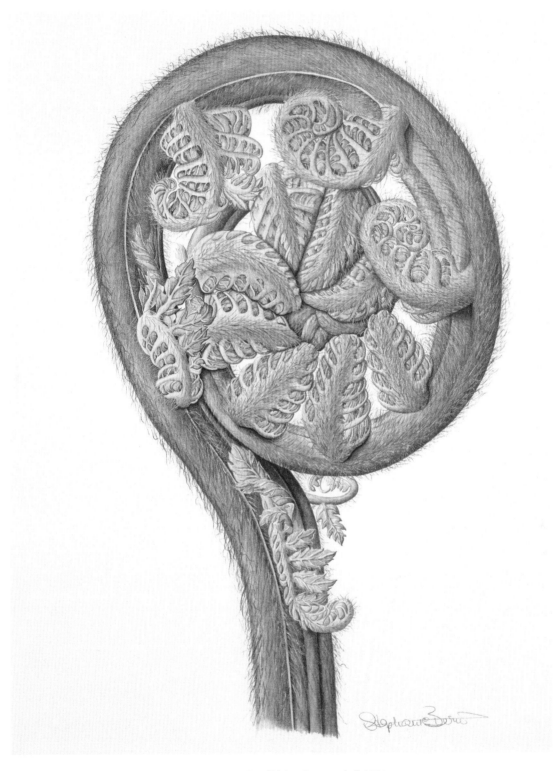

Australian tree fern (*Dicksonia antarctica*), 2004
Watercolour over pencil on paper, 29 × 20 cm / 11½ × 7¾ in
Shirley Sherwood Collection, London

In this watercolour by the contemporary British artist Stephanie Berni, an unfurling leaf of the Australian tree fern (*Dicksonia antarctica*) fills the page. The image's large scale and the soft orange hairs that protect the tightly compressed fronds inside the curled stem echo a study of a treasured golden artefact – perhaps the bishop's crook that gave uncurled fern leaves their name, 'croziers'. Berni's highly original style is almost photographic in its careful portrayal of detail, using accurate observation and meticulous technique to reveal the minutest features of the plant. In the wild this tree fern favours shady gullies in wet forests in eastern Australia and Tasmania, where it can achieve a height of several metres, although its habitat has been reduced by land clearance. It is popular as a garden ornamental, but its slow growth means that fully grown specimens are often harvested from the wild, creating another threat to its survival. In the past, Aboriginal peoples in Tasmania ate the starch-rich pith in the centre of the trunk, and the rather bitter, slimy leaves. Berni, who had been a nursery teacher, changed career after studying botanical illustration at Chelsea Physic Garden under the direction of Anne-Marie Evans.

Liquidambar styraciflua, 1944
Gouache on black board, 41.9 × 29.2 cm / 16½ × 11½ in
Brooklyn Botanic Garden, New York

The most striking element of Maud Purdy's electrifying painting of sweet gum, *Liquidambar styraciflua*, is the way the black background throws forward the separate details of the plant. Purdy painted the tree's most familiar features – a single globular seed head and a flowering branch with its large maple-like leaves – smaller than life-size in the upper corners of the painting. Her composition is dominated by magnified, strongly illuminated repro-ductive structures floating on a dark background: a pistil's curved stigma lobes, glistening ovules, winged seeds and Medusa-like female flower heads that develop into the spiky capsular fruits. Employed as staff artist in 1913 by the then new Brooklyn Botanic Garden, Purdy was principal artist there for more than thirty years. Her paintings and drawings generally followed the conventions for scientific illustration and botanical art, but she upended convention with her electrifying paintings on black boards. *L. styraciflua*, named for the thick, aromatic resin the tree exudes when wounded, has been one of the eastern United States' most valuable and useful forest trees since the seventeenth century. Beginning in the 1730s the early American naturalist John Bartram sent thousands of the spiny seed heads to England for the establishment of American groves in landscape gardens.

GUO HONGWEI

Plant No. 8, 2012
Watercolour on paper, 67 × 101 cm / 26½ × 39¾ in
Private collection

The Chinese artist Guo Hongwei brings meticulous order to this watercolour of pressed flowers and foliage, an assemblage that is more than the sum of its parts. At first sight a work of straightforward documentation, the piece is titled so as to suggest that the carefully depicted plants are incidental to the artist's wider purposes; the title of the series from which it comes, *Painting as Collecting*, has the same effect. The son of a renowned calligrapher, Guo grew up and studied in Sichuan province and now represents a contemporary generation of artists working in Beijing. His understated work is a reduction of the visible world in two dimensions, and seeks to answer a fundamental question posed by illustration: what does it mean for one thing to resemble another? Guo is especially concerned with the functional aspects of art, the natural forms of his subject matter mirrored by precise attention to the artist's mat- erials and the physical processes of recording. The reality of the plants corresponds with a parallel world of images made actual on paper and gathered together like a series of memories. Similarities in the subject matter reveal the subtleties of individual perception in both the artist and the viewer.

Vera effigie della grandiglia dett' fior dell' passione (*A True Likeness of the Granadilla*), 1619
Hand-coloured woodcut engraving, 33.2 × 21.7 cm / 13 × 8½ in
Natural History Museum, London

This early seventeenth-century depiction of the wild passion flower or granadilla (now *Passiflora ligularis*), a tropical climber found in South America – is stylized, in particular the treatment of the flowers. However, for contemporaries of the Dominican friar and apothecary Fra Donato d'Eremita, who commissioned the engraving in 1619, this was a remarkably accurate representation of a flower that had previously been depicted in a more symbolic manner. The

first mention of the plant comes from an account published in 1569. The flower itself was said to be full of symbols of Christ's Crucifixion: its corona resembled the crown of thorns; its five stamens echoed the five wounds Christ was said to have suffered; the three stigmas represented the three nails with which he had been nailed to the Cross; and the pistil column was taken as the post against which he had been whipped. The plant was therefore called *flos*

passionis, or passion flower. In 1619 one blossomed in the Farnese Gardens in Rome (there had been a previous flowering in Paris, but the Italian observers may not have known this). D'Eremita dedicated this engraving to his friend Johannes Faber, a member of the Accademia dei Lincei, Europe's first scientific society.

JONATHAN SINGER

Passiflora quadrangularis,
from *Botanica Magnifica: Portraits of the World's Most Extraordinary Flowers and Plants,* 2009
Photograph, 100 × 73.6 cm / 39.5 × 29 in
Smithsonian Libraries, Washington, DC

The rich blues and reds of this grandilla, *Passiflora quadrangularis*, a vine native to the American tropics, loom out of the black background, emphasizing the remarkable petals whose stripes resemble the spines of a tropical fish. The lustrous colours – achieved by photographing in low light on a H2D-39 Hasselbad digital camera – have been likened to those of Old Master painters, above all, the preeminent flower artist 'Velvet' Brueghel, nicknamed for the lifelike texture of his petals. The image is one of hundreds taken by the American podiatrist-turned-photographer Jonathan Singer after his early large-scale images impressed curators enough to gain him access to the collections of the Smithsonian Institution. The result was *Botanica Magnifica*, a collection of 250 photographs divided into five volumes (including one on gingers alone), published in 2009 in a limited edition of ten hand-bound copies. At Singer's insistence, the book was published in double-elephant folio, a huge antique format 100 × 73.6 centimetres (39½ x 29 inches) he selected as a tribute to the *Birds of America* by John James Audubon (see p.206), the last work for which it was employed. The resulting images are often larger than life size, not only creating intense drama and beauty, but also revealing hidden anatomical details.

Buddha's Hand Fruit (*Citrus medica* 'Buddha's Hand'),
from *Ten Bamboo Studio Collection of Calligraphy and Painting*, c.1633
Ink and colour on paper, 25 × 27 cm / 9¾ × 10½ in
British Museum, London

This coloured woodblock print from seventeenth-century China shows the fine outline of the curiously shaped yellow fruits of *fo-shou* or Buddha's hand, with their characteristic white pitting and a gradation of green on the extremities or 'fingers' of the fruit. This illustration by Gao You comes from one of the earliest known picture collections in China to be printed in colour. Gao You, an artist working for the calligrapher and Chinese seal artist Hu Zengyan in the Ten Bamboo Studio in Nanjing, produced several works on fruits for the eight-volume collection. The Buddha's hand citron, with its long, fleshy, finger-like extensions, is an auspicious fruit in China, where it is offered in Buddhist temples at New Year for good luck and longevity. It is an aberrant form of *Citrus medica* the citron. These fruits are prized more highly if the fruit appears to have the fingers closed rather than splayed out. In Buddhism, a closed hand symbolizes the act of praying. The fruit can also be candied as a sweetmeat and is used in flavourings, tea and incense. At the time Gao You created the image, China was in crisis: the Ming Dynasty was crumbling, and would soon be replaced by the Manchu Qing Dynasty from the north.

MONIKA E. DE VRIES GOHLKE

Citrus medica, 2009
Hand-coloured aquatint, 30.5 × 22.9 cm / 12 × 9 in
LuEsther T. Mertz Library, New York Botanical Gardens

This modern representation of an ancient fruit reflects the artist's familiarity with five centuries of Western printing techniques. The German-born American artist Monika de Vries Gohlke presents the freakish-looking fruit – known as Buddha's hand – whole and in cross section. Buddha's hand is a form of citron (*Citrus medica*), probably the first citrus cultivated in Europe. The long, baroque fingers of the pulp-less fruit curl at the ends, and a canopy of leaves provides

a muted grey and black background where yellow fruit hangs heavily from slender, thorny branches. Citron, one of very few naturally occurring wild citrus species, reached the Mediterranean long before lemon and sour orange. It was described in the third century BC by the ancient Greek naturalist Theophrastus, having possibly originated in Asia. In the early modern endeavour to record and classify nature, the unpredictable shape and pockmarked skin of

citron made it a fascinating curiosity. Among the botanists attracted to citron as part of this exploration were Abraham Munting in 1696 (see p.62) and Johann Christoph Volkamer in 1708 (see p.273). Gohlke's print combines etching, aquatint and hand-colouring in a chromatically rich, botanically precise and original image.

PHILIP REINAGLE

Large Flowering Sensitive Plant, from Robert John Thornton, *The Temple of Flora*, 1799
Hand-coloured engraving, 44 × 35.7 cm / 17¼ × 14 in
National Gallery of Victoria, Melbourne

A Jamaican man in the background of this print gives an idea of the imposing size of *Calliandra grandiflora*, a native of tropical Central America whose reddish-purple stamens trail in tassels above its fine pinnate leaves. As the hummingbirds in this imaginary scene suggest, the British artist Philip Reinagle was known as an animal painter before he was commissioned by the doctor and botanist Robert John Thornton to work as an artist on *The Temple of Flora*. The book – more properly known as *New Illustration of the Sexual System of Carolus von Linnaeus, and the Temple of Flora and the Garden of Nature* – was a tribute to the Swedish botanist and natural historian Carl Linnaeus, who a few decades earlier had established the binomial system of naming plant and animal species that is still used today. Reinagle's setting of what was then called *Mimosa grandiflora* against a darkening, romantic background is typical of the majestic plates Thornton commissioned from the leading flower painters of the time, including also Sydenham Edwards (see p.127). Reinagle contributed eleven illustrations, which were engraved by Joseph Constantine Stadler. The ambitious scheme proved a commercial failure when it was published in 1799, however, and Thornton died destitute in 1837.

HELENE SCHMITZ

Mimosa (*Acacia saligna*; syn. *A. cyanophylla*), 2003–5,
from *A Passion for Systems: Linnaeus and the Dream of Order in Nature*, 2007
C-print, 90 × 70 cm / 35½ × 27½ in
Private collection

This somewhat surreal-looking image shows *Acacia saligna* covered with brilliant yellow flowers; its seeds are distributed by ants. The photograph was taken by the Swedish photographer Helene Schmitz as part of a project published in 2007 to coincide with the tercentennial celebration of the birth of her countryman the eighteenth-century botanist Carl Linnaeus (see p.63). The book discusses Linnaeus's 'Sexual System' of classification and illustrates its twenty-four categories with close-up views of selected plants from each Linnaean category or class, photographed against a black background in order to highlight colour and detail, including the reproductive parts. Taken with Georg Dionysius Ehret's plate depicting the twenty-four classes (1736; see p.28), Schmitz's photographs bring these classification categories to life, showing how the number of stamens and pistils (plant reproductive organs) can be counted and providing real-life examples of Ehret's icons. The *Acacia* shown here was assigned to the penultimate category, Polygamia, which contains plants having unisexual and bisexual flowers on the same individual plant, or on different plants of the same species. Schmitz was already taking close-range views of plants when she read Linnaeus's work and was inspired to make this book, which won several awards in Sweden in 2007.

Perennial cornflower (*Centaurea montana*), c.1875–86
Pencil and brown ink on paper, 11.2 × 10.2 cm / 4½ × 4 in
Ruskin Foundation, Lancaster University

This lively sketch clearly demonstrates the enthusiasm of an artist who is not put off by the lowly status of his subject. The Victorian John Ruskin, better known today as an art critic than as an artist, was a particular admirer of J.M.W. Turner (see p.224), and himself took a similar romantic approach to nature (he declared himself 'at war with' botanical precision). Ruskin's studies of wayside flowers were published in *Proserpina*, a curious series of lessons in how to draw wild plants. He describes thistles as 'a vast company of rough, knotty, half-black or brown, and generally unluminous plants – flower I can scarcely call them and weeds I will not.' He was more interested in the form and beauty of a flower than in its name – which is why it is difficult to identify this study precisely. In 1871 Ruskin founded the Ruskin School of Drawing and Fine Art in Oxford to challenge conventional art-teaching methods. He also founded the Guild of St George, a charity to promote the rural lifestyle and crafts, a utopian vision shared by his Pre-Raphaelite followers, including artist William Morris (see p.299).

MARGARET STONES

Spiny thistle (*Cirsium horridulum*), 1980
Watercolour on paper, 57 × 38 cm / 22½ × 15 in
Louisiana State University Libraries, Baton Rouge

The attention to detail lavished on this illustration of the spiny thistle (*Cirsium horridulum*), with its dissected and enlarged details, belies its status as a lowly roadside and field weed in the state of Louisiana in the southern United States. The flowers are either pale yellow or, as with this specimen collected near Baton Rouge in early April 1980, pale mauve. The young stems are edible. The Australian botanical artist Margaret Stones painted the thistle as part of a project she had begun four years earlier, painting the wild flowers of Louisiana to celebrate the state's bicentenary. The collection of more than 200 paintings was published as *Flora of Louisiana* in 1991. Having studied art in Melbourne, Stones was a nurse during World War II, and she started to paint flowers while convalescing from tuberculosis. In 1951 she moved to England and worked as a botanical artist, becoming chief artist on *Curtis's Botanical Magazine* in 1958 and holding that position for twenty-five years. Meanwhile, she worked on the six-volume *Endemic Flora of Tasmania* (1967–78), as well as making lily paintings for the supplements to the Royal Horticultural Society's *Monograph of the Genus Lilium*. Stones's extremely accurate paintings are annotated clearly with the specimen's date and place of origin.

Cabbage gum (*Eucalyptus pauciflora* subsp. *parvifructa*), *c.*1955
Watercolour, 28 × 30 cm / 11 × 11¾ in
Royal Botanic Gardens, Melbourne

Bold diagonal lines give a formal quality to this watercolour of the red stems, dark green leaves, buds, flowers and seeds of *Eucalyptus pauciflora* subsp. *parvifructa*, the cabbage gum, which was based on a specimen collected in 1955 at the top of Mount William, near Ararat, Victoria, by the Australian artist Stan Kelly. Kelly combined botanical painting with his job as an engine driver, and often made expeditions into the bush to collect plants and observe them in their natural habitats. His special interest was the eucalypts, of which there are some 680 species in the genus *Eucalyptus*, most of them native to Australia. They are often referred to as gum trees because of their sticky resin, or as stringybarks from their habit of shedding strips of bark from their trunks. Kelly published his first book, *40 Australian Eucalypts in Colour*, in 1949; twenty years later he produced the work for which he is best known, the two-volume *Eucalypts*, illustrated with 250 watercolours that Kelly later gifted to the National Herbarium of Victoria. In the 1970s and 1980s he turned his attention to fungi. In 1980 Kelly received the Order of Australia medal in recognition of his influence on the appreciation of Australian plants and conservation.

JEAN-BAPTISTE HUYNH

Nature – Eucalyptus, 1997
Inkjet print on Baryta paper, 120 × 120 cm / 47¼ × 47¼ in
Private collection

The varied angles of these leaf pairs, the shadow tones on their undersides, the asymmetry of their shape and the thinnest white outline that helps them to stand out against the gradated background give this print of a young sprig of eucalyptus a three-dimensional sculptural solidity. Reproduced at a huge size – it is 1.2 metres (4 feet) square – it almost resembles a series of steps the viewer could climb (perhaps with echoes of Jack's beanstalk). The self-taught French-Vietnamese photographer Jean-Baptiste Huynh is best known for his portraits, but he has also produced many photographs of plants, in particular of leaves taken in positions that yield interesting effects of light and shadow. This image is a study of the juvenile foliage of a eucalyptus (species not identified; perhaps *E. gunnii*): in most species the leaves lengthen and hang downwards as the plant becomes mature. The photograph emphasizes the varying geometry of the leaf pairs, which range from parallel towards decussate or angled placing. Huynh is one of the great success stories of recent times, working mainly in the medium of the photobook. His career culminated in a one-man exhibition at the Louvre, Paris, in 2012.

99

Rose and poppy, c.1760
Gouache and gold on paper, 11.8 × 13.2 cm / 4¾ × 5¼ in
Victoria and Albert Museum, London

The bold red makes for a pleasing echo between a rose and a poppy painted side by side, one on a salmon-pink background, the other on painted gold. The flowers – the work of the Mughal painter, poet and philosopher Mola Ram in India in the late eighteenth century – are highly stylized, with flowers and leaves outlined in gold and filled in with blocks of colour. The rose on the left appears flattened, with three flowers in full bloom and two tiny buds; the poppy's seed head is clearly visible inside the flower, with two buds yet to bloom. It may be an opium poppy, which has always been an important flower in northern India, where several Mughal emperors were addicted to the drug. Flower painting was also an important part of the Mughals' Islamic tradition of art, and flower imagery appears frequently – one renowned portrait of the third Mughal emperor, Akbar, showed him holding a rose, helping increase the flower's popularity in India. Ram, who is noted for introducing natural colours to his paintings, founded the Garhwal School of Painting, following Mughal traditions that had arrived in Garhwal a century earlier. He more typically painted highly stylized women, with large breasts, small waists and large eyes, in the Mughal style of miniature paintings. This painting is a rare example of his interest in flora.

European Columbines and Sweet Cherry, 1561–2, illumination added 1591–6
Watercolour, gold paint and ink on parchment, 16.6 × 12.4 cm / 6½ × 4¾ in
The Getty Museum, Los Angeles, California

This small manuscript – only about 16 × 12 centimetres (6¼ × 4¾ inches) – is nevertheless one of the most spectacular of all illuminated manuscripts. It was created by two outstanding artists who never met: the Hungarian calligrapher György Bocskay wrote the texts in Latin, German, Italian, Greek and Hebrew, while the Flemish illuminator Joris Hoefnagel added the plant and animal illustrations later. This page shows the titles of the Holy Roman Emperor Ferdinand I, painted in ink by Bocskay, plus two sweet cherries (*Prunus avium*) and two forms of European columbine (*Aquilegia vulgaris*) added by Hoefnagel. Shadows are given to the cherries while the columbines are painted as if stuck to the page with paper strips in typical trompe l'oeil style. Bocskay, secretary to the Royal Hungarian Chamber, worked for Ferdinand I in Vienna in 1561–2. After Ferdinand's death the manuscript passed to his grandson, Emperor Rudolph II who commissioned Hoefnagel to add the miniatures in the 1590s. Rudolph probably included the work in his famed Kunstkammer ('cabinet of curiosities') in Prague. Today the manuscript is generally known as *Mira calligraphiae monumenta* ('Miraculous monuments of calligraphy') or as the *Getty Codex* after the Museum in Los Angeles, California, where it is conserved.

Flowers, 1632–53
Carved and inlaid marble, approx. 175 × 400 cm / 68¾ × 157½ in
Taj Mahal, Agra, India

This carved marble panel is perhaps less significant for its rather fanciful depiction of flowers – some of which seem to resemble tulips – than for its location, on one of the world's most famous symbols of love: the Taj Mahal in Agra, India. Constructed under the orders of the seventeenth-century Mughal emperor Shah Jahan, the marble mausoleum was intended as a magnificent tomb for his favourite wife, Mumtaz Mahal. Work began in 1632 and took more than twenty years. The white marble is adorned with calligraphy, geometric patterns and many depictions of flowers, which in this large frieze are surrounded by a decorative *pietra dura* border of inlaid semi-precious stones. These flowers are thought to represent the paradise where Shah Jahan and Mumtaz would eventually be reunited. Plants and gardens played an important role in the Islamic concept of paradise, and the Taj Mahal and the formal gardens that surround it can be seen as a symbolic re-creation of paradise on Earth. The building carries many inscriptions referring to paradise, the day of judgement or divine mercy. Indeed, the word 'paradise' derives from an ancient Persian word that referred to a walled enclosure and thence to a park or garden.

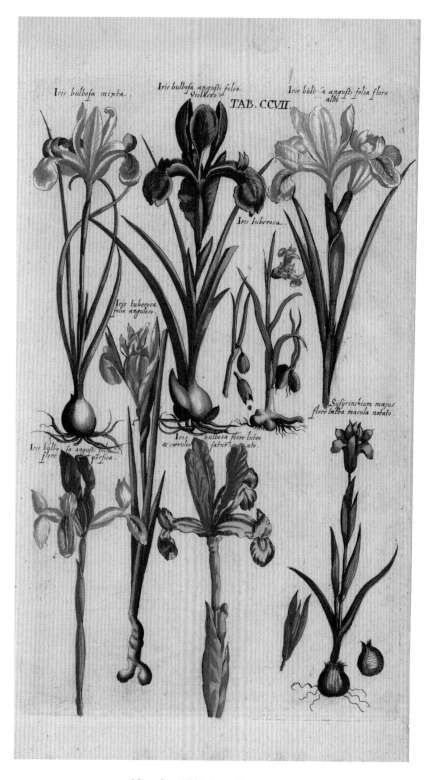

Irises, from *Viridarium reformatum*, 1719
Hand-coloured copper engraving, 39.8 × 25.3 cm / 15¾ × 10 in
Private collection

By including a yellow-flowered bulb of what is today known as *Sisyrinchium majus* in the bottom right-hand corner of his plate of irises, the Swiss-born artist Matthew Merian highlights the close relationship between the genera *Sisyrinchium* and *Iris* (he labels the yellow flower 'Sysyrinchium with large yellow flowers and notable blotching'). The iris was a challenge to classification. This plate shows *Iris xiphium*, the Spanish or bulbous iris – its bulbs differen-

tiate it from the larger *Iris germanica*, which grows from rhizomes – but confusion existed with blue English irises, which grew around Bristol in southwestern Britain, where they must originally have been dumped from a ship's ballast, and with Dutch cultivars. The Spanish iris, which was introduced northwards across Europe during the sixteenth century, was appreciated for its colours: mainly purple or blue with yellow or orange marks on the falls, but also with

yellow, white or bronze variations. *Viridarium reformatum* was remarkable for its time, for its scope and for its rich and detailed illustrations. It included almost 500 plates, including this one by Merian, who linked two generations of botanical artists. His father-in-law was the renowned Flemish publisher Theodor de Bry and Merian's daughter was the celebrated botanical painter Maria Sibylla Merian.

EDWARD STEICHEN

Delphiniums, 1940
Dye imbibition print, 33 × 23.4 cm / 13 × 9¼ in
George Eastman Museum, Rochester, New York

The American photographer Edward Steichen is renowned as one of the leading practitioners of the twentieth century; less widely known is his passion for delphiniums (he was president of the Delphinium Society of America). This magnificent photograph brings together both of Steichen's interests. Its composition displays the varying growth habits and heights of the subjects, while the sense of balance is underlined by the darkest shades appearing at the bottom of the image. Colour-coding emphasizes the height of the palest blooms, while added tension is created by the knowledge that the photograph was taken when World War II was already raging in Europe. Steichen pursued his passion for gardening alongside his career as a photographer. From his twenties, he focused on breeding delphiniums at his farm in Connecticut, where he devoted 4 hectares (10 acres) to the programme, selecting only about one plant in forty and ploughing the rest under. Real cut flowers of Steichen's delphiniums were shown in a dedicated exhibition at the Museum of Modern Art, New York, in June 1936, in what can be seen as one of the earliest bio art events. The flowering spikes were displayed in colour-coded relays during the week-long event; first the true or pure blue, then the fog and mist shades.

HEINRICH FÜLLMAURER

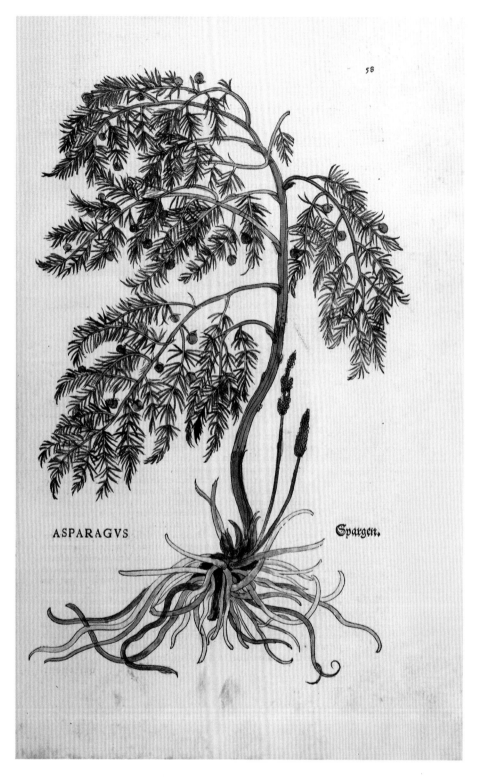

Asparagus (*Asparagus officinalis*), 1542
Coloured woodcut, 34.5 × 23 cm / 13¾ × 9 in
Biblioteca Nazionale Universitaria di Torino

This coloured woodcut of an asparagus plant (*Asparagus officinalis*), showing its berries and rhizoms as well as the edible shoots, comes from *De stirpium historia*, one of three books published within two years that changed the course of science. In 1542 *De revolutionibus orbium coelestium* by Nicolaus Copernicus proposed for the first time the idea of a heliocentric universe, while *De humani corporis fabrica* by Andreas Vesalius was the first modern textbook on human anatomy. The following year, *De stirpium historia* by Leonhart Fuchs, a professor at Tübingen University in what is now Germany, was the first modern herbal with long-lasting impact. It was printed at the height of the Renaissance in Basel, in both Latin and German, a tribute to the spirit of the Reformation (of which Fuchs was a major proponent). It is outstanding because of the remarkable quality of its woodcuts – which mark the beginning of printed plant illustrations that are true to nature – and because it includes portraits of the artists at work: the plant illustrators Heinrich Füllmaurer and Albrecht Mayer and the woodcutter Veyt Rudolf Speckle (this illustration from the Latin version is based on a watercolour by Füllmaurer). Fuchs's magnum opus appeared in several variants and translations, making him one of the 'fathers of herbal lore'.

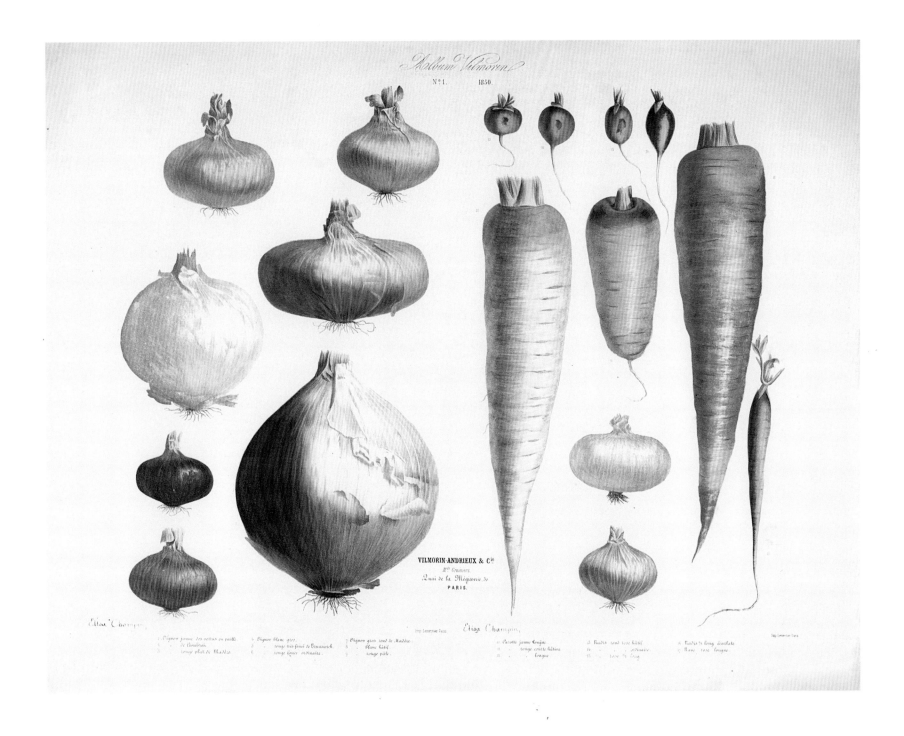

Album Vilmorin No. 1, 1850
Colour lithograph, 49 × 34.5 cm / 19¼ × 13¾ in
Private collection

This plate by the French painter Elisa-Honorine Champin was the first in a series of annual posters distributed by the Parisian seed firm of Vilmorin-Andrieux – founded in 1815 by a descendant of Pierre Andrieux, seedsman to King Louis XV – to advertise the vegetables it sold. Champin uses typically vibrant colour to depict realistically the various cultivars of carrot and onion available at that time, and lists the names of each cultivar at the bottom. Vilmorin-Andrieux distributed a large-format chromolithograph poster each year from 1850 to 1895. Brightly coloured, realistic and detailed, the posters also formed part of the seed catalogues sold as *Le Jardin Potager*. Although fifteen artists were involved in the production of the plates, many of the finest were painted by Champin. Born Elisa-Honorine Pitet in Paris, she was inspired by the plants in the Jardin des Plantes to create highly decorative floral art. In 1837 she married the French landscape watercolourist Jean-Jacques Champin, and from 1850 until her death in 1871 both she and her husband contributed posters to *Le Jardin Potager*. A book of all forty-six posters was published in 1899 with the title *Album Vilmorin*. The chromolithographs were produced by the highly reputable firm of Lemercier & Cie of Paris.

CHRISTABEL KING

Saxifrage (*Chrysosplenium macrophyllum*), from *Curtis's Botanical Magazine*, 2011
Watercolour, 21 × 12 cm / 8¼ x 4¾ in
Royal Botanical Gardens, Kew, London

The precise hairs on the stems of this specimen of *Chrysosplenium macrophyllum* – a robust ground-covering saxifrage found by streams in dark forests in western China, where its white flowers appear to shine in low light – are evidence of a botanical artist at the height of her powers. Christabel King, who prepared the illustration for *Curtis's Botanical Magazine* in 2011, has been the chief botanical artist at Kew Gardens since 1994, working mainly on illustrations for *Curtis's* and for monographs such as *The Genus Galanthus* (1999), *The Genus Lavandula* (2004) and *The Genus Roscoea* (2007). In her early years at Kew, King worked with Margaret Stones (see p.97) under the tutelage of the cactus specialist David Hunt, and she is renowned for her representations of spines and hairs, as seen here. King has travelled widely, notably with an expedition to the Rwenzori in Uganda in 1987; some of her paintings from that trip were published in *Africa's Mountains of the Moon: Journeys to the Snowy Sources of the Nile* (1989). She is also highly regarded as a teacher of botanical illustration, several of whose international pupils are now in the first rank of botanical artists, and she wrote *The Kew Book of Botanical Illustration* (2015).

Nepenthes truncata, 1999
Watercolour on paper, 54 × 38.5 cm / 26¼ × 15 in
Shirley Sherwood Collection, London

This watercolour depicts the remarkable traps that grow from the modified leaves of rare species of carnivorous pitcher plant, *Nepenthes truncata* from the Philippines, where it grows on open mountainsides at altitudes between about 230 and 600 metres (750–2,000 feet). Mariko Imai is one of the world's finest botanical illustrators, as is evident here in the meticulous detail of the shiny, striped lip of the pitcher. *N. truncata* has characteristically heart-shaped leaves and produces very large pitchers, up to 40 centimetres (16 inches) long. One of about ninety species in the genus, it is listed as endangered in the wild since its habitat is under threat. Pitcher plants have evolved their remarkably adapted leaves to ensnare animals, usually invertebrates such as flies, which drown in the liquid at the base of the pitcher, allowing the plant to absorb nutrients from them as they decay. A pitcher of this species at the Botanical Gardens in Lyon, France, was once found to contain the corpse of a mouse – the first record of a pitcher plant trapping a mammal. Imai has exhibited her work in her native Japan and overseas, and has illustrated several books, including *Endangered Plants of Japan: A Florilegium* (2004).

Cystoseira fibrosa, Delesseria sanguinea, Alaria esculenta, Sargassum plumosum,
Delesseria sinuosa and *Furcellaria fastigiata,* from *British Algae: Cyanotype Impressions,* 1853
Cyanotype, each 25 × 19 / 9¾ × 7½ in
New York Public Library

Only two of these beautiful shapes fanned out against the characteristic cyan blue background of the early photographs known as cyanotypes are plants – the *Delesseria* (top middle and bottom left). The others are seaweeds, which share some characteristics with plants but are actually algae. These images from the middle of the nineteenth century – a period of rapid development in photographic techniques – are remarkable because their creator was,

unusually for the time, a woman. Through her father and husband, John Pelly Atkins, both scientists, Anna Atkins was friendly with two photographic pioneers: Henry Fox Talbot (see p.221) and the astronomer Sir John Herschel. Talbot taught her the calotype and photogenic drawing techniques he had developed, and from Herschel she learned how to produce 'blueprints' using insoluble Prussian Blue dye. Atkins became a pioneer of the cyanotype

method, photographing first algae – these examples were some of her first – and later plants. The algae were placed on cyanotype light-sensitive paper and then exposed to light, creating a negative shadow image. After her husband died in 1837, Atkins produced three volumes of *Photographs of British Algae: Cyanotype Impressions* (1843–53).

BRYAN WHITNEY

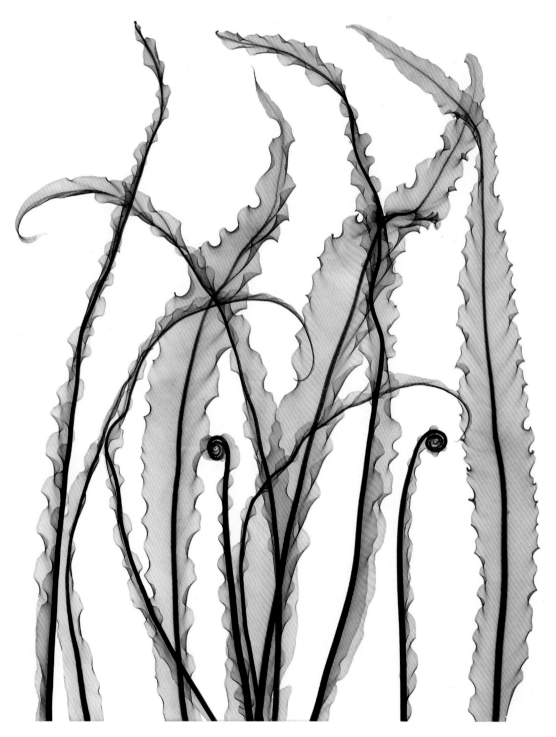

Bird's Nest Fern, 2010
Pigment print, 40.6 × 50.8 cm / 16 × 20 in
Private collection

This composition of upright and curling fronds, combining mature fronds with those whose heads are still furled at the tip, is the creation of the American photographer Bryan Whitney. Whitney employs a range of techniques, including using X-rays as here, to produce remarkable images that reveal the internal structures of his subjects, which include buildings and other man-made objects as well as animals and plants. Instead of a conventional camera, Whitney uses an X-ray machine to produce beams that penetrate the subject and create an image on a plate or photographic paper. This monochrome image is then digitally adjusted or coloured to produce the finished artwork. In some cases such images are worked on further to create animated sequences. In Whitney's portraits of plants, this method reveals otherwise invisible elements of the internal structure. In this study of a group of fern fronds, their general shape is visible, but they are also imbued with a beautiful translucency – an effect not achievable in traditional photography. Whitney studied the psychology of art at the University of Michigan and has also taught at the International Center of Photography and at the Center for Alternative Photography in New York. His work has been widely exhibited.

'Four tulips', c.1635–45
Watercolour on vellum, 34 × 44.9 cm / 13½ × 18 in
Metropolitan Museum of Art, New York

A peacock butterfly and a bush cricket highlight the scale of four rare Dutch tulips, whose subtle patterns are meticulously observed – because they were highly valuable. The German artist Jacob Marrel worked in Utrecht, Holland, at the height of 'Tulipomania', a remarkable craze in the mid-seventeenth century when tulip bulbs changed hands for huge prices. The wealthy Dutch middle classes rushed to speculate on the bulbs, which had been introduced from Turkey a century earlier. A wide range of tulips were cultivated in Holland, and the rarest fetched the highest prices. Especially prized were those with striped or streaked flowers, as here – from left to right, Boter man (Butter Man), Joncker (Nobleman), Grote geplumaceerde (Great Plumed One) and Voorwind (With the Wind). The streaks are now known to be the result of a mosaic virus infection, which makes the main colours split but also weakens the bulb and hinders propagation – increasing rarity and value. The vivid colours and detailed depiction are typical of Marrel's albums of tulip paintings (*Tulpenboeken*). In about 1650 he returned to Frankfurt, where his stepdaughter Maria Sibylla Merian (see p.207) became a noted flower artist. In Holland, meanwhile, the sudden end of the tulip bubble left many people ruined.

BRASSAÏ

Pistil, 1932
Silver gelatin print, 30 × 23 cm / 12 × 9 in
Centre Pompidou, Paris

The prolific Hungarian-born photographer Brassaï gives this close-up image of the reproductive organs of a tulip the same erotic quality that he gives the lovers in his better-known pioneering photographs of the streets of Paris. Pollen is scattered over the shiny petals and the stigma appears to glow with fecundity. The flower is in full bloom, but its moment has almost passed. Its precise stage of development is unclear, and that is part of Brassaï's intention: 'For me the photograph must suggest rather than insist or explain.' Brassaï – who was born Gyula Halász – is hailed as the father of street photography thanks to his grainily textured photographs of the nocturnal *demi-monde* of 1930s Paris. Having studied fine art and worked as a journalist, he did not pick up a camera professionally until he was thirty years old. Once he started, however, he did not stop. He captured both the sordid and smart sides of his adopted city: nightclubs, parties, dances, lovers and foggy, damp streets, as well as such contemporary writers as Thomas Mann, Colette and Lawrence Durrell and artists including Pablo Picasso, Georges Braque and Salvador Dalí. His obsession with the city's graffiti led to a myriad of photographs of walls.

JEHAN GIRAULT

Herbarium sheet, 1558
Dried and pressed sewn plants on paper, 30.5 × 24 cm / 12 × 9½ in
Muséum National d'Histoire Naturelle, Paris

These plants were collected near Lyon, France, about 460 years ago, dried carefully and then mounted with thread in this unique eighty-one-page volume of medicinal plants. This page comes from the earliest known herbarium of its kind in France. According to the inscription inside, the creator, Jehan Girault, began this collection of 310 plants in August 1558. We know little about Girault, who tells us that he was a pupil of the sixteenth-century French physician and botanist Jacques Daléchamps before training as a surgeon under Jehan Canappe at the faculty of medicine in Lyon. At the time botany was a vital part of medical studies, and students would have been encouraged to make a *hortus siccus*, or collection of dried plants. Most of the plants Girault collected are local to Lyon, which may have been where he lived and worked. The book came into the possession of a Mr Boissier, who in 1721 gave it to the doctor and botanist Antoine de Jussieu at the Jardin du Roi in Paris with the message, 'Here, sir, is a bouquet that I beg you to accept … It has its merits for the leaves and herbs which have been preserved for a very long time.' The Jardin du Roi is now part of MNHN, where this precious volume can now be found.

Herbarium sheet, *c.*1839–46
Pressed flowers on woven paper, 33 × 49.5 cm / 13 × 19½ in
Houghton Library, Harvard University, Cambridge, Massachusetts

These flowers are more important for the identity of the person who pressed them than for themselves. This is a page from a sixty-six-leaf herbarium, or album of dried flowers, put together in the mid-nineteenth century by fourteen-year-old Emily Dickinson, later one of America's most beloved poets, as a schoolgirl in Massachusetts. The flowers reflected her lifelong fascination with death: by drying and preserving them, she granted them immor-tality. She wrote to a friend: 'Did you ever know that a flower, once withered and freshened again, becomes an immortal flower, – that is, that it rises again?' Of the ten specimens shown on this page, Dickinson has labelled eight, including the potato, the white lettuce, the common foxglove and the marsh marigold. In total, her herbarium contained 424 specimens, most of which she labelled, with only a few errors. More than half were native to Massachu-setts; the remainder were yard, garden and houseplants. Flower-pressing was a popular hobby for young girls in the nineteenth century, but Dickinson often included a single flower she had dried herself when she wrote to her friends, frequently with a poem. When she was older, her father built her a conservatory at the family home, and she used it to study her beloved flowers.

Agapanthus umbellatus, 1700
Watercolour on paper, 46 × 33 cm / 18 × 13 in
Muséum National d'Histoire Naturelle, Paris

This illustration from 1700 of what was then known as the 'African hyacinth' shows the plant emerging on a short stem from the earth, its evergreen leaves breaking out of the frame of the painting. The inflorescence is shown cut off from the stem in order to fit within the image. Details show individual flowers from the side and in reverse with dissections, together with a seed capsule and seeds. The artist, Claude Aubriet, was royal painter to the Sun King, Louis XIV of France; as such he was expected to paint many of the exciting new plants growing in the Jardin du Roi in Paris. The paintings, mostly in bodycolour on vellum, were scientifically accurate and true to nature rather than in the more aesthetically influenced style of Aubriet's predecessor, Nicolas Robert. Aubriet's African hyacinth is now well known as *Agapanthus africanus*, but the genus *Agapanthus* was not given a separate name until 1788, long after Aubriet's death. He was commissioned to produce artwork for three of France's most distinguished botanists at the Jardin du Roi: the director Joseph Pitton de Tournefort, Sébastien Vaillant and Tournefort's successor, Antoine de Jussieu.

RON VAN DONGEN

Pennisetum glaucum 'Purple Majesty', 2005
Ultrachrome archival pigment print, dimensions variable
Private collection

By singling out just one tall, willowy stem of *Pennisetum glaucum* 'Purple Majesty'– an ornamental millet that grows up to 1.5 metres (5 feet) tall and that today is often grown in clumps for its dramatic colour – the Venezuelan-born photographer Ron Van Dongen captures the moment at which the young stalk matures and its stem begins to change from green to black. As it matures in turn, the spike will stand upright – some grow 30 centimetres (12 inches) tall – and

turn chocolate-brown, becoming a magnet for pollinating birds. By using his trademark tone-on-tone background, in this case purple, Van Dongen heightens the intensity of the stem's colour change in contrast to the delicate, barely maturing head. Unlike most of his contemporaries, Van Dongen, who was raised in Holland but now lives in the United States, grows the plants and flowers he photographs. Watching them grow allows him to gain an intimate

understanding of each stem's potential. As he says, 'I have a different relationship with the plants because I've literally grown up with them ... my everyday experience with the plants is very extensive, and I think the images are a result of that experience.'

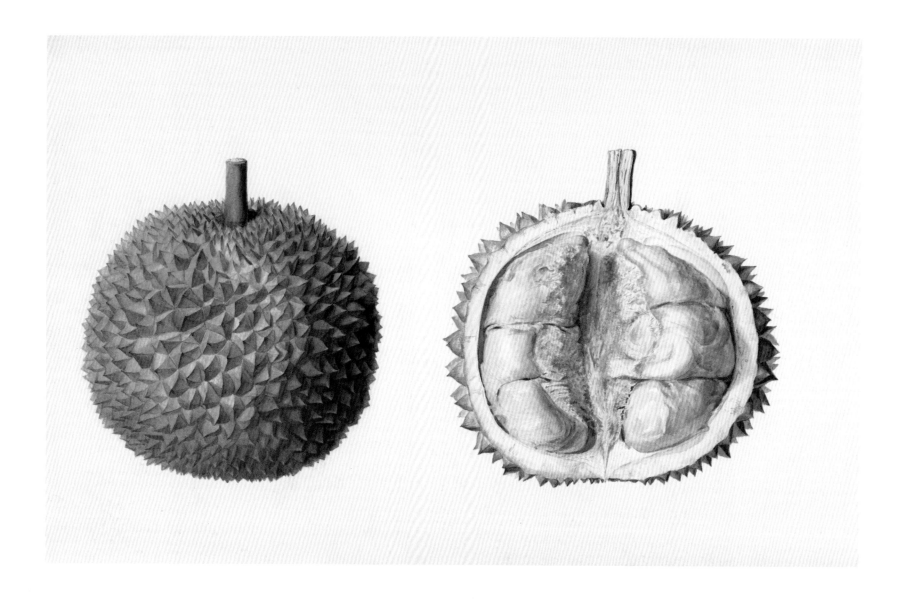

Durian (*Durio zibethinus*), c.1863
Watercolour on paper, 32 × 24 cm / 12¾ × 9½ in
Lindley Library, Royal Horticultural Society, London

Pity the artist who painted this fruit of the spiky-skinned durian, notorious for its strong smell, which many people find revolting. Despite this, the fruit's flesh is eaten raw, or cooked and used to flavour Southeast Asian dishes. It's also used in traditional Asian medicine, as both an anti-fever treatment and a aphrodisiac. This is one of nine watercolours depicting exotic edible fruit by the Javanese artist Radhen Salikin found in an album belonging to the nineteenth-century Dutch botanical artist Berthe Hoola van Nooten (see p.153). Born in Utrecht, van Nooten became interested in botany when she travelled to the Americas with her husband. After his death in 1839, van Nooten joined her merchant brother in the Dutch colony of Batavia (now Jakarta) on the north coast of Java. The connection between van Nooten and Radhen Salikin is unknown, but the artist's local knowledge would have been helpful to the widowed mother of five who conceived an ambition to produce an illustrated flora of Java. The durian tree is pollinated by fruit bats; there are many different cultivars, some smelling worse than others. In an effort to reduce complaints from tourists, an almost odourless variety was introduced in 2007.

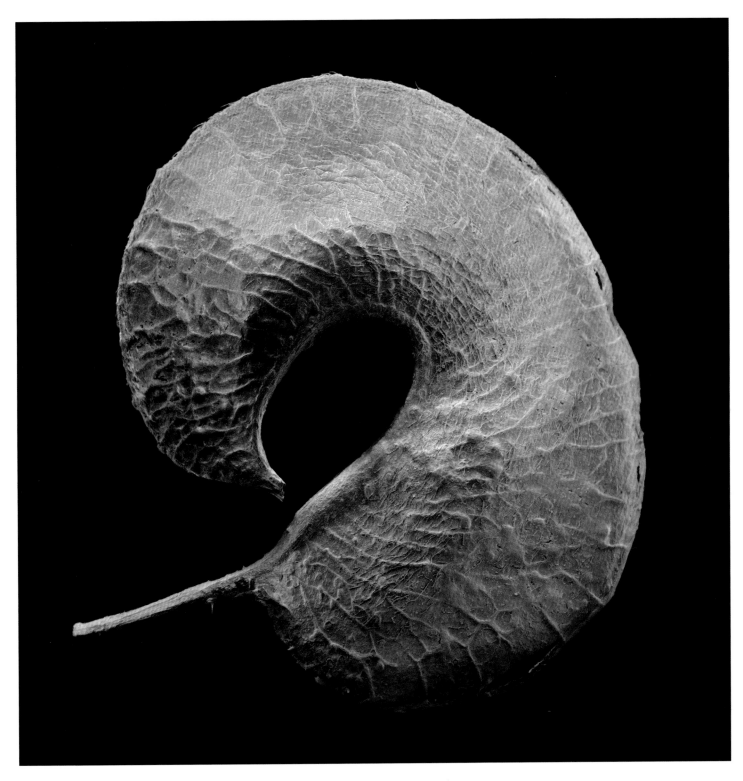

Fruit of moon trefoil (*Medicago arborea*), 2013
Photograph, 35 × 35.5 cm / 13¾ × 14 in
Private collection

Texture and shade give a solidity to the dramatic hook shape of the seed pod that gives *Medicago arborea* its common name, the moon trefoil. The fruit is distinctive, with its flattened spiral husk that remains hanging on the bush throughout the summer. The Spanish photographer Albert Lleal Moya places the magnified pod against a dramatic black background. In eighteenth-century Germany such an approach was characteristic of a school of natural history cabinet painting, as distinct from using local darkening to make pale colours stand out better. The occasional revival of this technique in twentieth-century photography is more probably a reflection of the influence of the neutral and unexpressive backgrounds of *neue Sachlichkeit* ('New Objectivity') photographers, such as Albert Renger-Patzsch. Lleal Moya has been a professional photographer since the mid-1990s, specializing in microscopy and other nature photography, and has worked for Spanish and French editions of *National Geographic* (so he may have been aware of Erich J. Geske's dark-background plant paintings, see p.13, published in the American edition of the magazine in the 1920s). Lleal Moya once observed that, growing up in the large urban sprawl of Barcelona, 'curiosity taught me to discover wildlife under flowerpots and large oceans in a drop of water.'

Horikiri Iris Garden, 1857
Coloured woodblock print, plate 33.7 × 22.3 cm /13¼ × 8¾ in
Minneapolis Institute of Art, Minnesota

The unusual composition of this woodblock print from 1857 is typical of the work of the famous Japanese artist Utagawa Hiroshige, with three nearly life-size flowers of the *hanashobu* (*Iris ensata*) cultivars partially obscuring the view of visitors enjoying the gardens of Horikiri, then a marshy wetland on the edge of Edo (now Tokyo). Hiroshige often used unusual vantage points in his work. Horikiri, with its naturally damp soil, was already famous for its displays of flowers when it was found to be perfect for cultivating species of iris and was developed for this purpose between 1801 and 1803. *Hanashobu* irises became much sought-after, and the gardeners of Horikiri enjoyed a booming export market towards the end of the nineteenth century. Part of the once extensive plantation has been preserved as the Horikiri Iris Garden, a tourist attraction that is still tended for its displays of colourful iris species and cultivars.

Hiroshige, a revered artist of the Edo period, produced landscapes as well as portraits of people, birds and flowers, and was part of the Utagawa school, whose members were renowned for their use of woodblock printing. *Horikiri Iris Garden* is from the famous series 'One Hundred Famous Views of Edo'.

JOHANN MICHAEL SELIGMANN

Great spotted iris (*Iris susiana*), from *Hortus nitidissimis*, 1768
Hand-coloured copperplate engraving, 36.4 × 23.4 cm / 14½ × 9¼ in
Real Jardín Botánico de Madrid

High-quality work like the shading on this near life-size iris, with its fine engraving and naturalistic hand-coloured speckled flower head, does not come cheap. The collection from which this plate comes, *Hortus nitidissimis* (*nitidus* being Latin for 'shining'), was so expensive to produce that it was published in stages over a period of forty years. The result was a dazzling collection of 188 colour plates by various artists depicting 'The flower garden in finest bloom throughout the year, or, pictures of the most beautiful flowers'. The plates by the exceptional Nuremberg artist and engraver Johann Michael Seligmann were based largely on coloured drawings by the work's first illustrator, the outstanding eighteenth-century botanical artist Georg Dionysius Ehret (see p.158), who had drawn the plants from life in the garden of the wealthy Nuremberg physician Christoph Jacob Trew. The text describing Trew's garden was issued separately from the plates and included horticultural advice as well as a brief history of each genus. The work contains mainly hardy cultivars of such popular plants as tulips, hyacinths and other bulbs. *Iris susiana*, the great spotted iris, originated in the Middle East and was the first iris of its type to be cultivated in northern Europe.

GARRY FABIAN MILLER

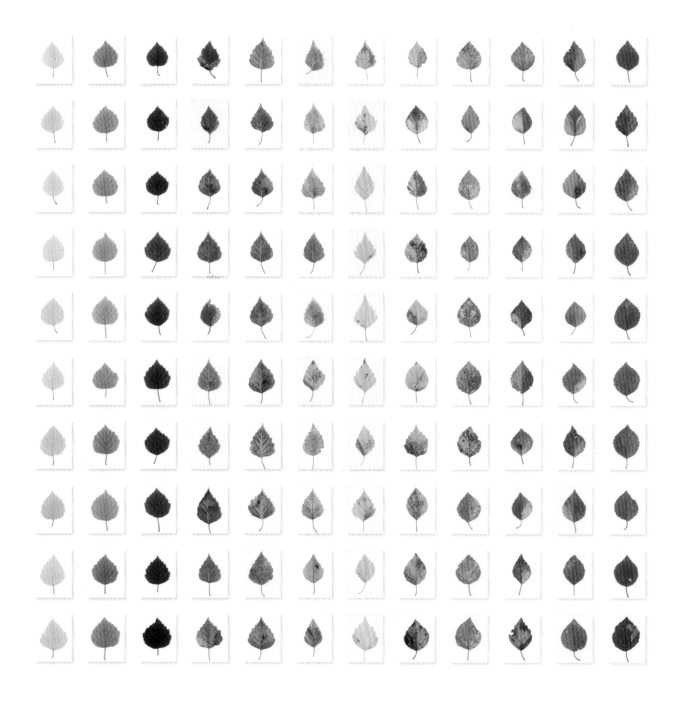

The Waiting, 2011
Leaf, light, 120 unique dye destruction prints, 211 × 211 cm / 83 × 83 in
Private collection

From a distance, this grid of 120 birch leaves from various times of the year 'reads' like a set of uniformly coloured shade cards. On closer inspection, however, it becomes clear that no two leaves are identical in either shape or colour. A deeper study along rows and up and down columns reveals the full diversity of their forms. The British photographic artist Garry Fabian Miller has worked without a camera since 1984, creating images directly on light-sensitive paper, a method that recalls the earliest days of photography in the mid-nineteenth century, in which light is both medium and subject. His use of long exposures gives his work an inevitable chronological aspect that in one sense replicates the processes of photosynthesis and the changing of the seasons. For example, increased spring daylight triggers the chemical changes induced by photosynthesis; on deciduous trees, leaf colour changes from pale yellow-green to deeper green. As summer moves through autumn into winter, the leaves change again, from green shades to yellow then warmer russet hues. In contrast to traditional and digital photographic exposures that last for a fragment of a second, Miller's exposures last anywhere between one and twenty hours to create his unique, luminous images.

WATARU YAMAMOTO

A Chrysanth leaf 7, from the series 'Leaf of Electric Light', 2012
Gelatin silver print, 35.4 × 27.9 cm / 14 × 11 in
Private collection

Although it is clearly distinguishable as a leaf – if one of indeterminate species – this artwork by the young Japanese artist Wataru Yamamoto is more like some kind of light show from a fairground or circus. In fact, it depicts not only the shape of an actual physical leaf but also what Yamamoto calls its 'aura'. Using a technique known as Kirlian photography, he captures the luminescence that is given off when he stimulates the leaf with a high-frequency, high-voltage electrical charge. The technique is named after Semyon Kirlian, who discovered by chance in 1939 that an object on a photographic plate will leave an image when electricity is passed through it. Because the technique uses no camera or lens, the composition is achieved by the careful arrangement of the specimen on the plate. Yamamoto, much of whose work explores the ambiguous understanding of 'nature' in a modern urban world, uses the technique to examine the discrepancy between what we 'see' in a leaf and what its 'material' reality might be. He explains that the different patterns reflect the thickness of the leaf, how much moisture it contains and the environment in which it is created – thus questioning the idea that a leaf has a 'material' reality even as he attempts to picture it.

Bulbus liliaceus vomitorius capitis bonae spei,
from *Exoticarum aliarumque minus cognitarum plantarum centuria prima*, 1678
Engraving, 30.4 × 19 cm / 12 × 7½ in
Dumbarton Oaks Library, Washington, DC

This engraving from 1678 by the artist Stephanus Cousius, clearly illustrates the clumsiness of plant-naming before the introduction of Carl Linnaeus's binomial ('two-name') system in 1753. *Bulbus liliaceus vomitorius capitis bonae spei* refers to both the poisonous properties and the geographical origin of the plant, which was eventually standardized to *Drimia elata*. Cousius clearly shows the large, loosely scaly bulb, which is often only partially buried or sits on the surface of the soil; however, the leaves and flower spike are not usually produced together by the plant, suggesting either that Cousius's plate was composed from several sketches made over the course of a year at the Cape of South Africa, or that the plant's growth cycle was disrupted by cultivation or import and subsequent cultivation in the northern hemisphere. Like their Mediterranean counterpart the squill, *Drimia* bulbs are toxic but also have medicinal uses. The epithet *elata* refers to the tall flower scape, which the artist has cut in two and skilfully used either side of the plate to frame the leafy bulb. Cousius provided many of the illustrations for the German botanist Jakob Breyne's work on the plants of southern Africa, *Exoticarumque minus cognitarum plantarum centuria prima*, which was published in 1678.

JEAN EMMONS

Ixia viridiflora, 2008
Watercolour on calfskin vellum, 45.7 × 30.5 cm / 18 × 12 in
Akridge/Peterson Foundation, Seattle, Washington

The dynamic composition and graceful lines of work by the contemporary American botanical artist Jean Emmons invoke the rocky, windswept environment where the endangered *Ixia viridiflora* grows in the southwestern Cape of South Africa. Emmons's painting was commissioned by the Brooklyn Botanic Garden Florilegium Project, set up in 2000 to recruit dozens of leading flower artists to record the garden's herbarium. Cut flowers and a small plant were posted over 4,500 kilometres (2,800 miles) from Brooklyn across the USA to Emmons's home near Seattle, so the original samples did not have the best start. Nevertheless, Emmons was bewitched by the exquisitely rare turquoise flowers, and painted them in this less traditional manner. Working on calfskin vellum to add brilliancy, Emmons builds up sometimes forty or more layers of translucent washes and dry brushwork to lend richness to her paintings. She works from life whenever possible, preferably with a plant she has grown herself, so she can observe it over time. This painting was used as the catalogue cover and exhibition invitation for 'Losing Paradise? Endangered Plants Here and Around the World', a travelling exhibition by the American Society of Botanical Artists from 2009 to 2011.

Three and Four of Cyclamen, c.1440
Copper engraving, each approx. 11 × 7 cm / 4¼ × 2¾ in
Kupferstich-Kabinett, Staatliche Kunstsammlungen, Dresden

With their upswept, twisted petals, the flowers on these fifteenth-century playing cards leave little doubt that they are intended to show a species of cyclamen, probably the European cyclamen (*Cyclamen purpurascens*). The anonymous artist – named the Master of the Playing Cards – is known for his extremely early copper engravings, mostly playing cards, of which two botanical sets are known, one showing roses, the other cyclamen. (The

Kupferstich-Kabinett in Dresden possesses five 'cyclamen' cards.) It has been suggested that the Master of the Playing Cards – dubbed 'the first personality in the history of engraving' – was a goldsmith working in Alsace, possibly Strasbourg. Certainly, his small-format prints precede the first botanical woodcuts, which were also produced in the region along the Upper Rhine. It is notable that the so-called Scheide Bible, produced by the pioneering printer

Johannes Gutenberg in Mainz in 1454–5, contains in the marginal scrolls a few painted flowers that agree almost perfectly with the cyclamen of the Master of the Playing Cards. These were clearly added by hand after the printing process had been completed. Prints of work by the Master of the Playing Cards are exceedingly rare; when they do occasionally reach the market, they fetch colossal prices.

N.º 1001

[1001]

CYCLAMEN HEDERÆFOLIUM. IVY-LEAVED CYCLAMEN, or SOW-BREAD.

****

Class and Order.

PENTANDRIA MONOGYNIA.

Generic Character.

Cor. rotata, reflexa, tubo breviffimo: fauce prominente. *Bacca* tecta capfula.

Specific Character and Synonyms.

CYCLAMEN *hederæfolium;* foliis cordatis angulatis denti-culatis. *Hort. Kew.* 1. *p.* 196. *Willd. Sp. Pl.* 810.
CYCLAMEN *europæum. Mill. Dict.* 1.
CYCLAMEN folio hederæ et vernum. *Lob. Icon.* 605.
CYCLAMEN romanum foliis hederæ, flore carneo et flore purpureo. *Swert. Florileg. t.* 59.
CYCLAMINUS orbicularis. *Dod. Pempt.* 337.
CYCLAMINUS verno tempore florens. *Cluf. Pan.* 234. *Hift.* 265.
CYCLAMEN hederæfolium. *Bauh. Pin.* 308. *Ger. emac.* 844. 2. *f.* 5. *Raii Hift.* 1206.
CYCLAMEN vernum flore purpureo. *Park. Parad.* 195. *t.* 197. *f.* 1.

The ivy-leaved Cyclamen is faid to be a native of Italy; is a very valuable plant, on account of its early flowering, fweet fcent, and beautiful foliage. It is not fo hardy as *europæum*, but can be cultivated in the open ground. May be propagated by cuttings of the root. Cultivated by GERARD, in 1596.

Syd. Edwards del. Pub. by T. Curtis, St Geo: Crefcent Mar 1 1807. F. Sanfom sculp

Cyclamen hederaefolium, 1807
Watercolour, 22.7 × 13.7 cm / 9 × 5½ in
Private collection

In Sydenham Edwards's illustration of the spring-flowering *Cyclamen repandum*, four vibrant magenta flowers with their typically reflexed petals rise above a mass of ivy-like leaves. When this illustration was published in 1807, the editor of *Curtis's Botanical Magazine*, John Sims, mistakenly identified the plant as *C. hederaefolium*, an autumn-flowering cyclamen from which the spring-flowering *C. repandum* had been distinguished only the previous year. For twenty-eight years around the start of the nineteenth century, Edwards was the main artist for the influential British journal *Curtis's Botanical Magazine*, to which he contributed all but seventy-five of the 1,721 illustrations published in that time. His simple, accurate and uncluttered style was in contrast with William Curtis's earlier artists, William Kilburn and James Sowerby, whose 'whole plant, roots and all' methods were well established.

Edwards was born in Wales, and his skill in botanical drawing was spotted by a friend of Curtis on a visit to Abergavenny in 1779. He moved to Walworth, near Curtis's Botanic Garden in Lambeth Marsh, London, and contributed twenty-seven illustrations to Curtis's *Flora Londinensis* before moving on to the *Botanical Magazine*. In 1815 Edwards launched a rival magazine, the *Botanical Register*, for which he produced all 349 plates until his death in 1819.

Cereus scandens, 1756
Hand-coloured copperplate engraving, 26 × 41.9 cm / 10¼ × 16½ in
Private collection

The enormous flower of this climbing cactus nearly fills the page above the angular stems with their characteristic spines. This hand-coloured engraving by the English artist Richard Lancake is remarkable not only for its craftsmanship but also for the fact that Lancake must have painted it by candlelight because, as its name suggests, the West Indian night-flowering cactus *Selenicereus grandiflorus*, or Queen of the Night torch lily, opens only at night. The huge flowers and heady fragrance made the plant highly fashionable in mid-eighteenth-century London. Lancake's engravings were included in *Figures of the Most Beautiful, Useful and Uncommon Plants described in the Gardeners Dictionary* (1755–60), published to complement the first comprehensive *Gardeners Dictionary*, written in 1731 by Philip Miller, head gardener at the Chelsea Physic Garden in London. The supplement contained 300 plates, of which Lancake produced just over half; the other artists included John Miller, Georg Ehret (see p.158) and William Houstoun. This night-flowering cactus still bore the Latin name given to it by Paul Hermann in 1698, because Miller did not adopt Linnaeus's shortened two-name system until the eighth edition of his dictionary, in 1768. Lancake's later career took an unfortunate turn: he started a paper manufactory in Paris that went bankrupt.

ADAM FUSS

Sunflower, 1992
Unique cibachrome photogram, 152.4 × 101.6 cm / 60 × 40 in
Private collection

If this photogram of a sunflower by the British photographer Adam Fuss seems more reminiscent of the early nineteenth than the early twenty-first century, there is good reason. Fuss, who worked extensively in Australia before moving to New York City, specializes in experimenting with old photographic techniques. Rejecting the digital manipulation used by many contemporary photographers, he works with daguerreotypes, platinum prints and, as here, photograms, created using a process invented by William Henry Fox Talbot (see p.221) in the mid-nineteenth century that removes the camera entirely from the photographic process. Fuss lays objects directly on to light-sensitive paper and uses a variety of exposures to create images that are at once abstract and realistic, transient and fixed. For Fuss, as for such artists as Vincent Van Gogh (see p.291), the close association of the sunflower (*Helianthus annus*) with the sun itself makes the flower a symbol of both the fleeting transience of beauty and the power of regeneration. The yellow corona flaming around a seed head that resembles a black hole above the shapes of ghostly leaves gives the image a poignant quality. The flower's decline has already begun. Fuss himself remarked about photograms, 'Photograms let you see what has never been in a camera. Life itself is the image.'

REGINE HAGEDORN

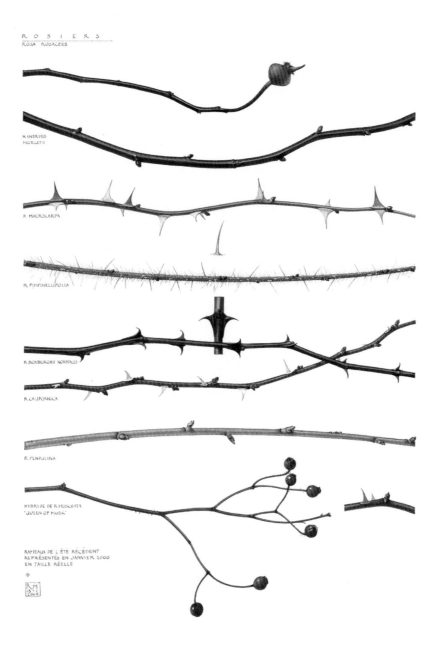

Rosiers, 2000
Watercolour on paper, 49.7 × 35.7 cm / 19½ × 14 in
Shirley Sherwood Collection, London

This watercolour by the contemporary German artist Regine Hagedorn concentrates on one of the most frequently overlooked parts of the rose: the stem. Hagedorn finds great variety in eight meticulously drawn rose stems, which are supplemented by details of the thorns of specific species. While the image is best seen through a magnifying glass in order to appreciate the precision with which she renders each stem, even with the naked eye it is easy to see how the different kinds of roses differ. To ensure scientific accuracy, Hagedorn labels each stem with its botanical name (with more than 100 species of rose and thousands of cultivars, this is the only way to ensure accurate classification). In the bottom left-hand corner she introduces a more personal note, recording that these are stems gathered the previous summer and drawn and painted in January 2000. Hagedorn's strikingly modern treatment of the rose perhaps reflects her early training in jewellery at the École des Arts Décoratifs in Geneva, as she seeks a different way to represent the roses she loves. Her remarkably detailed watercolours combine scientific precision with a lushly romantic quality.

Acorns from Brunei, 1997
Watercolour on paper, 20 × 13 cm / 7¾ × 5 in
Shirley Sherwood Collection, London

Attracted by the shapes of acorns from oak tree relatives found in Brunei, the Japanese artist Mieko Ishikawa represents a selection of them arranged in fourteen dorsal and lateral views as they would be in a field guide – but here with a delicacy that makes them resemble precious jewels. Painting with fine kolinsky and cat-hair brushes, Ishikawa captures the contrasting textures of the hard, shiny surface of the nuts and the rough outer cupule. Born in Tokyo in 1950, Ishikawa studied graphic design before turning in 1989 to botanical art, painting a series of cherry blossoms that were subsequently shown at the Japanese Embassy in Washington, DC. When she visited Borneo for the first time, in 1994, she was immediately fascinated by the mystery and magnificence of the rainforest flora. It was there that she discovered such strange plants as *Rafflesia*, *Nepenthes* (the pitcher plant), *Camponotus* (the ant plant) and the oaks native to Borneo. Trees that bear acorns are usually evergreen in Borneo. There are many *Lithocarpus* (from the Greek *lithos*, stone, and *carpos*, fruit), including *Quercus* (oak) and *Castanopsis* (similar to *Castanea*, the Spanish edible chestnut). Compelled to draw these plants, Ishikawa visited Borneo twelve times to continue her research and sketching, and that led her in 1997 to paint the fascinating acorns of Brunei.

Pages from Pseudo-Apuleius Herbal, c.1070–1100
Ink and colours on parchment, 26 × 19 cm / 10¼ × 7½ in
British Library, London

These pages from an eleventh-century herbal produced by an unidentified monk at St Augustine's Abbey in Canterbury include water mint (*Mentha aquatica*), elder (*Sambucus*), hypericum or St John's wort (*Hypericum*) and a mandrake – the most remarkable of all the plants to be found in medieval herbals – shown in the shape of a curvaceous naked woman. Mandrake had genuine medicinal value as an anaesthetic, but Greek and biblical tradition turned it into an aphrodisiac. This, together with the humanoid form of the roots, signified the plant's powers. But superstitions accumulated around the plant, especially that its shriek on being uprooted was fatal to hear (male mandrakes were generally illustrated being dragged from the earth by a chained dog). The other plants in the herbal are decorative, though stylized, and sometimes identifiable only by recourse to their Latin names, scripted in red rubrics. The herbal was based on the text of Apuleius Platonicus, a fourth-century compiler of medicinal recipes spiced with magical folklore who himself relied on classical sources, including Pliny the Elder, and whose work was in turn copied for centuries. A few unfinished pages in the Canterbury manuscript, where the text surrounds blank spaces of varying sizes, suggests that the illustrations were copied last, from an earlier exemplar.

JACOPO LIGOZZI

Mandrake *(Atropa mandragora)*, 1575–1600
Gouache and watercolour on paper, 67.5 × 46 cm / 26¾ × 18 in
Galleria degli Uffizi, Florence

When this delicate image was painted in the late sixteenth century, the mandrake *(Mandragora officinarum)* was still surrounded by superstition. The plant's root – which has narcotic and hallucinogenic properties – was often depicted in a quasi-human form: it was said to shriek as it was pulled from the ground. There is no hint of such a fanciful approach in this painting by the Italian Renaissance artist Jacopo Ligozzi, who adopted a realistic approach that perhaps reflects the fact that he also worked for the naturalist Ulisse Aldrovandi (see p.220). Having worked for the Habsburg court in Vienna, Ligozzi settled in Florence in about 1577 and became painter to the Medici court and head of the Accademia del Disegno. In Florence he found a broad outlet for his skills as a portraitist, miniaturist, designer and illustrator. Alongside the historical religious and mythical subjects typical of the period, he also pro-duced beautiful paintings of subjects from the natural world. These gouache and watercolour drawings of animals and plants – known as *naturalia* – were much in demand from connoisseurs who created 'paper museums'. The exot-ica reaching Europe from the voyages of exploration were particularly popular, but plants such as mandrake were a mainstay of the older herbal tradition of the Mediterranean.

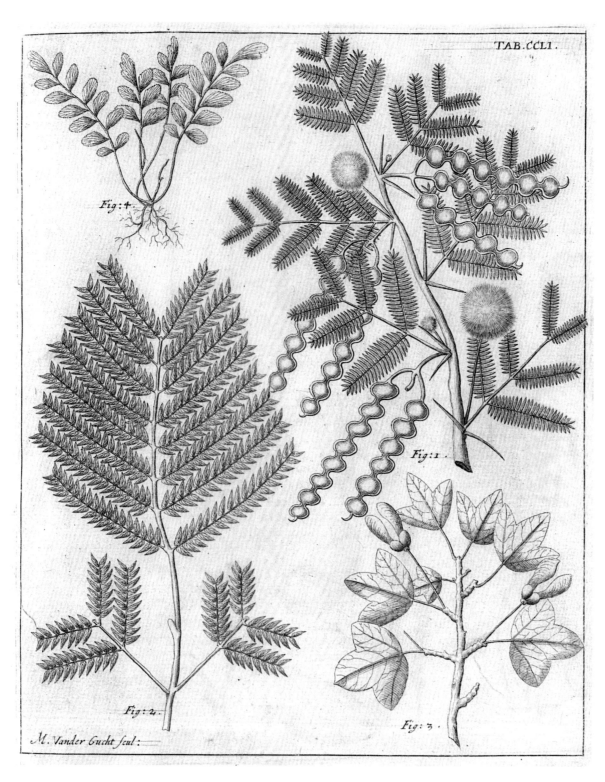

Acacia and other plants, from *Phytographia*, 1691–6
Engraving, 23.5 × 16.7 cm / 9 × 6¾ in
Real Jardín Botánico de Madrid

The seventeenth-century English physician and botanist Leonard Plukenet did not group the plants in his plates according to a classification scheme, yet his ability to present a large amount of information accessibly made his four-volume *Phytographia* (1691–6) an important work. This image of acacia with other plants is a good example of the way he grouped many species on a page, with plate and figure numbers to link them to his plant descriptions. The

largest collection of plant images then available, the *Phytographia* is based largely on specimens from Plukenet's own herbarium, a collection of some 8,000 plant specimens about which he wrote extensively. Later Royal Professor of Botany and gardener to Queen Mary, Plukenet is best known for a series of books published between 1691 and 1705 (*Phytographia*, *Almagestum Botanicum*, *Almagesti Botanici Mantissa* and *Amaltheum Botanicum*) that contain

some 2,740 images and descriptions of new and rare plants, along with a catalogue of his herbarium. Plukenet's published work was consulted by contemporary and later botanists, and was much valued by Carl Linnaeus (see p.63), who cited Plukenet in his landmark publication *Species Plantarum* (1753). Plukenet's herbarium is now held at the Natural History Museum in London.

MIEKO KONISHI

Bamboos and Bamboo Shoots
Acrylic and gouache on paper, 53 × 36 cm / 20¾ × 14 in
Hunt Institute for Botanical Documentation, Carnegie Mellon University, Pittsburgh, Pennsylvania

The contemporary Japanese artist Mieko Konishi achieves an almost photographic precision in her acrylic and gouache depiction of four species of bamboo, together with details of their respective shoots and stems for ease of comparison. The four species the artist has chosen – all popular and decorative forms – help to suggest the wide variety within the bamboos (a subfamily of the grass family). *Pleioblastus gramineus* f. *monstrispiralis* (spiral bamboo),

at left, has an unusual twisted and contorted stem and is often planted for its eye-catching value. *Phyllostachys bambusoides* (timber bamboo) is one of the strongest and tallest of bamboos, capable of growing to over 20 metres (65 feet) tall, and is widely planted, especially in China and Japan; it is harvested for a multitude of uses, including for use in construction and as scaffolding. *Phyllostachys aurea* (golden bamboo) is graceful and decorative, with

golden-green foliage, while *Phyllostachys nigra* f. *henonis* (Henon bamboo, right) has glossy green leaves and produces graceful green canes. Mieko's illustration was part of an exhibition in 2006 at the Hunt Institute in Pittsburgh, of contemporary botanical watercolours from Japan distinguished by the Japanese word *yuuga* – 'elegant and gorgeous' – a fitting description of Mieko's plate.

Tab. 2.

Gladiolus tubiflorus.

Gladiolus bicolor.

Gladiolus anceps.

Gladiolus bicolor, Gladiolus tubiflorus and Gladiolus anceps, from *Gladiolus*, 1784
Engraving, 21 × 15 cm / 8¼ × 6 in
Smithsonian Libraries, Washington, DC

These three species of gladiolus were engraved to accompany a dissertation presented to the University of Uppsala, Sweden, by Carl Peter Thunberg, one of the seventeen famed 'Linnaean Apostles'. These favoured students of Carl Linnaeus (see p.63) made expeditions to faraway lands to explore and to collect plant and animal specimens, and many of them shared specimens, drawings and information with Linnaeus. Thunberg set out for Japan on a Dutch ship, but because Japan was then closed to foreigners other than Dutch traders, he first spent three years in South Africa to learn Dutch and to collect plant and animal specimens, before continuing to Japan for fifteen months as a physician and botanist. He published his *Flora Japonica* in 1784, the same year that this gladiolus dissertation was defended. Most of the estimated 260 species of gladiolus – the name means 'little sword', after the long, narrow leaves – are native to sub-Saharan Africa. Thunberg also published two works on his South African plant studies, documenting 3,100 species in the two-volume *Prodromus plantarum capensium* (1794 and 1800) and the unfinished *Flora capensium* (1807–13) with the German botanist J.A. Schultes. At the time, plants from the Cape in South Africa such as bulb plants, *Erica* and succulents were very popular in European gardens.

BRONWYN VAN DE GRAAFF

Grass tree (*Xanthorrhoea australis*), 2005
Watercolour on paper, 58 × 46.3 cm / 22 × 18¼ in
Shirley Sherwood Collection, London

This watercolour of the 'grass tree' – in fact a relative of the lily – which grows in dry, sandy habitats in mainland Australia and Tasmania, might resemble vintage botanical plates in its inclusion of different parts of the plant, but its striking composition and the abstract quality of the dark trunk mark it out as utterly contemporary. The Australian artist Bronwyn Van de Graaff highlights the trunk, which has a wooden core encased by the resin-compacted bases of thousands of spirally arranged leaves. In some species this trunk is buried, with the leaf rosettes appearing apparently stemless on the surface, while other species grow several metres tall. The twenty-eight or so species of *Xanthorrhoea* are a unique group of living fossils, notable for producing a rigid, vertical inflorescence (right) that bears the flowers. Aboriginal peoples used the leaf bases and new shoots as food and the resin as a glue for mounting spear and axe heads, and burned the resinous stems as torches for night fishing. The plants grow very slowly, and consequently are often taken from their habitat to create instant garden features in warmer countries, a practice that has led to concern about their survival in the wild.

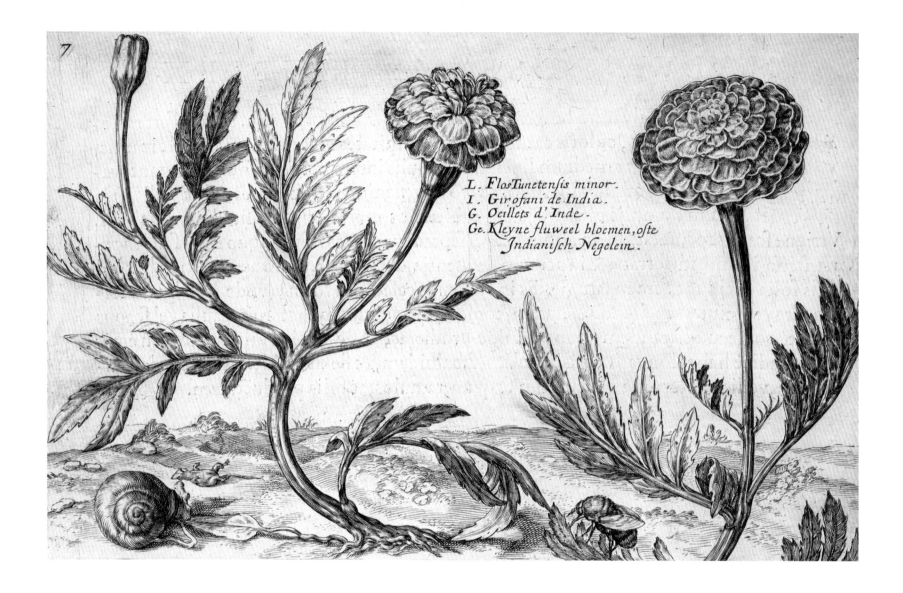

African marigolds (*Tagetes erecta*), from *Hortus Floridus*, 1622
Copper engraving, 13.5 × 25.7 cm / 5½ × 10 in
Natural History Museum, London

This seventeenth-century Dutch copperplate engraving of the African marigold (*Tagetes erecta*), originally from Mexico – complete with snail and bee – came with instructions for colouring the plate, should the reader wish to do so. It is from Crispijn van de Passe's florilegium *Hortus Floridus*, a collection of garden plants of the period, mostly created by him with his brothers Simon and Willem (the three brothers were part of a larger family of artist-engravers). *Hortus*

Floridus – one of the best-known seventeenth-century florilegia – was made at a time when increasing numbers of new plants were being introduced into Europe, and more people were collecting and growing them. The book is organized in two parts: the first is divided into four sections by season of flowering, beginning with spring, and contains nearly 175 illustrations; the second contains about sixty plates of fruit trees, fruits and medicinal plants. The heavier, less skilled

plates in the second part may have been made by Crispijn when he was learning his craft by copying from other drawings and engravings, including those of his father. The flowers depicted in the seasonal sections are engraved with greater delicacy than is common in other florilegia of the period, and many are shown growing in a Dutch landscape, rather than in isolation on the page. In some cases a bulb is also shown lying on the ground.

Proserpina 1, 2009
Cyanotype, 25 × 32 cm / 9¾ × 12¾ in
Private collection

The Scottish artist Alexander Hamilton has spent more than forty years using photograms to record stunning images of plants such as this crocus, which is shown complete with its root system. In his cyanotype process, Hamilton places plants and flowers on light-sensitive paper and exposes them to light, before the image is fixed using the 'blueprint' technique devised by the astronomer Sir John Herschel in the mid-nineteenth century, which used the insoluble Prus-sian blue dye that gave the process its name ('cyan' comes from the Greek for 'dark blue'). Having completed his art studies, Hamilton became interested in flora during a six-month project to catalogue the plants on an uninhabited Scottish island, Stroma, where he made his first cyano-types. He saw the process as an antidote to the manipu-lated images that offer a filtered and processed view of the natural world. He finds an emotional response in a method that allows the sun to draw out the image from the plant, which he calls 'allowing nature to speak for itself'. The crocus was one of the subjects Hamilton studied during a one-year period (2008–9) as artist in residence at Brantwood, the Lake District home of the Victorian art critic and photographer John Ruskin (see p.96), during which Hamilton investigated Ruskin's own efforts to create a holistic approach to botany.

JOHN ELLIS

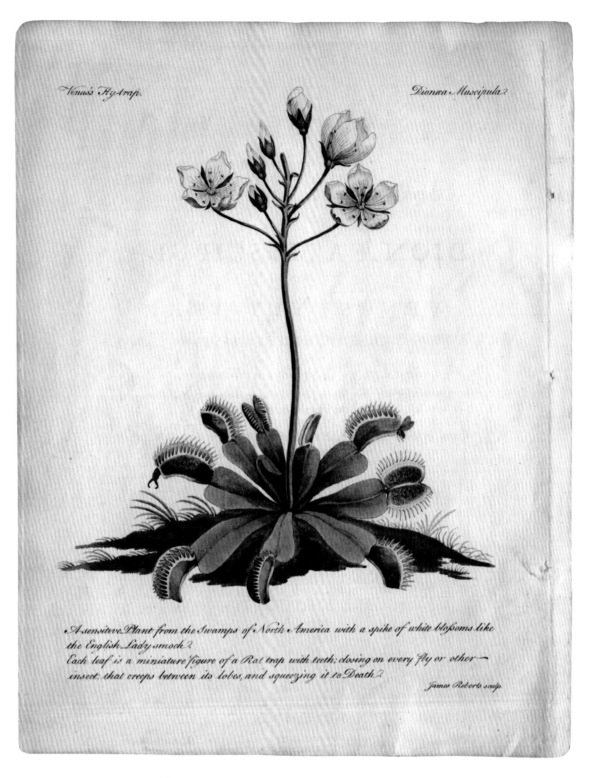

Venus Fly-trap, from *A botanical description of the Dionaea muscipula*, 1770
Hand-coloured engraving, 23.6 × 18.9 cm/ 9¼ × 7½ in
Linnean Society of London

This lifelike coloured engraving shows a single *Dionaea muscipula* – the Venus flytrap – with an inflorescence of white flowers above radiating leaves that end in the 'traps' that give the plant its name. It was drawn by John Ellis, a London merchant and enthusiastic naturalist, correspondent of Linnaeus (see p.63) and major importer of plants in his role as London agent for both Florida and the Dominican Republic. Ellis originally used dried specimens, sent to him indirectly by John Bartram, to describe this remarkable North American plant in a London newspaper in 1768. In 1770 he became the first artist to illustrate it for publication – engraved by James Roberts – in his book *Directions for Bringing over Plants and Seeds from the East Indies and Other Distant Countries ....* The Venus flytrap was native to subtropical North and South Carolina, where it was discovered by Bartram in 1765. *Dionaea* means 'daughter of Dione', the Greek godddess Aphrodite – the Roman Venus – and *muscipula* means mouse trap. The Carolina wetlands are poor in nutrients, so the plant has adapted to attract insects by producing nectar in its hinged leaves, which close to form cage-like traps inside which the insect is subsequently digested.

1 Pitcher Plant, 1 Purple Iris, 1 Lady Slipper Orchid, 2013
Pigment print on watercolour paper, 152.4 × 152.4 cm / 60 × 60 in
Private collection

A trio of remarkably different plants – the carnivorous pitcher plant, the ubiquitous purple iris and a cultivated relative of the rare lady slipper orchid – are captured in a image that pays homage to the Dutch heritage of husband-and-wife photographers Inez Van Lamsweerde and Vinoodh Matadin. This is Dutch Old Master flower-painting for the twenty-first century: the uprooted pitcher plant (*Nepenthes*) appears to hover above the iris and orchid as its tendrils embrace the two flowers. Its pitcher has already partly consumed the iris, whose purple flower appears withered and shrunken. In contrast, the lady or lady's slipper orchid (*Cypripedium*) is in full bloom, its petals shiny and vibrant. This photograph is an unexpected departure for the highly stylish pair, who are better known for their groundbreaking fashion and advertising photography. But Van Lamsweerde explains that photographing flowers is not such a huge leap: 'Working with flowers, for me, is about coming as close as I can get to abstract painting; it's very intuitive. We go to the New York City flower market in the morning and get everything we love, and with a very fast tempo we create these still lifes. It's about bringing out the heroic side of each element, and that's what we do with people.'

WILHELM LUDWIG PETERMANN

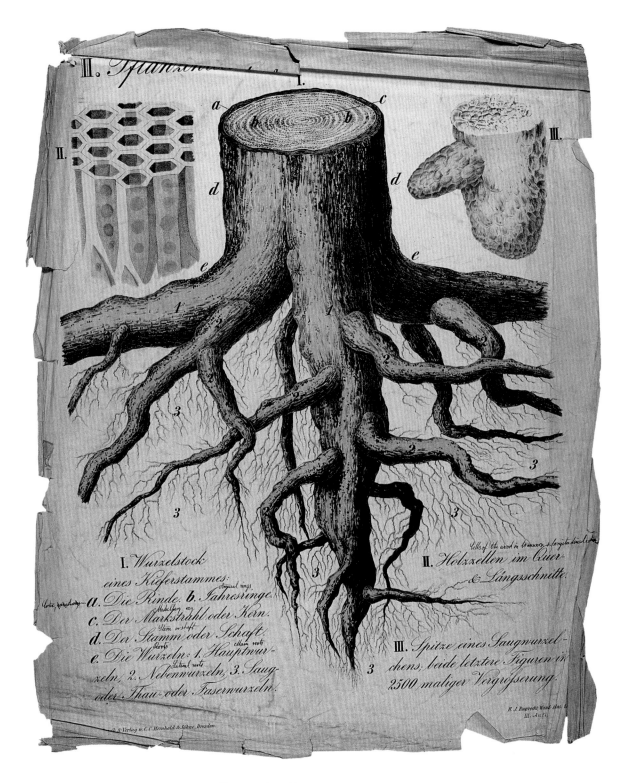

Tree root, from *The Plant Kingdom*, c.1850
Chromolithograph, 62.5 × 55.3 cm / 24¾ × 21¾ in
Wellcome Library, London

This coloured plate comes from *The Plant Kingdom*, published from the 1840s onwards by the German academic Wilhelm Ludwig Petermann, in which he classified plants by what he termed their 'natural systems'. An unidentified root dominates the page, with details of its cell structure and root tips at the top; the labels for the key are squeezed into the available space around the roots, which Petermann illustrates down to the thinnest

tendrils. Just as interesting, however, is Petermann's depiction of the rings in the trunk (labelled 'b'). The existence of tree rings had been known since ancient times, and during the Renaissance Leonardo da Vinci had noted that they formed annually and that their width depended on the growing conditions each year. It was only in the mid-nineteenth century, however, that scientists began trying to use such rings to calculate the changing

climate of the past, and realized that they could be used to calculate the age of wooden samples from, say, historical buildings or archaeological sites, a science now known as dendrochronology. Petermann – a student and later professor of botany at the University of Leipzig, where he was also director of the herbarium of the botanical garden – classified dozens of species for the first time in *The Plant Kingdom*.

LAUREN PIEDMONT

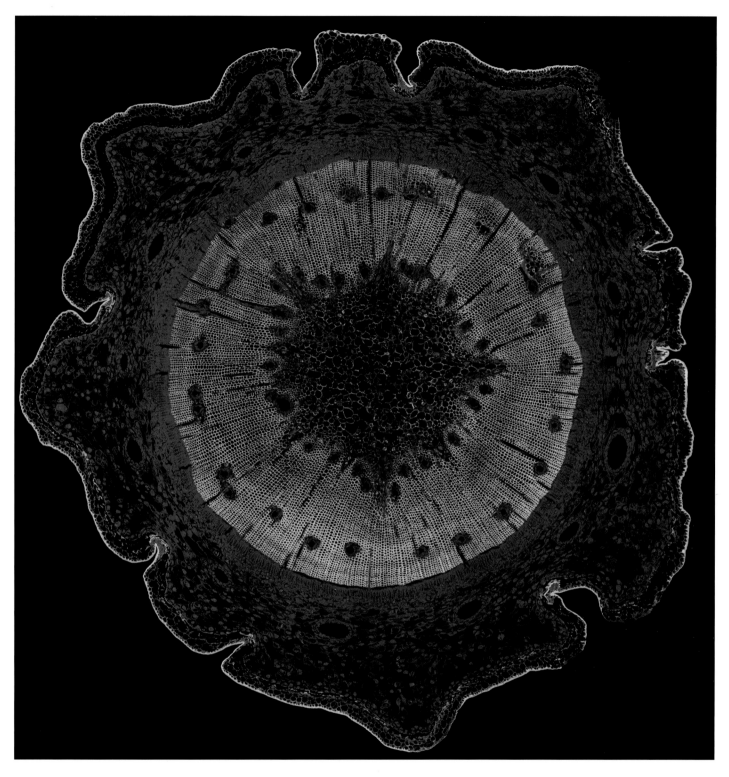

Light micrograph of pine stem, 2011
Light micrograph, two-colour fluorescence
Dimensions variable

This stunning image demonstrates that fluorescence adds another dimension to microscopy, turning it into an art form. As well as being a powerful scientific research tool, fluorescence microscopy defines the intersection of art and science. Lauren Piedmont, a technician at Harvard Medical School in Boston, MA, entered this image into the international digital imaging competition Olympus BioScapes in 2011 – the foremost showcase for outstanding digital images. It received an honourable mention.

In this cross section of a pine branch, the irregular green line defines the craggy edge of the pine's bark. A single row of larger, dark vascular cambium cells shows the dividing line between the Chartreuse-coloured wood and the orange-tinged bark. The British scientist Sir George Stokes described and named fluorescence in 1852, observing that mineral fluorite emitted red light when illuminated by ultraviolet excitation, and that the fluorescence was always at a longer wavelength than the excitation light. In the later nineteenth century, experiments with specimens showed that they fluoresce when irradiated with ultraviolet light. But it was not until the 1930s that the potential for using fluorochrome (fluorescent dye) in biological investigations was fully understood.

Golden leather fern (*Acrostichum aureum*), from *Ferns of North America*, 1880
Hand-coloured copperplate engraving, 23.5 × 41.9 cm / 9¼ × 16 ½ in
University of Alberta Libraries, Edmonton

This detailed and accurate illustration of the golden leather fern (*Acrostichum aureum*) has been laid out on the page in the manner of a herbarium specimen so as to reveal as much of the plant as possible. The main illustration shows the fertile frond, while Figure 2 is a detail showing how it is given a brown felted texture by what the American artist Charles Edward Faxon calls 'a mass of naked sporangia'. Figure 3 shows a spore and Figure 4 a cross section of the stalk. Eaton noted that, although this fern can be found in tropical regions worldwide, it is the largest of all the ferns in the United States, growing up to 3 metres (10 feet) tall in brackish saltwater marshes in Florida. Along with James Henry Emerton, an expert in spiders, Faxon produced many of the illustrations for Daniel Cady Eaton's *Ferns of North America* (1880). A trained civil engineer, Faxon was also a skilled botanical illustrator and was asked by the first director of Harvard's Arnold Arboretum, Charles Sprague Sargent, to be his assistant. Faxon spent the next twenty-one years producing 744 plates for Sargent's *Silva of North America*. Some 1,825 of Faxon's drawings were published between 1879 and 1913.

ALOIS AUER

Trichophorum germanicum (deergrass), *Caltha palustris* (marsh marigold),
Symphytum officinale (comfrey) and *Primula elatior* (oxlip)
Electrotype print, Private collection

These four images printed from actual plants in the middle of the nineteenth century – clockwise from top left: *Trichophorum germanicum* (deergrass), *Caltha palustris* (marsh marigold), *Symphytum officinale* (comfrey) and *Primula elatior* (oxlip), – do not both achieve the same level of clarity, but the technology of the nature printing method employed by the Austrian printer Alois Auer was in its infancy. The plate was created using Auer's own

new 'electrotype' method of nature printing. Rather than simply pressing an object covered in ink onto paper, as in traditional nature printing, Auer took a wax mould of the plant that he coated in graphite and immersed in an electrolytic bath containing copper that formed a thin shell over the mould. The shell was removed from the mould and reinforced with lead alloy to create the printing plate. As director of the Imperial Printing House in Vienna, Auer

also developed many other typographical inventions, such as the use of a continuous roll of paper for newspaper production. The English nature printer Henry Bradbury (see p.300) read Auer's work and patented a similar printing technique without acknowledging Auer. In the ensuing controversy Auer accused him of plagiarism and Bradbury committed suicide, aged just twenty-nine.

Blackberry (*Rubus fruticosus*), from *Codex Aniciae Julianae*, before AD 512
Tempera and ink on vellum, approx. 30 × 37 cm / 11 ¾ × 14½ in
Österreichische Nationalbibliothek, Vienna

The importance of the codex to which this illustration of a blackberry belongs is unparalleled. Known variously as the *Codex Aniciae Julianae* after its first owner, the sixth-century Byzantine princess Juliana Anicia; the *Codex Constantinopolitanus* after Constantinople, where it was created; and the *Codex Vindobonensis* or *Vienna Dioscorides*, after the place where it has been kept since 1453, it is listed in the UNESCO Memory of the World Register, a list of documents of outstanding historical importance. The work is the most significant secular Byzantine manuscript and the oldest illuminated version of the writings of the first-century physician Pedanios Dioscorides. Known more widely as *De Materia Medica* (*On Pharmaceutical Material*), Dioscorides' book never left circulation during the medieval period, and eventually became the precursor of modern pharmacopoeias. The illustration of the blackberry is more or less true to nature; it is accompanied by a pharmaceutical text in Greek minuscules and later vernacular plant names in Arabic and Hebrew added by subsequent owners. Ghislain de Busbecq, the imperial ambassador to the Ottoman Porte, discovered the codex in Istanbul and arranged for its acquisition by Emperor Maximilian II. Brought to Vienna, it was immediately deposited in the Imperial Library and created a sensation among scholars.

GEORGE BROOKSHAW

Gooseberry cultivars, from *Pomona Britannica*, 1817
Hand-coloured stipple engraving, 27.9 × 22.9 cm / 11 × 9 in
Natural History Museum, London

George Brookshaw's precise depiction of sixteen types of gooseberry is both a celebration of domesticated diversity and a reminder of the huge variety to be found in a kitchen garden in the early nineteenth century. Its regular spatial arrangement also suggests the order contemporaries sought to achieve both physically in the garden and intellectually in their understanding of the natural world. This plate comes from Brookshaw's *Pomona Britannica*

(first published in 1812), a book of hand-coloured aquatints illustrating 256 kinds of fruit. Brookshaw's career began as an apprentice to Samuel Troughton, a painter and 'japanner' in Birmingham, but his marriage in 1778 to the daughter of a wealthy Birmingham gunsmith allowed him to establish his own workshop in London, where he produced painted and stove-japanned furniture. In about 1795 he gave up this business and became a professional botanical illustrator.

Under the aliases John or G. Brown, he produced painting manuals and taught flower painting to ladies; he then produced *Pomona Britannica* under his own name. The gooseberry remains a popular soft fruit, as is the closely related blackcurrant. In about 1880 a hybrid of the two was raised by William Culverwell, a gardener on the estate of Thorp Perrow in North Yorkshire, and subsequently named *Ribes × culverwellii*.

Flowers, 1931
Woodcut, 18.1 × 13.7 cm / 7 × 5½ in
Private collection

All three components of this woodcut of the trumpet flowers of the fragrant Asiatic lily (*Lilium speciosum*) – the lilies, the Dutch poem and the Latin motto – have at their heart the concept of beauty and transience. By showing the lily beyond its first bloom, the artist M.C. Escher captures its momentary beauty and, by implication, life's impermanence. The Latin motto urges the viewer to 'Rejoice and marvel at another stage', while the Dutch reminds us: 'We die an early death, so feast your eyes.' Better known for 'impossible structures' such as his never-ending staircase, the Dutch graphic artist Maurits Cornelis Escher produced a number of floral and landscape images early in his career. In 1931, while living in Rome, he started to experiment with woodcuts and collaborated with the scholar G.J. Hoogewerff, then director of the Dutch Institute in the city, to produce this woodcut to illustrate a collection of art and literature. Hoogewerff contributed the Latin and Dutch text, which Escher incorporated into his design. The lily's name reflects its role in the story of Christ's Passion at Easter: Christians believed the lilies had grown where Christ's tears fell in the Garden of Gethsemane.

Pamianthe peruviana, 1933
Watercolour and pencil on paper, 25.2 × 35.3 cm / 9¾ × 13¾ in
Royal Botanic Gardens, Kew, London

This illustration of *Pamianthe peruviana*, the Peruvian daffodil, was painted by Lilian Snelling, and demonstrates her remarkable skill for depicting delicate white flowers. The accompanying pencil studies depict cross sections and magnifications of elements of the plant to aid in its identification. For thirty years from 1922 Snelling was chief artist for *Curtis's Botanical Magazine*, during which time she established a reputation as the most important British botanical artist of the era. Snelling, who had trained in Edinburgh before being commissioned by the plant collector Henry Elwes to complete the posthumously published supplement for his *Monograph of the Genus Lilium* (1933–40), was lauded for her technically precise, scientifically accurate and closely observed approach. This striking plant – its common name reflects its resemblance to the narcissus – is now extinct in the wild owing to the destruction of its habitat. The bulbous plant grows epiphytically, that is, it is supported nonparasitically by another plant. Snelling's elegant style was achieved by building up thin layers of watercolour to accomplish a delicate effect. Until the 1940s *Curtis's* plates were hand-coloured; as the official artist, Snelling would copy a zinc plate from her original painting. Then she would add colour to the printed plate as a model for the colourists.

Plate from *Das Buch der Natur* (*The Book of Nature*), 1482
Hand-coloured woodcut, 31 × 38 cm / 12¼ × 15 in
Library of Congress, Washington, DC

This hand-coloured woodcut is one of two botanical plates included in *The Book of Nature*, an incunabula, or early printed book, created in Germany in 1475, making it the earliest printed botanical illustration known in Europe. Earlier manuscript plant illustrations had been highly stylized and had also suffered from frequent copying. This is one of the earliest examples in which most of the depicted plants are recognizable: lily of the valley (*Convallaria majalis*), sweet violet (*Viola odorata*), meadow buttercup (*Ranunculus acris*), and possibly cornflower (*Centaurea cyanus*) and a type of gourd. Although the full potential of woodblock printing was still to be realized, the technique is more refined, with detailed line work and larger areas of black on some of the leaves. *The Book of Nature* was compiled in the mid-fourteenth century by the Bavarian scholar Konrad von Megenberg as a survey of natural history, from physiology to astronomy and descriptions of sea monsters. The section on plants lists eighty-nine herbs and vegetables. Konrad's work was popular in manuscript, and was an early candidate for printing after the introduction of movable type by Johannes Gutenberg in the mid-fifteenth century.

ANONYMOUS

Cipher manuscript (Voynich manuscript), 1404–38
Ink and colour on vellum, 31 × 48 cm / 8¼ × 18¾ in
Beinecke Rare Book and Manuscript Library, Yale University, New Haven, Connecticut

For centuries cryptographers have failed to decipher the Voynich manuscript, a 204-page herbal from the early fifteenth century, shown here with a fold-out page. Occasional patterns in the characters tantalize linguists, and the planetary diagrams and zodiacal signs make no sense. While some of the plants illustrated resemble real ones, other pages are filled with dismembered roots, far from the style of any herbal. The tall columns are pharmaceu-

tical jars containing coloured liquids – sometimes naked ladies are attached to them by tubes, or else tethered to stars. On other pages the ladies disport themselves in pools alongside turreted domes. Might these elements constitute some kind of search for the elixir of life? Or are they the hallucinations of a visionary? Whatever the answer, the manuscript is genuine, with vellum, ink and paints dating from the early fifteenth century. Although it is named after

Wilfrid Voynich, a Polish book dealer who purchased it in 1912, the manuscript once belonged to the sixteenth-century emperor Rudolph II, and passed to his head gardener, Jacobus Hořčický de Tepenec, whose name is still visible under ultraviolet light. They believed it was a manuscript of Roger Bacon, possibly acquired from the English alchemist John Dee – but the manuscript continues to guard its secrets closely.

Pineapple, from *Historia general y natural de las Indias*, 1547
Woodcut, 15 × 7.2 cm / 5¾ × 2¾ in
Middle Temple Library, London

Gonzalo Fernández de Oviedo y Valdés, who made this first depiction of a pineapple in Europe in the mid-sixteenth century, was an important chronicler of the Spanish conquest of the Caribbean, where Europeans first encountered the fruit. Christopher Columbus had tasted pineapple on Guadeloupe during his second voyage in 1493, but long before Europeans arrived, pineapples are believed to have originated from Paraguay and Brazil: used for food and to make alcohol, they also provided medicines and poison for the tips of arrows. In 1496 Columbus brought back a pineapple for King Ferdinand of Spain, and when Oviedo, who arrived in Panama in 1514, wrote his *General and Natural History of the Indies* (1535 and 1552), the fruit was very rare and valuable in Europe. Oviedo established the pineapple's reputation as the fruit of a new Eden, not only of excellent sweetness but also 'unequalled in composition and beauty' (the curving rows of 'eyes' on a pineapple follow the Fibonacci sequence). Pineapple fruits seldom survived the Atlantic crossing, but it proved possible to cultivate the crown of leaves in European hothouses. The first mention of a pineapple grown in England came in August 1661, when a fruit was grown by the Earl of Essex's gardener, John Rose, and presented to King Charles II.

BERTHE HOOLA VAN NOOTEN

Point d'après nature par Mᵐᵉ Berthe Hoola van Nooten, à Batavia.   Chromolith. par P. Depannemaeker, à Ledeberg-lez-Gand. (Belgique).

CITRUS DECUMANA.

Librairie C. Muquardt, éditeur Bruxelles.

Citrus decumana, 1885
Chromolithograph, 38.9 × 55.3 cm / 15¼ × 21¾ in
Wellcome Library, London

This delicate watercolour by Berthe Hoola van Nooten shows the huge, strangely shaped, pale green-yellow *Citrus maxima* and a pale-pink segment of the fruit (the artist notes that the flesh can also be white). The grapefruit-like flesh is sweet to eat, and the flowers are highly fragrant. The fruit is also known as pomelo, pamplemousse, shaddick or shaddock, the last two of which commemorate Captain Philip Chaddock of the British East India Company, who brought the fruit from Asia to the West Indies in the mid-seventeenth century. Berthe van Dolder was born in Utrecht but moved overseas after she married Dirk Hoola van Nooten, a judge in Suriname in South America, from where she sent plants back to botanical gardens in the Netherlands. The couple started a Protestant seminary in Louisiana, but following her husband's death a second seminary in Texas ended in financial disaster for Berthe. She travelled with her brother to Java, where she hoped to raise money by painting forty plates for a book of local fruits and flowers, *Fleurs, fruits et feuillages choisis de l'Ile de Java peints d'après nature*. The book was published in 1863–4, using the new technique of chromolithography and with the patronage of Sophia, wife of King Willem III of the Netherlands.

Native Vanilla Hanging from the Wild Orange, Praslin, Seychelles, c.1883
Oil on board, 50.6 × 35.3 cm / 20 × 13¾ in
Royal Botanic Gardens, Kew, London

A wild vanilla (*Vanilla phalaenopsis*) grows over rocks and through a bush of naturalised orange (*Citrus*) in this painting of the island of Praslin in the Seychelles. For a generation who had never seen coloured photographs of exotic flowers growing in their natural habitat or viewed tropical forests on television, the paintings of the late nineteenth-century British artist Marianne North were a revelation that complemented perfectly the exotics they could see growing in the hothouses at Kew (where today there is a gallery dedicated to North's work). North visited the Seychelles in 1883 to photograph the coco de mer, a large endemic palm – a typical expedition for an artist who had been left enough money to enable her to travel and paint, and whose poor health was helped by wintering in warm climates. North, who had studied flower-painting, made her first painting expedition to Sicily, before visiting Canada, the United States, Jamaica and Brazil. For thirteen years in the 1870s and 1880s she travelled almost continuously, visiting nearly every continent. Although she was primarily an artist who loved flowers, rather than a botanist, some of the plants North painted were new to science, and the giant red-hot poker, *Kniphofia northiae*, was named in her honour.

WENCESLAUS BOJER

Colville's glory (*Colvillea racemosa*), 1834
Drawing, 24 × 19.2 cm / 9½ × 7½ in
Peter H. Raven Library, Missouri Botanical Garden, St Louis

This painting of a vivid orange flower cluster from the attractive Madagascan tree *Colvillea racemosa* (Colville's glory) is all the more striking because parts of it are left uncoloured. In the first half of the nineteenth century the botanist and artist Wenceslas Bojer left his homeland of Bohemia (now the Czech Republic) to explore Africa, including the islands of Madagascar and Mauritius. He made many collections of plants, and several species of animal and plant are named in his honour. He became head of natural history at the Royal College in Mauritius in 1826, where he was in charge of teaching science. Bojer discovered this member of the pea family in 1824 and named it after Sir Charles Colville, the Governor of Mauritius from 1828 until 1834. The tree is endemic to Madagascar, where it grows mainly in the southern, western and northern regions, in dry lowland forests. Locally its timber is used for posts and fences, and the trunks hollowed out to make canoes. Its fine, feathery foliage and vivid flowers make it a popular ornamental plant, especially in Australia and North America. This illustration by Bojer appeared in *Curtis's Botanical Magazine* in 1834.

Millefleurs Tapestry, c.1500
Silk and wool, 183 × 212 cm / 72 × 3½ in
Victoria and Albert Museum, London

Nestled among the blue, red, white and yellow spring flowers in this fragment of a 500-year-old tapestry are partridges and a cockerel, and at its very heart is a mythical white unicorn. The unicorn was a common feature of medieval tapestries; it was revered as a creature of the forest that symbolized chastity and invulnerability – it was said a unicorn could be caught only by a virgin – and was linked to Christ. This style of tapestry, known as *millefleurs* ('a thousand flowers') was very popular in the late fifteenth and early sixteenth centuries in northern France and Flanders, at the time a cultural centre of Europe. It lacks the usual detail of people, biblical scenes, castles or battlefields, instead presenting a profusion of flowers, small animals and birds in a symbolic celebration of the natural world. In late medieval and Renaissance Europe, tapestries were not only a sign of wealth; they also insulated and decorated cold stone castles and halls. Weavers became skilled at creating detailed pictures using wool, silk and gilt metallic thread. This example, which hangs in the Victoria and Albert Museum in London, is all that remains of what was probably a much larger work: a typical tapestry might measure 4.5 × 9 metres (15 × 30 feet).

The Flight into Egypt, from the *Hastings Hours*, c.1480
Ink and colour on parchment, 16.5 × 12 cm / 6½ x 4¾ in
British Library, London

The flowers in the borders of this late fifteenth-century prayer book look as if they have just landed on the page, echoing the religious festivals when statues of saints were carried through the streets and flowers were cast around them. The blue speedwells echo the colour of the Virgin Mary's robe in the depiction of the biblical Flight into Egypt; there are also pink wild roses, red pinks and bicoloured pea flowers, while tiny strawberries develop in the centre of their pure white flowers. The opposite page features butterflies, snails and insects among the depictions of irises. These borders, which were both symbolic and decorative, contained lifelike studies of well-known plants, either depicting one significant flower such as irises, roses or lilies from every angle, or arranged in a pattern. They came from manuscript prayer books from Flanders, from the Ghent–Bruges School. The English king Edward IV, who gained power after the Wars of the Roses, was a great bibliophile. He and his chief minister, William Lord Hastings, regularly commissioned illuminated manuscripts from Flanders, where Edward's sister reigned as Duchess of Burgundy. Examination shows that in each manuscript a team of different artists were at work, and surviving contracts suggest that they worked to deadlines.

GEORG DIONYSIUS EHRET

American Turk's cap lily (*Lilium superbum*), 1738
Gouache and watercolour on vellum, 53 × 37 cm / 21 × 14½ in
Victoria and Albert Museum, London

This remarkably vivid and detailed painting of an American Turk's cap lily (*Lilium superbum*) is by one of the most skilled of all botanical illustrators, the German Georg Dionysius Ehret, but is only part of the collaborative undertaking behind the discovery and naming of the species. A specimen of this species was cultivated in the garden of Peter Collinson in London. When it flowered in August 1738, Ehret documented it in this drawing on vellum. Before 1751

a copy of this illustration, probably by Ehret though now untraceable, must have been sent to Christoph Jacob Trew, a rich city physician in Nuremberg and an important promoter of natural history publishing. Learning from Jan Frederick Gronovius, a botanist based in Leiden, that the plant originated from Pennsylvania, Trew arranged to have Ehret's drawing engraved in copper by Johann Jacob Haid in Augsburg and prepared a description of the illustration.

Both were included Trew's *Plantae selectae* published in 1751, probably in Nuremberg. When Carl Linnaeus, professor of medicine and director of the botanic garden of Uppsala University, studied Trew's book in around 1760 he realized that this spectacular lily had not yet received a modern name. Although he never saw a specimen of the plant, he called it 'Lilium superbum', which is the name still used today.

GARY YEOH

Amazonia (Amazon Lily – Eucharis × grandiflora), 2011
Radiography, Lambda print on metallic paper, 75.2 × 80 cm / 29¾ × 31½ in
Private collection

In this X-ray by the Hong Kong-based histopathologist Dr Gary Yeoh, the hybrid Amazon lily (*Eucharis × grandiflora*) takes on some of the qualities of a designer's blueprint for the creation of some kind of organic structure, with ethereal blue shapes held together by struts of white against a black background. Yeoh's medical career spent peering through a microscope has given him a perspective on life and death that few people ever experience, and this is reflected in his flower X-rays. A self-taught photographer, he uses modern medical X-ray machines to create what he calls 'floragraphy': digital images that reveal the unseen beauty within the flowers. Commonly known as the Amazon lily, this shade-loving plant with its fragrant white flowers in some ways resembles a daffodil, with its long, straight stalk and delicate blooms. Here, the shiny dark leaves are absent – instead, Yeoh concentrates on a lily that has several buds alongside its open flowers in order to reveal the inner essences of the flower with the bright white of the cone-like buds suggesting potential for life and growth. As part of a larger body of work, Yeoh has utilized technical skills from medicine to create unique art as part of the 'Mystical Garden Project', an international collaboration to promote cutting-edge botanical illustration and benefit various charitable organizations.

NEHEMIAH GREW

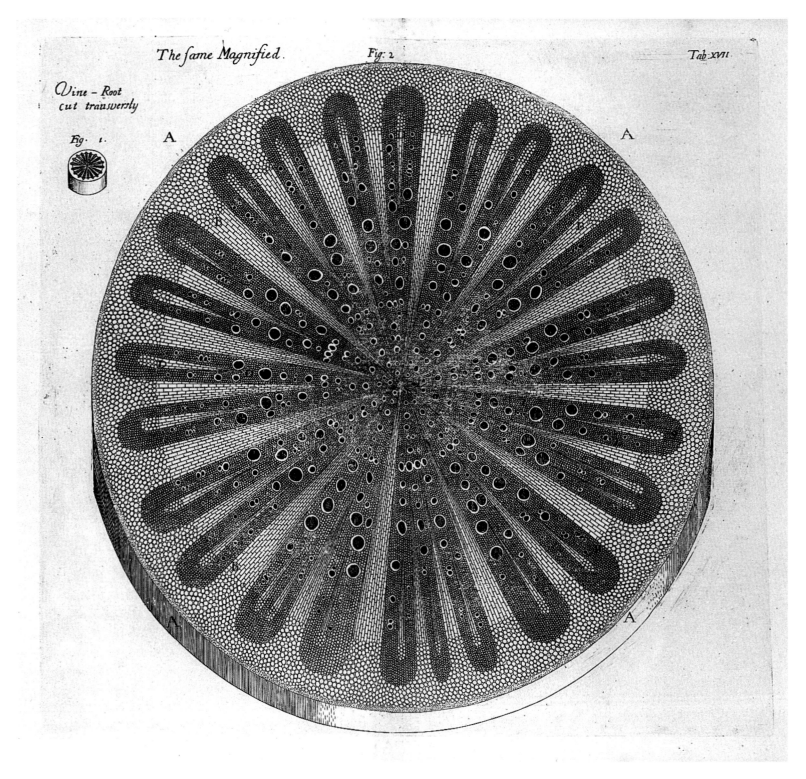

The same Magnified. Fig: 2 Tab·XVII·

Vine - Root
cut transversly

Fig· 1. A A

A A

Cross section of vine roots, from *The Anatomy of Plants*, 1682
Engraving, 36.4 × 43.8 cm / 14¼ × 17¼ in
Wellcome Library, London

This masterpiece of seventeenth-century engraving – drawn and engraved by the English natural philosopher Nehemiah Grew – was published in Grew's *The Anatomy of Plants* in 1682. The public had been introduced to microscopic drawings of plants seventeen years earlier by Robert Hooke (see p.214), but not in such detail: Grew used his superior microscopes to show the 'cells' – a name coined by Hooke – of a vine root. Believing that 'accurate Observa-tion' of plant structure 'must be made by the Microscope', Grew studied the structure of roots and stems and experi-mented with different ways of representing dissections on the page: triangular wedges for portions of stems, stepped structures to reveal three layers of tissue, and here a full cross section with a section of the root at life-size along-side the magnified version. In this plate, A indicates outer skin; the radiating lozenges are 'sap-vessels', and B indi-cates 'parenchymous [i.e. functional] insertions betwixt the parcels of wood'. As secretary of the Royal Society from 1677 until his death in 1712, Grew was at the centre of English scientific life. His advocacy, and the fine detail of his engravings, helped to promote microscopy as a tool for the scientist.

LOUISA HOWARD

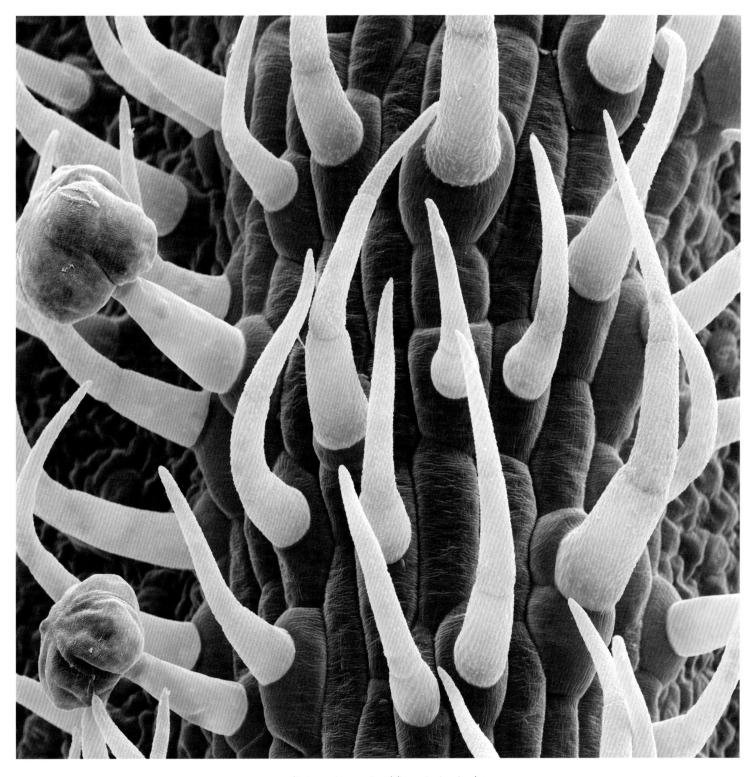

Tomato (*Solanum lycopersicum*) (lower leaf surface), 2011
Coloured scanning electron micrograph (SEM), dimensions variable
Dartmouth College, Hanover, New Hampshire

The structures in this image – what appears to be two mushrooms and many tentacles – might look as though they were growing in some alien forest, but they come from the leaf of one of the most homely and familiar of plants: the tomato. Under a scanning electron microscope, the hairs on the leaf are revealed as being of two different types. The pinheads of the 'mushrooms' are secretory glands, which exude an oily compound, which gives the plant the highly distinctive odour, familiar to anyone who grows tomatoes. The oil in these hairs acts as an important deterrent against foraging herbivores. The apparently threatening lance-like hairs are in fact the benign soft downy simple hairs found all over the tomato plant. They may also deter foraging animals by making the plant less palatable to eat. Both glandular and simple hairs have also been found to prevent water loss form the leaf surface of plants that have to survive in hot, dry climates. Louisa Howard, who works in the Electron Microscope Facility at Dartmouth College in Hanover, New Hampshire, has photographed algae, bacteria, insects and plant and animal cells.

ANONYMOUS

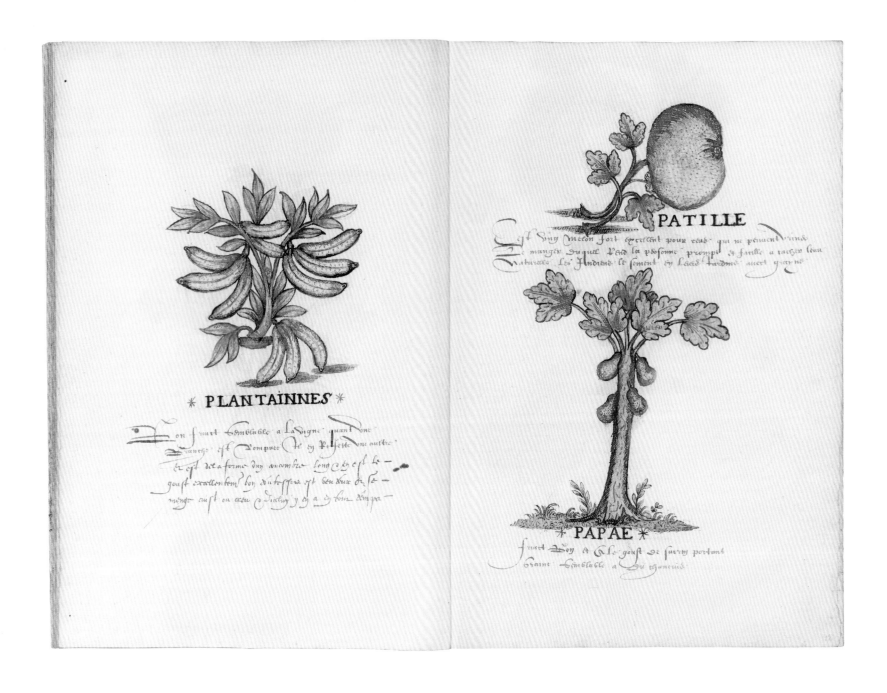

Plantain (Plantainnes), *Patille* (Watermelon) and *Papae* (Papaya), from *Histoire Naturelle des Indes*, 1586
Black chalk, pen and ink with watercolour, each page 29.3 × 19.7 / 11½ x 7¾ in
The Morgan Library & Museum, New York

A century before an unknown artist drew these fruits in the Caribbean in the sixteenth century – *Plantain* (Plantainnes), *Patille* (Watermelon) and *Papae* (Papaya) – it would have been impossible for the plants to be found in the same place. Papaya originated in the Americas, or the New World, plantains and watermelon in the Old World. This depiction of Old World plants growing in the New World is early evidence of the 'Columbian exchange', the great two-way movement of plants, animals, people and knowledge that took place between the two regions following Christopher Columbus's arrival in the Bahamas in 1492. These watercolours are believed to have been drawn by one or two French Huguenot sailors in what is now called the 'Drake manuscript', because it twice mentions the English seafarer Francis Drake, who made the second circumnavigation of the world between 1577 and 1580. Many geographical references in the text correspond with places Drake visited. The manuscript's images present an engaging, although sometimes inaccurate, picture of the plants, animals and people the sailors encountered on their travels. Elsewhere the manuscript illustrates tomatoes, mammee apple and 'siroveles'. The accompanying texts, as here, reveal the illustrators' interest in plants for both food and medicine, as well as in how they might be cultivated.

162

BRYAN POOLE

Musa paradisica sapientum.

Banana Palm Flower and Fruit: *Musa paradisica sapientum*
Hand-coloured copperplate etching, 53 × 40 cm / 21 × 15¾ in
Shirley Sherwood Collection, London

For those who have ever wondered about where a banana comes from, the rhythmic curve of studies of flowers opening and forming into fruit (technically they are both fruit and herbs, because they carry seeds but do not grow on a tree) will be just as interesting as the dramatic, hand-coloured flower head and bunched bananas that dominate this etching of *Musa × paradisiaca* by the contemporary New Zealand-born artist Bryan Poole. Poole himself, who now lives and works in the United Kingdom, was drawn to a banana plant while on holiday in Greece, having never seen one before. The bold colours of the finished work reflect the vibrancy of the Mediterranean climate, where he could get close to the plant only during the hottest part of the day: at other times it was surrounded by clouds of nectar-seeking wasps and hornets. 'After making detailed sketches in the field, I brought the flower head back to my studio and immediately set about making a master cartoon,' he says. Poole specializes in etching, using the same techniques as great seventeenth-century botanical illustrators, such as Pierre-Joseph Redouté (see p.10), using an etching needle to produce a plate from which he makes only 100 prints that are hand-finished with watercolours.

Vine, c.1900
Ink and colour on paper, 24 × 25.1 cm / 9½ × 9¾ in
Arthur M. Sackler Gallery, Smithsonian Institution, Washington, DC

The solitary yellow flower on this loofah plant (*hechima*, known botanically as *Luffa aegyptiaca*) has succeeded in attracting a single bee, which is about to land on it. It is a typical detail from romanticized Japanese *kacho-e*, or 'bird and flower', prints such as this woodblock print from about 1900. The cucumber-like plant trails and climbs from the left of the image, and its delicate tendrils and the off-white background emphasize the pendulous mature loofah fruit; beyond it is a curling immature fruit. The artist, Kōgyo Tsukioka, was born just after the Meiji Restoration of 1868, when Japan began to open up to trade with the Western world for the first time, and he lived through a period of monumental change. The romanticized nature of Japanese images like this was designed to appeal to Western taste. Kōgyo is known principally for the more than 550 prints he made of traditional Noh theatre, but he also produced a number of artistic – and accurate – *kacho-e* prints. *Luffa aegyptiaca* originated in South and Southeast Asia. Its young fruits are used in Japan as a vegetable, while the fibrous, old, dried fruits are familiar in the West as bath sponges. Its oil has some medicinal properties.

LVFFÆ ARABICÆ, Flos & Fructus.

Luffa aegyptiaca, 1640
Copper engraving, 21.9 × 15 cm / 8¾ × 6 in
Real Jardín Botánico, Madrid

This copper engraving shows a climbing plant new to the Europeans who discovered it in Egypt in the late sixteenth century: the sponge gourd (*Luffa aegyptiaca*). Over the centuries, the Republic of Venice maintained a network of consuls throughout the Ottoman Empire, including in Cairo. The Venetian consuls were often accompanied by their physicians, some of whom were interested in plants for their medicinal uses. The first was Prospero Alpino, who later became prefect of the botanic garden of Padua University. In 1592 he published *De plantis Aegypti liber* ('Book of Egyptian Plants'), which included the first printed illustration of a twig of the coffee tree (*Coffea arabica*). Alpino was followed by Johannes Vesling, who published *De plantis Aegyptiis observationes* (Observations on Egyptian Plants). Both Alpino and Vesling included illustrations of the sponge gourd in their publications. This engraving, based on an anonymous drawing prepared for Vesling, is superior to the drawing made for Alpino, as it shows the flower in more detail and also the ripe fruit with its dry exocarp partially removed. Vesling's book is dedicated to Doge Niccolò Contarini, who died after only fifteen months in office, probably of the plague, seven years before the text appeared.

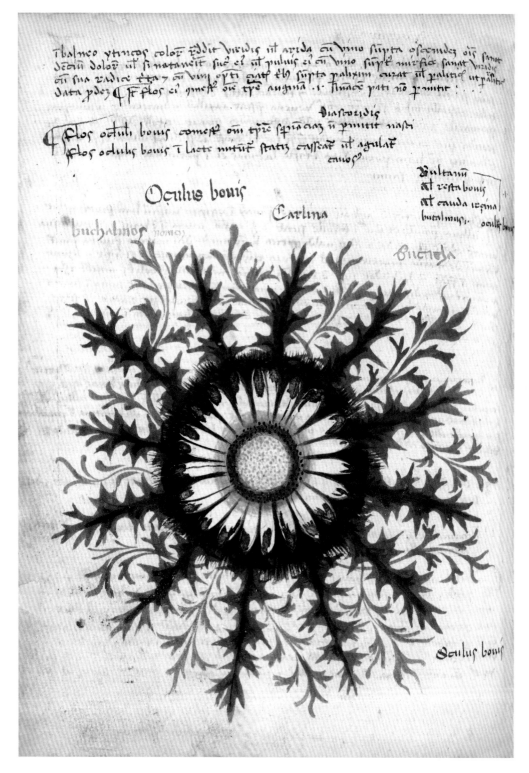

Carline thistle ('*oculus bonis*'), from *Codex Bellunensis* (Belluno Herbal), early 15th century
Watercolour on manuscript, 31 × 23 cm / 12¼ × 9 in
British Library, London

This circular early fifteenth-century depiction of the carline thistle (*Carlina acaulis*), then also known as *oculus bonis*, emphasizes the flower's resemblance to the rays of the sun, with its petals and leaves that radiate from the centre. The image comes from the Belluno Herbal, a work produced in northern Italy that, like the Carrara Herbal (see p.80), depicted live plants rather than traditional images, although with a measure of stylization. The Latin text was still taken mainly from the work of the first-century physician Dioscorides, but additional notes were written in Italian, and it featured indigenous plants gathered and used in the area of the Venetian Alps around Belluno, including green hellebores, orchids and edelweiss, and the ground-hugging alpine thistle. Carline thistles were named after the ninth-century emperor Charlemagne, who was pursuing his dreams of a united Europe when his army was struck down by fever. According to legend, he was guided by an angel to use this plant to cure his men. The flowers also had a protective reputation and were hung over the doorways of homes and barns to repel evil spirits; the name *oculus bonis* suggested the all-seeing protective eye of heaven, an image that sometimes appears in medieval churches in southern Europe.

OLEKSANDER HOLOVACHOV

Pulsatilla grandis, 2013
Digital photograph, 25.4 × 25.4 cm / 10 × 10 in
Private collection

This highly magnified photograph gives what could be something like a bee's-eye view of the centre of the greater pasque flower (*Pulsatilla vulgaris* subsp. *grandis*), showing the anthers as a ring of white, pollen-dusted cones around the pistils (in reality the petals are pinky-purple and the centre of the flower is yellow). Oleksander Holovachov, a post-doctorate researcher in the department of zoology at the Swedish Museum of Natural History, Stockholm,

uses electromagnetic radiation to generate ultraviolet (UV) light to stimulate fluorescence in plant and animal samples – partly because the resulting images are stunningly beautiful, as here, and partly in order to investigate the poorly understood role of fluorescence in nature. While some experts have suggested that fluorescence may help pollinators navigate to pollen-rich areas of particular plants, for example, this now seems unlikely: Holovachov

has discovered that patterns of fluorescence are far less straightforward than this purpose might suggest. The greater pasque flower, which takes its name from the fact that it flowers around Easter, is native to central, southeastern and eastern Europe. In the past, however, its beauty meant that it was frequently picked, and it has become locally endangered in specific areas, particularly Germany.

Stapelia ciliata, from *Stapeliæ novæ*, 1796
Hand-coloured engraving, 22.2 × 35.1 cm / 8¾ x 13¾ in
Royal Botanic Gardens, Kew, London

What looks like a marine creature that has crept into the top of this coloured engraving is the fleshy five-lobed flower that gives the starfish stapelia, *Orbea ciliata* (*Stapelia ciliata*), its name. The low-growing succulent is a member of the dogbane family, the *Apocynaceae*, and a native of the Cape Province of South Africa. The plate comes from *Stapeliæ Novae: or, A Collection of Several New Species of that Genus; Discovered in the Interior Parts* of Africa (1796–7) by the Scottish gardener Francis Masson, the first official plant-hunter for the Royal Botanic Gardens at Kew in London. Masson spent a total of twelve years in South Africa and described many plants of the Cape region, the world's smallest yet richest floral kingdom. The plants and seeds he sent back to England sparked considerable interest in the Cape: about a third of the plates in the first twenty volumes of *Curtis's Botanical Magazine* were based on specimens he supplied. In all, Masson introduced more than a thousand species to Britain. When he sailed for Africa in 1772, only two species of *Stapelia* were known: Masson collected about forty, which, in his words, he was able to 'humbly present to the lovers of Botany'.

Inflorescence of Bertholletia excelsa, 2015
Photograph, dimensions variable
New York Botanical Garden

The cream flowers of the Brazil nut tree, *Bertholletia excelsa*, are captured in numerous stages as they emerge from the green buds in this revealing photograph by the American botanist Scott Mori, who works at the New York Botanical Garden. Originally published in the scientific journal *Phytoneuron* in 2015 – Mori and four others contributed an article that included photographs showing dissections of the flowers – with a pale background, it is reproduced here with a dark background that enhances the contrasting green stem and creamy flowers. Mori's photograph reveals how technological advances have enabled botanists to use high-resolution colour photography as an equally detailed alternative to traditional botanical art. Mori is often to be found hanging on specialized climbing equipment high up in the South American jungle canopy, camera at the ready to capture similarly precise and revealing images of canopy flowers that are impossible to see from the ground. The Brazil nut tree, which is native to the Amazonian rainforest, can grow to more than 50 metres (160 feet) tall. The highly nutritious nuts are enclosed in a fruit with a hard shell that is the size of a baseball.

MADELEINE BASSEPORTE

Oxalis *cernua* (*Jacq:*)
Cap:

Bermuda buttercup (*Oxalis pes-caprae*), 18th century
Watercolour on vellum, 46 × 33 cm / 18 × 13 in
Muséum National d'Histoire Naturelle, Paris

The green trefoil leaves, dark above and paler beneath, and the three short upright inflorescences of bright yellow flowers draw the eye in this watercolour by the eighteenth-century French botanical artist Madeleine Basseporte. She shows this South African bulbous rooted plant emerging from the ground, and paints a bulb, a flower bud and two flowers – one facing and the other in reverse – separately. The painting reflects the influence of Basseporte's tutor, the renowned botanical artist and Royal Painter Claude Aubriet (see p.116), at whose studio in Paris she met the visiting Carl Linnaeus (see p.63). When Aubriet died in 1742, Basseporte succeeded him as Royal Painter to King Louis XV, who also asked her to teach his daughters how to paint flowers. This painting was created for the *Vélins du Roi* (*The King's Vellums*), a remarkable work begun in 1631 to record the royal collections of plants and animals. Although the plant is here named *Oxalis cernua*, this must have been added after Basseporte's death. The species had in fact already been named *Oxalis pes-caprae* by Linnaeus in 1753. Linnaeus called it the 'wood sorrel with goat's feet' because of its ability to spread. It is now a rampant weed in Australia and parts of the USA, but then, as a plant newly introduced to the Jardin du Roi, it would have been culti-vated under glass to flower early in spring.

170

GÉRARD VAN SPAENDONCK

'Jacinthe double. *Hyacinthus orientalis*', from *Fleurs dessinées d'après nature*, 1801
Stipple engraving, 44.5 × 31.7 cm / 17½ x 12½ in
Minneapolis Institute of Arts, MN

This double-flowered hyacinth lends weight to the case made by experts who rate the flower engravings of the Dutch artist Gérard van Spaendonck among the finest ever made. It is one of twenty-four stipple engravings he produced for *Fleurs dessinées d'après nature* (1799–1801), showing popular garden trees, shrubs and perennials of the time. The stipple method, where a copper plate is engraved with a dense grid of fine dots, allowed the artist to convey fine gradations of tone. The oriental hyacinth or jacinth, *Hyacinthus orientalis*, originated in the Middle East and was probably sent from Turkey to Charles de l'Ecluse (Carolus Clusius), who helped to create the Dutch bulb industry in the mid-sixteenth century. The popularity of the fragrant plants was greatly boosted 200 years later by Madame de Pompadour, mistress of the French king Louis XV, who grew hundreds of hyacinths indoors and outside at Versailles. In 1780 Spaendonck replaced Madeleine Basseporte (see p.170) as professor of botanical art at the Jardin du Roi in Paris (now the Jardin des Plantes). In 1795, during the French Revolution, he became a founding member of the Institut de France. Among his most famous pupils were Henriette Vincent and the Belgian brothers Pierre-Joseph and Henri-Joseph Redouté (see p.10).

Tulips 'Le Miroir' and 'Pandora' (*Tulipa*), c.1927
Autochrome photograph, 18 × 13 cm / 7 × 5 ¼ in
Spaarnestad Collection, Nationaal Archief, The Hague

This simple image of four flowers from two tulip cultivars is an eloquent testimony both to the importance of the bulb industry to the Netherlands and to the tremendous advances made in photography at the start of the twentieth century. The first commercially successful process for printing photographs in colour was the Autochrome process, patented by the Lumière brothers in 1903. It was more laborious than monochrome processes, because the various filters used required longer exposures – with the result that many photographers turned to plant photography, which had the advantage that its subjects remained still. One of the early masters of the use of autochromes for horticultural purposes was the Dutch photographer Leendert Blok, who made many images of tulips and other plants in the nursery gardens around Lisse (now the site of the renowned Keukenhof bulb display garden), near Leiden.

Because Blok's work was published mainly in nursery catalogues, it escaped the notice of historians of photography until recently, when the historian Frido Troost rediscovered it. The two tulip cultivars shown – 'Le Miroir' and 'Pandora' – both disappeared from cultivation before the compilation of the *Classified List of Tulip Names* in 1996 (there is a more recent 'Pandora', quite different from this one).

HUANG XU

Flower No. 1 (Chrysanthemum), 2008
Giclee print, 150 × 150 cm / 59 × 59 in
Private collection

The primary focus of interest in this depiction of a chry-santhemum flower lies in the quilled structure of the petals and the patterns that are formed as they curve in different directions. The flower's supporting structure is concealed by what the Chinese photographer Huang Xu calls 'the immersion of the flower into a void of blackness'. He created his 'Flower' series of photographs in 2008 in order to explore 'mortality, seduction, vulnerability and

contradiction'. His choice of plants reflects Confucian sym-bolism, in which the four noble flowers – chrysanthemum, orchid, bamboo and plum blossom, also known as the 'Four Gentlemen' – symbolize the qualities of a scholar. Chry-santhemum, which blooms in the autumn, stands for the ability to withstand adversity; the orchid symbolizes both humility and nobility; bamboo represents tolerance and adaptability; while plum blossom stands for inner beauty.

Huang's use of black and white also places the images in a photographic tradition dating from the late nineteenth century, when gardening books began to be published with monochrome images of flowers. Sometimes, as with Henry James Jones's *Chrysanthemum Album* of 1896, the images were presented as art prints, even though, as portraits of named varieties, they could hardly have helped with identi-fication in the absence of colour.

Page from *Libellus de Medicinalibus Indorum Herbis*, 1552
Watercolour on paper, 15.5 × 20 cm / 6 × 7¾ in
Instituto Nacional de Antropología e Historia, Mexico City

This page from a herbal produced by an indigenous artist of the Aztec Empire in the mid-sixteenth century depicts ten medicinal plants. The plant second from right in the bottom row is thought to be *Bourreria huanita*, a borage tree native to the Americas whose scented flowers were used to add flavour to beverages and tobacco. Its Nahuatl name is translated as 'popcorn flower.' The manuscript, known as the *Libellus* or the *Codex Cruz-Badianus*, was produced at a school founded by Spanish Franciscans in Mexico in the 1530s in order to educate Aztec boys for the priesthood. The manuscript was commissioned by Governor Don Francisco de Mendoza to present to King Charles V of Spain, to demonstrate the talents of the local people and inspire Charles V to send financial support for the school. The text was written in the Aztec language, Nahuatl, by the school's Aztec physician, Martín de la Cruz, and translated into Latin by a student, Juan Badianus. It is not known who made the illustrations. The manuscript passed through the hands of several European owners before coming to the Vatican in the early twentieth century, where it remained until 1990, when it was returned to Mexico by Pope John Paul II.

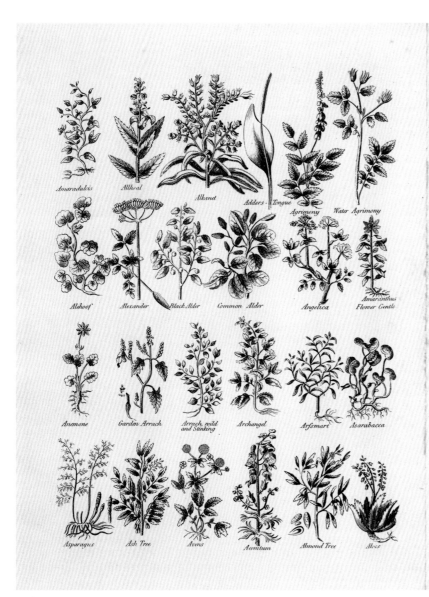

CULPEPER's ENGLISH PHYSICIAN,

CONTAINING THE

HERBAL.

AMARA - DULCIS.

CONSIDERING diverse shires in this nation give divers names to one and the same herb, and that common name which it bears in one county, is not known in another; I shall take the pains to set down all the names that I know of each herb. Pardon me for setting that name first which is most common to myself; besides amara-dulcis, some call it morral, others bitter-sweet, some woody-nightshade, and others felon-wort.

DESCRIPTION. It grows up with woody stalks even to a man's height, and sometimes higher: the leaves fall off at the approach of winter, and spring out of the same stalk again at spring time; the branch is encompassed about with a whitish bark, and hath a peth in the middle of it; the main branch brancheth itself out into many small ones, with clafpers, laying hold on what is next to them, as vines do; it bears many leaves, they grow in no order at all, or at leastwise in no vulgar order; the leaves are longish, though somewhat broad and pointed at the ends; many of them have two little leaves growing at the end of their foot stalk, some of them have but one, and some none; the leaves are of a pale green colour; the flowers are of a purple colour, or of a perfect blue, like to violets, and they stand many of them together in knots; the berries are green at the first, but when they are ripe, they are very red; if you taste them, you shall find them just as the crabs which we in Sussex call bitter-sweet, viz. sweet at first, and bitter afterwards.

No. 5.   P   PLACE.

Plants and herbs from *The Complete Herbal*, 1789
Engraving, each page 25.2 × 19.5 cm / 9¾ × 7¾ in
Royal Botanic Gardens, Kew, London

This plate of common English flowers, among which are allheal (*Prunella vulgaris*), alkanet (*Alkanna tinctoria*), adders-tongue fern (*Ophioglossum vulgatum*), asarabacca (*Asarum europaeum*) and the potentially lethal *Aconitum napellus*, comes from an eighteenth-century edition of a seventeenth-century herbal so successful that it is still in print today. It was drawn by the astrologer and physician Ebenezer Sibly before 1789 to illustrate a new edition of

Culpeper's Complete Herbal. The original work, *English Physician and Complete Herbal*, had been written by the maverick apothecary Nicholas Culpeper in 1652. It was not illustrated, but that did not diminish the book's revolutionary impact. In Culpeper's time, the Royal College of Physicians had a monopoly on all medicinally related literature, which was written in Latin. Culpeper, who was well educated and trained as an apothecary, was incensed

at this stranglehold and translated the physicians' standard work, the *Pharmacopoeia Londinensis*, into English so that everyone could have access to it. Culpeper then produced his herbal at a lower price than other contemporary herbals, audaciously criticizing much of the quackery within the *Pharmacopoeia Londinensis*. Culpeper also made his book less formal and more witty, with reference to plants, ailments and of course remedies.

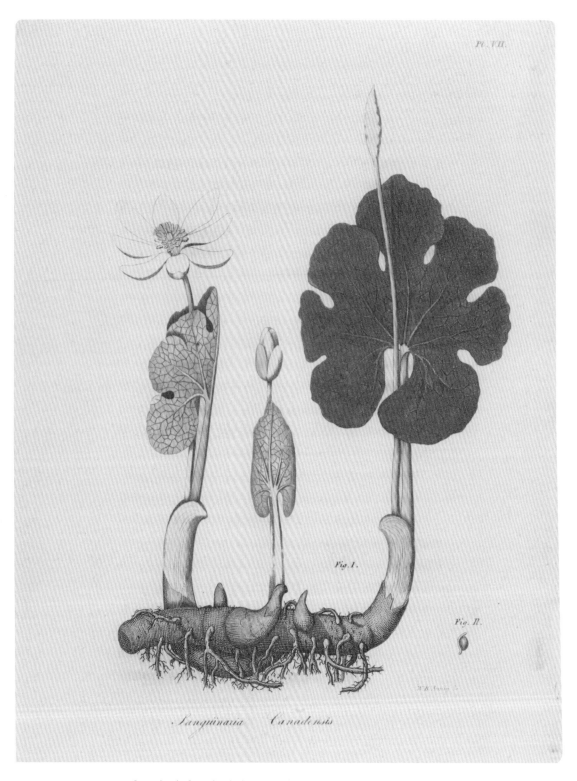

Sanguinaria Canadensis, from *American Medical Botany*, 1817
Coloured engraving, 26 × 18 cm / 10¼ × 7 in
Peter H. Raven Library, Missouri Botanic Garden, St Louis

Jacob Bigelow's portrayal of bloodroot (*Sanguinaria canadensis*) takes advantage of the fact that his *American Medical Botany* (1817–20) was the first such book in America printed in colour to show the bright red root that gives the plant its name. This member of the poppy family comes from eastern North America, where native peoples used the root to make medicines and dye. The three-volume publication, an early American herbal, described native plants of medicinal value – their chemistry and their use – with illustrations by the author. Bigelow taught both medicine and botany at Harvard University, and was also president of the American Academy of Arts and Sciences from 1847 to 1863. He was much concerned with public health, and with replacing traditional procedures such as blood-letting and purging with useful remedies from the world of plants. His philosophy is summed up in the preface to his book: 'Yet when we consider how small a portion of the vegetable kingdom has been *medically* examined, there can be little doubt that a vast number of active substances, many perhaps of specific efficacy, remain for future inquirers to discover.' A statement that still holds true today.

HANNAH COLLINS

Magic in Nature, 2013
Silver gelatin print, 34 × 23.8 cm / 13½ × 9½ in
Private collection

This black-and-white image of the fragrant, pendulous flowers of the borrachero tree *Brugmansia suaveolens* – they are known as angel's trumpets – against the darkened foliage of the Amazonian rainforest captures their deceptive beauty. Used by indigenous peoples during religious ceremonies, the flowers in fact produce a powerful hallucinogenic drug that can easily be misused, with fatal results. For the British artist Hannah Collins, documenting such ritually important plants in the field in remote, marginalized places gives them the value of a found object, as she explains: 'The most important thing for me is that my work develops deep links with the environment in which it is made.' For her series of photographs 'The Fertile Forest 2013–2015', Collins – who is known for her wide use of photography including images produced on an environmental scale in the East End of London – travelled to the Amazon rainforest of Colombia. Working alongside the indigenous Cofan and Inga people, she documented hundreds of Amazonian plants used by indigenous peoples either in shamanic rituals or as medicines. Collins intends the project to create a corporeal map of the Amazon's vast reserve of useful plants, most of which are unknown outside the forest, in order to show that the Amazon is the world's primary pharmacy as well as its lungs.

Ginger (*Zingiber elatum*), 1832
Watercolour on paper, 53.5 × 37.3 cm / 21 × 14¾ in
Royal Botanic Gardens, Kew, London

These detailed illustrations by an unknown artist of the flower and roots of a species of ginger (*Zingiber elatum*) barely fit on the page. They come from the three-volume *Plants of the Coast of Coromandel* (1795–1820) by the Scottish botanist William Roxburgh, the first such work to be devoted to Coromandel, the southeastern coastal region of India, which features both wetlands and dry evergreen forests. The book contains more than 300 illustrations and descriptions of selected local species. The first fascicle, of twenty-five plates, appeared in 1795; the completed work contained a total of 300 plates. The genus *Zingiber* contains about 100 species of tropical herb found mainly from India to New Guinea, many of which are used as spices. Roxburgh studied medicine and botany at the University of Edinburgh before becoming assistant surgeon to the Madras (now Chennai) base of the East India Company in 1776. In 1789 he was appointed the company's botanist. He moved in 1781 to Samulcotah (now Samalkota), where he established a garden for economic plants, and in 1793 to Calcutta (now Kolkata), where he took charge of the Company's botanic garden. He was a meticulous field botanist who produced accurate descriptions and oversaw the production of large numbers of botanical illustrations.

Black peppercorn (*Piper nigrum*), from *A History of East Indian Trees
and Plants, and of their Medicinal Properties*, 1600–25
Ink and watercolour on paper
British Library, London

In the early seventeenth century, when this manuscript drawing was made of black peppercorn (*Piper nigrum*) climbing around a thorny bush, peppercorns – seen here on the left as spikes of round, berry-like red fruit – were one of the most valuable commodities in the world, thanks to their role in flavouring and preserving food. *Piper nigrum*, a native of India, provides black, white and green peppercorns depending on the time of harvest, and had

been traded widely for centuries (in the first century AD the Roman writer Pliny the Elder complained about the price of pepper). The plant on the left is *Erythrina variegata*, which is also known as tiger's claw, Indian coral tree and sunshine tree. This illustration by an unknown European explorer of the 'East Indies' – loosely South and Southeast Asia – is one of a series of plant portraits in a volume of manuscripts collected by the English physician Sir Hans Sloane and

now held at the British Library in London. The volume also depicts plantain, tamarind, coconut, pomegranate and durian, each accompanied by a description in English of the plant and its uses. The information was probably gathered for use by a local 'factory', as European trading stations were called. The artist did not depict only plants, however: one image shows two snake charmers with the tools of their trade.

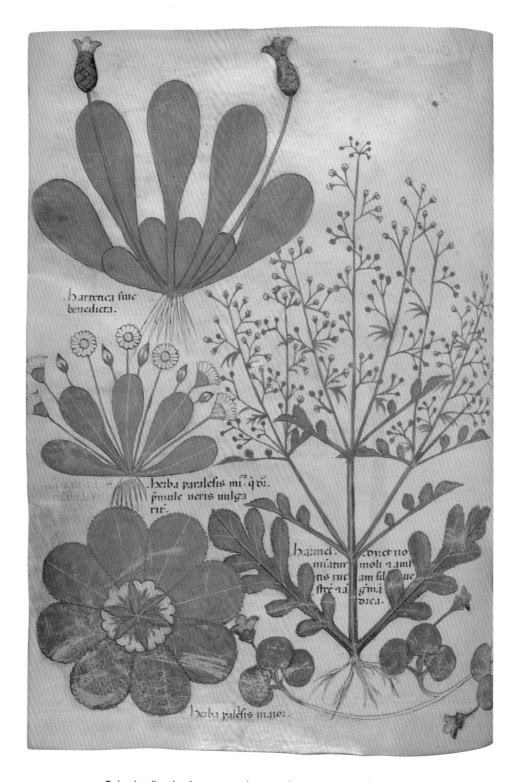

Daisy, hardhead, primrose, asarabacca and sweet wormwood, c.1440
Ink and colours on parchment, 36 × 25.5 cm / 14¼ × 10 in
British Library, London

The anonymous fifteenth-century artist who copied these plants from a 200-year-old herbal was not a botanist, and the plants he copied are highly stylized. The daisy at centre left is instantly recognizable, but the primrose beneath it is harder to identify, being viewed from above. Above the daisy is what appears to be a hardhead (*Centaurea*); beside the primrose creeps asarabacca (*Asarum europaeum*), identifiable by its purple flowers. It was used as an aid to childbirth. The plant on the right is sweet wormwood (*Artemisia annua*), which was also an important medicinal herb during the middle ages. The slight curve of the stalks and the lower part of the flowers are correct, but the purple petals are an example of medieval artistic licence. In the original version of this manuscript, the artist dressed the human figures that illustrated medical conditions in fashionable clothes, which enables the manuscript to be dated to the 1440s. Copies were often made of herbals with attractive illustrations, although the scientific text was sometimes reduced or omitted altogether, suggesting that they were being re-created as picture books for wealthy bibliophiles. Here the original was a medical treatise created in Salerno in about 1300, the *Tractatus de Herbis*.

WILLIAM KILBURN

Daisy (*Bellis perennis*), 1777, from *Flora Londinensis*, 1777–98
Hand-coloured engraving, 15.2 × 10.7 cm / 6 × 4¼ in
Private collection

The Irishman William Kilburn painted this small but highly naturalistic image of a common daisy, with magnified and numbered details, in 1777 for one of the great botanical figures of contemporary London: William Curtis. In 1771 Curtis had founded his own botanic garden in Lambeth and been made director of the prestigious Chelsea Physic Garden. He also undertook to identify and describe all the wild plants found within 16 kilometres (10 miles) of London.

Kilburn's illustration, from the first volume of *Flora Londinensis*, is small in comparison to others in the six-volume work, but its proportions are perfect. The accurate colouring may have been done by Curtis's friend the colourist William Graves. Curtis's *Flora* turned out to be hugely costly, but he recouped some of that money in 1787 when he founded the first illustrated botanical journal, *Curtis's Botanical Magazine*, which was a huge success. It remains

a successful publication today. After working for Curtis, Kilburn developed a more fluid style, painting on fine cotton, and bought a cloth-printing business that transferred floral paintings on calico and muslin to woodblock prints for large-scale reproduction.

SEBASTIAN SCHEDEL

Opium Poppy (*Papaver somniferum*), 1610
Watercolour on paper, 17.2 × 27.3 cm / 6¾ × 10¾ in
Royal Botanic Gardens, Kew, London

This simple watercolour of a flowering head of a red opium poppy was a study for one of the greatest florilegia of the seventeenth century – one that placed its emphasis on beautiful rather than useful plants, and that began life in a bishop's garden. In essence the *Hortus Eystettensis* (1613) by Basilius Besler captured the magnificent garden of Bishop Johann Conrad von Gemmingen at Eichstätt in Bavaria and translated it on to the page through a series of stylized hand-coloured copperplate engravings. The book was published in both a deluxe hand-coloured edition and a cheaper black-and-white version. Besler, who served as the bishop's apothecary, lived in Nuremberg, which was then a centre of German science and publishing. This poppy was painted by Sebastian Schedel, a local artist who also worked as a steward for the Butchers' Guild. Along with other of his watercolours and those by various – now unknown – artists, it was worked up into various plates for the *Hortus*. Schedel also bound his working drawings together into a manuscript volume entitled *Calendarium* (from which this page comes), complete with his bookplate. Whereas the *Hortus* was broadly divided into the four seasons, Schedel chose to make his volume a monthly record that reflected the time each plant flowered.

LÁSZLÓ MOHOLY-NAGY

Flower, 1925–7
Photogram, 23 × 17.2 cm / 9 × 6¾ in
Centre Pompidou, Paris

The rich black and stark white of this composite flower of a *Chrysanthemum indicum* plat. make it seem almost as if it is a three-dimensional model that has been sculpted out of marble or plaster. In fact, the image is a 'photogram' – a photographic image created without using a lens – by one of the outstanding photographers of the first half of the twentieth century, the Hungarian László Moholy-Nagy. Moholy-Nagy experimented with camera-less photography in the early 1920s, placing objects directly on to chemically prepared paper and fixing the resulting image. While his most famous photograms used combinations of geometric forms in an almost abstract manner, overlapping to create 'a new space created with light directly', he continued to experiment with the realistic representation of objects, only varied in this case by the double exposure of the inflorescence. For Moholy-Nagy, the photogram was convincing evidence that 'even the complete mechanization of technics may not constitute a menace to its essential creativeness'. Like his contemporary Man Ray (see p.320), Moholy-Nagy drew on a tradition of camera-less photography that may even have preceded the origins of photography in the first half of the nineteenth century, as in the renowned cyanotypes of Anna Atkins (see p.110).

AMY SHELTON

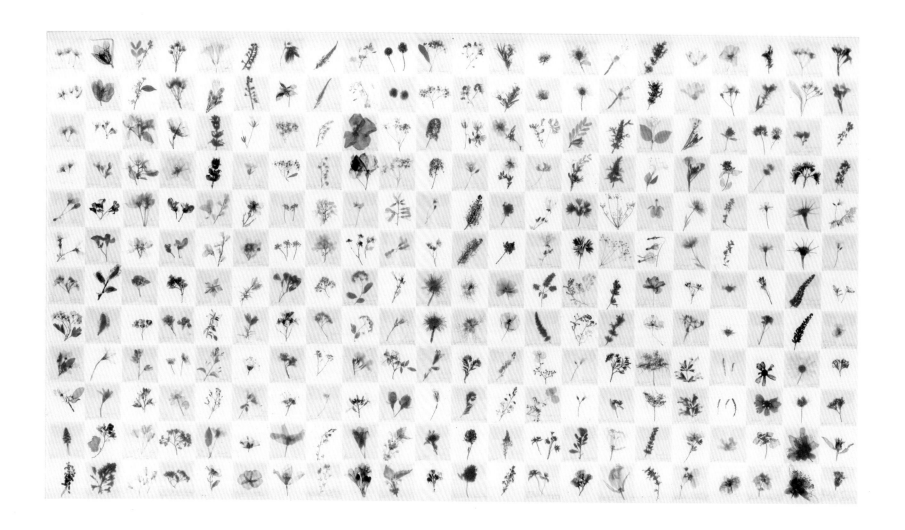

Florilegium: Honey Flow II Late Spring/Early Summer (May/June), 2014
Light-box installation, dimensions variable
Wellcome Library, London

These pressed flowers in glassine envelopes, each secured by delicate linen tape and labelled by its collector, the British artist Amy Shelton, are like a modern herbarium – with a twist. Shelton set out to collect samples of all the mellifluous (honey-bearing) flowers a honey bee pollinates during an entire year, from the sparse offerings of January and February through the riches of spring and summer back to the quieter autumn and early winter. Over five years, Shelton gathered and pressed some 30,000 flowers at peak bloom and arranged the best 1,056 samples chronologically, reflecting the subtle relationship between bees and flowers through the year. Some occur only once in the display, which is spread over four light boxes (this selection of 264 covers spring and early summer), but others, such as the dandelion, crop up at regular intervals. Shelton, a trained art historian based in Devon in southwest England, is particularly drawn to the natural world and explains that *Florilegium: Honey Flow I–IV* is intended as a map from a bee's-eye view, 'illuminating the invisible landscape'. It is part of the artist's broader interest in bees and their relationship with humans, inspired by Shelton's bee-keeping aunt.

LISA CREAGH

Floriculture 2, 2015
Lightjet print, 182.9 × 111.8 cm / 72 × 44 in
Private collection

This photograph is created from a painstaking arrangement of many images of commercially grown flowers, fitted carefully together in order to make an artificial 'garden' that visually evokes not only a garden but also the traditions of Persian carpets or elaborately crafted quilts. The British photographer and digital artist Lisa Creagh created the work as part of her project *The Instant Garden*, begun in 2009 and inspired by Dutch flower paintings, particularly those of the seventeenth- and eighteenth-century artist Rachel Ruysch. Creagh presents her composite images as having been made or assembled rather than 'taken' in the standard photographic sense, and the resulting images evoke the decorative arts, with pieces of images of living plants placed together in larger, somewhat abstract flower patterns, highlighting their colours and forms against a black background that allows the plants to produce their own light. This makes the garden images seem at once both natural and artificial. Creagh says that her use of the word 'garden' in the title of the project refers to the origins of gardens as enclosed spaces in which plants are grown, in much the same way that the frames of her photographs are themselves enclosures for the plant images she arranges within.

*Lilium chalcedonicum, c.*15th century BC
Fresco, dimensions variable
Thera, Santorini

Graceful swallows fly between clumps of long-stemmed red flowers (possibly *Lilium chalcedonicum*, the red lily of Greece) painted by an anonymous artist as part of a mural that covers three sides of a room in a house built on the Greek island of Santorini during the Minoan age, sometime before 1600 BC. That places them among the oldest pictures of recognizable plants currently known – they predate ancient Egyptian images of plants by around 300 years (see p.45). There remains some dispute about how precisely identifiable the plants are, however. They are probably stylized representations of lilies growing among equally stylized and highly colourful volcanic rocks. Whatever the species, the flowers – depicted in various stages from buds to full bloom – are so lifelike that they seem to sway in a breeze. The paintings were discovered in the 1960s during archaeological investigations on Santorini that revealed a Minoan city which had been destroyed during the Thera eruption, in approximately 1600 BC. They may mark the very beginning of botanical art – if only we could be certain what plants they show.

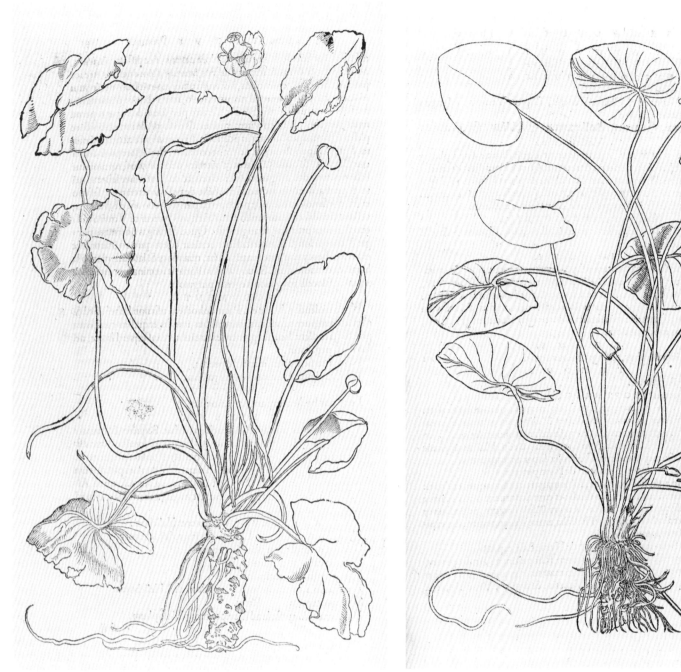
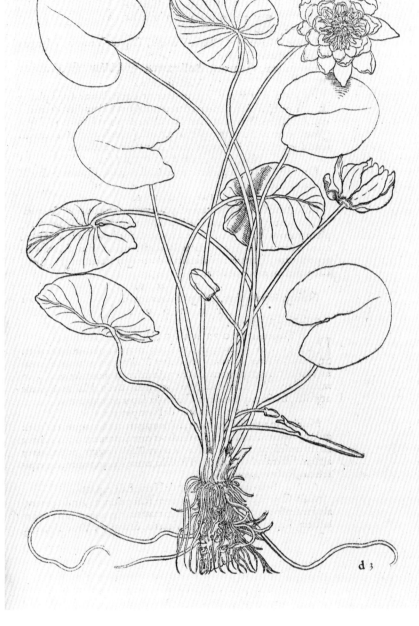

Waterlilies (*Nuphar lutea* and *Nymphaea alba*), from *Herbarum vivae eicones*, 1530–6
Woodcuts, each 25.6 × 16.2 cm / 10 × 6¼ in
Peter H. Raven Library, Missouri Botanical Garden, St Louis

These two woodcut illustrations of waterlilies – easily identifiable as the European natives *Nuphar lutea* (left) and *Nymphaea alba* (right) – appeared more than 480 years ago in a work that is generally regarded as marking the true beginning of modern botanical art. They are free of the stiffness, heavy lines and schematic rendering found in previous printed plant portraits. Hans Weiditz was the first artist commissioned to illustrate a book on plants by drawing actual specimens found in the wild or in gardens, rather than by copying earlier images. The title of the book testifies to the importance attached to this innovation: *Herbarum vivae eicones*, 'living pictures of plants'. The text, by the apothecary Otto Brunfels, was not so much a traditional herbal, or treatise on medicinal plants, as a call for the reinvigoration of plant studies by field research rather than by recycling information from ancient writers. Some of Weiditz's watercolours survive in the Felix Platter Herbarium in Berne; they have been praised for their colouring and are seen as superior to the printed versions, but it was the woodcuts that were circulated throughout Europe and stimulated a generation of artists to start observing and recording real plants.

BARBARA COTTON

'Hybrid Amaryllis Regina Vittata' (*Hippeastrum × johnsonii*),
from *Transactions of the Royal Horticultural Society of London*, 1824
Hand-coloured stipple engraving, 42.2 × 28.2 cm / 16¾ × 11 in
Museum of Fine Arts, Boston, Massachusetts

There is an architectural, three-dimensional quality to the English botanical artist Barbara Cotton's bold painting of this hybrid of two South American bulbs known then as *Amaryllis reginae* and *A. vittata*. The three large, lily-like flowers carried on a single stem – with characteristic white stripes along each petal – are set above deep green strap-shaped leaves. Cotton's lifelike artwork (engraved by William Say) was probably influenced by the 'true to nature'

style of William Hooker, a former pupil of the celebrated botanical artist Franz Bauer (see p.15) and official artist of the Horticultural Society of London. Cotton and the botanical artist Augusta Withers helped Hooker to complete his ten-volume treatise on fruit trees after he suffered a stroke in 1820. It was not until 1821 that the South American *Amaryllis* species were separated from the African ones into the genus *Hippeastrum*. When John Lindley, assistant secretary

to the Horticultural Society, wrote the article on the hybrid that accompanied Cotton's image, he did not use the new name. Lindley's post involved caring for the society's garden in Chiswick, west London, and Cotton probably painted the *Hippeastrum* for him from a plant grown under glass there.

Red Amaryllis with Blue Background, c.1907
Watercolour on paper, 46.5 × 33 cm / 18½ × 13 in
Museum of Modern Art, New York

The striking contrast of red and blue in this *Hippeastrum* is a non-traditional approach to capturing the essence of the amaryllis in this bold study by the renowned Dutch abstract artist Piet Mondrian. Bearing little resemblance to the later geometric abstract work for which Mondrian became famous, this painting dates from an earlier period when he made many plant drawings and paintings, always produced as single specimens. He did not try to copy the living beauty of nature – believing it was impossible – but instead tried to express such beauty from a personal perspective. The central placement of the stem evokes a strong characteristic of the flower and creates an axis that bisects the central bloom, although the three blooms are not identical nor axially symmetrical. The use of strong primary colours prefigures Mondrian's later abstract work. This represents a key period in the artist's shift away from a purely representational approach, while still achieving aesthetic beauty. As a founder of the De Stijl movement, Mondrian found ideas of reduction and creating abstract art central to his approach, and he placed an emphasis on the new art forms introduced at the start of the twentieth century. His style ultimately became entirely nonrepresentational, but this painting pre-dates his change to pure abstraction.

HENRIËTTE GEERTRUIDA KNIP

Primulas, 1803–42
Pencil and watercolour on paper, 38 × 26.8 cm / 15 × 10½ in
Teylers Museum, Haarlem, Netherlands

This watercolour of two cultivated polyantha primulas owes much to the naturalistic style and precision of Gérard van Spaendonck, with whom the artist Henriëtte Knip studied in Paris after 1802. One primula is shown as a whole plant, with the inflorescence of five red-rimmed, golden-centred flowers borne high above the near-perfect primrose-like foliage. Another inflorescence behind it has several pale blue-rimmed, yellow-centred flowers. Together the two cultivars make a fine composition set against a white background. Knip principally painted landscapes and floral bouquets, but her botanical work befits the Age of Enlightenment, in which she lived. She was part of the age in which the system of classifying and naming new plants from around the world devised by Carl Linnaeus (see p.63) was in the ascendant. This new science was coupled with an increasing desire to grow plants and paint them for pos-terity. *Primula × polyantha* cultivars, bred between coloured variants of the primrose and the wild cowslip, were almost as popular in Europe from the sixteenth to the eighteenth centuries as were the choice cultivars of the shorter-flowered, mealy-leaved *Primula auricula*. These last, so-called florists' flowers, were often displayed in wooden 'theatres' along with choice varieties of tulip, carnation, hyacinth, anemone, pink and ranunculus.

Primula menziesiana: Pot Plant in Flower, 1921
Photograph, dimensions variable
Royal Botanic Garden Edinburgh

This photograph of two flowering plants of the Himalayan primula *P. bellidifolia* seems to be an exposé of the photographer's methods. Robert Moyes Adam, official photographer at the Royal Botanic Garden in Edinburgh from 1914, took the picture with his own Watson & Son halfplate field camera, placing the flowers against a black background in order to enhance the lollipop-like inflorescences on long, thin stems. The ruler propped up alongside the plants shows their height. It is very likely that the plants are still in their clay pots, submerged in a thick layer of soil to give them a more natural appearance. On the left, their white wooden label has been left on a brick. Adam's photograph may have been intended to honour Private Alan Menzies, a gardener from the Royal Botanic Garden in Edinburgh who died in World War I. The plant was collected in Bhutan in 1914 and named after Menzies by Isaac Bayley Balfour and William Wright Smith – but it was later reclassified, along with four other primula species described by them, into *P. bellidifolia*. The species has fragrant blue, mauve or violet flowers and the leaves are sometimes densely covered beneath with a white farina or meal.

PAUL JONES

Blue star waterlily (*Nymphaea nouchali*), from *Flora Superba*, 1971
Acrylic on paper, 76.2 × 77.5 cm / 30 × 30½ in
Private collection

These blue star waterlilies (*Nymphaea nouchali*) by the twentieth-century Australian artist Paul Jones combine remarkable botanical accuracy in the depiction of the flowers with a frankly romantic background and composition of blacks and greens that echo the murky waters. Jones specialized in painting similarly showy, attractive blooms, and is perhaps best known for his *Flora Magnifica* (1976), which contains a series of studies in the romantic style of

Robert John Thornton's famous *Temple of Flora*, which was originally published in 1799 (see p.94). Jones summed up his thoughts about botanical painting: 'Sureness of touch comes with unrelenting practice … But the real worth and true quality of a memorable drawing can only come from the heart. Flawless technique can astonish only, but fails to capture that particular "something" which can only be described as "magic".' The blue star waterlily – native to

southern and eastern Asia, from India, Sri Lanka and China to Borneo, the Philippines and Australia – is not only beautiful but also an important medicinal plant, especially in traditions such as Ayurveda. Extracts from the plant are used to treat indigestion and have anti-inflammatory and anti-diabetic properties. Born in New South Wales, Jones studied at East Sydney Technical College before gaining a global reputation for his work.

E.V. DAY

Waterlily Transporter – Six Stages, 2014
Laser-etched, hand-tinted Plexiglas in six sections
61 × 26.7 × 165 cm / 24 × 10½ × 65 in
Private collection

The delicate tracery of this three-dimensional image of a waterlily might resemble a kind of mathematical exercise in angles and tension; that is certainly part of the point. But it is also an echo of earlier, more famous images of waterlilies – some of the most well-known flower paintings ever produced – those painted by Claude Monet in his celebrated garden at Giverny outside Paris in the 1890s. In 2010 the New York installation artist E.V. Day spent three months in Giverny as artist in residence, and was handed a key that allowed her to enter the garden at any time, even when it was closed to visitors. She was fascinated by the famous waterlilies, and began to contemplate 'transporting' them back to the United States in a process similar to that of the transporter on the television series *Star Trek*, which dissolved people or objects in one location to reconstitute them in another. Day used a computer programme to render a three-dimensional model of a flower in curving wire, which she coloured pink (there is also a monochrome version) and enclosed in layers of resin to represent the six stages of transportation. Day equates the process to stretching and shaping fishnet stockings, a material she often uses in her work.

ANONYMOUS

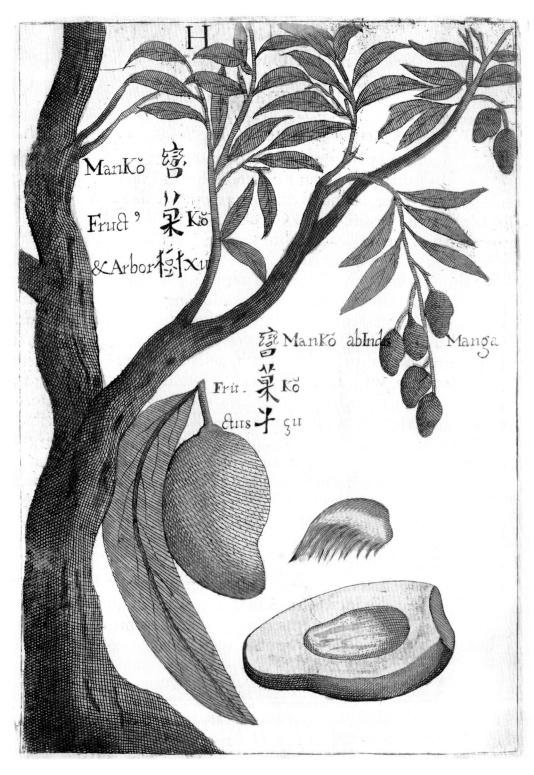

Mango tree and fruit (*Mangifera indica*), from *Flora sinensis*, 1656
Coloured woodcut, 34.4 × 23.6 cm / 13½ × 9¼ in
Natural History Museum, London

Even to the uninitiated, the Chinese characters in this seventeenth-century woodcut of the mango tree and its fruit look odd. That is not surprising, since they were produced by an anonymous woodcutter in Vienna in 1655 in the absence of the author of the book in which the image appears, the Jesuit missionary Michał Piotr Boym. Dedicated to Leopold I, the newly crowned king of Hungary, *Flora sinensis* was intended to praise the Jesuit mission in China and to offer the first glimpses of its flora and fauna, then almost completely unknown in the West. In fact, the work's title is misleading, since Boym deals with plants he had seen not only in China but also in India. The work is also an important source of information about the early transfer of economic plants from the Americas to Asia, including the pineapple, the papaya and the cashew. Boym, who was born in what is now Ukraine, had become a Jesuit in Cracow and travelled via Rome and Lisbon to southern China, then in the throes of a civil war. In early 1651 he returned to Europe via India and Turkey, eventually reaching Venice, from where his manuscript and drawings may have been sent to Vienna.

Still Life with Quince, Cabbage, Melon and Cucumber (after Cotán), 2008
Watercolour on paper, 71 × 88cm /28 × 35 in
Private collection

This painting by artist Lizzie Sanders is based on an original by an early master of still life, the seventeenth-century Spaniard Juan Sánchez Cotán. Cotán's original was radically austere for the time in portraying not the abundance typical of a *vanitas* painting, but individual fruit and vegetables. Sanders faithfully replicates the lighting and composition of Cotán's painting but shows the objects against a white background rather than the dense, enigmatic blackness of Cotán's original, in which the quince and cabbage hang from invisible hooks to prevent them from rotting, and the melon and cucumber sit on a stone sill. The effect lends the modern illustration an altogether cleaner, more scientific feel. Sanders' subjects are the same as the original, but in more modern cultivars: a greener quince; a crinkled, light-veined Savoy cabbage rather than a dark green cabbage; a rosier, more modern variety of melon; and a more uniform kirby cucumber. Sanders' composition preserves the tension in the space between the objects in Cotán's painting, and the elegant curve that swoops from upper left to lower right. Both artists paint their subjects in meticulous detail, but by eliminating the sill and the blackness beyond Sanders keeps her focus on observable rather than mystical reality.

GIUSEPPE CASTIGLIONE

Opium poppies (*Papaver somniferum*), 18th century
Album leaf, ink and colours on silk, 33.3 × 27.8 cm / 13 × 11 in
National Palace Museum, Taipei

This delicate eighteenth-century silk painting of the opium poppy (*Papaver somniferum*) brings together Western artistic traditions – seen in the baroque shading and use of perspective in the flowers and leaves – with Chinese taste, as reflected in the fringing of the petals and the 'true to nature' bent and curving flower stems. This is one of sixteen paintings in ink and Chinese pigments on silk by the Italian Jesuit Giuseppe Castiglione gathered in the *Album*

of Immortal Blossoms in an Everlasting Spring. Castiglione arrived in China in 1715, during a period of great reform. He studied traditional Chinese art with contemporary painters and adapted it over time into what became known as the Sino-European or Chinese Palace art style. The missionary's skill was recognized by the Kangxi Emperor while Castiglione was working as an enameller in the workshops of the Imperial Palace; he later became court painter for

Kangxi's successor, the Yongzheng Emperor, and helped to decorate the expanded Yuanming Yuan Palace in 1725. During the reign of the Qianlong Emperor, Castiglione's painting skill was recognized when he was given the Chinese name Lang Shining. Aside from his paintings, Castiglione devised engravings, designs on porcelain and plans for buildings in Beijing.

Spiders I: no. 5, 2013
Charge-coupled device flatbed scan, 1.2 × 1.8 m / 4 × 6 ft
Edge Foundation, New York

This huge canvas by the New York-based artist Katinka Matson – it is 1.8 metres (6 feet) wide – uses magnification to emphasize the spider-like forms of the long, narrow petals of the spider chrysanthemum (*Chrysanthemum morifolium*) against a black background that draws attention to the first signs of decay at the edges of the delicate flowers. At the start of the twenty-first century Matson developed a new way of portraying flowers by using no more than a flatbed scanner, Adobe Photoshop and an ink-jet printer. Slowly scanning the flowers captures their exact appearance, without the distortion that is inevitably created by a single-lens photograph. Chrysanthemums have long been revered by the Chinese and Japanese, and in Germany white chrysanthemums are used at Christmas to symbolize the Nativity. Matson came upon the idea of making flower images in this way when, out of curiosity, she placed a bunch of flowers on a scanner and immediately liked what she saw: 'I was rather frustrated that day. But the very first flower scans had already inspired me.' Matson is the first artist to have taken scanning into the realm of high art, and has worked for over a decade to perfect her technique. As she says, 'New technologies equal new perceptions.'

Magnolia Blossom, 1925
Silver gelatin print, 25.4 × 32.4 cm / 10 × 12¾ in
Private collection

A flower of *Magnolia grandiflora* will last no more than four days before it begins to decay, so the American photographer Imogen Cunningham's photograph captures this specimen at its peak. Lighting the flower from the top right-hand corner, Cunningham casts a strong shadow on the lower petals that fill the frame, giving them an abstract, architectural quality. At the centre of the flower are the pistil and stamen, with its cone of tiny hooks, which give the image its context. Cunningham – who turned to sharp-focus plant photography when she was at home raising her three young sons in the 1920s – was a contemporary of Anselm Adams and Edward Weston, with whom she was a member of the influential San Francisco-based photography group f64. Cunningham's black-and-white photograph from 1925 of a magnolia flower reflects the group's philosophy of producing sharply detailed, un-manipulated and un-retouched photographs, and is one of a series of studies she made of the flower. Symbolizing purity and dignity, the magnolia, the flowers of which can reach 25 centimetres (10 inches) wide, has a heady, intoxicating fragrance. *M. grandiflora* is widely found in the United States: the evergreen tree can grow up to 24 metres (80 feet) tall and 12 metres (40 feet) wide.

Magnolia sieboldii subsp. *sinensis*, from *The Highgrove Florilegium*, 2008
Watercolour on paper, 46 × 57 cm / 18 × 22½ in
Private collection

The magnolia tree whose blossom is seen here in three stages of its life – the opening flower cup; the fully open, ten-petalled flower; and the fruit with red seeds hanging by tiny threads – belongs to Prince Charles and grows in his garden at Highgrove, Gloucestershire. There exist some 210 species of magnolia, one of the most ancient of plant genera, and many are highly prized for their beautiful blossom in early spring, although its short flowering makes it a somewhat wistful symbol of fleeting beauty. This exquisite watercolour of *Magnolia sieboldii* subsp. *sinensis* by the Japanese-born British artist Mayumi Hashi comes from *The Highgrove Florilegium*, a collection of watercolours painted over seven years by about seventy invited botanical artists from around the world. The resulting 124 plates of flowers, fruits and vegetables from the Prince's garden were printed on hand-marbled paper and published in two volumes in an edition of only 175 copies. Hashi started painting at an early age, often choosing wild flowers as her subject, before studying botanical illustration at Bromley Adult Education College, Kent, where she now teaches, having meanwhile painted orchids in Peru and served as artist in residence at the Royal College of Physicians.

Tordylium, Eyed garden poppy with fringed petals, from *Hortus Eystettensis*, 1613
Hand-coloured copperplate engraving, 55.9 × 41.9 cm / 22 × 16½ in
Royal Botanic Gardens, Kew, London

The bright red, deep purple and vivid yellow of these two poppies leap out from the otherwise subdued colouring of this plate from a florilegium produced in Germany in the early seventeenth century; they stand either side of a drawing of what may be *Tordylium syriacum*. Basilius Besler's *Hortus Eystettensis* was a collection of copperplate engravings in a very large-format work showcasing the plants, mostly exotics, that grew in the garden of Johann Conrad von Gemmingen, the Prince Bishop of Eichstätt (see p.102). Von Gemmingen employed the Nuremberg apothecary Besler to help with the garden, and then to create a book depicting the plants in grand style. Besler worked on the book for sixteen years, hiring ten engravers to translate his drawings into what turned out to be 367 elegant plates showing more than 1,000 plants, presented with accompanying letterpress. Von Gemmingen died a year before the book was published, however, so his promised funding for the project disappeared. Still, Besler completed the work and published at least 300 copies the following year (two further editions were published in 1640 and 1713). Deluxe copies were printed on better paper and some were hand-coloured, but even the uncoloured images are riveting, their style easily recognizable.

Single Oriental Poppy (C), 1968
Pigment print, 30 × 40 cm / 11¾ × 15¾ in
Private collection

This cut specimen of the oriental poppy (*Papaver orientale*) is already beginning to wilt: its delicacy is a far cry from a robust growing plant. Instead, this photograph by the leading twentieth-century US photographer Irving Penn echoes the tradition of seventeenth-century Dutch still-life painting, with elements turning towards decay. *Poppies* was Penn's second series of flower photographs, produced over seven years for *Vogue* magazine. Penn claimed no particular knowledge of horticulture, a fact that freed him from the need to represent perfection. The sensibility he had developed working in contemporary advertising and fashion lends a lush quality and high finish to this study of ephemeral beauty, a critical meditation on fashion. As a depiction of something just past its prime, the poppy is a deliberate inversion of fashion – a *vanitas*, a reminder that beauty does not fully compensate for death. Native to the near Middle East, this hardy perennial species produces brilliant scarlet-orange flowers in the wild. What is depicted here is rather different, a garden hybrid with its close relative the great scarlet poppy, *Papaver bracteatum*. Selective breeding has produced a wide range of colours including the deep maroon shown here, and the sense of artifice in this photograph is heightened by removing the poppy from any kind of natural setting.

JOHN GERARD

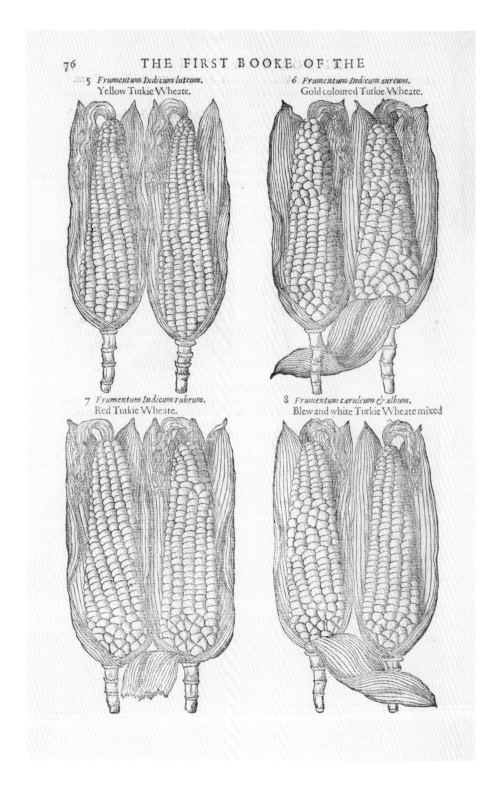

Varieties of maize, from Gerard's *Herball*, 1597
Woodcut, 34.2 × 21.5 cm / 13½ × 8½ in
Boston Public Library

In this woodcut from John Gerard's *Herball* of 1597 – probably the most famous of all English herbals – the differences between these four types of maize, or corn, are very minor, apart from the labels that specify the respective colours: yellow, gold, red and blue-and-white. At the time, maize was known in England as 'Turkie wheat', suggesting that it had been introduced from Turkey – in fact, it had been brought to Europe from Mexico after the

Spanish voyages to the New World started by Columbus in 1492 (the name of the turkey itself reflects a similar misleading association). Few of the woodblocks used for Gerard's *Herball* – as few as sixteen out of 1,800 – were by Gerard himself. Most had originated in Antwerp, where artists such as Pieter van der Borcht had produced them for the publisher Christophe Plantin. As was the custom of the time, the woodcuts were recycled for numerous later

herbals and published in 1590 as a collection of illustrations alone. The English printer John Norton saw them in the herbal of Tabernaemontanus (Jacob Theodor, 1588) at the Frankfurt Book Fair and arranged to borrow the blocks for use in an English herbal. He hired Gerard as a writer after his original choice died. The book was a great success, and in 1633 a revised edition was published.

Solanum tuberosum 'Danshaku', 2015
Watercolour on paper, 69 × 84.5 cm / 27 × 35¼ in
Lindley Library, Royal Horticultural Society, London

The arrangement of this watercolour of a potato plant – arranged carefully to show the tubers, leaves, flower and shoots – clearly reflects the European botanical tradition of the eighteenth and nineteenth centuries, but in fact the illustration comes from contemporary Japan. Although the potato originated in South America, this cultivar, 'Irish Cobbler' (*Solanum tuberosum* 'Danshaku'), was first imported there in the early twentieth century by Danshaku (Baron) Ryokichi Kawada. Since then it has become the most popular cultivar of potato in the country, and is used in a number of local dishes. This particular specimen was grown among seventy different cultivar of vegetable crammed into the small allotment of the artist Hideo Horikoshi in Tokyo. Horikoshi trained in agriculture and technology before turning to botanical illustration, under the mentorship of Mieko Ishikawa. He painted the different stages of the plant's development over a period of five months at his home before including it in his exhibition of watercolours 'Traditional Root and Tuber Crops in Japan' at the Royal Horticultural Society's London Botanical Art Show in 2015 (where he won a gold medal and was also awarded Best Botanical Painting for an illustration of the carrot cultivar *Daucus carota* 'Kintokininjin', another local delicacy).

CARL JULIUS FRITZSCHE

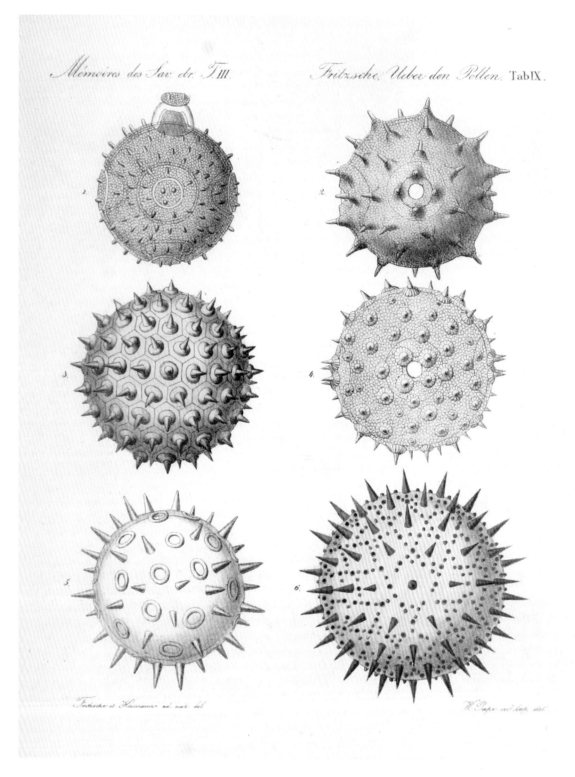

Pollen grains, from *Ueber den Pollen*, 1837
Chromolithograph, 25 × 20 cm / 9¾ x 7¾ in
University Library, University of Illinois at Urbana-Champaign, Champaign

This striking image shows six pollen grains from different flowering plants and vegetables viewed through a microscope at a magnification of 500. They are the work of the nineteenth-century German-born chemist and botanist Carl Julius Fritzsche, and form an entry in his work *Ueber den Pollen* (*About Pollen*) of 1837. Fritzsche was able to draw the grains with such precision because his microscope contained a new lens, invented just seven years previously, that removed the coloured edge around an image that had dogged earlier lenses. Fritzsche's training as a chemist is evident in the labelled image (6), which shows a pollen grain from the *Alcea rosea* (common hollyhock) that he has treated with sulphuric acid. The grains numbered (3) and (4) both come from the beautiful Indian mallow *Abutilon indicum*: on the left, the pollen is dried and seen from above; on the right, the same grain has been rehydrated. Fritzsche catalogued his pollen grains from different angles in an attempt to understand their structure through close observation. Drawing them allowed him to study the grains in even closer detail. He coined new terminology in the study of pollen, including the terms 'exine' for the outer wall of a pollen grain or spore, and 'intine' for the inner wall.

HEITI PAVES

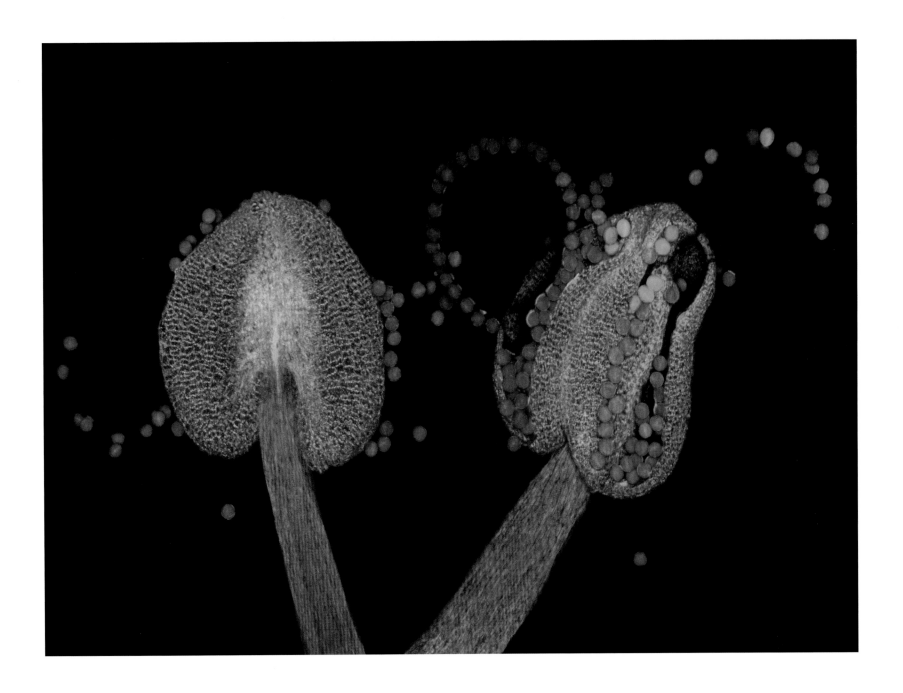

Anther of a flowering plant (Arabidopsis thaliana) (20x), 2015
Photograph, dimensions variable
Private collection

These toadstool-shaped structures are anthers, the male sex organs of flowering plants; the green beads that trace delicate loops are grains of pollen released from the anther on the right. Since the images of Robert Hooke in the seventeenth century (see p.214), each advance in microscopy has revealed new depths of beauty on a tiny scale. This image of part of the stamen of thale cress (*Arabidopsis thaliana*), magnified twenty times, was created by the Estonian scientist Heiti Paves at Tallinn University of Technology using a confocal microscope. Confocal microscopy produces a very small depth of field: the operator combines many wafer-thin section views of a subject to create a three-dimensional image. Paves has been using such technology for thirty years to investigate processes in living cells. Thale cress – related to cabbage and mustard – has celebrity status in the plant world. In 2000 it became the first plant to have its entire genome sequenced. It was also the first plant to undergo its entire lifecycle in space, from germination to flowering and setting seed. In 2015 scientists on the International Space Station used thale cress to investigate the influence of gravity on genes, research that may help us learn how best to grow plants in space.

Cuvier's Wren, *Regulus cuvieri*, from *Birds of America*, 1827–38
Hand-coloured aquatint, plate 49.5 × 31.1 cm / 19½ × 12¼ in
Natural History Museum, London

Although the evergreen North American shrub *Kalmia latifolia* dominates this huge hand-coloured aquatint – the page itself is a double elephant folio, 127 centimetres (50 inches) high – for John James Audubon the plant was little more than a perch for his real subject: the Cuvier's kinglet. Setting out to record American birds in their natural habitats meant that Audubon inevitably became a skilled botanical observer and painter, and both the birds and plants that eventually appeared in the four-volume *Birds of America* (of which this is plate 55), published over twelve years from 1827, were groundbreaking in their detail and beauty. Kalmia had been introduced to England by the naturalist Mark Catesby (see p.25) in 1726, but it proved difficult to propagate and was not recorded to flower until the 1740s. Soon afterwards kalmia was named by Linnaeus after Pehr Kalm, who searched America from 1748 to 1751 for plants that might successfully be transplanted to Scandinavia. Audubon shot this kinglet in Pennsylvania in 1812 – he often shot the specimens he painted – and named it Cuvier's kinglet after the French zoologist Georges Cuvier; but no other specimen has ever been recorded. It now seems likely that Audubon had wrongly identified a golden-crowned kinglet and given it a bright red – and probably misleading – crown instead.

MARIA SIBYLLA MERIAN

Swamp Immortelle with Giant Silk Moth, 1702–3
Watercolour and bodycolour with gum arabic on vellum, 35.9 × 28.5 cm / 14 × 11¼ in
Royal Collection Trust, London

Maria Sibylla Merian's flowering branch of the coral tree (*Erythrina fusca*) comes complete with leaves riddled with caterpillar holes, the caterpillars of three different moths, a chrysalis and two flying giant silk moths (*Arsenura armida*). In fact, the insects rather than the tree were Merian's main interest for her seminal work on the insects of Suriname, *Metamorphosis Insectorum Surinamensium* (1705). Merian had demonstrated her talents as a botan-

ical artist – producing sets of drawings in 1675, 1677 and 1680 – but her remarkable skill in recording the life cycles of insects and their plant hosts became so prized that her work was purchased by Peter the Great of Russia. Merian had travelled to Suriname in 1699, aged fifty-two, with a grant from the burghers of Amsterdam to paint the plants and insects of the recently established Dutch colony there. Maria and her daughter Dorothea Maria lived for two years

in a Protestant plantation until her illness forced her to return to Europe in 1701, leaving her daughter behind to carry on painting. This tree – a tropical member of the pea family, more typically seen with red flowers – was also sometimes known as 'palisade tree', a term used for a number of hardwood plants that could be made into fences.

Japanese Witch Hazel, 1915
Pencil and watercolour on paper, 26.3 × 21.1cm / 10½ × 8¼ in
Hunterian Museum and Art Gallery, University of Glasgow

The strong outlines and carefully separated colours of these branches of Japanese witch hazel reflect the art nouveau background of the artist, Charles Rennie Mackintosh. Better known as a designer and architect, especially in his home city of Glasgow, Mackintosh was also a talented painter who produced detailed depictions of plants as well as landscapes. The detached flower at bottom right, painted at an enlarged scale, shows its structure clearly,

with narrow, crumpled petals, each with a brown spot at its base. The uncoloured sections of the main drawing reflect Mackintosh's fascination with Japanese art. The panel at the bottom of the page dates the painting to 1915, and gives its location, the village of Walberswick on the Suffolk coast, to which Mackintosh and his wife Margaret had moved the previous year. The picture may have had an emotional significance for the couple, as the panel vertically spells

out their initials: Charles Rennie Mackintosh and Margaret Macdonald Mackintosh. Japanese witch hazel, *Hamamelis japonica*, is native to the mountains of Japan and Korea, where it grows in the understorey, but it thrives in cultivation and is a popular garden shrub, providing colour and fragrance in winter and early spring when few other plants are in flower.

ELLSWORTH KELLY

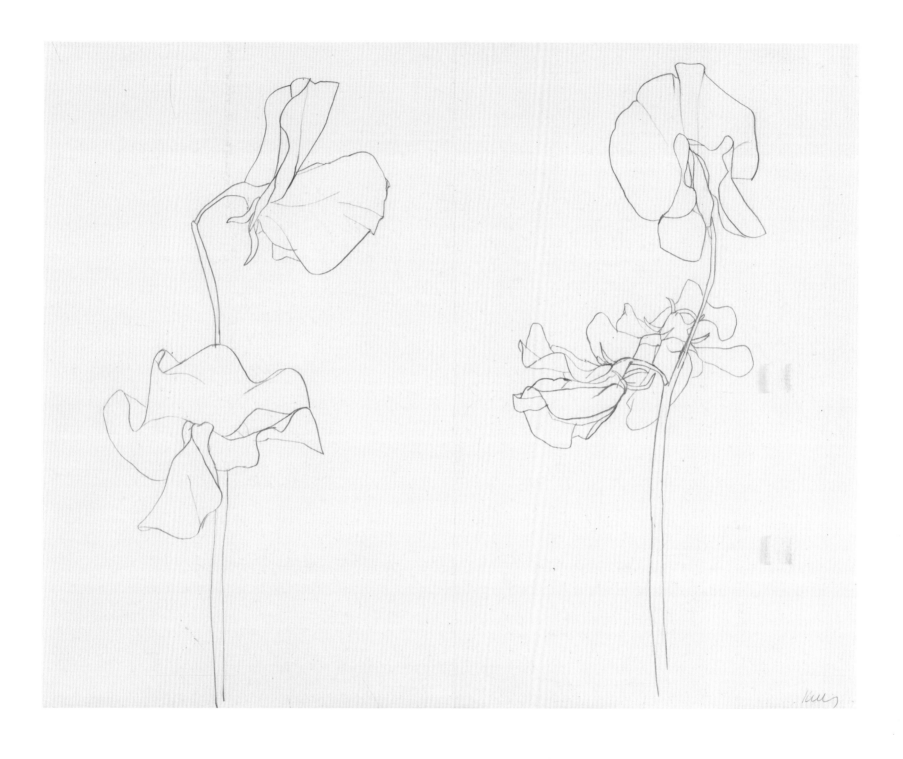

Sweet Pea, 1960
Graphite on paper, 57.3 × 72.4 cm / 22½ × 28½ in
Baltimore Museum of Art, Maryland

Using only a minimal line, the celebrated twentieth-century US artist Ellsworth Kelly – better known for large, vividly coloured, hard-edged abstract forms in his paintings and sculptures – captures the delicacy and beauty of a sweet pea (*Lathyrus odoratus*) through the use of contour alone, abstracting form from its other qualities. Close observation of natural forms was a point of departure for Kelly, who was influenced as a child by illustrations of birds and developed his interest as an applied artist in a World War II Camouflage Battalion. This slight, small monochrome drawing is a study of a fragile plant seen from two angles. The artist notes idiosyncrasies in the subject and also honestly records inconsistencies in his own perception, but with a characteristically precise attention to the outline of the motif. The subject is a well-loved annual – called a 'pea' as a climbing legume and 'sweet' for the fragrance of the essential oils, which are attractive to pollinators and gardeners alike. Sweet peas were first noted in the seventeenth century and were actively bred to develop a range of pastel colours. Enthusiasm for these cultivars reached a peak with Henry Eckford's work in the late Victorian period; larger flowers appeared later in the United States.

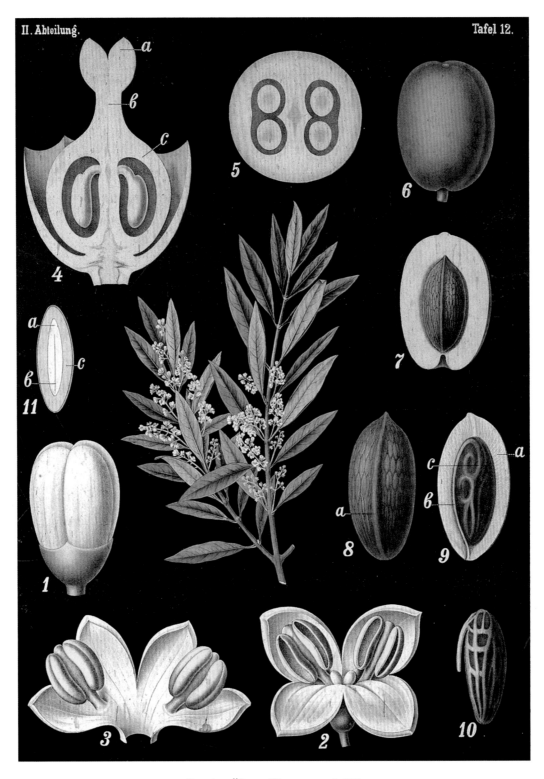

Gemeiner Ölbaum *(Olea europaea)*, 1897
Chromolithograph, 70 × 49.5 cm / 27½ × 19½ in
Private collection

Many people have their first experience of botanical illustration at school, and this German poster from 1889 was clearly designed for classroom use. A twig of European olive (*Olea europaea*) with leaves and flowers is surrounded by enlarged, detailed depictions of the dissected flower (1–5) and the fruit and stone (6–11). The important parts are labelled clearly with numbers and letters relating to a key that was presumably accessible by teacher, students or both. The quality of the illustration is less important than precision and clarity, so the different elements are set against a black background. This is plate twelve of a series entitled *Ausländische Kulturpflanzen in farbigen Wandtafeln* (*Exotic Cultivated Plants in Coloured Wall Posters*), which reflected the tradition in the late nineteenth and early twentieth centuries of using posters in the teaching of biological and other subjects. Such large-scale charts became fundamental tools for classroom instruction across much of Europe, particularly in Germany. The development of colour lithography from about 1850 to 1890 enabled the production of charts of greater detail and containing more information. This set of educational botanical wall charts was edited by the botanist Hermann Zippel with illustrations by the lithographer Carl Bollmann.

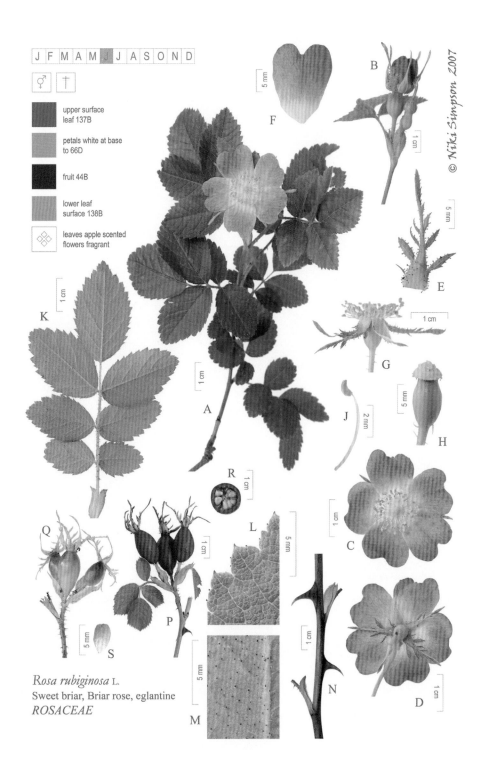

© Niki Simpson 2007

Rosa rubiginosa L.
Sweet briar, Briar rose, eglantine
ROSACEAE

Sweet briar (*Rosa rubiginosa*), 2007
Digital composite image, dimensions variable
Private collection

This illustration of *Rosa rubiginosa* or sweet briar – also known as eglantine – is intended to be scientifically informative, as is clear from the colour reference, the scale bars that accompany the separate plant parts, and the careful noting of scientific and English names, family name and flowering season (indicated in the calendar bar at the top of the page). Although it echoes botanical plates of the past, however, this plate is the creation of cutting-edge

technology. The British plant artist Niki Simpson has pioneered the use of digital photography to record each stage of a plant's life cycle in season, assembling the images of leaves, buds, flowers and fruit on to one plate: leaves photographed in different seasons may be overlapped, and important details may be dissected and enlarged. Simpson and her colleague the botanist Peter Barnes are creating a library of images of British native wild flowers and plants.

Eglantine, which is mentioned in *A Midsummer Night's Dream*, grows wild over much of southern England, and Europe. Simpson's illustration shows its important features: the bright pink flowers, the curved thorns, the glandular sepals on top of the ripe hips, and the glands on the underside of the leaves, which release a sweet apple scent.

ROSÁLIA DEMONTE

Aristolochia gigantea, 1985
Gouache on vellum, 55 × 41 cm / 21¾ × 16 in
Shirley Sherwood Collection, London

This gigantic tube-shaped flower, mottled with white and maroon netting that darkens near the middle, is as striking in the flesh as in the Brazilian painter Rosália Demonte's gouache depiction: not only is it gigantic – over 35 centimetres (14 inches) long – but also it emits a foul smell similar to rotting meat in order to attract the flies that pollinate it. The huge bloom belongs to the Brazilian vine *Aristolochia gigantea*, also known as giant Dutchman's pipe

and used in traditional medicine to help with childbirth and abortion. The yellow spot in the middle of the flower leads to a closed pouch, where the flies following the smell are steered deeper inside and trapped by stiff hairs as they deposit pollen from other plants. After a time, the plant stops releasing the scent, the hairs soften and the flies escape, now carrying its pollen. Demonte, who came from a family of artists but herself had no formal artistic training,

drew attention through her work to the beauty, diversity and fragility of flora and fauna of the Brazilian tropical forest, hoping to inspire a reverence for the natural world, even as parts of it were disappearing because of industrial and residential development.

HONOUR HIERS STEWART

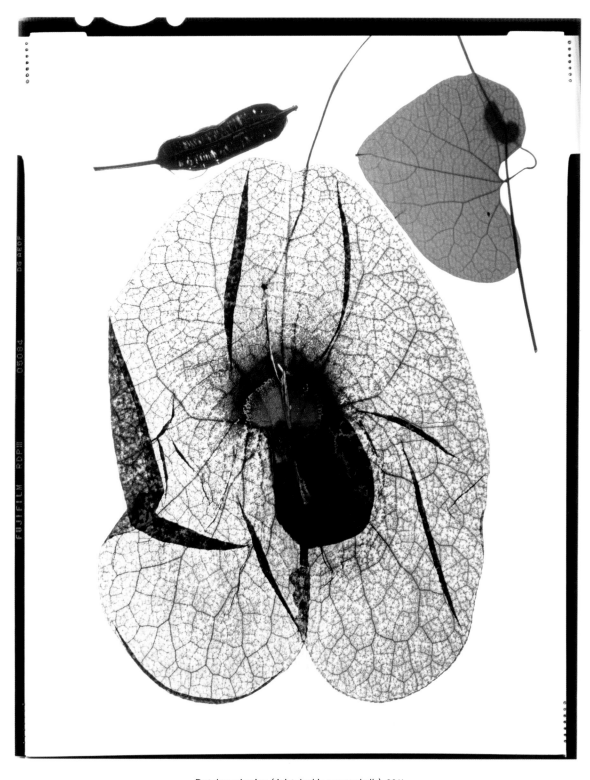

Dutchman's pipe (*Aristolochia macrophylla*), 2011
Transparency film with botanical specimen, 101.6 × 81.3 cm / 40 × 32 in
Private collection

Displaying a single distinctive heart-shaped leaf of Dutchman's pipe (*Aristolochia macrophylla*), a vigorous deciduous climbing vine native to eastern North America, next to a plan view of the curiously shaped flower creates a clarity rarely seen in nature, where the foliage generally obscures the flowers. This view underlines the delicate tracery of the brown-purple lobes around its open-mouthed top; the dark, mysterious void of the 'pipe' adds a sense of drama to the composition. The US photographer Honour Hiers Stewart is dedicated to creating a contemporary herbarium that she hopes will help to stimulate Americans' interest in native plant species, so guaranteeing their future existence. Hiers Stewart – who in 2008 gave up the use of digital cameras in favour of large-format film with a 1960s Tachihara bellows camera made of cherry wood – takes a contemplative approach, carefully considering the plants to photograph in particular regions and being careful not to disturb fragile environments. Some specimens are photographed within a day or two of being gathered, others after several months. Working in such an ecologically sensitive way requires patience in order to gain an understanding of her subjects before capturing their images. Given the ambitious scope of her project, Hiers Stewart accepts that her work may never be considered complete.

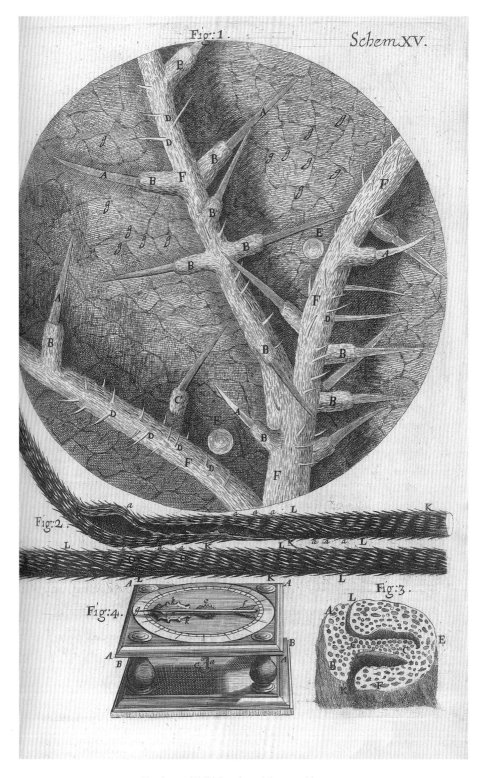

Nettles and Wild Oat, from *Micrographia*, 1665
Copperplate engraving, 31 × 20 cm / 12¼ × 7¾ in
United States National Library of Medicine, Bethesda, Maryland

The English natural philosopher Robert Hooke changed not just botany but all other sciences when he published *Micrographia* in 1665. Engravings of this kind were the first published illustrations of plants, insects and objects seen through a microscope, and they introduced the public to a previously invisible world. This plate illustrates the under-surface of a nettle leaf (fig. 1), two parts of the beard of a wild oat (fig. 2), a cross-section of the beard of a wild oat (fig. 3) and a proposed hygrometer to measure humidity using the reaction of wild oat beard to atmospheric moisture (fig. 4). Of the nettle leaf, Hooke describes seeing 'the whole surface of it very thick set' with spines (F) from which protrude hollow spikes that taper to a point (B, A). Hooke's text explains how he stung himself repeatedly in order to discover that these spikes pierced the skin with a 'liquor' that led to the 'burning pain' of the sting. As a pioneer of microscopy, along with his contemporaries Malpighi (see p.52) and Nehemiah Grew (see p.160), Hooke promoted his new method of investigation enthusiastically – although, in fact, his three-lensed microscope produced distorted, poor-quality images. His plates did more than any other work of the period to convey the excitement of microscopy and to encourage others to look at plants through lenses as well as with the naked eye.

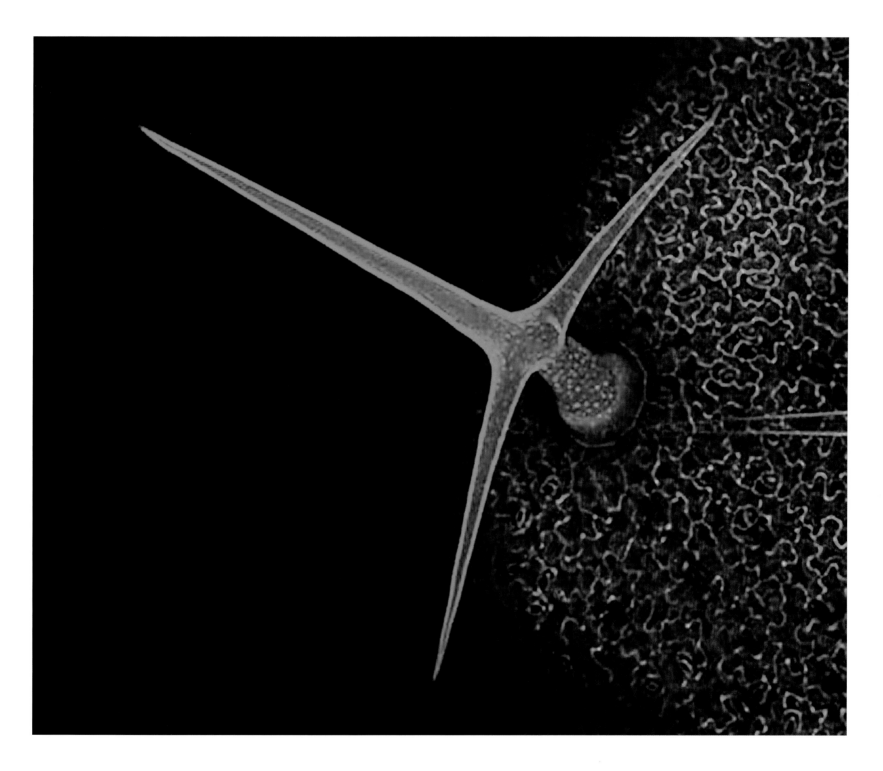

Trichome (haircell) of the leaf epidermis of *Arabidopsis thaliana*, 2003
Confocal microscopic image, magnification 600x,
dimensions variable

This formidable-looking trichome – a tiny outgrowth on the surface of a leaf – is most abundant on new leaves, as in this case of *Arabidopsis thaliana* (thale cress). It probably affords the succulent new leaves some protection from insects that feed on them. At the base of the trichome, the cells of the leaf surface include epidermal cells that resemble jigsaw pieces and the stomata, the pores through which leaves absorb carbon dioxide as the first step of photosyn-thesis. The image was created using a technique known as confocal microscopy, in which plant cells are modified by the insertion of a jellyfish gene called green fluorescent protein (GFP). The GFP is made visible by activation with lasers to produce three-dimensional images, even in living cells. The red visible inside the leaf-surface cells is fluores-cence emanating from chloroplasts, the cellular structures that use sunlight and carbon dioxide to produce sugar and, incidentally, the oxygen we breathe. *Arabidopsis thaliana* was a small, seemingly insignificant plant in the brassica family before it rose to prominence in the early 1990s as a model organism for the study of genetics. In 2000 it became the first plant to have its entire genome sequenced.

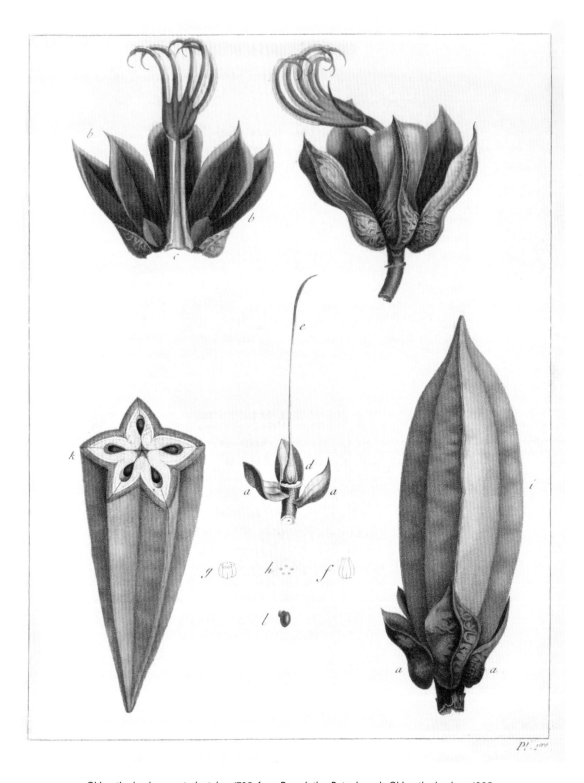

Chiranthodendron pentadactylon, 1795, from *Description Botanique du Chiranthodendron*, 1805
Hand-coloured stipple engraving, 27 × 21 cm / 10¾ × 8¼ in
Smithsonian Institution, Washington, DC

At the top of this watercolour from the end of the eighteenth century are a cross section and a full illustration of the vivid red flowers that give the Mexican hand tree its name, thanks to the five elongated stamens that resemble the fingers of upturned hands. Beneath are the characteristic five-ribbed fruits. Their similarity to okra is no surprise given that both okra and *Chiranthodendron pentadactylon* belong to the same mallow family. Little is known about

the artist who created this carefully balanced composition. José Dionisio Larreátegui studied medicine and botany in Mexico City, where he gave an admiring address on the still relatively new classification system of Carl Linnaeus; it was published in 1795 as *Descripciones de Plantas*, and the book from which this engraving comes is the French translation of that work. Larreátegui studied botany with Vicente Cervantes, a veteran of the Spanish botanical expedition

to Mexico led by Martín de Sessé y Lacasta and José Mariano Mociño from 1787 to 1820. The expedition's botanical artists included Atanasio Echeverría y Godoy (see p.317) and Juan Vicente de la Cerda, who painted the Mexican hand tree under the name *Cheirostemon platanoides*. Cerda's drawing was only published posthumously in the 1890s, however, so Larreátegui's illustration and description validate the name *Chiranthodendron pentadactylon*.

WILLIAM T. COOPER

Barringtonia asiatica. No. 653
Cape Tribulation - Coll.-S. Breeden
Oct.-90.

Beach Barringtonia *(Barringtonia asiatica)*, from *Australian Rainforest Fruits: A Field Guide*, 1994
Watercolour, 21 × 27 cm / 8¼ × 10¾ in
State Library of New South Wales, Sydney

This strongly geometric composition – balancing circle and square, brown and green – combines side-on and plan views of the distinctive lantern-shaped fruit of *Barringtonia asiatica*, which turn brown as they mature. The plant is native to mangrove swamps in the Indian Ocean and western Pacific. Inside each 'lantern' is a spongy middle layer full of tiny air sacs that add buoyancy, so that, once shed, the fruit can float vast distances on the ocean, surviving for up to two years; a hard innermost layer protects the seed. All parts of *Barrington asiatica* contain poisonous saponins. Traditionally, the seeds are pounded and thrown into rivers, where the poison stuns fish without affecting the flesh. The leaves, seeds and juice are also used in traditional medicine. The Australian William T. Cooper began his career as a landscape and seascape artist, but became renowned for his natural-history illustrations, particularly his ornitho-logical painting. This watercolour comes from *Australian Rainforest Fruits: A Field Guide* (1994), written by Cooper's botanist wife, Wendy, with whom he collaborated on the book over seventeen years. In the year it was published, Cooper received the Order of Australia for his contribution to natural history and art.

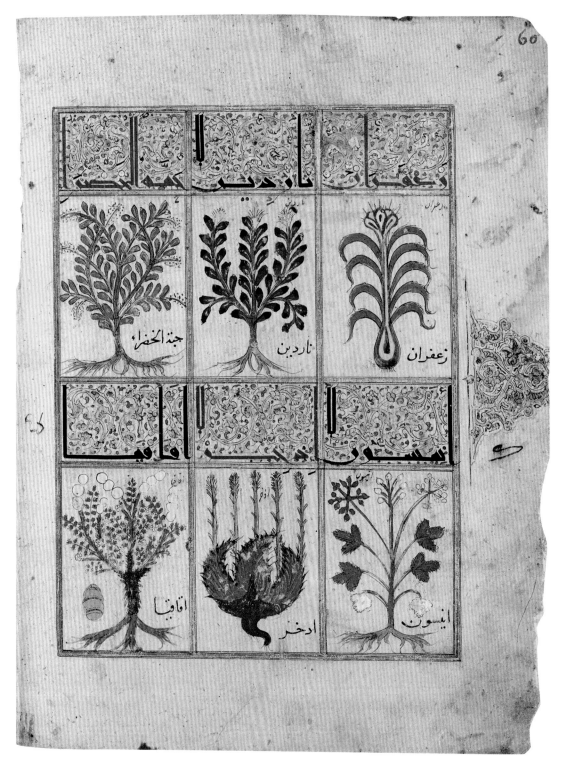

The Book of Theriac (*Kitāb al-Diryāq*), 1199
Ink and gouache on paper, 36.5 × 27.5 cm / 14 ½ × 10¾ in
Bibliothèque nationale de France, Paris

This beautiful illuminated page with precise illustrations of six plants comes from what is essentially a medieval Islamic recipe book, or *theriac*, for making up antidotes to deal with specific ailments. It was produced by an unknown author in northern Iraq in about 1199; the miniatures may have been produced by the scribe responsible for copying the manuscript, Muhammad ibn Abi i-Fath. Each plant is listed with its cursive name below a title in Kufic script,

with instructions on how it should be prepared and used in remedy. Other pages of the book include illustrations of minerals or animals whose body parts were included in particular cures. The manuscript was presented under the guise of a translation of Galen, the second-century Arab writer whose medical encyclopedia dominated the Islamic world for more than a millennium, but who himself had adopted many elements of classical Greek learning. Galen

himself is illustrated near the start of the *Kitāb*, along with other medical authorities, who are shown discovering the antidotes it describes. The compendium contained some sixty specific cures (*theriac* means snake venom) using ingredients such as ground snakeskin, opium and an onion-like plant known as *moly* (possibly top right) The drugs were mixed in honey to make them more palatable.

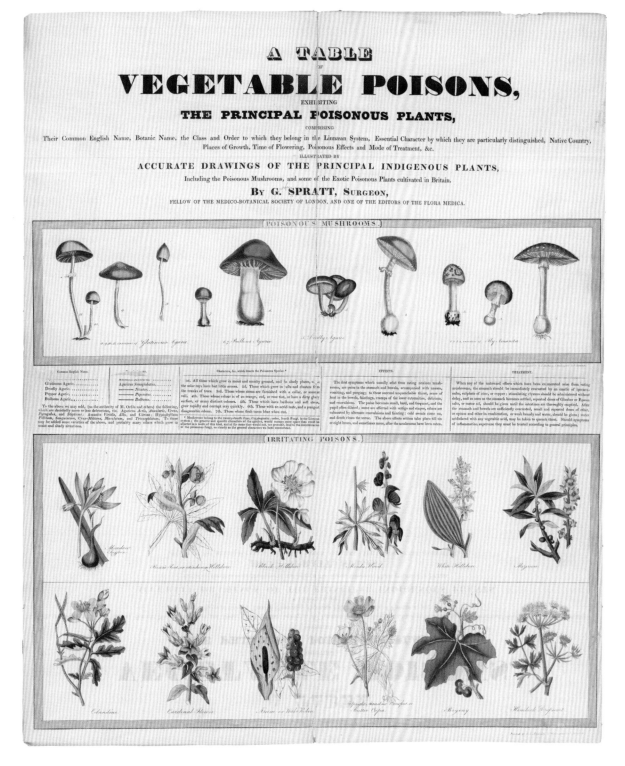

A Table of Vegetable Poisons, 1843
Hand-coloured lithograph, 63 × 52 cm / 24¾ × 20½ in
Library of Congress, Washington, DC

This unusual mid-nineteenth-century medical chart, rather ponderously entitled *A Table of Vegetable Poisons, Exhibiting the Principal Poisonous Plants*, is an illustrated guide to identifying many of the poisonous species known in Britain at the time, including both fungi and flowering plants. The first table depicts ten species of poisonous fungus, which are named in the text below, accompanied by medical notes on the symptoms experienced by unfortunate victims and the suggested treatment (which tends to be general rather than specific to each poison). The illustration at the far right is clearly the fly agaric (*Amanita muscaria*) with its distinctive white-flecked red cap, a poisonous (although rarely fatal) fungus with hallucinogenic properties. The lower table, entitled 'Irritating Poisons', features twelve flowering plants with poisonous properties, all identified carefully, including meadow saffron, hellebores, monks-hood and wild arum. This unusual table was the combined work of the surgeon George Spratt and the engraver, lithographer and printer George Edward Madeley. Spratt was a member of the Medico-Botanical Society of London, and illustrated a number of botanical and other works. His best-known publication is *Flora Medica* (1829–30), a two-volume work containing 184 hand-coloured plates of plants of particular medicinal interest.

Squash Vine (*Cucurbita peregrina alba maior
seu cucurbita Indica Mathioli florida*), from *Piante Fiori Frutti*, c.1560
Pencil and opaque watercolour on paper, 46.5 × 36 cm / 18¼ × 14¼ in
Private collection

Gracefully curved to fit the page, this image portrays a result of the botanical exchange between the Old and New worlds, showing both the flowers and the fruit of one of the earliest squashes brought to Europe. *Cucurbita* is a genus of herbaceous vines from the Andes and Mesoamerica, where its gourds were a major source of food for indigenous peoples such as the Inca. This colourful plate, in which orange flowers contrast strikingly with the green leaves, is remarkable among the output of Ulisse Aldrovandi, one of the most important botanical artists of the sixteenth century, since most of his works were black-and-white woodcuts. Aldrovandi was the first professor of natural sciences at the University of Bologna, where in 1568 he founded one of the earliest botanic gardens. Aldrovandi was also a noted collector. He gathered some 18,000 natural objects, while his plant-hunting trips yielded a fifteen-volume herbarium containing more than 5,000 mounted specimens. He wrote hundreds of books and papers, of which the few published were illustrated with woodcuts that mingled scientific observation with medievally fanciful 'monsters'. He also produced some 3,000 dramatic yet accurate paintings like this one, using densely opaque paint to illustrate plants, fruit, birds and animals.

Bryonia dioica – The English Wild Vine, c.1839
Photogenic drawing negative, 18.3 × 22.4 cm / 7 × 8¾ in
National Media Museum, London

In this ghostly image of white bryony, a member of the cucumber family, thin tendrils curl around the stem and five-lobed leaves, the veins of which are perfectly clear. This specimen was picked from a hedge at Lacock Abbey, Wiltshire, home of the photographic pioneer William Henry Fox Talbot. A few years before making this picture, Fox Talbot's frustration at being unable to draw – even with the aid of a camera obscura – led him to experiment with creating what he termed photograms. In the summer of 1835 he placed a plant on a sheet of paper coated with silver nitrate, following a process used ten years previously by the French inventor Nicéphore Niépce to produce the earliest photographic image. Fox Talbot observed that wherever sunlight struck the paper it darkened, but where the plant blocked the light it left an outline image on the paper in negative. He worked out that the negative outline could be turned positive by being printed on light-sensitive paper. Fox Talbot's friend Sir John Herschel, meanwhile, discovered that sodium thiosulphate 'fixed' images printed in this way, so that they did not fade. Fox Talbot patented his images as 'calotypes', and published them in the first photographic book, his *Pencil of Nature*, which appeared in instalments between 1844 and 1846.

Pages from *Das Grosse Stammbuch*, 1596–1633
Pen and ink and watercolour on vellum, 20.8 × 16 cm / 8¼ × 6½ in
Private collection

Philipp Hainhofer, the Augsburg merchant for whom this page of flowers was drawn – complete with a scroll of tendrils marking the margin, a snake and a frame of seashells – was one of the most important art collectors of the early seventeenth century. He stood at the centre of an interchange of art and political ideas that were closely linked at the time, and kept an extensive record of his travels, studying law in Siena and Padua and learning about a range of artistic styles throughout Europe, especially in Italy and the Netherlands. He is probably best known for the many 'cabinets of curiosities' (*Kunstschränke*) – collections of remarkable objects linked to natural history, antiquities, ethnography and so on – that he created with the help of local craftsmen and artists. One renowned example was produced for Duke Philip II of Pomerania. Hainhofer's *Grosse Stammbuch* (*Book of Friendship*), which dates from 1596 to 1633, is a lavishly illustrated work in pen and ink and watercolour on vellum and paper with text in German, Latin and Italian. It is a rare and valuable object, although some pages have been reproduced widely. This plate, which includes a crown imperial and tulips which were recent introductions from the Middle East, may be the work of the late sixteenth-century Flemish artist Joris Hoefnagel.

Star of Bethlehem (*Ornithogalum umbellatum*), wood anemone (*Anemone nemorosa*)
and sun spurge (*Euphorbia helioscopia*), c.1505–10
Pen and ink with red chalk on paper, 19.8 × 16 cm / 7¾ × 6¼ in
Royal Collection Trust, London

If there is one overriding characteristic of Leonardo's drawings, it is his quest to go beyond mere description. A supreme draughtsman, he captured the smallest details with great accuracy by spending hours in focused observation as he sought to reach a deeper understanding of his subject. Driven by an insatiable curiosity about the world around him, the original Renaissance man used drawing not only to sketch details for his larger paintings but also almost as an analysis of life forces: the flow patterns of turbulence in water, the tension within the muscles of the human body and, in this drawing of Star of Bethlehem, the dynamic energy of the swirl of leaves from which the flowers burst forth. On the same sheet, a drawing of a wood anemone reveals the more delicate fragility of the flowers on their stems, while the close-up observations of the cupped seed heads of the sun spurge (bottom left) show his forensic fascination with the anatomical arrangement of parts. It was through such deep observation that Leonardo was able to integrate the living world so convincingly into his paintings. These particular drawings may have been used to create the foreground of his painting of *Leda and the Swan*, which was lost in the seventeenth century but is known in copy.

Study of Weeds, Etc. Plantain, Nettle, Cat's Tail, Daisy, Lady's Smock, Grass, Willow – May, c.1815–17
Ink on paper, 16 × 11.2 cm / 6¼ × 4½ in
Tate, London

This sketch depicts a rather ordinary collection of weeds that caught the eye of one of the leading British painters of the early nineteenth century, J.M.W. Turner. The relatively detailed study of tangled leaves and stems the lower page passes up into a quickly scratched overhang of skeletal trees on the opposite page within what is called the 'Walmer Ferry' sketchbook, and notes record the names of the weeds in typically illegible handwriting. Turner used this small brown leather sketchbook, with its stained cover and broken clasp, between 1815 and 1817, halfway through his career. Before using it, Turner applied a wash of warm slate colour to the pages, which allowed him to work in the mid-range of shades, using his pen or pencil to render shadows or scratching off the wash to create highlights, as in the edges of the larger leaves and flowers here. The sketchbooks give an impression of a man in a hurry to record all around him, in either a few rapidly applied ink strokes or more carefully observed studies such as this. When Turner died, in 1851, the contents of his studio – more than 30,000 artworks – became the property of the nation.

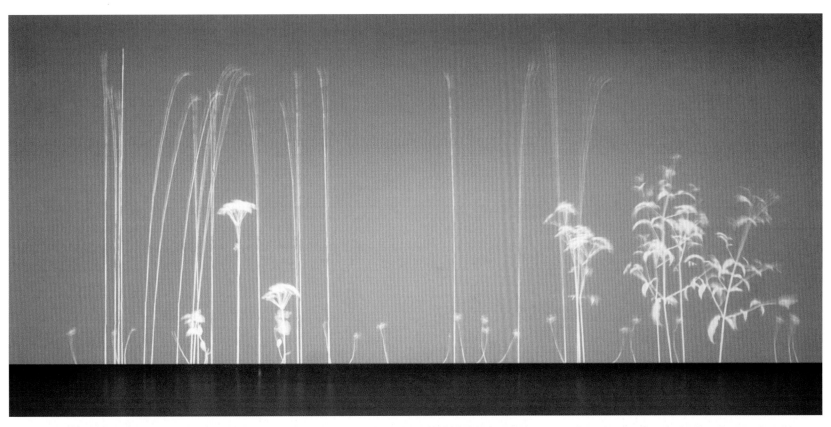

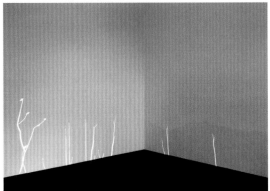
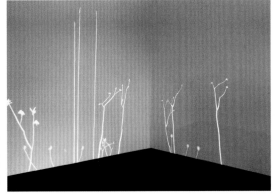

Lightweeds, 2006
Location sensitive light projection, dimensions variable
Museum of Modern Art, New York

These weeds and grasses grow before our eyes on a gallery wall in a light projection by the Dutch-born artist Simon Heijdens – but they grow differently every time, their development being affected by the climate outside the gallery and the passage of viewers within. In this installation, which Heijdens calls *Lightweeds*, plant silhouettes appear to grow on several walls around the gallery, each plant being generated from a digital 'seed' containing the specific genetic details of its family. Outdoor sensors meanwhile measure light, rainfall and wind, providing a stream of data that affect seedling growth: each plant reacts differently to the changing external physical conditions. Plants also flex as viewers pass, reflecting their presence and patterns of movement. After several passages of viewers, the plants shed their seeds, which then travel to another wall – and so a new plant grows. This 'pollination' sequence is affected directly by footfall, so the positions of the new plants on the walls reveal which areas of the gallery are used more than others at different times of day. Heijdens creates site-specific installations to reintroduce the effects of unpredictable natural elements into urban environments that are increasingly dominated by twenty-four-hour lighting and climate-controlled buildings.

JACQUES LE MOYNE DE MORGUES

Snowdrops with a Lady Butterfly, c.1575
Watercolour on paper, 27.3 × 19 cm / 10¾ × 7½ in
Victoria and Albert Museum, London

The rich orange and black of the Lady butterfly (now more commonly known as the painted lady) in this sixteenth-century watercolour contrast with the delicacy of the three views of a snowdrop (back, front and profile), with white flowers and green-tipped perianths. The artist Jacques Le Moyne de Morgues was once best known mainly for relatively simple woodcuts – or for his adventurous life. In 1564 he was the artist and cartographer on a French expedition to Florida, but was almost the only survivor after the Spanish attacked the group's settlement. His drawings of the expedition were destroyed, but subsequently re-created, possibly earning him an appointment as a court artist. His album of fifty-nine flower paintings on paper – discovered only at the start of the twentieth century, when it established his reputation – belongs to this period. Le Moyne de Morgues was a Huguenot, and in 1572 he fled to England to avoid the growing hostility to the Hugenots which was to culminate in the Massacre of St. Bartholomew's Day. In London, under the patronage of Sir Walter Raleigh, he published *La Clef des Champs* (1586), a pattern book containing woodcuts of flowers, birds and animals. By including the butterfly in this plate, Le Moyne de Morgues continued the artistic tradition of linking plants and insects begun by medieval manuscript illuminators.

EDWARD AUGUSTUS BOWLES

Snowdrops (*Galanthus plicatus* subsp. *byzantinus*), 1906–7
Watercolour, 32 × 23 cm / 12¾ × 9 in
Lindley Library, Royal Horticultural Society, London

This delicate study of snowdrops, painted by the renowned British gardener Edward Augustus Bowles in the winter of 1906, shows the green markings on the inner segments of each flower, which differentiates the subspecies *byzantinus* from the subspecies *Galanthus plicatus*. Snowdrops grew in Bowles's celebrated 3.2-hectare (8-acre) garden) at his family home in Enfield, north London, Myddelton House, which is still known for its bulb collection: he collected 130

species of crocus and *colchicum* alone. Bowles had studied divinity at Cambridge and became a keen entomologist, but after the death of his brother and sister from tuberculosis in 1887 he dedicated himself to the garden. Despite losing the sight in his right eye and having no formal art training, he was a keen watercolourist. The first of his many books, *My Garden in Spring*, was published in 1914, at the beginning of World War I. After his death in 1956,

Sir Frederick Stern published the monograph *Garden Varieties of Galanthus*, which included Bowles's list of 137 named snowdrops, some of which were no longer in cultivation. In February 2011 a single bulb of a pure white *G. p.* 'E. A. Bowles', that had been found growing at Myddelton House, sold for a record £357 in an online auction.

'Solis flos Peruvianus. Solis flos minor', from *Florilegium*, 1612
Hand-coloured copperplate engraving, 39.7 × 22.5 cm / 15¾ × 8¾ in
Private collection

The Dutch plantsman Emanuel Sweert was a talented artist, as this pair of sunflower cultivars shows, with the carefully delineated petals and seed heads – but he was also a merchant. His *Florilegium* of 110 hand-coloured engravings was essentially a catalogue of the plants he had for sale, with explanatory text in Latin, Dutch, German and French. Florilegia, or books of garden flowers, became a popular genre in the early seventeenth century. Originally intended as sourcebooks for embroiderers and weavers, they soon became popular simply as collections of flowers, engraved in modern copperplate to show more intricate detail than old-style woodcuts. Such books often showcased plants that had been brought back to Europe by explorers – like these sunflowers from the New World – inspiring both wealthy garden owners and horticulturists (Sweert included instructions for planting unusual bulbs). Sweert, who sold plants in Amsterdam and at the annual Frankfurt Fair, worked for the Holy Roman Emperor Rudolph II, who granted him copyright for the *Floregium*. In fact, Sweert was himself no respecter of copyright, having copied some of his images from earlier works. His sunflowers are a reversed copy of an engraving of about 1612 by Johann Theodor de Bry.

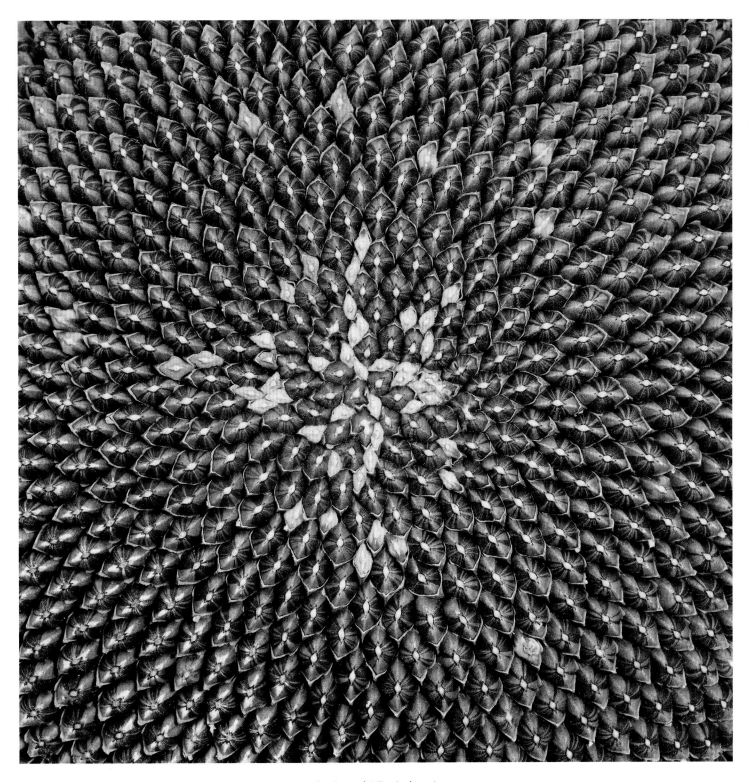

Sunflower (*Helianthus*) seeds
Photograph, dimensions variable

This close-up photograph of the seeds in the head of a sunflower (*Helianthus*) combines the imperfections of the organic world with a precision that is almost mathematical. The occasional opened seed breaks up the perfect regularity of the florets, which form an inward spiral best seen in their thin yellow outlines. The resulting pattern seems more architectural than botanical – it is no coincidence that the contemporary British photographer, Mark Sykes, specializes in architectural images – as if it were a plan for a structure built from individual plates. Sunflower seeds are arranged in a series of intersecting spirals that allow the maximum number to fit into the available space. The pattern follows a special sequence of numbers known as the Fibonacci sequence – named after its thirteenth-century discoverer, the Italian mathematician Leonardo Fibonacci – in which the next number is the sum of the previous two: 1, 1, 2, 3, 5, 8.... The sequence is widely observed in nature, as in, for example, the distribution of florets in the scales of a pineapple, the arrangement of petals in a rose or the spiral in the shell of a snail. There is a particular poignancy in finding this enduring mathematical perfection in a sunflower, traditionally a symbol of the transient nature of beauty and of life itself.

GIROLAMO PINI

Étude de Botanique, 1614–15
Oil on canvas, 92 × 120 cm / 36¼ × 47¼ in
Musée des Arts Décoratifs, Paris

This luminous oil painting is one of the few traces left of the early seventeenth-century Italian artist Girolamo Pini. It is also a permanent record of a period of great advances in botanical science. Pini was active at a time when botanic gardens were being developed at the universities in Padua, Pisa, Florence and Bologna, and it may well have been a wealthy patron of one of these gardens who commissioned this remarkably detailed study. Every aspect of the plants,

from their roots and bulbs to their flowers are displayed, including the all-important insects associated with them. To the joy of botanists, Pini identifies clearly all forty-three flowering plants featured on a paper scroll in the bottom left-hand corner. Pini may have been influenced by the work of his more celebrated contemporary Jacopo Ligozzi, whose botanically accurate paintings were commissioned by the Medici in Florence and was celebrated for his

paintings of plants and animals. Ligozzi was also employed by the naturalist Ulisse Aldrovandi to paint his extensive botanical collections in Bologna. Pini may not have had Ligozzi's privileges, but whoever commissioned this work, carried out some twenty years before fortunes were made and lost speculating on the price of bulbs in Europe, *Étude de Botanique* would have been a very secure investment.

REGULA DETTWILER

Narzisse Magenta/Grün: Made in China, 2007
Watercolour, 77 × 57 cm / 30¼ × 22½ in
Private collection

There is a strong irony in showing an artificial flower – here a make-believe red flowered daffodil – in a way that recalls traditional botanical studies. This specimen is easily deconstructed, since its parts are not joined as they are in nature. On the left, the ordering of the elements of the flower is botanically correct, as well as aesthetically appealing. Anthers and filaments are perpetually pollen-laden, as sterile as many garden varieties of real daffodils.

The distinctive trumpet shape of the inner flower is lost in this plan view, but the delicate frill of its opening is underlined. Two layers of outer petals – the perianth – are placed as they would be were the flower intact. At the bottom, the pale sepals that make a protective cover over the emerging flower bud are shown folded back. The flower is frankly artificial, however: daffodils of this colour do not occur in nature. The Swiss artist Regula Dettwiler travels

the world collecting artificial flowers, just as botanists and plant-hunters did real ones, and she draws and paints them in much the same way as botanical artists would have done centuries ago with new plant discoveries. One of her main interests is to analyse the artificial 'nature' that has become part of our everyday surroundings.

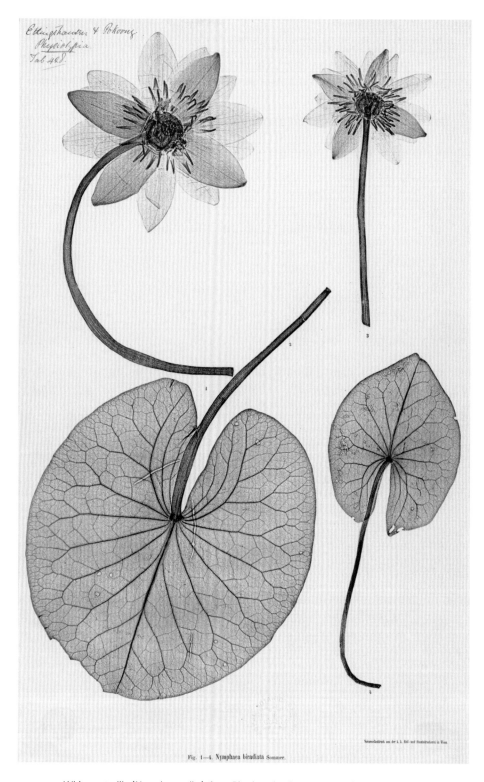

White waterlily (*Nymphaea alba*), from *Physiotypia plantarum austriacarum*, 1854–6
Nature print, 47 × 30 cm / 18½ × 11¾ in
Royal Botanic Gardens, Kew, London

When plants or plant parts are pressed and dried, and printing ink is applied to them, it is possible to use them as 'plates' to produce precise monochrome prints on paper. Because of the pressure exerted on the originals, however, they deteriorated rapidly and only a few prints were possible, before a breakthrough in the process occurred in the middle of the nineteenth century in the State Printing Works in Vienna. In 1852 the foreman there, Andreas

Worring, had the idea of laying 'a plant ... between a copper and a lead plate' and passing both 'between two rollers firmly screwed together', creating an impression of the plant in the soft lead. The impressed lead plate was further worked over and then used in the same way as a copper plate for printing, creating deceptively natural copies known as nature prints. This print of *Nymphaea alba* (identified on the illustration as *N. biradiata*) from

the five-volume *Physiotypia plantarum austriacarum* (1856) by Constantin Freiherr von Ettingshausen, professor of botany at Graz University, and the naturalist Alois Pokorny, is considered the apotheosis of this new method. Despite the hopes of its pioneers, however, the new technique proved too expensive to become an alternative to traditional herbaria.

Lotus, 1894
Collotype with lithographic overprinting in colour, 26.1 × 27.1 cm / 10¼ × 10¾ in
Victoria and Albert Museum, London

This crisp, uncluttered photograph of a sacred lotus (*Nelumbo nucifera*) – a partial, oblique view of the leaf, a tightly closed bud and an open flower with a tangle of stamens around the developing receptacle – was taken at the end of the nineteenth century by the Japanese photographer Ogawa Kazumasa. Born into a samurai family at the time when Japan's self-imposed 250-year isolation from the West was ending, Ogawa became in 1882 the first Japanese to study photography abroad when he travelled to Boston and Philadelphia to study printing and collotype. After returning to Japan, he pioneered the use of photomechanical printing processes as a publisher, and was also an energetic promoter of photography as art, becoming well-known for his photographs of temples, art, scenic places and traditional Japanese life and culture. In the 1890s Ogawa created colour collotypes of Japanese flowers, some of which were used as frontispieces for the lavish, multi-volume *Japan: Described and Illustrated by the Japanese* (1897), edited by Francis Brinkley. The stately lotus, which has a central place in Buddhist iconography, opens the second volume. The image is quite different from Ogawa's more typical pictorialist tableaux: it prefigures a later modernist photograph by Edward Steichen (see p.105).

ANTOINE GOUARIN

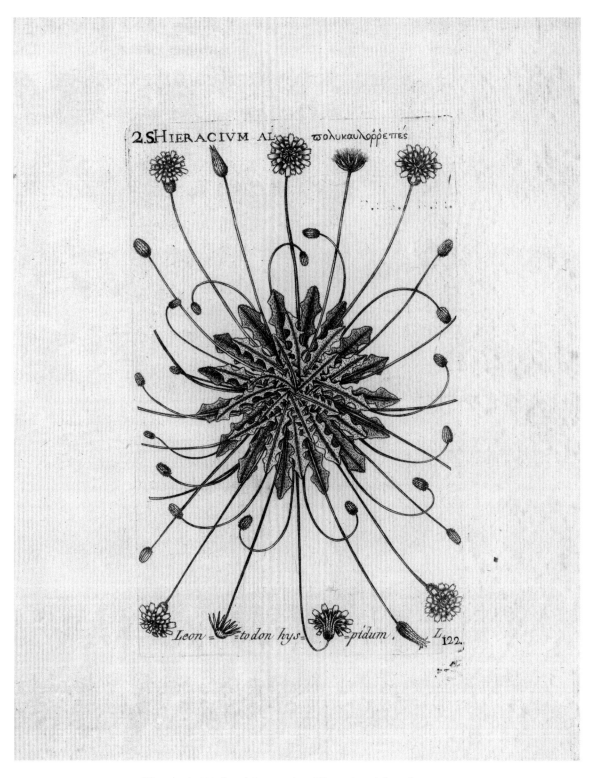

'Hieracium', 1600, from *Démonstrations élémentaires de botanique*, 1796
Engraving, 17 × 10.8 cm / 6¾ × 4¼ in
Muséum d'Histoire Naturelle de Grenoble

In this artful 'bird's-eye' engraving, the stalks of the rough hawkbit *Leontodon hirtus* radiate like spokes from the narrow, rough-haired, dandelion-like leaves. *Leontodon hirtus* is native to southern France and Italy, where the French botanist Pierre Richer de Belleval carried out his explorations. In 1593 Belleval – supported by his patron, the Duc de Montmorency, and King Henry IV of France – founded the Montpellier Botanic Garden, the oldest in France, which he based on Italian forerunners in Pisa and Padua. Belleval employed the artist Antoine Gouarin to produce 500 copperplate engravings – including this one, which Belleval called 'Hieracium' – for a proposed flora of the Languedoc, the region surrounding Montpellier. Belleval died before the work was published, however, and Gouarin's plates passed to his heirs, to be discovered by the famous French botanist Joseph Pitton de Tournefort while he was a student in Montpellier in 1679. Belleval's family clearly sold the plates, since the botanist Jean-Emmanuel Gilibert of Lyon later acquired 300 of them from a bookshop in Montpellier. Gilibert published 282 of Gouarin's plates in his *Démonstrations élémentaires de botanique* (1796). L'Institut de Botanique Montpellier now holds 459 of the original plates.

MAT COLLISHAW

Whispering Weeds, 2011
Fan, hard drive, LCD screen, wooden frame, 29.9 × 26 × 6.3 cm / 11¾ × 10¼ × 2½ in
Private collection

If these images – they are a still from a video created by the British artist Mat Collishaw – look familiar, it is no accident. Lying in hospital after what he terms a near-death experience, Collishaw decided to re-create Albrecht Dürer's renowned watercolour *Das Grosse Rasenstück* (*The Great Piece of Turf*; 1503), in constant motion as the grasses are blown softly by a fan. Collishaw explained how his brush with death brought an appreciation of the ordinary and mundane in Dürer's collection of common grasses, flowers and weeds that include dandelion, cock's foot, daisy, greater plantain and smooth meadow-grass. By cropping out any background, honing in on the plants and adding gentle movement, Collishaw set out to capture the viewer's attention and focus it on the overlooked value of mundanity: 'They are endowed with life even though they are weeds. They are nothing, they are on the wayside.'

In Collishaw's reinterpretation, however, the weeds and grasses are as worthy of close attention as Dürer's original. The work was a considerable departure for Collishaw, who earned the nickname 'Mr Nasty' for such early works as *Bullet Hole* (1988) (in fact an ice-pick hole) or his sculpted orchids infected by venereal disease and cancer.

WENCESLAUS HOLLAR

Large peony (*Paeonia officinalis* cultivar), surrounded by various flowers and moths, 1663
Etching, 17.5 × 27.4 cm / 6¾ × 10¾ in
Wellcome Library, London

Wenceslaus Hollar has been dubbed 'the man who drew London' for his engravings of the city both before and after the Great Fire of 1666. Here, he uses his great adaptability as an engraver to capture a collection of exotic and less exotic flowers – the Latin names were added later – interspersed with butterflies and moths. The central flower is a peony, surrounded by (clockwise from top left) an anemone, a daisy, a double narcissus, a rose and an African marigold. (The last originated in South America, in fact, but it was naturalized in North Africa after being taken there by the Spanish.) Born in Prague, Bohemia, Hollar moved to Frankfurt, where he worked for the engraver Matthew Merian (see p.104), father of the famous flower artist Maria Sibylla Merian (see p.207). He published a book of etchings in Cologne before travelling to England with the wealthy art collector Thomas Howard, Earl of Arundel.

Apart from an eight-year break during and after the English Civil War (in which he supported the defeated Royalists), Hollar spent the rest of his career in England, where he became the most celebrated engraver of the time, drawing maps, buildings and women's fashions as well as plants and wildlife. Despite leaving some 3,000 engraved plates, however, Hollar died destitute in 1677.

KONAN TANIGAMI

Lunar Peony, 1917
Coloured woodblock print, 42 × 56 cm / 16½ × 22 in
Private collection

Fine detail and intense colours – from subtle variations of green and pink to the bold red and yellow at the heart of the flower – make this depiction of a *Paeonia suffruticosa* tree peony one of what observers sometimes cite as the finest Japanese woodblock prints ever made. Unusually large for a woodblock – it measures 56 centimetres (22 inches) across – the hand-coloured image is printed on handmade paper with a 'natural' untrimmed edge. It is

one of twenty-four pictures of peonies commissioned from the artist Konan Tanigami for the Imperial Academy Art Exhibition, or Teiten, in 1917, where the level of both materials and craftsmanship had to be remarkable. Konan belonged to the Japanese tradition of *kacho-e* – artists who painted birds and flowers – but was the first Japanese artist to concentrate on depicting plants that came from outside the country. The tree peonies he painted were bred

in Japan from original stock that had been introduced from China in the eighth century. They were initially planted in Japanese Buddhist temples and the gardens of the nobility, but they became widely cultivated in the Meiji period in the nineteenth century, and are seen as bringing good fortune and a noble spirit to those who grow them.

237

MARTIN RÖSSLER

Flora Danica Tab. DLXXXIX.

Tormentil (*Potentilla erecta*), from *Flora Danica*, 1771
Hand-coloured engraving, 37 × 22.6 cm / 14¾ × 8¾ in
Det Kongelige Bibliotek, Copenhagen

This plate, which was probably painted by the eighteenth-century German artist Martin Rössler, depicts tormentil (*Potentilla erecta*), a common wild flower of rough grassland, open woodland and heathland in northern and western Europe. Its stocky root, leaves, flowers and fruiting heads are all clearly visible. The plate was prepared for the Bavarian doctor and botanist Georg Christian Oeder, who in 1752 became a professor at the Royal Botanical Institute in Copenhagen. In 1753 Oeder proposed the creation of an illustrated flora, *Flora Danica*, a comprehensive guide to the plants of Denmark. The first part of this ambitious work, financed by the Crown, was published in 1761, but it was not completed until 1883: twelve more editors followed Oeder. Consisting of fifty-one parts and three supplements, the Flora contained thousands of engravings and illustrations of Danish wild flowers. Oeder travelled widely to seek suitable artists, and employed Michael Rössler, an engraver from Nuremberg, and his artist son, Martin. The Rösslers moved to Copenhagen in 1755 to concentrate on the great work, which eventually contained 3,240 plates. Some were used to decorate porcelain, including the famous banquet service ordered by Crown Prince Frederik in 1790 as a gift for Catherine II, the Russian empress.

Buttercup with Veined White, 2015
Copper, brass and oil-based paint, 30.5 × 33 × 30.5 cm / 12 × 13 × 12 in
Private collection

This buttercup rising from a branching root seems so delicate and lifelike that it is difficult to believe that it is constructed from copper and brass. Carmen Almon, a contemporary artist based in France, creates botanical works using wire, copper sheeting and enamel paints. She was born in Guatemala to an American father and a Spanish mother, an amateur artist who painted birds and flowers. Almon became a watercolour painter but was inspired to develop her sculptural technique when a friend asked her to restore some pieces of *tole*, a process that involves decorative painting on metal or wood. Each piece is very time-consuming but creates a permanent representation of what is by its nature fragile and ephemeral, such as a plant or flower. Almon's inspiration comes from actual plants but also from her study of seventeenth- and eighteenth-century botanical illustrations. She regards herself as building a branch or plant in the way that it grows in nature, slowly forming it over a process that takes weeks: 'I think about the will of a plant to live, its fight towards the sun, each leaf positioning itself like a small solar panel. Along with its struggle against gravity, and its own demise.'

PIERRE PLAUSZEWSKI

ENCYCLOPÉDIE DE LA PLANTE

COBÉE GRIMPANTE

Cobée grimpante, from *Encyclopédie artistique et documentaire de la Plante*, 1904–8
Collotype, 39 × 34 cm / 15¼ × 13¼ in
Private collection

There is a naturalistic quality but also a scientific accuracy about the way these strands of '*Cobée grimpante*', the climbing cobaea, trail across the pale background, showing the cup-shaped flowers, the texture of the leaves and the fragility of the new tendrils. This image by the French photographer Pierre Plauszewski was designed both to perpetuate the beauty of flowers beyond their brief flowering season and to capture them in as much detail as possible.

Plauszewski chose to photograph the white-flowered form, *alba*, of this very vigorous, rather tender climbing plant *Cobaea scandens* from Mexico, which typically has deep-purple flowers that are pollinated at night by bats. He contributed all the collotypes to illustrate Maurice Pillard Verneuil's four-volume *Encyclopédie artistique et documentaire de la Plante* (1904–8), a work that reflects the creativity and ambition of Europe in the Belle Époque.

Verneuil, himself a student of the great Swiss designer Eugène Grasset, had been impressed with Plauszewski's earlier photographic work on plants, the two-volume *Encyclopédie Florale* (1899–1900). For the new *Encyclopédie*, Verneuil did not wish to rely solely on photographs, and so he commissioned artwork from the Czech artist Alphonse Mucha and paintings and engravings from Mathurin Méheut.

NICK KNIGHT

Schizaeaceae: Lygodium palmatum, from *Flora*, 1997
Hand-coated pigment print, 73 × 46.5 cm / 28¾ × 18¼ in
Natural History Museum, London

The British fashion photographer Nick Knight was not the first person to appreciate the delicate beauty of angel's fingers, *Lygodium palmatum*, the only native North American species of this predominantly Asian genus. No less an authority than the writer and naturalist Henry David Thoreau called it 'a most beautiful, slender, and delicate fern', and its fronds were such a popular Christmas decoration in nineteenth-century America that in 1869

Connecticut passed a law to prevent it from being picked (the first such law in the United States). But Knight's graphic aesthetic lends an almost wreath-like quality to this cutting from the renowned Herbarium in the Natural History Museum, London, combining palmate sterile leaves with smaller fertile segments near the ends of the frond. Introduced to the collection while working on a commission, Knight spent four years searching its 6 million items

to select forty-six specimens for his book *Flora* (1997). Each specimen was mounted on white card and photographed against a light box, transforming the originals into something more architectural than plant-like. As Knight remarks, 'Photographs of live flowers have a ready-made tragic quality because you know they're going to fade and die ... But these flowers were permanent, bold and strong. They had escaped their fate.'

Alstroemeria salsilla (*Bomarea salsilla*), 1783–1810
Watercolour on paper, 53.9 × 38 cm / 21¼ × 15 in
Real Jardín Botánico de Madrid

Delicate pink flowers in an umbel (a flower cluster in which stalks of nearly equal length spring from a common centre and form a flat or curved surface) are documented in this eighteenth-century watercolour of the tropical climber *Alstroemeria salsilla* (now known as *Bomarea salsilla*), which grows in South and Central America. The region fell into Spain's immense American possessions and was the destination of three major expeditions sent by the Spanish Crown to gather botanical information. This illustration relates to the second of these, from 1783 to 1816, led by José Mutis, a physician, polymath and later priest, who was succeeded by his nephew Sinforoso. They studied plant life in what are now Colombia, Ecuador, Panama, Venezuela, Peru, Brazil and Guyana, collecting a considerable number of herbarium specimens and arranging for the preparation of botanical illustrations. Francisco Javier Matís, who painted this *Bomarea*, was the most prolific of the expedition's artists, of whom Mutis noted: 'They must be between the ages of twenty and thirty, work nine hours a day and accept a salary between 8 and 12 reales per day. They will be provided with lodgings and a midday meal ... They must have a great capacity for work and be of docile character.' For various reasons the publication of the expedition's materials began only in 1954, and is not yet complete.

ALBERTO BARAYA

Orchidea Vanda purpura, from *Herbario de plantas artificiales*, 2014
Photographs and drawings on cardboard, 112 × 82 × 8 cm / 44 × 32¼ × 3¼ in
Private collection

If the purple of this orchid looks too intense to be natural, that is because it is. The 'herbarium' collected by the Colombian artist Alberto Baraya comprises only plastic plants, displayed in the tradition of an eighteenth-century herbarium. The provenance of the fake specimens, found lying in the street or gathered from restaurants and waiting rooms, determines a rigorous but idiosyncratic system of documentation. Baraya's classification is meticulous but absurd, reminding us that stories and imagination offer alternatives to a narrow view of nature. The work also echoes the classification of Latin America by colonial powers, as when the Spanish Royal Botanical Expedition set out in 1783 to New Grenada (present-day Colombia, Ecuador, Panama, Venezuela, Peru, northern Brazil and western Guyana), led first by José Mutis (see opposite). Over the next thirty-three years, some 6,000 new species were catalogued according to their potential medicinal or commercial use, using the new scientific method of Linnaean taxonomy. As the plants of the Americas were classified, so too were its peoples, as the colonial powers imposed their own reality. Baraya subverts these taxonomic strategies to remind us that constructions of the natural world are not innocent, and that they continue to shape reality in an age of globalization.

FREDERICK ANDREWS WALPOLE

Lodgepole pine (*Pinus contorta*), 1898
Ink on paper, 29.5 × 19 cm / 11¾ × 7½ in
National Museum of Natural History, Smithsonian Institution, Washington, DC

This remarkable drawing of a branch of *Pinus contorta* is an exercise in precise observation, accurate draughtsmanship – and endless patience. The American artist Frederick Andrews Walpole has drawn every needle and every scale of the cones separately. The drawing exemplifies his customary attention to detail: he inked the preliminary drawings he had made in the field with a sable brush stripped down to just a few bristles. Born in New York, Walpole may have studied with the landscape painter Junius Sloan in Chicago before moving to Portland, Oregon, in 1886 as an illustrator for a printing company. A decade later his work came to the attention of Frederick V. Coville, a botanist with the United States Department of Agriculture (USDA). At Coville's urging, Walpole was appointed Artist for the Division of Botany of the USDA in 1896. Walpole's career was divided between working in Washington, DC, at the USDA and field trips to the northwest, including Alaska, where he drew, botanized, collected and identified specimens by their scientific Latin names. A willow he discovered on the tundra of Alaska bears his name. Coville described Walpole's drawing technique as holding a brush parallel to the surface of the paper to make lines as delicate as those of a fine engraving.

244

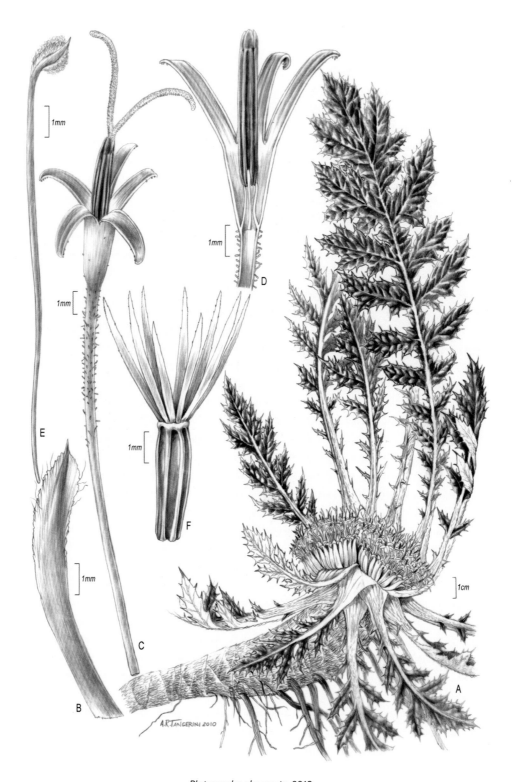

Platycarpha glomerata, 2010
Polycarbonate pencil on film, 43.2 × 33 cm / 17 × 13 in
National Museum of Natural History, Smithsonian Institution, Washington, DC

This pencil drawing of a South African member of the aster family might seem more traditional than contemporary were it not for the remarkable detail achieved by Alice Tangerini, an illustrator in the botanical department at the Smithsonian National Museum of Natural History. By some estimates, 10 per cent of all plants belong to the aster family, so relationships are complex: how *Platycarpha glomerata* fits in with the rest of its enormous family is not yet clear. However, Tangerini is used to working with unusual specimens. Since joining the Smithsonian in 1972 she has illustrated over a thousand plants, most of which were not even found in botanic gardens – and many of which were new to science. She works with whatever she can get: dried and pressed herbarium specimens, photographs, rehydrated plants. This plant was first described in 1800 by Carl Peter Thunberg (see p.136), who put it in the genus that includes the common artichoke (*Cynara*). Later botanists instead assigned it to a genus of just three South African species, all of which Tangerini illustrated in 2010. Two of the species have since been tentatively reassigned to a new genus, leaving *Platycarpha glomerata* on its own.

WERNER BISCHOF

Photomontage, 1941
Photograph, 40.6 × 30.5 cm / 16 × 12 in
Private collection

At first glance this photomontage created in neutral Switzerland in 1941, as World War II raged across Europe, may look like a convincing botanical study, since the structure of the ray flower has been rendered distinctly. But this is the exact opposite of a botanical photograph: it conveys not reality but fiction. Its primary effect is achieved by the juxtaposition of positive and negative images that fight against each other's interpretation. Not only is the thirteen-petalled composite flower unidentified, but also its central disc has been obscured by the overlay of a fluffy pappus; meanwhile, the bleached image of a pair of stems or branches crosses the main image. Small, dark round objects – seeds with or without the seed coats – are scattered at random over the whole print. An early member of the photographic cooperative Magnum, the Swiss photographer Werner Bischof worked mainly as a war reporter and documentary photographer; he died in a car accident in Peru at the age of thirty-eight. He also experimented with photomontages such as the one shown here, which was published in an edition of 25 copies. His goal in the photomontages was, as here, to create spatial ambiguity through the combination of geometric forms.

ROB KESSELER

Scabiosa crenata. Fruit – diameter 7.2mm, 2013
Hand-coloured scanning electron micrograph (SEM), dimensions variable
Private collection

What at first appears to be a design for an exotic ballet costume is in fact a vastly magnified micrograph image of a tiny seed of *Scabiosa crenata*, the pincushion flower, a member of the honeysuckle family. For more than a decade the British artist Rob Kesseler has been working on the frontier between art and science, producing microscopic views of plant material such as seeds and pollen grains, and highlighting how little we know about the mysterious workings of plant propagation. Kesseler applies a fine coating of platinum to his specimens before scanning them with a high-magnification scanning electron microscope to produce black-and-white images, which he then begins to tint with thin washes of colour. He does not necessarily reproduce the hues of the objects themselves; instead, he uses colour to enhance the seemingly mysterious forms, revealing their delicate structure. The results are intended to evoke a sense of the unfamiliar and an impromptu symbolism that inspires curiosity and wonder in those contemplating the possible functions underlying the forms. Through his art, Kesseler makes the invisible features of plants visible, and his extreme highlights of nature reveal the extraordinary diversity of plant forms.

JOSEPH DALTON HOOKER

Rhododendron argenteum, c.1849
Lithograph, 47 × 30.5 cm / 18½ × 12 in
Royal Botanic Gardens, Kew, London

A glimpse of the very silver underside of these leaves explains why the botanist and artist Joseph Dalton Hooker named this plant *Rhododendron argenteum*, or 'silver'. In fact, it had been classified as *R. grande* – by which name it is still known – by Robert Wight of Edinburgh three years earlier, in 1847, based on the collections of William Griffith. Hooker, son of the renowned director of Kew Gardens in London, William Jackson Hooker (see p.292), found the plant during an expedition to the Himalayas from 1847 to 1851 – a period of early British colonial and scientific interest in the mountainous region. He noted that he discovered the plant on a mountain summit in Sikkim in April 1848, and that it was so reluctant to flower that he was hard-pressed to be able to finish his drawing, which eventually showed the large, white tubular flowers beneath the evanescent pale pink bracts that enclose the young growth at the apex of the flowering shoot. Hooker collaborated with Kew's official botanical artist, Walter Hood Fitch (see p.267), to convert his drawings into coloured lithographs for his authoritative work, *The Rhododendrons of Sikkim-Himalaya* (1849–51).

FIONA STRICKLAND

Rhododendron 'Horizon Monarch', 2014
Watercolour on paper, 77 × 91 cm / 30¼ × 35¾ in
Private collection

The stem and flat, dark green leaves lend an unusual diagonal composition to this detailed portrait of a bud of *Rhododendron* 'Horizon Monarch' as – unusually – two flowers emerge simultaneously from the bud scales. This large-scale watercolour reveals the vivid use of colour and meticulous detail characteristic of the work of the Scottish botanical artist Fiona Strickland, who came across this specimen on a visit to the famous collection of rhododen-

drons at the Royal Botanic Garden in Edinburgh. Strickland set out to communicate the sense of discovery that came with finding the emerging pair of flowers. She also wanted to try painting the white hairs on the bud scales with a technique called 'negative painting', in which the background between the hairs is painted so that the hairs themselves are indicated by the white paper: 'The challenge in this instance was to communicate this surface to the viewer

whilst conveying the form convincingly, taking account of the changing underlying colour of the bud scales, and the effect of the light on them and on the very fine hairs.' The painting won 'Best in Show' at the Annual International Exhibition of the American Society of Botanical Artists and the Horticultural Society of New York in 2015.

ANONYMOUS

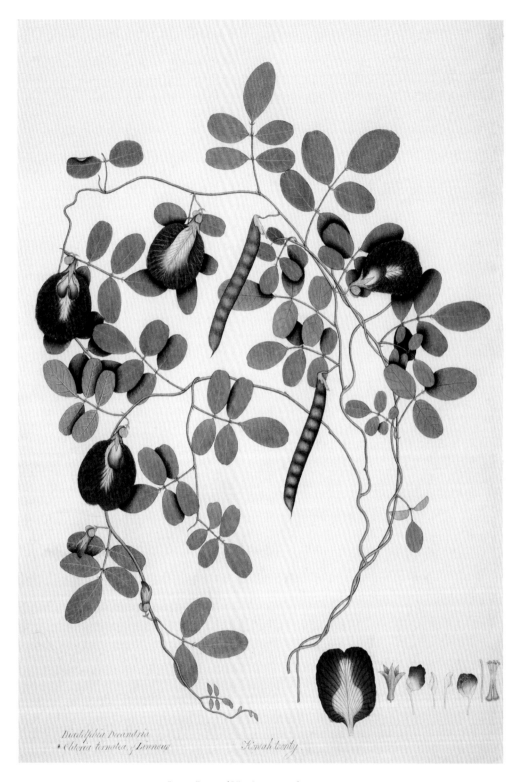

Butterfly pea (*Clitoria ternatea*) , c.1840–60
Watercolour on paper, 50 × 36.8 cm / 19¾ × 14½ in
Natural History Museum, London

This beautiful image of the climbing butterfly pea combines the Mughal heritage of its unknown Indian artist, evident in its swirling arrangement, with the scientific detail required by the European botanist who asked him to paint it – particularly visible in the floral dissections at bottom right. The artist painted the plant in the classic Anglo-Indian style known as the Company School, and his eye for detail is evident in the brilliant blue of the broad pea-like flowers streaked with white veins (their supposed resemblance to human female genitalia earned them their Latin name of *Clitoria ternatea*) and the loose naturalistic arrangement of the scrambling plant. The British East India Company set up the Calcutta Botanic Garden at Sibpur in 1787 under the directorship of Colonel Robert Kyd, who set out to document the remarkable flora of Britain's Indian colony. Under Kyd's successors, notably William Roxburgh and the Dane Nathaniel Wallich, many local artists were employed to paint the plants collected for the garden. By 1844 the botanist William Griffith was in charge of the garden, and he lamented the fact that only some 3,000 drawings of Indian plants had been produced under his predecessors. It is not known when this particular painting was made.

Sundew *(Drosera burmannii)*, from *Icones Plantarum Indiae Orientalis*, 1846
Hand-coloured lithograph, 16.6 × 23 cm / 6½ × 9 in
Royal Botanic Garden Edinburgh

The flattened, tipped-up perspective in this lithograph of *Drosera burmannii*, a tiny sundew, is characteristic of Indian art and suggests – correctly – that the artist came from the Subcontinent. As well as stylistic convention, however, it might also reflect the fact that the prolific artist, Rungiah, drew the main image from pressed herbarium material. The later, more three-dimensional flower dissections incorporated into this print suggest that Rungiah may then have had access to fresh plant material. Rungiah was employed by the Edinburgh-trained surgeon-botanist Robert Wight, who was posted to Madras by the East India Company in the 1820s. For thirty years, alongside his administrative duties, Wight collected plants assiduously, training local people as artists and amassing a vast herbarium. Returning to Edinburgh on three years' leave – with 100,000 herbarium specimens – Wight mastered lithography, hoping to disseminate knowledge of Indian botanical diversity widely through illustrated publications (lithography was at the time a new and potentially far cheaper alternative to engraving). Taking a lithographic printing press back to India, he set about realizing this aim and was joined by other lithographers. This lithograph, coloured by Wight-trained artists, was one of 200 images Wight chose for his *Spicilegium Neilgherrense* (*Plants of the Nilgiri Hills*; 1846–51).

Herbarium Specimen Painting, 2006–09
Pencil and watercolour on paper, 59 cm × 5.3 m / 23 in × 18 ft
Royal Botanic Gardens, Kew, London

The level of variety and detail here is almost overwhelming – *Herbarium Specimen Painting* is nearly 5.5 metres (18 feet) in length and illustrates 506 plant families. The British artist Rachel Pedder-Smith set out to illustrate a representative of every flowering plant family drawn from the herbarium at Kew Gardens. Another criterion was that she had to include specimens from every year since the herbarium was founded in 1853. Accurate reproduction of the colours of old pressed and dried specimens means the work is dominated by shades of brown, although other colours survive on some of the more recent flowers. Such an ambitious undertaking is typical of Pedder-Smith's work, which is instantly recognizable from its combination of a large number of related images into a single image. One early example, for instance, was devoted to the fruits and seeds of the family *Leguminosae* (peas and beans), with a wonderful array of different examples – again based on the collection at Kew. After studying graphic art and design at Leeds Metropolitan University and natural-history illustration at the Royal College of Art in London Pedder-Smith now teaches art as well as being a natural-history painter.

Spring Crocus in UV Light
Photograph with UV filter, coloured digitally
dimensions variable

This photograph of the spring crocus (*C. vernus*) looks very different from what we see with the naked eye: pale petals that darken to lilac at their tips, with a stamen that is white at its base and bright yellow at its tip, and a heavy coating of pollen. In this image by the Norwegian nature photographer Bjørn Rørslett, ultraviolet (UV) light – invisible to humans, but very visible to bees – reveals a new view of the flower. Bees' colour preferences are yellow, blue,

purple and ultraviolet: they cannot see the longer wavelengths of red shades. Rørslett has developed a non-representational style that uses UV and infrared light to explore the 'unseen' natural world. He took this image using a digital camera adapted to filter UV light, then coloured the resulting monochrome image on a computer to show areas that reflect or absorb UV light (yellow and dark respectively): these petals have high UV reflectance.

Such patterns, which are known as 'nectar guides', may act as visual cues to attract pollinating insects, an evolutionary adaptation that helps plants to survive the strong competition to attract in-flight pollinators and ensure pollination. Rørslett's technique is laborious, but it reflects the high level of scientific interest in understanding how pollinators see colour.

MOHAMMAD REZA DADPOUR

Tribulus Bud, 2010
Epi-illumination, dimensions variable

This dramatic image of a bud of the weedy flower *Tribulus terrestris* in the final stages of its development has a pronounced three-dimensional quality. At this magnification the bud has the qualities of an abstract artwork; epi-illumination, in which light is shone on to the object under the microscope, adds an attractive iridescent appearance. Distinctive shape, texture and shading define each separate layer of the bud; the veined lower one resembles the folded wings of an insect. This contrasts with the spear-shaped middle layer, the pale, slim, striped and margined central 'tongues' of which screen thinner petals, shown here coloured lime, and hold the fuzzy-textured emergent tip. Mohammad Reza Dadpour of the department of horticultural sciences at the University of Tabriz, Iran, created the image by effectively building it from a series of horizontal sections through the bud. The devil's thorn, *Tribulus terrestris*, is a tap-rooted herbaceous perennial plant that has adapted to grow in extremely dry conditions where few other plants can survive. Widely distributed around the world, it is invasive in North America. Its stems radiate from the crown up to a metre (3 feet) across the ground, bearing small oval leaves and tiny flowers, each with five lemon-yellow petals.

JAMES SOWERBY

Grey-headed coneflower (*Rudbeckia pinnata*)
from *Curtis's Botanical Magazine*, 1815
Watercolour, 24 × 19.4 cm / 9½ × 7¾ in
Lindley Library, Royal Horticultural Society, London

The pronounced and highly fragrant 'cone' of dark brown florets at the top of James Sowerby's painting from 1815 gives the coneflower its name. Beneath the pendulous, yellow ray florets is the dissected or 'pinnate' leaf, which gives the plant its Latin name, *Ratibida pinnata*. Sowerby's painting is simple – one leaf and one flower filling the whole page – but it would have interested readers of the popular journal *Curtis's Botanical Magazine*, for which it

was created. The coneflower – also known as the grey-headed coneflower – originated on the prairies of North America but was introduced to France by the exiled royal botanist André Michaux in 1795, before being introduced to England from Madrid by Lady Amelia Long in 1803. Sowerby's sample of this still rare plant was obtained in 1815 from the second botanical garden of the late William Curtis, a neighbour of Sowerby in Lambeth, south London.

Sowerby trained as a natural history illustrator at the Royal Academy before – in his twenties – encountering Curtis, who opened his first botanic garden in Lambeth in 1779. Sowerby contributed illustrations to Curtis's *Flora Londinensis* and fifty-six plates to the *Botanical Magazine*. In 1790 he began his thirty-six-volume collaboration with James Edward Smith, *English Botany,* and in 1804 he illustrated Smith's *Exotic Botany.*

Melanorrhoea usitata, 1830
Hand-coloured lithograph, 38.1 × 33.5 cm / 15 × 13¼ in
Peter H. Raven Library, Missouri Botanical Garden, St Louis

The bright-pink flowers of *Melanorrhoea usitata*, a deciduous tree from Burma, leap out from this plate by Vishnupersaud (also known as Vishnu Prasad), an Indian artist at the Calcutta Botanical Gardens in the early nineteenth century. The foot of the page shows (from left to right) a ripe fruit with persistent petals that act as wings helping disperse the seeds. Vishnupersaud's exceptional attention to detail and use of vibrant colours were highly sought-after by European botanists in India. From 1817 to 1828 he prepared hundreds of drawings of various Asian plants under the direction of the Danish botanist in charge of the Calcutta Botanical Gardens, Nathaniel Wallich. Some of Vishnupersaud's watercolours appeared between 1830 and 1832 in *Plantae Asiaticae Rariores*, Wallich's three-volume description of plants from the British East Indies. This example, which was printed in London by the Maltese lithographer Maxim Gauci and hand-painted by the British colourist John Clark, shows a plant that Wallich discovered and named in Myanmar in 1827. The dark-brown sap of this tall tree from the cashew family, also known as Burmese lacquer, is used in Southeast Asia as a source of a waterproof varnish.

A Rose, 1936
Gelatin silver print, 28.6 × 23.2cm / 11¼ × 9¼ in
Private collection

A generation before this photograph of a rose was made in 1936, the only way of portraying the internal anatomy of a flower was by cutting it in cross section, as was done by such notable early twentieth-century illustrators as Arthur Harry Church (see p.60). But the rapid development of X-ray photography made it possible to create images that were seemingly unmediated expressions of the plant's structure, in the same way that early photographs seemed to their initial audience to be unmediated presentations of reality. The American doctor and radiologist Dain Tasker played an important role in developing X-ray photography as a medium, experimenting with a wide range of subjects and having his work displayed in galleries and published in popular magazines. This image of a rose would be less helpful to a botanical student than Church's lithographs, which, with their deliberate stylization and use of distinct blocks of colour to differentiate organs, made the floral structure intelligible. Here it is difficult to assign the different layers of tissue to their correct planes. Tasker's image has its own value and beauty, however, conveying as it does the messiness and complexity of a floral dissection rather than the clarity of an artificially coloured diagram.

ALICE CAZENAVE

Untitled, from *Honesty pictures*, 2015
Gelatin silver print on fibre-based paper, each 24.1 × 30.5 cm / 9½ × 12 in
Private collection

These four ghostly photographs of leaves come from a series of eight created by the young British artist Alice Cazenave, who presents them anonymously, leaving the viewer to identify (or not) the species from which they come. For Cazenave, the customary criteria of identification are less important than the plants' inner workings of the leaves and stems. Cazenave named her series *Honesty pictures*, reflecting the fact that they were taken without a camera or lens, using direct contact between the plants and the photographic paper. She sees the resulting images as 'commenting on the concept of vulnerability' with their depictions of semi-transparent, outstretched plants. Cazenave's interest in alternative methods of photography is in part a reaction to what she calls the 'photo-saturated culture' that has made viewers over-familiar with and apathetic towards conventional photography – hence her return to the photogram technique associated with such pioneers as Anna Atkins at the very beginning of photography. In her most famous pictures, Cazenave refines her photographic processes further by using a combination of photosynthesis and photographic chemicals to create a portrait within the leaf itself, rather than by superimposing images on the surface during processing.

Chinese hollyhock (*Alcea rosea*), c.960–1279
Ink and watercolour on silk, 25 × 26.2 cm / 9¾ × 10¼ in
National Palace Museum, Taiwan

The unusual shape of this beautiful painting of the Chinese hollyhock (*Alcea rosea*) reflects the painting's original purpose, which was to decorate a rigid oval fan that probably belonged to a member of aristocratic court circles under the Southern Song Dynasty of the twelfth to thirteenth centuries; it was later removed and mounted in a small album. Although the identity of the artist is unknown, the style shows the influence of the Southern Song Imperial Painting Academy, which encouraged high technical standards and a common approach to painting during one of the great ages of the visual arts in China. Under the influence of neo-Confucian philosophy, Song artists became increasingly concerned with the accurate depiction of objects in order to understand their nature more fully, and paintings were often accompanied by poems describing this 'essence'. The artist's precision is evident in the outlines of the petals and serrated leaf edges, as well as in the delicate and realistic shading of the leaves and petals. The Chinese hollyhock was introduced into European gardens before the fifteenth century and the English herbalist William Turner named it holyoke in the mid sixteenth-century.

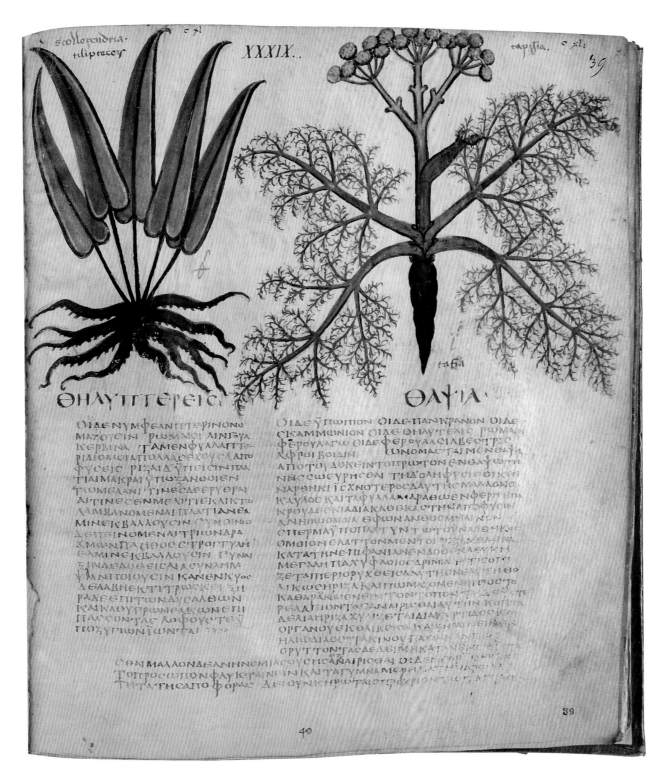

Hart's-tongue (*Asplenium scolopendrium*) and *Thapsia garganica*, c.600 AD
Tempera and ink on vellum, 29 × 26 cm / 11½ × 10¼ in
Biblioteca Nazionale di Napoli

The two plants portrayed on this page from an early Byzantine manuscript – hart's tongue (*Asplenium scolopendrium*) on the left and *Thapsia garganica*, on the right – are fairly widespread. Both were commonly used in medieval medicine. The manuscript also depicts species that are far more limited in their distribution, however, such as *Euphorbia resinifera*, a species of spurge that occurs only from what is now northwestern Morocco. Being a medicinal plant used since antiquity, it comes as no surprise that it should be included in this manuscript herbal. At the same time, its inclusion demonstrates the wide contacts existing in the Mediterranean in the early medieval period. There is general agreement that the manuscript, usually called *Codex Napoletanus* after the city in which it has been kept for several centuries, is significantly younger than the *Codex Aniciae Julianae* (see p.146), and based at least partly on the same exemplar. By contrast, opinion is divided on where it was produced: in a scriptorium in Ravenna or in the southern part of the Italian peninsula. All plant illustrations are placed on recto pages; the text in Greek majuscules is arranged as a rule in two columns below, with the Greek plant names in red.

MOHAMMAD KHAN

Page from Dara Shikoh Album, c.1633
Opaque watercolour and gold on paper, 16.9 × 10.1 cm / 6¾ × 4 in
British Library, London

The iris in the bottom left-hand corner of this miniature from the early 1630s is easily recognizable, but while the other flowers may include hibiscus, they are too stylized to be identified precisely. The stylization reflects the painting's twin influences, the Persian traditions of the artist on the one hand and the European florilegia, or printed herbals, that inspired its balanced layout. The painting appears in the Dara Shikoh Album, named after the Mughal prince who collected its paintings and calligraphy as a gift for his future wife. Dara Shikoh was a favoured son of Shah Jahan, emperor of the Islamic Mughal dynasty that ruled India from 1526 to 1857. The Persian rulers set up ateliers of artists whose flowing floral borders reflected the importance of flowers and gardens in Islam, where they are symbolic of paradise. The only signed painting in this album is a portrait by Mohammad Khan, who is also credited with these flowers. The Mughal library held florilegia, illuminated psalters and a Bible donated by visiting Europeans. Khan's composition clearly suggests that he had studied the printed Western herbals, but the refined drawing, colouring and brushwork of this painted page is purely Persian.

ALBRECHT DÜRER

89

Iris, c.1503
Pen and watercolour on paper, 77.5 × 31.3 cm / 30½ × 12¼ in
Kunsthalle Bremen

The most important aspect of this famous watercolour is rarely appreciated: its size. Painted on two sheets of paper glued together, it measures about 77 × 31 centimetres (30 × 12 inches) and is clear evidence of the German Renaissance artist Albrecht Dürer's intention to document an iris at its natural size. The dry, matter-of-fact approach makes it an icon of botanical illustration, of superb quality and truth to nature. There is general agreement among specialists that this watercolour is the only one of its kind to be undoubtedly by Dürer (probably painted about 1503). The monogram at the top and the date are believed to be a later addition by an unknown hand. The iris depicted is generally accepted to be *Iris × germanica* (known also as *I. trojana*), which is native to what is now Turkey. Dürer's iris was copied by members of his workshop in Nuremberg and integrated into the famous *Virgin and Child* (*The Madonna with the Iris*, c.1500–10; now in the National Gallery in London) and its variants. Dürer's second botanical master-piece, *Das Grosse Rasenstück* (*The Great Piece of Turf*, now in the Albertina, Vienna) was apparently dated 1503 in his own hand, but is rightly regarded as a study more in plant sociology than in botanical illustration.

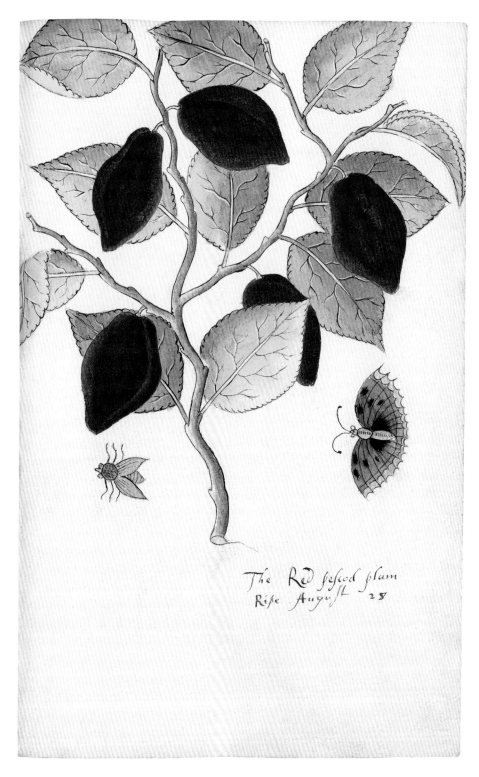

The Imperyall Plum, from *Tradescant's Orchard*, 1620s
Ink and colours on paper, 30.2 × 19.5 cm / 11¾ × 7¾
Bodleian Library, University of Oxford

The butterfly and fly attracted by these red peascod plums resemble a child's drawings, while the plums themselves are more realistic. The illustration comes from *Tradescant's Orchard*, a collection of sixty-six paintings of fruit grown by the celebrated English gardener and nurseryman John Tradescant the Elder, dating from the 1620s. The paintings – with their stylized branches and insects – evoke contemporary embroideries, but the fruits are lifelike and shine with vitality (an effect created by adding egg white to the pigments). Early in his career, when he was head gardener to Robert Cecil, 1st Earl of Salisbury, at Hatfield House in Hertfordshire, Tradescant began to introduce many new varieties of fruit tree from the continent – and later an apricot from Algeria. In 1629 John Parkinson (see p.302) listed sixty-four different plums that his friend Tradescant had 'wonderfully laboured' to obtain. The peascod plums were named for their resemblance to a pea pod, tapering at either end. Tradescant was an eager collector of seeds, bulbs and natural history curiosities. The 'Ark', where he displayed them, in Lambeth was a forerunner of the 'cabinet of curiosities', and one of the earliest public museums. This painting passed to Elias Ashmole, founder of the Ashmolean Museum in Oxford, among the Tradescants' collections, but without any record of the commission.

Pomegranate (*Punica granatum*), from *Traité des arbres fruitiers*, 1835
Hand-coloured stipple engraving
Private collection

The deep purple of pomegranate seeds in the cross section in this hand-coloured stipple engraving stands out against the more delicate colours of the fruit and flower, and careful shading gives depth to each individual seed. Such detail is characteristic of the illustrations produced by the Frenchman Pierre-Jean-François Turpin to illustrate *Traité des arbres fruitiers* (*Treatise on Fruit Trees*) by Henri-Louis Duhamel du Monceau, one of the most beautiful books

ever produced on the subject. From humble beginnings, Turpin became one of the great botanical artists of the early nineteenth century, thanks to both talent and serendipity. Having served in the army in the colony of Saint-Domingue (now Haiti), his artistic talent was noticed by a senior officer in France who offered him a promotion. Turpin chose instead to return to Saint-Domingue in 1794. This was a crucial decision, since it was there that he met the

botanist Pierre Antoine Poiteau, who taught him about plants (Turpin later developed his botanical work further, becoming an accomplished microscopist). In 1800 Turpin met Alexander von Humboldt, whose books he would subsequently illustrate, but Poiteau and Turpin were later reunited in France, and produced their stunning plates for an illustrated version of Monceau's book.

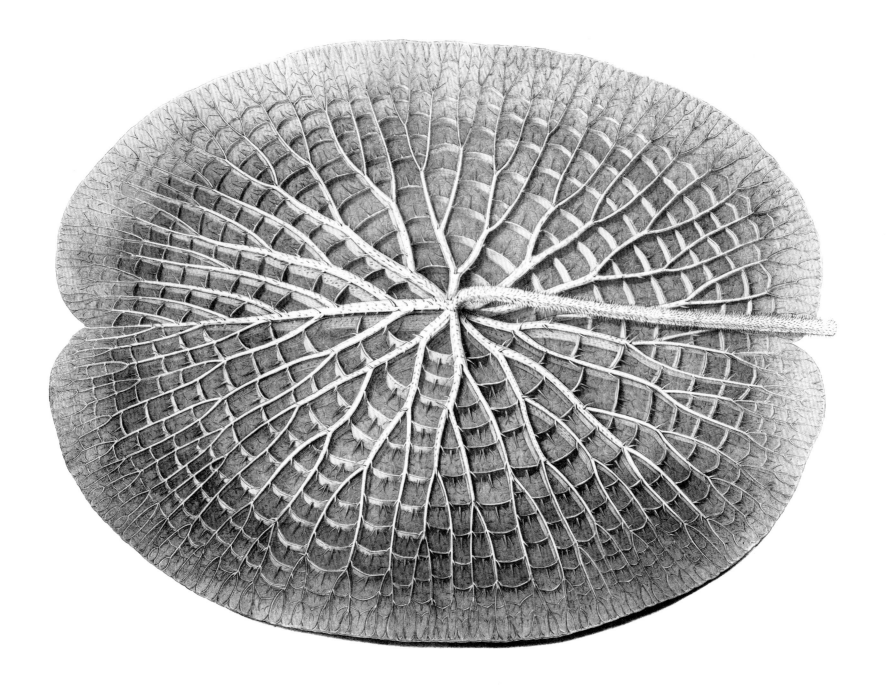

Victoria Regia, from *Victoria Regia, or the Great Water Lily of America*, 1854
Chromolithograph, 55.4 × 73.7 cm / 21¾ × 29 in
Natural History Museum, London

The fine pattern of ribs spreading across the underside of this leaf of *Victoria amazonica* is a remarkable example of natural engineering. The ribs support massive floating leaves that can grow up to 3 metres (10 feet) in diameter. This magnificent giant waterlily, which was discovered in 1801 by the Czech explorer and naturalist Thaddäus Haenke on an expedition to Peru arranged by the Spanish government, is native to the flooded lakes of South America.

In 1853 it flowered for the first time in the United States, in the greenhouse of John Fisk Allen in Salem, Massachusetts. Allen was inspired by it to write *Victoria regia, or the Great Water Lily of America*, which was published the following year. The book was illustrated by the English lithographer William Sharp, who is credited with introducing chromolithography to the United States in 1840. Named originally in honour of Queen Victoria, this largest of all

water lilies is now classified as *Victoria amazonica* and is widely grown in warm greenhouses around the world. In his book, Allen reported an account by the British botanist William Jackson Hooker (see p.292) of testing the leaves' strength by successfully placing his eight-year-old daughter on one.

WALTER HOOD FITCH

PLATE II

VICTORIA REGIA

Victoria regia Opening Flowers, 1851
Coloured lithograph on paper, 57 × 76 cm / 22½ × 29¾ in
Royal Botanic Gardens, Kew, London

The Glaswegian artist Walter Hood Fitch captures the remarkable giant waterlily *Victoria regia* – now known as *Victoria amazonica* – in the process of opening its huge 40-centimetre-diameter (15-inch) flowers, which bloom white on the first day and fade to deep pink on the second. The huge leaves, which are heavily armed beneath with spines that provide a supporting apparatus, float on the surface of the water and can be up to 2 metres (6½ feet)

in diameter. Fitch's illustration is one of several that he produced for a publication to commemorate the successful flowering of the plant in hothouses at Syon House, west London, and the Royal Botanic Gardens at Kew, where he was the official botanical artist. The text and description of the giant Amazon waterlily was written by William Jackson Hooker, director of Kew. The German botanist Eduard Friedrich Poeppig was the first to describe the plant in 1832

with the name *Euryale amazonica*, recognizing a new species of waterlily collected from Bolivia in 1801. The Scottish botanist John Lindley meanwhile had created the new waterlily genus *Victoria* in honour of Queen Victoria, and this waterlily was transferred into that genus in 1847.

Pages from *Kitāb-i hasha'ish* (*Book of Herbs*), 1595
Opaque watercolour and ink on paper, 40 × 51 cm / 15¾ × 20¼ in
Freer Gallery of Art, Smithsonian Institution, Washington, DC

The five plants illustrated in this double folio from a sixteenth-century herbal from Islamic India include a carrot relative (top left), a hollyhock (bottom right) and probably a waterlily (right centre) that were used in traditional medicine. The lifelike images, which show the complete plants, including their roots, are freely drawn, with subtle details of leaf shapes and careful differentiation of the tones of leaves and flowers, and the way in which they

break out of the ruled margins around the Persian text make them seem almost as if they are growing out of the pages. This manuscript herbal is a Persian translation of *materia medica* or knowledge of the medical uses of natural substances, entitled *Kitāb-i hasha'ish* (*Book of Herbs*). It is believed to have been created during the reign of the Indian king Ibrahim Adil Shah II, who ruled Bijapur in the Deccan from 1580 until his death in 1627, and who was

a noted artist, poet and patron of the arts. Throughout the medieval period and beyond, Islamic physicians and scholars translated Greek works on medicine and pharmacology, such as those by the second-century writer Galen and his predecessor Dioscorides. These later Islamic authorities added their own knowledge to this information, while also keeping the classical medical tradition alive.

Anthemis, that is, bābūnj, from *Kitāb fi al-adwiya al-mufrada* (*Book of Simple Drugs*), 1256
Ink and opaque watercolour on paper, 24.6 × 17.3 cm / 9¾ × 6¾ in
Osler Library of the History of Medicine, McGill University, Montreal, Quebec

This beautiful handwritten Arabic herbal is illustrated with nearly 400 colour paintings, mostly of plants but also of animals and minerals used therapeutically in the late Middle Ages. This image depicts plants from the family *Compositae*, showing their basic forms and key characteristics such as leaf and flower shapes. Although not all of the illustrations are detailed enough to identify their species, the plant bottom left is almost certainly *Matricaria*

discoidea known as pineapple weed due to its aroma and as an important medicinal plant. This is one of the few surviving manuscripts of the herbal written by Abu Ja'far al-Ghafiqi of Andalusia, said to have been one of the most knowledgeable pharmacologists of the twelfth century, from a copy made in 1256, nearly a century after his death. As with most medieval herbals, the core of al-Ghafiqi's herbal is based on the illustrated work of the first-century

Greek physician-botanist Dioscorides (see opposite), also incorporating information from Galen (second century) and Islamic authorities from the ninth to the eleventh centuries, Abu Hanifah al-Dinawari, Abu Bakr Muhammad ibn Zakariya al-Razi and Ibn Samajun. To this al-Ghafiqi added his own extensive knowledge of 'simple' drugs, or drugs made directly from plants, animals or minerals without being 'compounded' or mixed with other substances.

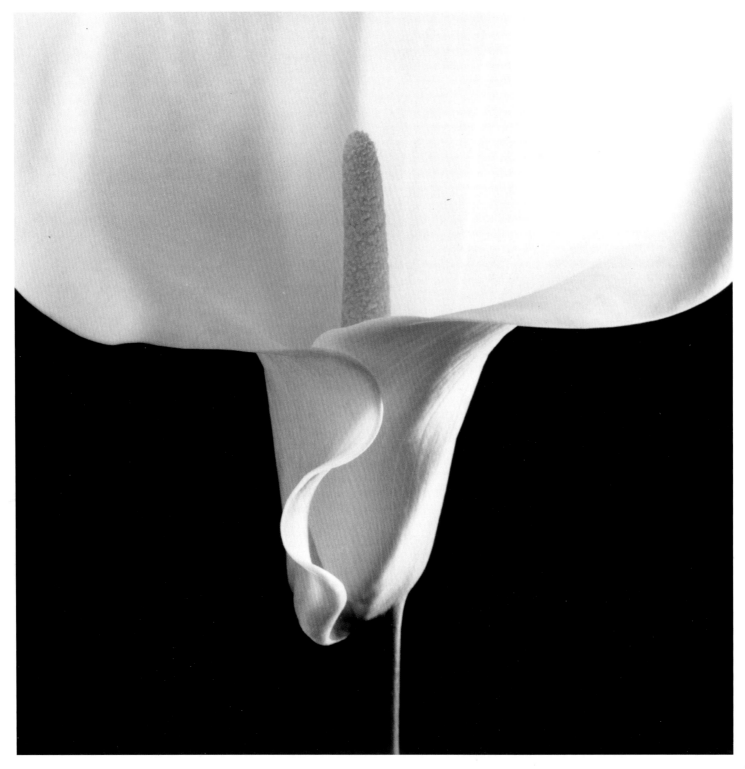

Calla Lily, 1988
Silver gelatin print
60.9 × 50.8 cm / 24 × 20 in

There is something unsettling about this silver gelatin print of a calla lily (*Zantedeschia aethiopica*). This is no botanical study. Instead, the tightly composed image concentrates on revealing physical beauty and fragility, emphasizing the contrast between the pure white of the flower and the dark background. This image, like much of the rest of American photographer Robert Mapplethorpe's body of work, also carries erotic overtones of male and female sexuality, with its concentration on the rigid upright pistil enfolded by the softer surrounding brilliant white spathe. Though floral subjects, which were a major focus of his artistic output, are associated with Mapplethorpe, he is sometimes better known for his sensitive and individual portraits. His subjects included many of his friends, including fellow artists and composers, and he also produced many self-portraits. His early work was with a Polaroid camera and he later used a medium-format Hasselblad. Native to southern Africa and widely naturalized and cultivated elsewhere, the calla lily is in fact not a lily at all, but an aroid. It is a popular garden plant and the cut flowers are used in floral displays and as a symbol of purity at weddings and funerals.

RORY MCEWEN

Fritillaria meleagris, 1981
Watercolour on vellum, 28 × 19 cm / 11 × 7½ in
Private collection

The renowned Scottish musician and artist Rory McEwen gives a combination of weight and translucent lightness to this portrayal of a snake's head fritillary (*Fritillaria meleagris*), a humble 5-centimetre-long (2-inch) flower once common in European meadows. McEwen, who began painting flowers at the age of eight, was an innovative artist who had learned from the celebrated art teacher Wilfrid Blunt. Having studied works by Pierre-Joseph Redouté (see p.10) on vellum, McEwen – inspired by their translucency – himself began painting exclusively on vellum, as few of his contemporaries were doing. His other innovation was to paint larger than life-size. His paintings were passionate, alive and modern in their definition of space. The first part of McEwen's tragically short life had been devoted to music – Scottish ballads, American blues and twelve-string guitar – but he continued to paint even after becoming a celebrity on the 1960s music scene. In 1964 he turned from music to the visual arts, professing 'I am glad I was so long in learning to see, after I had learned to hear.' Exhibitions of his work in the 1970s and a posthumous exhibition in 1988 were a revelation and a profound influence on botanical art that followed.

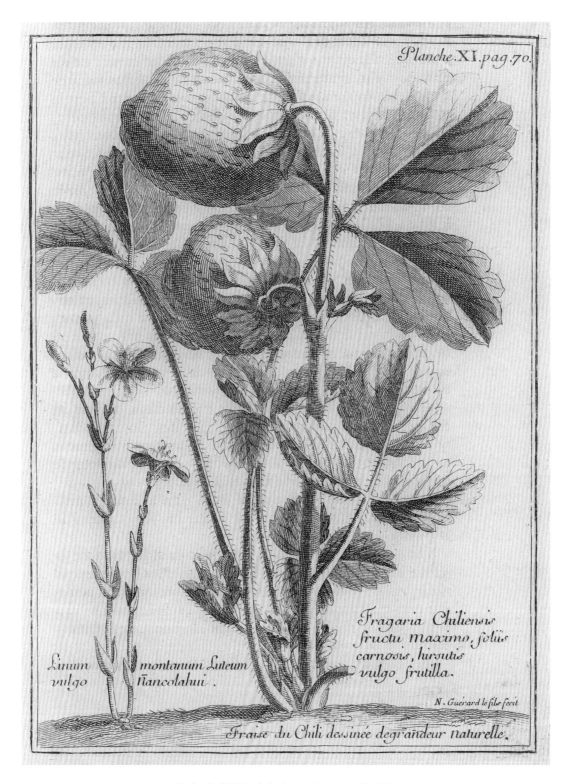

Fraise du Chili dessinée de grandeur naturelle, 1716
Engraving, 29 × 19.5 cm/ 11¼ × 7¾ in
Bibliothèque nationale de France, Paris

The small plant on the left of this engraving from 1716 is flax (*Linum*); the large plant that dominates the plate is the evergreen Chilean strawberry (*Fragaria chiloensis*), which was introduced to Europe in 1714 by Amédée-François Frézier. A spy sent by the French government to study harbours and fortifications along the Pacific coast of the Spanish colonies in what are now Peru and Chile, Frézier returned home from his two-year mission and published a travelogue of his journey with four plant illustrations, including this one. More significant than the intelligence Frézier gathered was his cargo of five specimens of the Chilean strawberry from Concepción, which he kept alive during the return trip. One of them was planted in the royal garden in Paris, another in Frézier's private property in Brittany; they multiplied and were distributed to other gardens. Being all male, however, the new species produced no fruit and so was not a success. But, many years later, in 1765, the French botanist Antoine-Nicolas Duchesne identified a specimen from Holland as a successful cross in cultivation between the white-fleshed Chilean strawberry and the cultivated red-fleshed Virginian strawberry (*Fragaria virginiana*), an introduction from North America. The result is now a plant of major economic importance – the garden strawberry (*Fragaria × ananassa*), which is cultivated today on five continents.

PAUL DECKER

Limon Bergamotto Personzin Gientile, from *Nürnbergische Hesperides*, 1708
Hand-coloured engraving, 31.8 × 21 cm / 12½ × 8¼ in
Private collection

This unusual illustration shows a bergamot bitter orange – famed for flavouring Earl Grey tea – above a scene that shows the Tucher family in their Nuremberg garden, complete with a gardener raking. The fruiting branch is wrapped with a ribbon bearing the fruit's name at the time, 'Limon bergamotto personzin gientile', while a cut-open fruit is in the top left corner. The orange is one of 200 citrus fruits contained in Johann Christoph Volkamer's two-volume *Nürnbergische Hesperides* (1708, 1714), many of the plates for which were drawn by the local artist and engraver Paul Decker. Decker's illustration resembles the paintings of Vincenzo Leonardi (see p.314), which Volkamer had probably seen in Italy when he visited in the 1660s. A rich merchant and clockmaker, Volkamer had one of the finest gardens in Nuremberg, with a greenhouse full of rare citrus plants. When he wanted to record them, he had Decker and six other artists prepare the drawings and backgrounds for the work. At the same time as Volkamer was describing the bergamot citrus, Giovanni (or Johann) Maria Farina took it to Cologne. There, in 1709, he started his perfumery, Johann Maria Farina gegenüber dem Jülichs-Platz, and used the fruit in his now famous formula for eau de cologne.

273

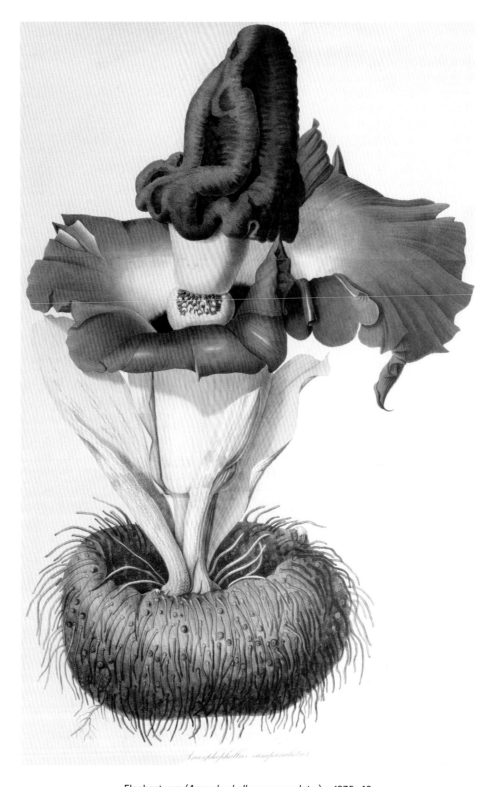

Elephant yam (*Amorphophallus campanulatus*), c.1835–48
Lithograph, 64.5 × 42.6 cm / 25¼ × 16¾ in
Royal Botanic Gardens, Kew, London

This fine depiction of elephant yam (*Amorphophallus paeonifolius*) fills a three-page fold-out of Carl Ludwig von Blume's four-volume flora of the island of Java, then part of the Dutch East Indies, which appeared between 1835 and 1848. The scale is appropriate, given the plant's size: its dark brown tuber can weigh as much as 15 kilograms (33 pounds) and the impressive flowering spike rises up to 70 centimetres (27½ inches) from a bell-shaped spathe that forms a shiny collar surrounding the spadix. Despite its name, the elephant yam is not related to other yams (*Dioscorea*); it actually belongs to the same genus as the titan arum. As with true yams, however, its tuber is rich in starch and is valued as a source of food from India to Myanmar, southern China, Indonesia and northern Australia; it is also cultivated widely as a fodder crop. Blume was a German botanist who spent much of his working life in the Netherlands as director of the state herbarium in Leiden, in which position he made detailed studies of the flora of Java, containing information about and illustrations of plants. The artist who illustrated his work, however, is unknown.

AGATHE HAEVERMANS

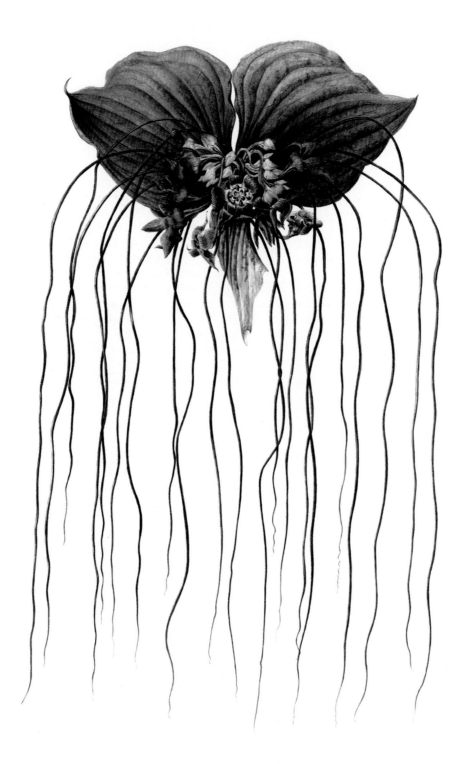

Bat plant (*Tacca chantrieri*), 2013
Watercolour on paper, 45.7 × 30.5 cm / 18 × 12 in
Private collection

Isolated against white space, without the long supporting stem that rises from the base of the plant, the 'floating' dark flowers and trailing tails of *Tacca chantrieri*, the bat plant or bat flower, seem as much animal as vegetable in this watercolour by the contemporary French botanical artist Agathe Haevermans. Large, spreading maroon-black bracts make a dramatic backdrop of 'bat wings' for the small flowers in front. Filament tails 10 centimetres (4 inches) long hang from the tip of each petal, leading to the plant's other common name, cat's whiskers. Mysterious and dark, this member of the yam family captivated Haevermans when she first saw it in the greenhouses of the Muséum National d'Histoire Naturelle in Paris, but her attempts to paint it were frustrated for several years by the difficulty of keeping the plant alive without the right tropical conditions. This bloom comes from a plant given to the artist by one of her students. Haevermans teaches botanical art after an early career as a tropical animal trainer was cut short by injury. An aptitude for drawing led her to become first a scientific illustrator and later a botanical illustrator. Haevermans has taken a leading role in re-establishing botanical art and illustration in her native country.

Amorphophallus titanum, 1891
Watercolour and pencil on paper, 29.4 × 26.3 cm / 11 ½ × 10½ in
Royal Botanic Gardens, Kew, London

The flowering spike of *Amorphophallus titanum*, the titan arum, is one of the tallest of all inflorescences, rising to over 2.5 metres (8 feet). Any flowering is a rare and unpredictable event, but this painting by Matilda Smith celebrates the plant's first flowering in Britain, at Kew Gardens in 1889. The bell-shaped spathe – green on the outside and purple and red within – surrounds the tall yellow-green spadix, at the base of which are female (pink) and male (cream) flowers. The experience was not enjoyable for the artist. The plant is pollinated by minute flies, attracted by a pungent odour resembling rotting meat (in its native Indonesia, it is known as corpse flower). Smith's second cousin, the director of Kew, Joseph Dalton Hooker, who had asked her to illustrate the long-running *Curtis's Botanical Magazine*, noted that recording the plant involved 'a prolonged martyrdom that terminated in illness'. When Smith first started working at Kew, aged just twenty-three, she lacked any knowledge of botany. With the guidance of Hooker, however, she worked there for forty-five years, producing more than 2,300 drawings and becoming the Civil Service's first botanical artist. *Amorphophallus titanum* was first collected by the Italian Odoardo Beccari in the central Sumatran rainforest in 1878.

AURIOL BATTEN

Gazania krebsiana subsp. *arctotoides*, from *Flowers of Southern Africa*, 1988
Watercolour and graphite on paper, 32 × 24 cm / 12¾ × 9½ in
South African National Biodiversity Institute, Silverton

Few botanical artists venture into the wild to observe wild plants in their native habitat; most work from garden plants or herbarium specimens. The South African artist Auriol Batten, who painted more than 1,000 plates before her death in 2015, was an exception. She developed a novel approach, as seen here, of accompanying the plant with a pencil sketch of its habitat (although most of her habitat sketches were drawn from photographs, in order not to delay getting the plant specimens back to her drawing board). She recorded this gazania beside the road near the Biedouw Valley in the Western Cape: 'In this dry area the vegetation is rather scanty and the soil sandy, with many small stones, but it is here that *Gazania krebsiana* subsp. *arctotoides* is seen in its best colour form of rich, blood red.' This is one of 100 such illustrations published in Batten's book *Flowers of Southern Africa* (1988), which helped to create international interest in her style. Batten's precision in description extended to her account of her methods: her watercolours were 'done on pure rag watercolour paper, using mainly Windsor and Newton paints and series 7 sable brushes'.

CAROL WOODIN

Trichoceros antennifer, 2013
Watercolour on vellum over panel, 28 × 38.1 cm / 11 × 15 in
Private collection

The expanse of pale sepia vellum behind the flower spikes creeping across this watercolour of the orchid *Trichoceros antennifer* by the contemporary US artist Carol Woodin emphasizes the orchid's delicacy in the same way as a drawing of the same orchid by Pierre-Jean-François Turpin for Humboldt and Bonpland. Rather than standing up stiffly as in that drawing though, these flower spikes stretch as if scrambling among shrubs on cloud-forest slopes in the high Andes, the orchid's native range. The tiny flowers (each under 2.5 centimetres across) bloom from autumn through to spring and are pollinated by male flies that are tricked into trying to copulate by their uncanny resemblance to female flies. Woodin is known for her paintings of rare orchids – from critically endangered slipper orchids of Vietnam to the no less exotic pink lady slippers around her home in the Catskill Mountains. As several thousand new plants are discovered and published each year, such paintings are examples of botanical illustrations that show how vital the relationship between art and science remains. Woodin has made numerous trips to South America and painted this antennae *Trichoceros* in Ecuador. Over two hundred years after its original publication as *Epidendrum antenniferum* by Humboldt and Bonpland, this fascinating, insect-mimicking orchid remains uncommon in cultivation.

MARC QUINN

Seed of the Baroque, 2014
Painted bronze, 47 × 41 × 30 cm / 18½ × 16¼ × 11¾ in
Private collection

The writhing petals of this large bronze sculpture of an orchid by the British artist Marc Quinn are reminiscent of *Apollo and Daphne* or *The Ecstasy of Saint Theresa* by the great seventeenth-century sculptor Gian Lorenzo Bernini. Like Bernini, Quinn is interested in the idea of transcendence or transformation, and the flower is for him a symbol of both beauty and impermanence. Quinn sets out to take ethereal, light and transient blooms and preserve them in heavy materials – here, bronze painted a clinical white. Flowers figure frequently in his work, both for their attractive shapes and for their symbolism. In *Garden* (2000), Quinn submerged dozens of plants in full bloom in a tank of refrigerated silicon oil, creating an image that he describes as 'all the flowers in the world coming up at the same time, in the same place, an idea of a perfect paradise'. This vision of perpetual life, however, is created from flowers that are already dead: if one were to touch the petals, they would be brittle and snap. Quinn's career has often led him into controversy, not least when he created a sculpture of his head using his own frozen blood.

Paphiopedilum spicerianum, Calathea roseopicta, Philodendron panduriforme, 1985
Watercolour on paper, 50.3 × 35.3 cm / 19¾ × 13¾ in
Royal Botanic Gardens, Kew, London

This painting of the orchid *Paphiopedilum spiceriana* with *Philodendron panduriforme* and *Calathea* (prayer plant) leaves is typical of the style of the British botanical artist Pandora Sellars, who is particularly renowned for her depiction of glossy and fleshy foliage. This orchid appeared in England in 1878 among a mixed collection of orchids from somewhere in India, but its exact habitat was unknown; it was propagated by the famous nursery James Veitch & Sons and was subsequently discovered to have originated in Assam, where it was said to grow on near-vertical rock faces. By the early 1880s it was available as an attractive flowering plant recommended 'for the warmest houses'. This particular specimen was grown by Sellars's late husband in his warm greenhouse. Pandora Sellars has been called 'one of the most important botanical artists of all time', not only for her botanical painting or her scientific illustration – she illustrated two Kew monographs, *The Genus Arum* (1993) and *The Genus Erythronium* (2015), and *Curtis's Botanical Magazine* from 1981 onwards, receiving the Jill Smythies Award for botanical illustration from the Linnean Society in 1999 – but also for her role as an inspiring teacher to many young botanical artists from around the world.

Yellow lantern banksia (*Banksia lemanniana*), 1988
Watercolour and pencil on paper, 55.8 × 76.2 cm / 22 × 30 in
Monash University Collection, Melbourne

This large watercolour and pencil drawing of a branch of yellow lantern banksia (*Banksia lemanniana*) shows three of the species' unusual hanging inflorescences – in most Banksia species, they grow upwards – one of which has produced woody follicles that open to release seeds. The Australian botanical artist Celia Rosser captures an enormous amount of detail in every flower by using tiny 00 brushes – and a steady hand. Rosser dedicated much of her career to illustrating the *Banksia* genus, which is in the *Proteaceae* family. The resulting three-volume work, *The Banksias*, which was completed in 2000, contains seventy-six of Rosser's watercolours, illustrating every *Banksia* species. Brought up during the Depression, Rosser held her first exhibition in Melbourne in 1965, and that was followed by her first book, *Wildflowers of Victoria*. By 1970 she was the Science Faculty Artist at Monash University, illustrating *The Saltmarsh Plants of Southern Australia* and *The Mosses of Southern Australia*, but it was the *Banksia* project initiated by the botanist Alex George in 1974 that motivated her to paint every *Banksia* species from living material. Thus began a twenty-five-year collaboration with George, including field trips collecting plants from Western Australia to Tasmania, where Rosser sketched *Banksia* in the wild and then meticulously re-created them in the studio.

Tsubaki, from *Amoenitatum exoticarum politico-physico-medicarum fasciculi V*, 1712
Engraving, 21 × 17.5 cm / 8¼ × 7 in
Natural History Museum, London

When this drawing of *tsubaki – Camellia japonica –* was made between 1691 and 1692, few Europeans were familiar with what is now a favourite ornamental plant, thanks to Japan's policy of closing its doors to the outside world. The German surgeon Engelbert Kaempfer shows the leaves, the opening buds, the full flower and the dry seed pods. From 1690 to 1692 Kaempfer was a physician for the Dutch East India Company in Japan, confined with all other Europeans on an artifical island in Nagasaki Harbour. He twice made the long journey inland to Edo (Tokyo) to pay homage to Japan's ruler, the Tokugawa Shogun. Somehow he also managed to record 420 plant species, many of which he illustrated himself. Back in Europe, Kaempfer practised medicine; he did not publish the observations in which this illustration appears until 1712. He uses the plant's Japanese name in his engraving; the name *Camellia* was given to it later by Carl Linnaeus (see p.63) in honour of the Jesuit botanist Georg Joseph Kamel. Thanks to intensive hybridization and selection, there are now more than 2,300 named cultivars of *Camellia*. Some plants near the Emperor's Palace in Japan are more than 500 years old – old enough to have been seen by Kaempfer himself.

Gossypium herbaceum, 1816
Hand-coloured stipple engraving, 15.2 × 25.4 cm / 6 × 10 in
Private collection

This delicate watercolour shows the herbaceous cotton plant's mallow-like flower in full bloom, with dissections of the floral parts, fruits and seeds below. The hand-coloured stipple engraving on copper clearly shows the papery folds of the flower petals and reveals the fluffy nature of the ripening cotton boll. The illustration was drawn by the French artist Pancrace Bessa as one of 572 he prepared for *Herbier Général de L'Amateur*, an ambi-tious attempt to illustrate and describe all the exotic plants cultivated in the gardens of Paris in order to rival English publications, such as *Curtis's Botanical Magazine* (1787–) and *The Botanist's Repository* (1797–1812). The work was conceived by the naturalist Jean-Claude-Michel Mordant De Launay, who recorded that he grew the cotton plant himself from seeds that he germinated in 1811. Delaunay died before publication of the first volume in 1816, and his work was continued by Jean-Louis-Auguste Loiseleur-De-slongchamps until the completion of the eighth volume, in 1827. Cotton, one of the world's most economically important plants, grows wild in sub-Saharan Africa and Arabia. The species pictured and *G. arboreum* have been cultivated for fibre and oil for thousands of years, although the New World species *G. hirsutum*, originally from Mexico, produces most of the world's cotton today.

CHARLES RÉMY & GASTON CONTREMOULINS

Radiographie de fleurs, from *Radiographies: Laboratoire des travaux
pratiques d'histologie de la faculté de médecine de Paris*, 1896
Radiograph, dimensions variable
Bibliothèque de l'Institut de France, Paris

Smaller *chrysanthemum* flower heads float like satellites around the larger central bloom in this beautiful, ghostly image, which marks a key moment in botanical art and science. Taken very shortly after the discovery of X-rays by Wilhelm Röntgen in 1895, it is one of the earliest examples of applying the new technology to a plant – and of using cutting-edge science to produce exceptional aesthetic results. The image is itself the result of a collaboration between an artist and a scientist. The painter Gaston Contremoulins had been led by his interest in photography to join the laboratory of Professor Étienne-Jules Marey, physiologist and inventor of chronophotography, where he became one of the first people to become technically proficient at taking X-rays. Contremoulins was approached by the surgeon Charles Rémy, who saw the potential of radiography as a diagnostic tool, and the pair experimented with the use of X-rays in anatomical research, including the finding of foreign bodies in the skull. Early X-rays had an exposure time of up to 90 minutes, so static plant material was an ideal subject for experimentation. Early machines generated much greater radiation than today's versions, and the two men became aware of the hazards; Contremoulins was a pioneer in shortening exposure times and developing ways to protect against radiation.

LEOPOLD AND RUDOLF BLASCHKA

California tree poppy (*Dendromecon rigida*), 1894
Glass, dimensions variable
Harvard University, Cambridge, Massachusetts

Bright butter-yellow four-petalled flowers with many golden radiating stamens are set among narrow grey-green leaves. What appears to be a real California tree poppy (*Dendromecon rigida*), however, is in fact a near-perfect nineteenth-century representation in glass by the Bohemian artists Leopold and Rudolf Blaschka. In Bohemia, Leopold was apprenticed to a goldsmith and gem-cutter, and developed a unique glass-spinning technique, making sixty model glass orchids for Prince Camille de Rohan in Prague (they were later destroyed in a fire). Blaschka moved to Dresden, where his son Rudolf was born in 1857, and began selling glass models of marine invertebrates to museums. In the late 1880s, by which time Rudolf was working with his father, some of these models were seen in Boston by George Goodale, a professor of botany at Harvard and the first director of the university's Botanical Museum. Realizing that models would constitute superior teaching aids to paintings or dried specimens, Goodale persuaded the Blaschkas to produce glass flowers – and persuaded Mary Lee Ware, one of his students, and her widowed mother to fund the project. In all, the Blaschkas made more than 3,000 glass flowers between 1890 and 1938 (Rudolf continued alone after Leopold's death in 1895).

PIETER VAN KOUWENHOORN

LILIVM *flo:* ALBO
LIS BLANCQ
lilien gants wеіs gemeine.

Lilium flo: albo, c.1630
Watercolour on paper, 45 × 31 cm / 17¾ × 12¼ in
Lindley Library, Royal Horticultural Society, London

The seventeenth-century Dutch artist and glass painter Pieter van Kouwenhoorn produced forty-six paintings for his *Verzameling van Bloemen naar de Natuur geteekend door* (*Collection of Flowers Drawn from Nature*), including this Madonna lily, *Lilium candidum*. The painting shows the entire plant in three sections, with the stem on the left, the inflorescence in the middle and the bulb exposed to reveal the diagnostic scales on the right. Van Kouwenhoorn gives the large white flowers extra depth by using darker shading on their reverse. He intended to paint the many bulbous plants that had recently arrived in the Netherlands – mainly from eastern Europe, Asia Minor and the Levant – during the late Renaissance. The Madonna lily originated in Greece, the Balkans and the Middle East, where it had been revered for millennia. It was depicted accurately on a fresco at Knossos on Crete more than 3,500 years ago, and was associated during the Renaissance with the Virgin Mary. Other spectacular new arrivals painted by van Kouwenhoorn included the crown imperial (*Fritillaria imperialis*), nodding star of Bethlehem (*Ornithogalum nutans*), dog's tooth violet (*Erythronium dens-canis*) and of course several tulips – this was, after all, the peak of the frenzied collecting fever known as Tulipomania.

Lilies of Japan, 1890
Colour lithograph, 26.5 × 39 cm / 10¼ x 15¼ in
Lindley Library, Royal Horticultural Society, London

You can almost smell the strong scent of the white-and-yellow golden-rayed lily of Japan (*Lilium auratum*) – its flowers are the largest of any in the lily family – in the centre of this woodblock print from the last decade of the nineteenth century. The lily features with three other cultivars of Asiatic lily species – including *L. speciosum* and *L. longiforum* – on the cover of the *Lilies of Japan* catalogue of 1890, produced by an unknown Japanese artist for the publisher Hasegawa Takejiro on behalf of the Yokohama Gardeners' Association, which produced such catalogues annually to promote exports to Europe. Written in English, the catalogues include lists of the plants for sale accompanied by impressive plates, which were all coloured by hand and very true to life. An enterprising German nurseryman, Louis Boehmer, had started exporting Japanese plants from Yokohama to the West in 1882 before Uhei Suzuki, a Japanese nurseryman who had worked for Boehmer, realized that he could do the same. With his nurseryman son Hamakichi and three other Japanese nurserymen, Suzuki formed the Yokohama Nursery Company in 1893 to export all kinds of Japanese trees, shrubs, herbaceous plants and seeds (Japanese bulbs, including lilies, were particularly successful exports). The company is still thriving today.

Orchis latifolia, Heath Spotted Orchid, 1884
Watercolour on paper, 33.1 × 23.6 cm / 13 × 9¼ in
Royal Botanic Gardens, Kew, London

The dramatic spike of this marsh orchid (*Dactylorhiza incarnata*) leaves little space for the notes of the artist, the Victorian orchid grower John Day. Day collected orchids from all over the tropics in glasshouses in Tottenham, north London, but this marsh orchid grew on his doorstep in the Lee Valley. At the height of Victorian orchidmania, Day inherited his interest in orchids – and the money to support it – from his wine-merchant father, and bought his first orchid collection in 1852. In the 1860s he learned to paint botanical illustrations of his orchids, and he subsequently filled fifty-three 'scrapbooks' with some 4,000 illustrations of great delicacy, with accompanying descriptions and dissections of the floral parts. Day's collections were mostly bought in the Covent Garden plant auctions, where, in 1881, he finally sold his own orchids – worth many thousands of pounds in today's terms. Day's orchidaceous friends included Joseph Dalton Hooker of Kew (see p.248) and Heinrich Reichenbach of Hamburg, the pre-eminent orchid authority who named numbers of new species from Day's paintings. Day named this species *Orchis latifolia*; the first part or genus name for it today, *Dactylorhiza* means 'finger roots' – in Shakespeare's *Hamlet*, Ophelia's garland included the flowers with the name 'dead men's fingers'.

Flowers, 1985
RP Direct Print, dimensions variable
Private collection

At the bottom of this close-up of a pink *Cymbidium* orchid by the Japanese photographer Nobuyoshi Araki is a fragile sprig of the popular bouquet-filler *Gypsophila*. Although orchids and bridal bouquets carry suggestions of innocence and femininity, Araki's tight focus on the petals makes the flower more reminiscent of the genital imagery of, say, the flower paintings of Georgia O'Keeffe (see p.51). The erotic potential of flowers is nothing new in art, but for the prolific Araki – he has published more than 350 books – female eroticism is a key part of his life's work. But Araki's flower photographs also contain a more spiritual element, *wabi-sabi*. This tenet of Taoist and Zen Buddhist belief reflects the idea that an object's inherent ageing must be understood in order to appreciate its beauty (loosely translated, *wabi* means 'simplicity'; *sabi* can be understood as the patina time gives an object). Araki's image already implies that the flower's beauty is transient and will fade. For him, this makes the flower a worthy subject for a botanical still life. Araki's approach goes against much of modern Japanese culture, however, which is obsessed with the new.

Bellflower and Dragonfly, c.1833–4
Polychrome woodblock print (*nishiki-e*), 26.8 × 39.2 cm / 10½ × 15½ in
Museum of Fine Arts, Boston, Massachusetts

A dragonfly hovers among blooms of bellflower (*Platycodon grandiflorus*) in this subtle woodblock print by Katsushika Hokusai, who probably had more influence on Western art than did any other Japanese artist. He was part of the *ukiyo-e* school during the Edo period (1615–1868). *Ukiyo-e* translates as 'the floating world', and these artists sought to capture the fleeting moments of everyday life and every-day subjects. The careful composition, empty space and imitation brushstrokes of this image are typical of Hokusai's series known as *Large Flowers*. *Kacho-e* (bird-and-flower) prints helped to fuel Japonisme, a vogue for Asian art that gripped Europe in the late nineteenth century and greatly influenced the Impressionists (Monet owned several prints in this series). Not only did such works influence artists' subject matter, composition, colour and line, but also their impact extended beyond art to garden design, sparking a demand for the type of flowers depicted, such as chry-santhemums, peonies and poppies. Polychrome printing involved transferring an original artwork on to semi-trans-parent paper that was pasted on to a wooden block and chiselled out. Each colour had its own woodblock, on which the areas to be printed were left raised. Paper made from the paper mulberry (*Broussonetia papyrifera*) was favoured for the prints because it was resilient to overprinting.

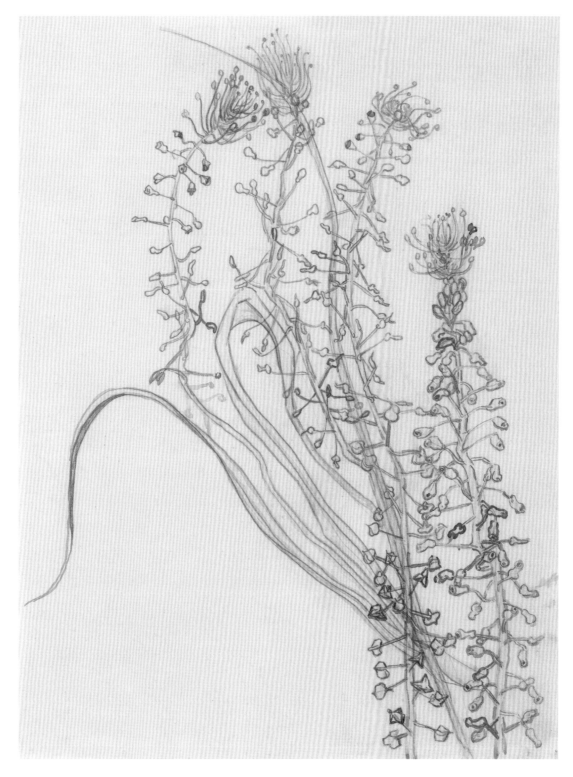

Tassel Hyacinth, 1889
Pencil, brush and ink on paper, 41.2 × 30.9 cm / 16¼ × 12¼ in
Van Gogh Museum, Amsterdam

This drawing may look a little clumsy, but it conveys perfectly the knobbly flowers and fruits of the unassuming tassel hyacinth (*Muscari comosum*), and it bears the hallmarks of a master draughtsman: the renowned Dutch artist Vincent Van Gogh. The drawing was part of Van Gogh's own therapy soon after he had admitted himself to the asylum at Saint-Rémy in Provence in May 1889. Confined to the grounds and wishing to avoid the over-stimulation of painting, Van Gogh drew the asylum garden and its plants to calm himself, gazing closely 'at a blade of grass, a pine tree branch, an ear of wheat'. In a letter to his brother Theo, Van Gogh mentions five 'hasty studies' – including this drawing – he is sending to Theo in Paris. The drawings, first roughly laid out in pencil, were inked in, sometimes with a brush but usually with pens he cut from reeds. In its simplicity, the drawing echoes a prized Japanese print of rice or millet that Van Gogh had aquired from an issue of the Parisian monthly magazine *Le Japon Artistique* of 1888. He noted: 'This,blade of grass leads [the artist] to draw all plants, then the seasons, the broad features of landscapes.'

Cycas circinalis, fern palm, from *Curtis's Botanical Magazine*, 1828
Coloured engraving, 22.9 × 29.2 cm / 9 × 11.5 in
Peter H. Raven Library, Missouri Botanical Garden, St Louis

The line drawing that stretches behind the whole of this plate is a single, spiny leaf of this male plant of the broad-leaved *Cycas*, a prehistoric plant native to southern India and Sri Lanka. It appears with a precise depiction of the whole tree and details of the crown, seed head and even grains of pollen. It was drawn by one of the nineteenth century's most influential English botanists, who was also a fine botanical artist: William Jackson Hooker published

his own drawing in volume 55 of *Curtis's Botanical Magazine* after he became its editor in 1826. He remained the journal's editor until 1845, and had contributed more than 640 plates by the time of his death in 1865. At first glance this plant resembles a palm tree or tree fern, but the woody trunk and stiff, spiny, evergreen leaves are very different from those of either. (Hooker included an illustration of the female form of this plant on the following page.)

Hooker was Regius professor of botany at the University of Glasgow when he made this painting, which reflects his interest in mosses and the so-called primitive plants, including the cycads. *Cycas circinalis* was first described by Carl Linnaeus in 1753 (see p.63).

MASUMI YAMANAKA

Japanese pagoda tree (*Styphnolobium japonicum*), 2013
Watercolour on paper, 72 × 100 cm / 28¼ × 39¼ in
Royal Botanic Gardens, Kew, London

Bent double as if to rest its weary limbs, supported by metal props and a brick pier, this venerable Japanese pagoda tree, planted in 1762, is undoubtedly approaching the end of its long life. It is one of the five 'Old Lions' at Kew Gardens, trees surviving from Princess Augusta's original botanic garden more than 250 years ago. The Kew-based Japanese artist Masumi Yamanaka, captivated by their history and majestic form, set herself the task of recording Kew's significant heritage trees as a permanent archive for Kew's art collections and to inspire others to appreciate the fundamental importance of trees to our planet. Yamanaka takes a respectful, spiritual approach to her subject, touching and stroking a tree and mentally 'seeking its permission' before taking photographs and making preliminary sketches. Each painting can take up to three months to complete. This watercolour was part of the exhibition 'Kew's Heritage Trees' at the Shirley Sherwood Gallery at Kew in 2015, and is featured in the accompanying book, *Treasured Trees* (2015). Despite its name, the Japanese pagoda tree (*Styphnolobium japonicum*), which was often planted in the grounds of Buddhist temples, is actually native to China and was first introduced to Britain in 1753 by the nurseryman James Gordon.

American Coral Tree (*Erythrina herbacea*), from *Flora of North America,* 1824
Hand-coloured copper engraving, 27.3 × 22.3 cm / 10¾ × 8¾ in
LuEsther T. Mertz Library, New York Botanical Gardens

William P.C. Barton's admiration for this gaudy herbaceous American Coral Tree is apparent from this drawing and his description in *Flora of North America*: 'The spikes were luxuriant and the flowers numerous, forming a full florescence of more than a foot in length.' Barton was lucky to find this specimen, normally native to Florida, growing in the greenhouse of William Bartram, who then ran the botanical garden opened by his father John in the 1720s at Kingessing, outside Philadelphia. Barton trained as a doctor of medicine but became more interested in botany under the influence of his uncle, the renowned botanist Benjamin Smith Barton, author of the first American textbook on botanical science. On the death of his uncle in 1815, William Barton became professor of botany at University of Pennsylvania, where he taught materia medica, medical botany (he would have known, for example, that the seeds of the Coral Tree were toxic and that the Native Americans used the yam-like roots to make a curative tea). Barton, who was elected president of the Philadelphia Linnean Society, was determined that the detailed descriptions of native plants in his flora would raise the profile of botany in North America. The Philadelphia Botanical Club's journal, *Bartonia*, which has been published since 1909, is named after him.

WILLIAM BARTRAM

Franklinia alatamaha, from *A beautiful flowering tree discovered growing
near the banks of the R. Alatamaha in Georgia*, 1788
Watercolour on paper, 47.8 × 35.8 cm / 18¾ × 141 in
Natural History Museum, London

The renowned American botanical gardener William Bartram drew this branch of the Franklin tree in full leaf – its open camellia-like flower revealing the large petals and mass of stamens, with two spherical fruits below – at a time when its namesake, Benjamin Franklin, one of the Founders of the United States, was still alive. Bartram and his father, John, were two of the most important plant-hunters of colonial America and the young republic.

They discovered this American relative of the camellia in a 1.2-hectare (3-acre) grove not far from the Altamaha River near Fort Barrington, Georgia, in October 1765 and named it *Franklinia alatamaha* after Franklin, John Bartram's friend and a co-founder of the American Philosophical Society. The tree is now extinct in the wild, the last reliable sighting having taken place in 1790, but it still exists in cultivation thanks to seed collected by William Bartram (illustrated

at the foot of the drawing). In cultivation the small tree suckers freely, and the deciduous leaves turn a deep red in the autumn. The original drawing was commissioned by the English apothecary and physician Dr John Fothergill; after Fothergill's death, it may have been sent to his friend John Coakley Lettsom, who catalogued Fothergill's garden.

Kakitsubata, early 18th century
Ink and colour on gold-foiled paper, each 151.2 × 358.8 cm / 59½ × 141¼ in
Nezu Museum, Tokyo

Ogata Kōrin's *Irises* looks so contemporary that it is difficult to believe that it was painted during the Edo period, in the early eighteenth century. It is easy to understand why the painting is one of Japan's national treasures, however. It depicts the fabled irises near the Yatsuhashi Bridge of Mikawa province, as described in the ancient Japanese classic *The Tales of Ise* – but Kōrin omits the bridge and stream. Instead, bold brushstrokes in three colours describe a 'stream' of moisture-loving *Iris laevigata* against a background of gold foil. Kōrin used *gunjo* (powdered azurite) to create a startlingly deep indigo-blue rather than violet for the flowers. One of the great early artists of the Rimpa School, Kōrin probably made the painting for the Nishi Hongan-ji temple in Kyoto, which he is known to have visited. The tradition of celebrating seasonal displays of flowering plants is entrenched in Japanese culture, and still persists. Today this masterpiece is displayed in the Nezu Museum in Tokyo in spring, when the irises are in flower in the museum's gardens. For this period, it becomes almost an object of veneration.

JOHANN JAKOB WALTER

Daffodil and Narcissi and Anemone,
from *Horti Itzeinensis*, 17th century
Gouache on vellum, Victoria and Albert Museum, London

The slightly naïve style gives these narcissi a realistic fragility, and the colours glow because the seventeenth-century artist, Johann Walter, painted with gouache on vellum. Behind the simple image is a story of religious strife, family upheaval and banishment. Walter's employer, Johann, Count of Nassau-Idstein, spent many years in exile in Strasbourg after his Protestant family fought unsuccessfully against the Catholic Holy Roman Emperor.

He returned in 1648 and remodelled the Garden of Idstein, near Frankfurt. Within a huge protective rectangle of walls and hedges, with niches for statues, he laid out his flowerbeds in eccentric designs shaped like various fruits. Here the Count cultivated fashionable flowers and exotica, including narcissi. The native yellow daffodils were augmented by new species from the south: sometimes double, with daintier trumpets – white, yellow and orange – and

able to sport several flowers to a stalk. The same enthusiasm that greeted tulips from Turkey welcomed these new narcissi to the garden. The Count invited Walter, whom he had met in Strasbourg, to spend the spring and summer at Idstein painting flowers, and Walther did so at least eight times between 1654 and 1674. Walter's paintings were collected into volumes (two survive) known as the *Horti Itzeinensis*.

CHRISTOPHER DRESSER

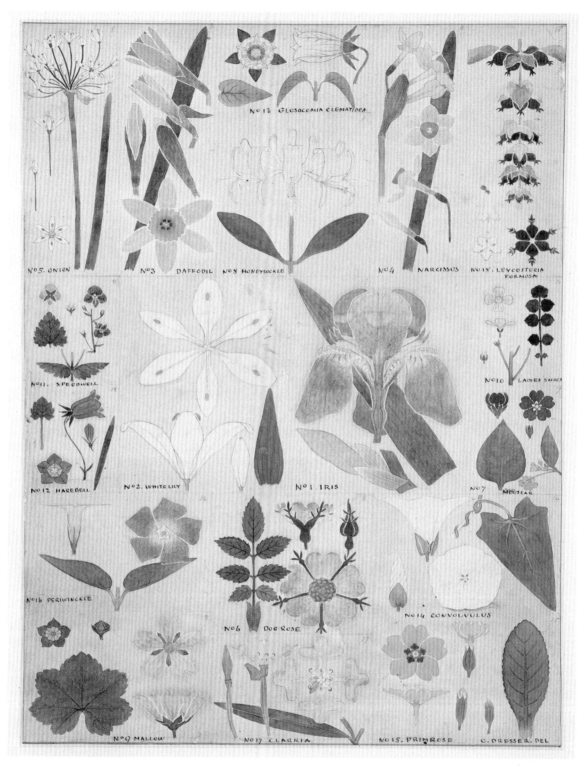

Leaves and Flowers from Nature, from *The Grammar of Ornament*, 1856
Pencil and watercolour on paper, 52.8 × 36.5 cm / 20¾ × 14¼ in
Victoria and Albert Museum, London

The eighteen labelled flowers in this Victorian plate – randomly numbered and arranged, from no. 1 *Iris* to no. 18 *Leycesteria formosa*, a Himalayan native introduced to Europe in the 1820s – are easily recognizable, but the English designer Christopher Dresser was far less interested in their individual characteristics than in their potential for incorporation into wider forms of design and architecture. Dresser – who is often identified as the first industrial designer – produced the drawing for Owen Jones's work *The Grammar of Ornament* (1856), a noted contribution to the design reform movement that attempted to combine beauty and utility in mass-produced domestic objects. There is no pattern to the relationships between any of the plants Dresser illustrates, but his eye for design is evident in the choices he made. His observations reflect natural patterns and symmetry, as for example in no. 13 *Glosocomia clematidea* (now *Codonopsis clematidea*), where he shows a flower with its several concentrically aligned internal structures. Dresser portrays the plants with very accurate shapes and colouring, but was more interested in what he called their geometric balance, which echoed his own scientific approach to art and design. He believed that within science truth was to be found, and that art reflected beauty.

WILLIAM MORRIS

Design for 'Vine' wallpaper, *c*.1872–6
Watercolour and pencil on paper, 81.4 × 64.6 cm / 32 × 25¼ in
Victoria and Albert Museum, London

This watercolour of twisting grapes and vine leaves reflects both a realistically accurate depiction of nature and a stylized geometric pattern. The image of lush fecundity and rhythmic lines was one of seventeen wallpaper designs the British artist William Morris made between 1872 and 1876. Morris was a man of varied talents: a poet, novelist and socialist activist, he is best known as a designer, particularly of textiles. He produced more than 600 designs for wallpaper, embroidery and textiles and more than 150 for stained glass, as well as borders for printed works and typefaces. Most of his designs are based on observation of the natural world, and require high-quality materials such as natural dyes and hand-processing techniques. Morris, who trained as an architect, was later closely connected with the Pre-Raphaelite movement, particularly Edward Burne-Jones and Dante Gabriel Rossetti, with whom he founded a decorative arts firm (eventually called Morris and Co.) that also involved the architect Philip Webb. Morris was one of the most influential figures of the Victorian age, and his legacy endures today. In particular, the impact and originality of his designs are such that they are still widely admired and used, and continue to be commercially available.

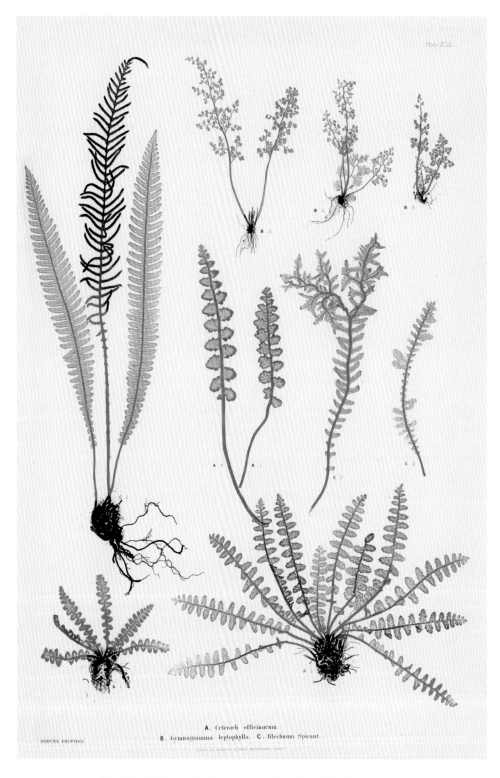

Ceterach officinarum, *Gymnogramma leptophylla* and *Blechnum spicant*
from *The Ferns of Great Britain and Ireland*, 1855
Green and brown ink on paper, 54.6 × 36.8 cm / 21½ × 14½ in
Peter H. Raven Library, Missouri Botanical Garden, St Louis

This illustration of British ferns, arranged carefully to show the different elements of the plants, comes from the height of the Victorian fern craze, or pteridomania. It was created in 1855 by Henry Bradbury, one of the last of the most skilful exponents of the craft of nature printing, which uses plant or animal specimens to create a plate from which a print is made. Nature printing was an ancient skill, but the technique as refined at the Imperial Printing House in Vienna by the director Alois Auer (see p.145) from about 1849 consisted of pressing a specimen into a soft lead plate with an iron roller, leaving an impression on the lead; this impression was transferred electrically to a copper plate that was used for the actual printing, using black, brown or green ink. Bradbury studied in Vienna and improved the technique, taking out his own patent in London. His masterpiece, *The Ferns of Great Britain and Ireland* (1855), a folio of fifty-one plates with text by Thomas Moore, was followed in 1859–60 by *Nature-printed British Seaweeds*. Bradbury set up his own printing works to produce the books, but at the age of only twenty-nine, after being accused by Auer of plagiarism, killed himself by drinking acid.

MAGDALENA TURZAŃSKA

Lepidozia reptans, 2013
Microphotograph,
dimensions variable

As modern technology pushes the boundaries of botanical knowledge, it also reveals breathtaking beauty. This alien-looking structure covered in mosaic is in fact a single stem of creeping fingerwort, a tiny plant that is often mistakenly referred to as a moss, which it resembles in the way it 'creeps' over soil or other surfaces in loose, green mats but it is in fact a liverwort. Without magnification, *Lepidozia reptans* resembles splashes of green, fuzzy-textured felt, and is commonly found in the acidic conditions of peaty banks, soft rock faces, rotting logs or the bark of living oaks, birches and conifers. Magdalena Turzańska of the Institute of Experimental Biology at the University of Wroctaw in Poland has won numerous photography awards for her work using a fluorescence microscope, which uses ultraviolet light to excite fluorescent molecules in the sample, producing a luminous effect. Here, reddish, earthy hues give fingerwort an almost reptilian appearance reminiscent in some ways of Aboriginal art. Microphotography makes it possible to explore the physical properties of tiny nonflowering plants that may appear insignificant, but that – as our increased knowledge of ecology has taught us – are just as important in ecosystems as larger, more showy specimens.

JOHN PARKINSON

1. The Crowne Imperiall 2. The Persian Lilly 3. The Martagon Imperials,
from *Paradisi in sole paradisus terrestris: A garden of all sorts of pleasant flowers*, 1629
Woodcut, 26.6 × 15.6 cm / 10 × 6 in
University of California Libraries, La Jolla

This is a plate from what may be the most famous English gardening book of the seventeenth century, John Parkinson's *Paradisi in sole paradisus terrestris*, taken from a facsimile edition of 1904. Largely using cultivars from his own garden, Parkinson – an apothecary and plantsman – described hundreds of plants that could be grown in English flower or kitchen gardens and orchards, including here, from top to bottom, the crown imperial (*Fritillaria imperi-

alis*), the Persian lily (*Fritillaria persica*) and the Martagon imperial (*Lilium martagon*). Parkinson gave practical gardening advice along with information that was standard in herbals, such as where exotics were imported from, when they flower, the names by which they were known and sometimes their medicinal uses. Parkinson had studied the work of Flemish plant authors and learned to grow tulips and other flowering bulbs from seed in order to produce

new cultivars; he listed scores of tulip cultivars, many of which he grew himself. Parkinson published his book when he was sixty-two, capitalizing on the demand for up-to-date plant information in English demonstrated by the success of John Gerard's *Herball*, first published in 1597. The title of his book, *Paradisi in sole*, is a Latin play on his name, 'park in sun'. He went on to publish *Theatrum Botanicum* (1640), a more botanical work describing nearly 4,000 plants.

Narcissus poeticus, Crown imperial, (*Fritillaria imperialis*),
auriculas (*Primula × pubescens* Jacq.), c.1650–82
Watercolour and bodycolour, 45.7 × 32.9 cm / 18 × 13 in
Royal Collection Trust, London

This watercolour folio by the seventeenth-century London gentleman-gardener Alexander Marshal is dominated by the crown imperial, *Fritillaria imperialis*, one of the most distinctive and imposing members of the lily family. The flowering stems are topped by green bracts above a whorl of orange-red flowers. The plant, which grows in the wild in an area from Turkey to the foothills of the Himalayas, reached Western Europe via Constantinople (now Istanbul) in 1576 and was soon widely cultivated in England. Marshal accompanies it with smaller depictions of two species of narcissus and two hybrid primulas, known as auriculas. The folio comes from Marshal's *Florilegium*, on which he worked for thirty years from about 1650. In all, the vast work contains 159 sheets illustrating more than 600 plants and flowers grown in English gardens at the time, as well as insects and birds. The *Florilegium* is regarded as a volume of great historical significance, although Marshal himself seems to have been motivated purely by an enjoyment of painting flowers, especially newly introduced species. Although he was not a trained artist, his independent wealth allowed him to devote much of his time to painting and gardening.

寄生花

Trumpet flowers (*Campsis grandiflora*), from *Ka-i*, 1759
Hand-coloured woodblock print
British Library, London

There is a deceptive simplicity to the regular outlines and simple colours of this eighteenth-century Japanese illustration of the Chinese trumpet vine (*Campsis grandiflora*), but in fact it is highly accurate. It shows two fully open flowers, together with five more in bud, and leafy shoots showing both the upper and lower leaf surfaces. The leaf veins are black on green for the upper surface and pale against a darker green underneath. The species, one of only two in the genus, is native to eastern and southeastern China but has long been grown in Japan, Korea and Taiwan and is widely cultivated elsewhere. The bright orange-red flowers are trumpet-shaped with a yellow throat. They produce a sweet nectar and are mainly pollinated by birds. This illustration appeared in a famous Japanese botanical work entitled *Ka-i* (1759), the first two volumes of which were completed by Shimada Mitsufusa and the remaining six mostly or possibly wholly by Ono Ranzan. In 1875 the *Ka-i* was published in a French translation, making it one of the first Japanese botanical books to be made available in a European language. Containing 200 woodcuts depicting selected flowering plants, it was bound in a concertina format.

GILLIAN BARLOW

Wisteria brachybotris 'Okayama', 2015
Watercolour on paper, 20.5 × 12.5 cm / 8 × 4¾ in
Royal Botanic Gardens, Kew, London

Violet, pea-like flowers cascade over the paper in this watercolour by the leading contemporary British flower painter Gillian Barlow, the careful composition framed by a sharp edge resembling a photographic snapshot. The painting was commissioned by Martyn Rix, editor of *Curtis's Botanical Magazine*, and Barlow found a good sample of the Japanese species *Wisteria brachybotris* 'Okayama' in the National Plant Collection of wisterias belonging to Chris Lane of Witch Hazel Nursery in Kent. The artist had to work quickly so as to set down the plant's likeness before its pendulous racemes and silky, bronze-tinged leaves began to droop. Barlow, who trained at the Slade School of Fine Art in London in the early 1960s but became an enthusiastic flower painter while living in New York City in the 1980s, works rapidly to capture the elusive freshness of her subjects. She makes sketches and colour notes in the field followed by more in the studio, taking measurements and making tracings before transferring her design to paper and, finally, adding colour. As well as teaching botanical art, she runs the growing archive of botanical paintings of the Chelsea Physic Garden's Florilegium Society. Her widely varied output includes work as a Herald painter for the London College of Arms, a post she has held since 1988.

ANYA GALLACCIO

Preserve 'Beauty', 1991–2003
2,000 gerberas, glass, metal and rubber
260 × 535 × 2.5 cm / 102¼ × 210¾ × 1 in
Tate, London

At first glance, this work by the British conceptual artist Anya Gallaccio resembles four red rugs, with random dark spots and a hanging fringe. Closer up, it becomes clear that *preserve 'beauty'* is created from rows of flowers of the hybrid *Gerbera* 'Beauty' – between 1,600 and 2,000 depending on their size in the installation. The irregularities in the distribution of the flowers occur when the glass panels on which they are arranged are raised and fixed to a wall, compressing the flowers to hold them in place. Some flowers slip, despite the dental floss that holds them temporarily (it is removed once the work is upright). Gallaccio first created the piece in 1991 and has since installed it several times in different locations. Despite the work's name, the flowers are not preserved: they are subject to decay, inviting reflection on various themes: time, life, death, beauty and renewal. The panels are adjusted to allow for the shrinkage of flowers as they decay, while dead flowers that fall are left to decompose on the floor. The process affects not only the work's appearance but also its smell, which changes from the sweet scent of fresh flowers to a rotting odor of decay.

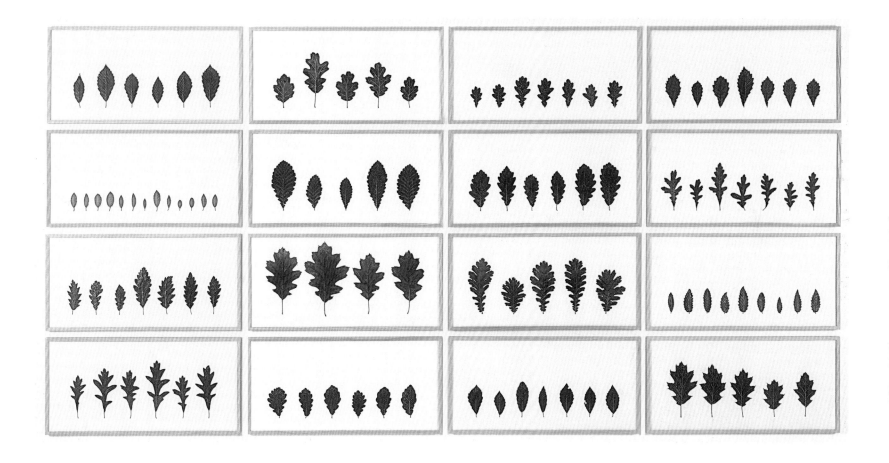

quercus, 1992
Leaves on paper, 144 × 537 cm / 56¾ × 211¼ in
Centre PasquArt, Biel

There are sixteen panels in this collage by the Dutch artist herman de vries – who styles his name in lower case in order to avoid connotations of hierarchy – each displaying a selection of leaves (between five and thirteen) from sixteen different species of oak (*Quercus*) mounted on paper. A smaller panel provides the title and a list of the species, together with de vries's signature. The leaves are real: de vries, who works only with nature rather than using

brushes or other equipment, collected them at the Royal Botanic Garden in Edinburgh. The sections of the collage are laid out in a regular grid but are not ordered by leaf size or alphabetically by species: no hierarchy is imposed. There is no set pattern to the composition, either: sections appear to be placed randomly rather than according to their relative visual 'weight'. The grid's straight lines are juxtaposed with the irregular lines and uneven edges of leaves

and stems, creating a subtly rhythmic work that isolates the subject, highlighting the diversity of the oak. Now working in the Black Forest, Germany, de vries believes the natural world contains great art without any intervention, and displaying natural objects for viewers to observe is central to his approach.

PIETER VAN DER BORCHT

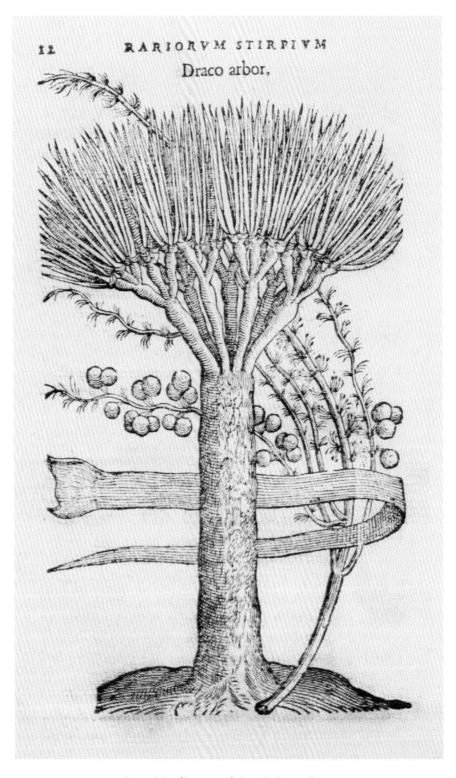

Draco Arbor (dragon tree), from *Rariorum aliquot
stirpium per Hispanias observatarum historia*, 1576
Woodcut, 13.7 × 7.7 cm / 5¼ × 3 in
Peter H. Raven Library, Missouri Botanical Garden, St Louis

This woodblock from 1576 was the first printed image of an object of great curiosity to Europeans who had never seen one: the dragon tree (*Dracaena draco*), a native of the Canary Islands that looked as exotic as its name suggested. The Flemish draughtsman Pieter van der Borcht shows the whole tree, with details of the leaves and berries. The tree was a source of a reddish resin known as dragon's blood, which it exuded as red drops that could be picked off the bark when dry. It had been used since ancient times for medical purposes as well as for varnish, dye and incense. From the mid-1560s van der Borcht worked for the famed Antwerp publisher Christophe Plantin, and he eventually led the Plantin team of draughtsmen. He is said to have made more than 3,180 botanical watercolours, and learned to engrave copperplates that eventually replaced the use of woodblocks. The Plantin woodblocks were one of five great sets of woodblocks used in European natural-history publications of the time, and appeared in the works of a number of authors. This image was published in Carolus Clusius's flora of Spain *Rariorum aliquot stirpium per Hispanias observatarum historia* (1576), the first national flora in Europe.

Pachypodium Plant, Andohahela National Park, Madagascar, 2010
Gelatin silver print, 127 × 172.7 cm / 50 × 68 in
Private collection

The spines of a Madagascan giant succulent *Pachypodium lamerei* add a blur to the outline of its trunk and branches as they reach across this black-and-white photograph – shot looking up into the tree – by the renowned Brazilian photographer Sebastião Salgado. Although Salgado is more famous for his images of our inhumanity towards other humans, he has also documented our brutalization and degradation of the planet. This image of *Pachypodium*'s bizarre tentacles was part of a huge eight-year project that took him to thirty-two countries to photograph unique ecosystems, as he explains: 'What we tried to do ... was to bring a new presentation of the planet; to present the planet mineral, the planet vegetable, the planet animal, putting us as one animal among all the others.' Salgado found this succulent in the Andohahela National Park in southeastern Madagascar in 2010. *Pachypodium*, a native of Madagascar and mainland Africa, is a succulent that in some ways resembles a cactus. Its Latin name means thick-footed and refers to the thick trunk, which has evolved to conserve water in dry environments. The spines grow in pairs or threes and wear with time, while the few stunted branches and sparse leaves reflect the lack of water.

Passion Flowers and Hummingbirds, c.1870–83
Oil on canvas, 39.4 × 54.9 cm / 15½ × 21¾ in
Museum of Fine Arts, Boston, Massachusetts

This scene set in the tropical forests of Central America is one of the first botanical paintings to reflect the evolutionary ideas published by Charles Darwin in 1859. The American artist Martin Johnson Heade shows two snowcaps (*Microchera albocoronata*) – a tiny species of hummingbird – amid the twisted stems and beautiful blooms of the red passion flower (*Passiflora racemosa*), thrown into the foreground by the steamy Brazilian forest behind as this passion flower is native there and he would have seen it in situ when painting the hummingbirds. Darwin had noted that their bills are adapted to enable them to feed from and thus pollinate the blooms of the passion flower, and his observation of such adaptations was crucial in the development of his theory of evolution. Heade, who was born and in Pennsylvania, exhibited his first work – mainly portraits – at the Pennsylvania Academy of the Fine Arts in Philadelphia. Later he moved to New York and began painting landscapes, notably coastal salt marshes. In 1863–4 he travelled to Brazil, where he made more than forty works depicting hummingbirds. He also visited Colombia, Nicaragua, Panama and Jamaica, where he painted tropical plants and birds. Later on he concentrated on still lifes. Although not widely appreciated in his lifetime, Heade's work is now held in many American museums, especially the Museum of Fine Arts in Boston.

SYDNEY PARKINSON

Banisteria atriplicifolia, 1769
Watercolour on paper, 27.9 × 47 cm / 11 × 18½ in
Natural History Museum, London

Sydney Parkinson's vivid image of *Stigmaphyllon auriculatum* – a twining vine with clusters of flowers, each with five bright-yellow petals, and leaves with reddish blush in their veins – is a record of an act of defiance. When Captain James Cook's ship *Endeavour* arrived in Rio de Janeiro in November 1768, on the explorer's circumnavigation of the globe, the city's Portuguese governor allowed the crew to disembark only for provisions. The expedition naturalist, Joseph Banks, stole ashore at night with a small party to collect plants. Banks and his fellow naturalist Daniel Solander identified this illicitly collected specimen as *Banisteria* although the name was later rejected. In Brazil, Society Islands, Madeira, Tierra del Fuego, Java, Australia and New Zealand, Banks and Solander ultimately collected 3,607 specimens of plants and animals; despite his diligence, Parkinson, the expedition's artist, could not keep up. This is one of thirty-eight finished paintings he made of the Brazilian specimens. Of more than 600 drawings he made in New Zealand and Australia, Parkinson was able to finish only thirty-three. To the rest he added colour references and made detailed notes on the verso. After Parkinson's death later in the voyage – he was only twenty-five – his notes allowed other artists to finish his *Endeavour* work.

Syzygium malaccense, 19th century
Watercolour, 41.5 × 48.6 cm / 16¼ × 19 in
Natural History Museum, London

This early nineteenth-century painting of the Malay rose plum (*Syzygium malaccense*), a favourite Southeast and East Asian sweet-flavoured fruit tree, records both a coming together of West and East and a glimpse into a closed world. It was painted in China, then still largely off-limits for Europeans, by a local artist working for the Englishman John Reeves, an inspector of tea (for the East India Company in Canton, Guangzhou) from 1812 to 1831. The illustration was painted to Reeves's instructions to echo a European botanical plate, with details of the fruit in various stages of ripening. The flowers, with their powder-puff of red stamens, are a feature of the myrtle family. Reeves has ensured that the artist shows the cluster of succulent pink tinged fruits, as well as a dissected fruit, seeds and flower parts. Reeves was gathering information for the English botanist Sir Joseph Banks, whom he had met before travelling to China. Banks had requested that Reeves send illustrations of Chinese plants to the recently formed Horticultural Society of London for assessment, so Reeves – no artist himself – employed Chinese artists to paint interesting plants cultivated in Canton, especially those growing in the Fa-tee flower market. Reeves also sent many Chinese plants back to the society's Chiswick garden for trial.

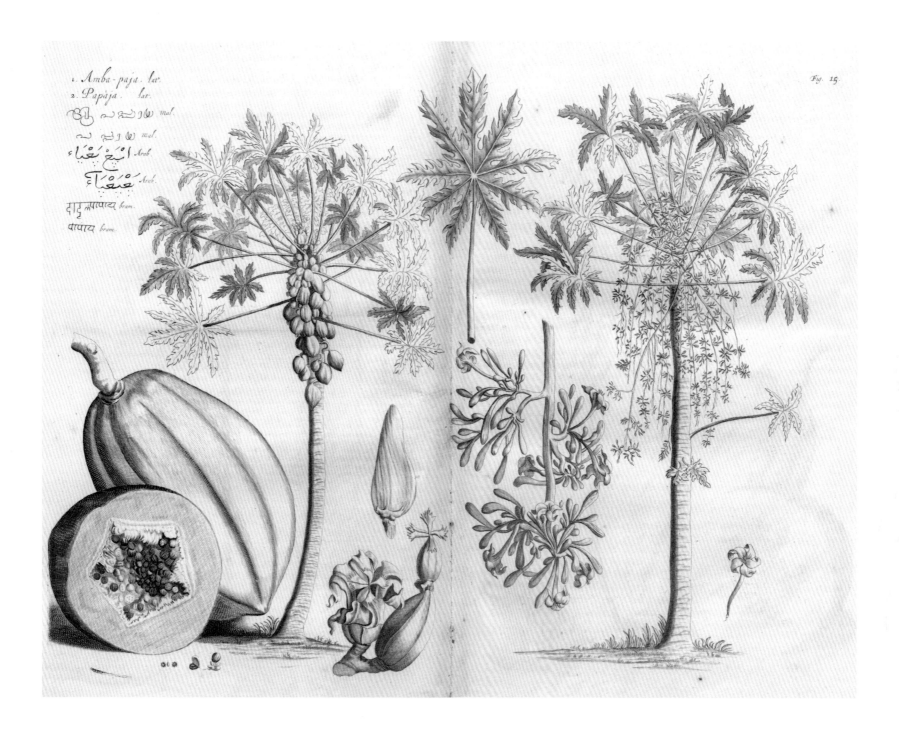

Amba-paja and Papaja, from *Hortus Malabaricus*, 1678
Engraving, 39 × 44.5 cm / 13¼ × 17½ in
Peter H. Raven Library, Missouri Botanical Garden, St Louis

These papayas from Malabar on the southwest coast of India show the scale of the images in the extraordinary twelve-volume *Hortus Malabaricus*, compiled by the Dutchman Hendrik van Reede tot Drakenstein in the late seventeenth century. The books are 39 centimetres (15¼ inches) tall, and most of the 793 illustrations are double-page spreads, showing the plants – or parts of them – at life-size whenever possible, as here with the cross section of fruit and details of the flowers. This South American fruiting plant (*Carica papaya*) was introduced by Spanish traders in the fifteenth century. Van Reede's survey of local flora was prompted by the need to find medicines for the army of the Dutch East India Company in Malabar. He put together an international team of collaborators, including tree-climbers to collect plant material, local artists and wise men to draw and describe the plants, local physicians to record knowledge about medical uses, and translators and editors to make the text readable for Europeans. In the process the text was translated three times: from Malayalam to Portuguese, Portuguese to Dutch and Dutch to Latin. Vernacular names appear on the plates in four scripts: Roman, Malayalam, Nagari and Arabic. *Hortus Malabaricus* was the first comprehensive account of the flora of the Indian subcontinent in a European language.

VINCENZO LEONARDI

Limon S. Remi, 1646
Hand-coloured engraving, 29.2 × 20.3 cm / 11½ × 8 in
Private collection

This coloured engraving of a lemon is typical of the style of the seventeenth-century Italian artist Vincenzo Leonardi, with the lemon's name – '*Limon S. Remi*' – written on a ribbon hanging from a leafy branch bearing a whole fruit, above a lemon cut in half to expose the pith and flesh. The engraving, possibly by the Dutch artist Cornelis Bloemaart, was one of many plates by Leonardi prepared to illustrate *Hesperides sive de Malorum Aureorum* (1646) by the Sienese botanist Giovanni Battista Ferrari. Ferrari and his associate, the scholar and collector of drawings Cassiano dal Pozzo, believed in the use of visuals to aide scientific study, and selected Leonardi to produce the first illustrated scientific study of the genus *Citrus*. The names on Leonardi's plates of lemons reflect the parts of Italy where Ferrari believed the particular shape to be most typically cultivated, in this case San Remi (now Sanremo) in Liguria. Leonardi had accompanied dal Pozzo from Rome to France in 1625 and produced many fine paintings of animals and plants for his Museo Cartaceo, or paper museum. This remarkable collection consisted of some 7,000 drawings of natural history subjects, including the eighty-two published paintings of *Citrus* for Ferrari's *Hesperides* and many more that were not published.

G.S. DELAHAYE

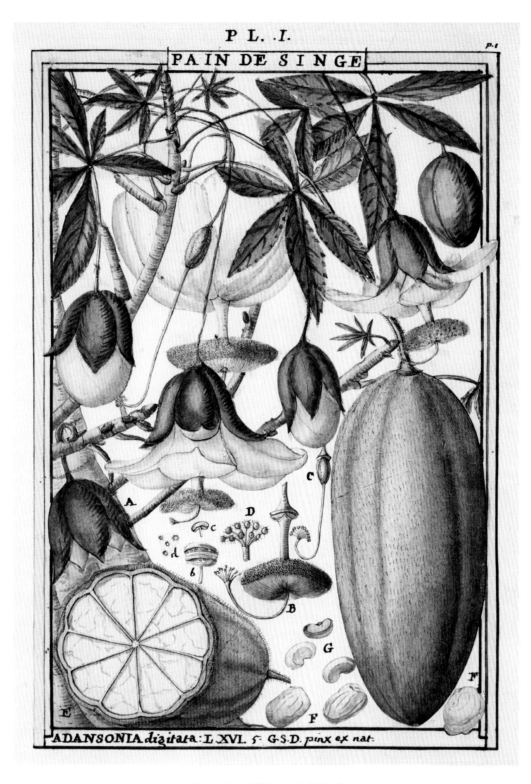

Monkey bread (*Adansonia digitata*),
from *Florindie, ou histoire physico-économique des végétaux de la Torride*, 1789
Watercolour on manuscript, 18.9 × 27.8 cm / 7½ × 11 in
Service Historique de la Marine, Vincennes

The large fruits shown at the foot of this plate both whole and in cross section earn the baobab (*Adansonia digitata*) its colloquial name of *pain de singe* – 'monkey bread': rich in calcium, antioxidants and vitamin C, baobab powder is marketed today as a 'superfood'. The rest of the plate is bursting with details of the foliage and pendulous flowers, crowded one on top of the other. The plate was drawn by an accomplished amateur botanist, the French curate abbé Delahaye, in the French colony of Saint-Domingue (now Haiti) on the Caribbean island of Hispaniola. There are eight species of baobab, most of which are native to Africa, but the tree had been introduced to the Caribbean through the slave trade with Africa. It is remarkable for both its distinctive swollen trunk and its longevity: it can live for more than 1,000 years. Delahaye's plate illustrated his *Florindie, ou histoire physico-économique des végétaux de la Torride* (*Physio-economic History of Tropical Plants*), an exploration of the benefits of the French colonies. At the time, however, France itself was in the convulsions of revolution, and only two years later Haiti's slaves would overthrow their French masters, establishing a self-governing republic that lasted until 1804. Delahaye was killed by Haitians loyal to their leader Toussaint Louverture in 1802.

315

ALEXANDER VON HUMBOLDT & AIMÉ BONPLAND

Berberis (Mahonia) moranensis,
from *Impression de plantes du voyage de MM. Humboldt et Bonpland*, c.1803
Ink on Spanish paper, 48 × 31.5 cm / 18¾ × 12¼ in
Bibliothèque de l'Institut de France, Paris

This unique image is a contact print of the pressed shoot of a shrub found in May 1803 by the French botanist Aimé Bonpland – whose annotation appears at the top of the sheet – on the slopes of Moran in central Mexico. The details of the leaves, flowers and shoot architecture are clearly visible, down to the primary veins on the leaflets. Bonpland accompanied the celebrated German naturalist Alexander von Humboldt on his explorations of North, Central and South America in 1799–1804. Faced with the difficulty of preserving their specimens from the ravages of insects and fungi in the tropical humidity, the two men resorted to making 'self-impressions', which they obtained simply by inking both surfaces of a specimen and pressing it between sheets of paper. The known examples are contained in a 252-leaf volume that is now held in the library of the Institut de France. More pressed material in the Herbarium of the Muséum National d'Histoire Naturelle in Paris contains what is clearly part of the same shrub, but a plate published in Humboldt and Bonpland's *Nova genera et species* (1822–23), produced with Carl Sigismund Kunth, may suggest that the original collection had been supplemented by additional material, possibly cultivated from seeds collected on the expedition.

ATANASIO ECHEVERRÍA Y GODOY

Erythrina variegata, c.1787–1803
Watercolour on paper, 24 × 35 cm / 9½ × 13¾ in
Hunt Institute, Pittsburgh, Pennsylvania

The late eighteenth-century Mexican artist Atanasio Echeverría y Godoy painted only the key elements of *Erythrina divaricata* (now known as *E. variegata*), a tree widely distributed in the tropics and subtropics, where it is used in traditional medicine. Flowers soon lose their colour in the heat, so the artist had to work quickly. Godoy spent over ten years travelling in Mexico, Cuba, Puerto Rico and the Pacific Coast with a team of Spanish botanists led by Martín de Sessé y Lacasta and José Mariano Mociño. Between 1787 and 1799 Echeverría and his colleagues accumulated over 1,800 botanical studies of potentially valuable plants. The expedition's records reached Spain in 1804, during the Napoleonic Wars, and it was only in 1815 that Mociño took them to Geneva, where the botanist Augustin Pyramus de Candolle made hurried duplicates before Mociño returned to Barcelona. Some eight years later Candolle named a genus of American flowering plants *Echeveria* after the artist, who became Director of Art at the Real Academia de San Carlos in Mexico City. The original material from the expedition was discovered in the library of the Torner family in Barcelona in 1980; much is now in the Hunt Institute in Pittsburgh.

Plates from *Concise British Flora in Colour*, 1965
Lithograph, 28.8 × 19.2 cm / 10¼ × 7½ in
Private collection

These carefully designed plates with close-fitting – but not overlapping – illustrations of the leaves, flowers and seeds of British wild plants are each identified by a carefully lettered label. They date from 1965, when the Reverend William Keble Martin published his *Concise British Flora in Colour*. The book quickly became a best-seller, establishing itself as the most authoritative illustrated flora, accessible equally to amateurs and more expert botanists. The groundbreaking book was the result of six decades of work as Keble Martin built up more than 1,400 plant portraits based on careful field studies: he was eighty-eight when the book finally appeared. Each plate is an individual work of art, with the plant portraits arranged in an aesthetically pleasing design and the related species displayed together for comparison. Keble Martin distilled the essence of each wild plant and flower into a portrait that not only is artistically pleasing but also captures the key features of each species, facilitating accurate identification – and demonstrating that botanically accurate paintings are usually superior to photographs in field guides. In 1967 the Post Office honoured Keble Martin's work by issuing British Flora commemorative stamps, bearing a selection of his beautiful paintings.

ROGER PHILLIPS

Winter aconite (*Eranthis hyemalis*), c.1977, from *The Wild Flowers of Britain*, 1977
Colour Cibachrome photograph, 13 × 10.5 cm / 5¼ × 4¼ in
Victoria and Albert Museum, London

Eranthis hyemalis, a member of the buttercup family and one of the earliest harbingers of spring, pushes up its yellow flower ahead of a neat ruff of leaves, even through a covering of snow. This sample, collected in 1977, was one of hundreds of wild flowers that fuelled the photographer Roger Phillips's enthusiasm on country expeditions with his young son. Using the photographic skills he had acquired in a career in advertising and applying them to botany, Phillips embarked on creating *The Wild Flowers of Britain* (1977), the first of more than twenty field guides he would produce with the botanist Martyn Rix, pioneering the use of photography for botanical illustration. A crate of water-filled milk bottles would rattle in the back of his car as he hastened back to his studio with samples, ready to photograph them with a De Vere large-format camera and Ektachrome transparency film. Clean white backgrounds and clinical, specimen-like layouts allow each detail to be examined closely. Phillips chose to photograph flowers in the order in which they flowered – as in seventeenth-century florilegia – with the aim of opening botany up to the general reader. In the decades since his first book appeared, Phillips has recorded more than 30,000 images, making him arguably the most prolific contemporary creator of plant illustrations.

Untitled, 1930
Gelatin silver print, 28.8 × 22.6 cm / 11¼ × 8¾ in
Museum of Modern Art, New York

The low camera angle and diagonal cropped composition of Man Ray's portrait of arum lilies (*Zantedeschia aethiopica*) enhances their ambiguous flattened, sculptural shapes and emphasizes the sensuality of the petals of this highly symbolic flower. Not actually a lily but an aroid, the plant has for centuries been associated with faith and purity. It is native to South Africa, where it was traditionally used to dress wounds – despite the fact that the plant is poisonous – but the arum lily (also known as the calla lily) was known to European botanists by the 1660s and is today one of the most popular ornamental plants in the world. Man Ray's photograph uses a technique discovered by his assistant and muse Lee Miller and known as solarization, which achieves a distinctive reversal of tones and dark outlines by exposing the photographic paper to light during developing. Such an experimental use of darkroom techniques helped to make Man Ray one of the most influential artists of the twentieth century. A key member of the Surrealist and Dada movements, his photographs – he also painted, sculpted and made films – defined new territory, elevating the medium beyond the functional and commercial to become truly recognized as artistic.

SPIROS HADJIDJANOS

Acanthus mollis, 2014
Alumide 3D print, 29.8 × 23.8 × 4.8 cm / 11¾ × 9¼ × 1¾ in
Private collection

This image of *Acanthus mollis* represents a revolutionary approache to botanical art. In *Urformen der Kunst (Art Forms in Nature*; 1928) by the German photographer Karl Blossfeldt (see p.86), highly magnified images were used to reveal the structures of plants and animals. In 2014 Blossfeldt's photographs were used by the Greek artist Spiros Hadjidjanos – who frequently works with plants – to generate a series of three-dimensional prints. Hadjid-janos scanned the original and used a series of algorithms to generate a three-dimensional image printed as a series of thousands of aluminium-nylon spikes of varying heights. The result is both a resurrection of the original plant and the creation of what is in many ways a fossil: the traces of a living, breathing plant preserved in solid form. In one variation of the work, Hadjidjanos placed the three-dimensional image behind a transparent screen on which he projected a video of the plant's reflection in moving water; in front was a dried *A. mollis* from Athens, close to where Blossfeldt had collected his own specimen.

DAVID KANDEL

naimen vnd würckung.   xxij

Das waffer / oder ein kochung von Roßmarein vnd Dictam gemacht /
feübert vnd heilet die faulen wunden / als des krebs / des wolffs / vnd der fi=
ftelen.
    Fomenta vnd bäder auß Roßmarein gemacht / haben die art der zamen
Müntzen / des Dictams vnd Poleyen.

Von Lafander vnd Spica / cap. xviij.

Lafander vnnd Spica / wie wol die zwen ftauden einander faft änlich
    feindt / mit wurtzeln / holtz / blettern / ftengelen / blümen / vñ famen. So   Caßid
ift doch der Spica in gemelten dingen / dem Lafander überlegen. Das aber   Nardus
die zwen ftauden nit einer art fein / kan ein jeder am geruch wol fülen. Dañ
Spica reücht faft anderft / vnd vil ftercker / dann Lafander . Die ftengel
feind an jn bedē vierecket / ein wenig hol. Die bletter gantz Æfchfarb grün /
breiter vnd lenger dañ der Roßmarin hat. Die blümen difer ftauden wach=
fen am oberftē des ftengels / wie ein Spica / oder äher am weyß oder dinckel
thūt. An welcher äher vil kleiner braun bloer blümlin wachfen. Der Some
                                                         D iiij

Lavender (*Lavandula*), from *Kreüter Buch*, 1546
Wood engraving, 12.9 × 13 cm / 5 × 5¼ in
Peter H. Raven Library, Missouri Botanical Garden, St Louis

These two types of lavender are drawn with remarkable detail for the middle of the sixteenth century, when they were created in Germany. The artist, David Kandel, differentiates carefully between the shape and arrangement of leaves on the two plants and the different arrangements of the root systems, one wide and fairly shallow, the other thicker and deeper. On the left, the characteristic purple flowers are starting to go to seed. The accompanying German text explains the plant's use in medicine. Kandel was a prolific illustrator who often added scenes of emblematic human activity to his plant portraits; since he was not specifically trained as a botanical artist, he frequently copied his plants from illustrations already published in recent German herbals by Otto Brunfels (see p.187) and Leonhart Fuchs. The lavenders are among some 550 distinctive plant portraits Kandel created for the botanist and physician Hieronymus Bock, who wrote under the Latin name of Tragus (both names mean 'goat'). Bock, who had published his herbal or *Kreüter Buch* in 1539, commissioned Kandel to illustrate the second edition, of 1546. Further editions followed in the sixteenth century, in Latin as well as in German, spreading Kandel's work throughout Europe.

322

Cannabis Plant, 2014
Colour-enhanced scanning electron micrograph (SEM),
dimensions variable

This alien form could be seen as the visual equivalent of being stoned. Beneath a scanning electron micrograph (SEM), the surface of the bracts on the cannabis plant inflorescence are magnified thirty-five times and its key parts illuminated. The small multicoloured pompoms are globules of resin on short glandular cells that contain tetrahydrocannabinol (THC), the active component of cannabis when used as a drug. Cannabis has been cultivated for centuries for a range of different uses. Classified by Carl Linnaeus in 1753, it is recognized today as having three main cultivars, although the distinction between them is nominal. The plant is grown and harvested differently according to its intended use: forms with long stems and few branches for their fibre and those with many seeds for the extraction of hemp oil. For medicinal or recreational use, flowers hold more cannabinoids – psychoactive chemical compounds – than the leaves, and it is the preparation of the flowers that is known as marijuana. Historically, medicinal and spiritual use has included ointments, teas and tinctures. Ted Kinsman, who created this image, is an assistant professor of photographic technology at the Rochester Institute of Technology in New York State, and his time-lapse films of flowers blooming have appeared in many commercials, music videos and films.

ZADOK BEN-DAVID

Blackflowers, 2010–12
Painted hand-cut aluminium, dimensions variable
Private collection

One of the most important qualities of any flower is its colour, so to reduce foxgloves, hibiscus and lilies to flat black shapes forces us to see the blooms anew. This is the game the Israel-born artist Zadok Ben-David plays with his audience, manipulating the viewer into undertaking a fresh exploration of each flower. His *Blackflowers* installation sets fifty-three different flowers against a white field. The sculptor takes his inspiration from botanical illustrations, which he reproduces on a vastly increased scale, laser-cutting the shapes from sheets of aluminium to create three-dimensional objects that sit on white bases. He paints each flower the same shade of black, and gives each its own foreshortened shadow and its own name – which bears no direct relation to the floral specimen it represents. Building on his widely seen *Blackfield* installation (2006–9), which comprised thousands of small hand-cut aluminium flowers embedded in sand, the London-based artist's installation of black flowers on a pure white field creates a permanent structure that causes the viewer to reconsider the transient quality of any flower and its fragile beauty. We see the flowers through Ben-David's perception, just as Victorian readers viewed flowers through the eyes of botanical illustrators. As Ben-David says, 'Like a magician, I enjoy surprising people, making them wonder.'

01

02

03

04

c. 9400 BC Fig cultivation is already taking place. An archaeological dig in Gilgal in the Jordan Valley, of a Neolithic house believed to be 11,400 years old, has produced figs lacking embryonic seeds, something that does not occur naturally.

c. 7000 BC In Africa, farming replaces simple 'gathering' to overcome the long periods of drought that had previously caused food shortages in eastern Sahara. Seeds start to be planted intentionally for food.

c. 5000 BC Flax is discovered, and, being one of the strongest natural fibres known at the time, it becomes the principal material for weaving cloth in ancient Egypt. The flax harvest is much celebrated as a festival.

c. 5000 A wide range of crops begins to be cultivated in Mesoamerica, including gourds, avocado, chilli pepper and cotton.

c. 4000 BC The Austronesian-speaking peoples start to cultivate rice.

c. 3500 BC Frankincense begins to be imported from the Arabian Peninsula to Mesopotamia.

c. 3000 BC In the early civilizations of Mesopotamia, Crete and Egypt, plant representations are scarce or far more simplistically drawn than those of animals and people.

Inhabitants of the Indus Valley in what is now Pakistan are weaving cloth from the fibres of the cotton plant.

Records show that olives are being grown extensively on the island of Crete by this time.

c. 2000 BC The medicinal use of *Aloe vera* is recorded on Egyptian papyri.

'Eranda' (*Ricinus communis*) is used in lamps and medicinally, as a laxative and purgative.

A Mediterranean cypress tree known as the Cypress of Abarkuh (*Cupressus sempervirens*), still alive today, is believed to have started growing in Iran. It is 25 metres (82 feet) high with a circumference of 18 metres (59 feet).

Gourds and squashes begin to be cultivated in the settlements of South America.

c. 1900 BC Farming begins in Peru.

c. 1600 BC On the island of Santorini, an unknown Minoan artist draws what is thought to be the red-flowered Greek lily (*Lilium chalcedonicum*). This may be the earliest extant botanical painting.
↑ 01, see p. 186

c. 1500 BC A frieze of 275 plants in the tomb of Thutmose III in Karnak, Egypt, depicts all the plants then known in Syria, which the Egyptians had recently conquered.

c. 1465 BC The fifth pharaoh of the Eighteenth Dynasty of Egypt, Hatshepsut, sends a trading expedition to Punt (thought to be Somalia or Arabia) to bring back aromatic resins for incense-making.

1352 BC Akhenaten accedes to the throne of Egypt; he encourages a less stylized form of art, including images of wheat and farming. ↑ 02, see p. 45

c. 1100 BC The first attempt is made to catalogue plants, in the sacred Indian texts known as the Avestan Writings.

c. 1000 BC A red cypress (*Chamaecyparis formosensis*) known as the Alishan Sacred Tree is said to have started growing in Taiwan. It is still alive today.

Wine made from grapes becomes widespread. It was previously made from dates, and beer from barley.

c. 800 BC The Etruscans, experts in horticultural engineering, cultivate the broccoli plant we know today. When it is introduced into England in the mid-eighteenth century, it is known as Italian asparagus.

c. 605 BC Work begins on the Hanging Gardens of Babylon.

c. 500 BC The practice of infusing tea leaves begins in China.

500 BC Greek coins are engraved with representations of important economic and cultural crops, including wheat, olives and silphion, a plant used for its resin.

440 BC The Greek writer Herodotus reports that the Scythians use cannabis in their steam baths.

c. 400 BC The island of Socotra in the Indian Ocean is annexed by the Greeks for its medicinal aloes. Legend has it that Alexander the Great acts on the advice of Aristotle, because he needs stronger aloe plants to heal his wounded soldiers.

c. 326 BC The fruit of *Citrus medica* is introduced into the West after Alexander the Great discovers it in India.

c. 300 BC The scientific study of plants is established in ancient Greece by the philosopher, scientist and 'father of botany' Theophrastus (died 287 BC), a pupil of Aristotle. His celebrated *Historia Plantarum* (*Enquiry into Plants*) survives today only in note form.

c. AD 3 Roman farmers build terraces on the Mosel River in order to cultivate grapes.

c. AD 30 A concoction for pain relief containing celery seeds is described by the Roman encyclopaedist Aulus Celsus in *De Medicina*.

c. AD 50 Dioscorides lists 600 species of plant and animal with curative properties in his *De Materia Medica*, which becomes a standard work for the next 1,500 years.

c. AD 210 Death of Galen, a Roman physician whose medical theories subsequently dominate European medicine for 1,500 years.

c. AD 400 A Roman writer known only as Pseudo-Apuleius writes a Latin herbal, which is influential in Europe for some 500 years.

AD 512 The *Vienna Dioscorides* or *Codex Vindobonensis*, an illuminated Greek manuscript, is produced by this date in Constantinople (now Istanbul) and contains about 435 full-page illustrations of plants; it is the oldest known illustrated version of the works of Dioscorides. ↑ 03, see p. 146

AD 538 Buddhist missionaries introduce flower-arranging to Japan; the craft later becomes known as *ikebana*.

AD 552 Agents from Byzantium impersonating monks smuggle silkworms and mulberry leaves to Europe in hollowed-out walking sticks, breaking China's monopoly on the production of silk.

AD 581–618 The earliest surviving Chinese scroll painting of a landscape is created by Chan Tzu-Chien in Beijing.

c. AD 600 The *Codex Neapolitanus*, a copy of Dioscorides' manuscript, is created in Constantinople.

AD 794 End of the Nara period in Japan. The habit of viewing cherry blossom is by now well established.

c. AD 896 Death of Abu Hanifa al-Dinawari, considered to be the founder of Arabic botany for his *Book of Plants*, a six-volume work that describes plant cycles and the production of flowers and fruit; the surviving portion describes 627 plants.

1030 King Duncan I of Scotland is said to have defeated an army of Danes by distributing a drink made from the berries of belladonna.

1090 The Hashashin group – from which we get the word assassin – is founded by Hassan-i Sabbah. Targeting Persian rulers for six centuries, the assassins were given hashish, derived from the cannabis plant, before every mission to steady their nerves.

c. 1100 The Song Dynasty emperor Huizong (Hui Tsung) accedes to the Chinese throne; he awards prizes to encourage court painters to depict the natural world accurately, from observation, in 'bird and flower' paintings.

c. 1121 Lambert, Canon of Saint-Omer, completes his encyclopedic *Liber Floridus* in France, including illustrations of biblical plants. ↑ 04, see p. 20

1190 Matthaeus Platearius, a physician at the School of Salerno, writes *Circa Instans*, a medicinal herbal.

1199 The *Book of Theriac*, based on the works of Galen, is written and illustrated in northern Iraq.

c. 1200 The apothecary's rose, *R. gallica* var. *officinalis*, becomes the foundation of a large medical industry around Provins, France, in the thirteenth century.

1200 Tibetan monks have by now completed the *Gyuschi*, a compilation of Tibetan medicines extracted from herbs, roots and minerals, often served as hot teas.

1200s Japanese farmers grow the banana for its fibre, which is woven into cloth.

1228 The writer Bihnam the Christian includes the first known nature print in a manuscript of Dioscorides created in Anatolia or Syria.

1248 Death of Ibn al-Baitar, a Spanish Islamic pharmacist and botanist who served as chief herbalist to the Ayyubid sultan al-Kamil and compiled two influential compendia of Islamic medical knowledge, including *Compendium on Simple Medicaments and Foods*, which lists 1,400 plants and foods and their uses.

1252 The future Edward I of England marries Eleanor of Castile, who brings gardeners from her native lands in Spain, introducing peaches and quinces to the royal garden.

c. 1272 The term 'green fingers' is understood to have derived from the passion of Edward I of England for green peas. It is said that after hours of pea-shelling, the servant with the greenest fingers would win a prize.

1280 The Venetian merchant and traveller Marco Polo is the first person to describe coconut trees, after seeing them in Sumatra.

05

06

07

08

c.1300   *Tractatus de Herbis*, a medicinal herbal, is created in Salerno near Naples.

Monastic illuminators begin to draw plants based on observation, rather than copying from earlier sources.

1348   Painful plague swellings called buboes are lanced and then treated with a mixture of tree resin, the root of the white lily and dried human excrement. The resulting concoction is applied to the open wounds.

1350s   Giovanni Boccaccio's character Neifile sings of the thorny rose and the lily white in his book *The Decameron*.

1380s   Geoffrey Chaucer's Wife of Bath compares herself to a flower's pith in the *Canterbury Tales*.

1403   When Venetians take over the city-state of Padua, production of the artistically innovative *Carrara Herbal* is abandoned with only fifty illustrations complete. ↑ 05, see p.80

1410–16   Farming scenes are included in the *Très Riches Heures*, a book of hours produced for the French Duc de Berry by the Limbourg brothers.

1418   The woodcut process is used to reproduce drawings in Germany.

c.1430   The Van Eyck brothers include highly accurate depictions of lilies and irises in the Ghent Altarpiece.

1430s   The first recorded use of intaglio printing in Europe is in Germany, to manufacture playing cards.

c.1439   Johannes Gutenberg introduces printing with movable type to Europe.

1447   Pope Nicholas V sets aside part of the Vatican grounds for a garden of medical plants that are used to promote the teaching of botany.

c.1450   Coffee beans are brewed for the first time in a Sufi monastery in Yemen, and recipes are recorded.

1461   The first European woodcut book illustration appears.

c.1470   The convention of decorating the margins of illuminated manuscripts with tendrils and curlicues is replaced by the use of realistic paintings of flowers.

1475   An edition of *The Book of Nature* by Konrad von Megenberg contains two woodcuts; they are the first printed botanical illustrations in Europe. ↑ 06, see p.150

Michael Wolgemut begins to improve German methods of woodcutting.

1477   A lavish Book of Hours is prepared for Mary of Burgundy.

c.1480   Around this time, English nobles commission many illuminated Books of Hours from Flanders, often with depictions of flowers in the margins.

1481   The first printed flower illustrations are published in Rome in the *Herbarium Apulei*, copied from hand-illustrated manuscripts.

1485   German printer Peter Schoeffer publishes the *Herbarius Latinus*, containing 379 woodcuts, 65 of which are believed to have been drawn from life.

1492   Christopher Columbus lands on Hispaniola in the Caribbean, initiating the Great Columbian Exchange, in which, over the following centuries, plants and animals native to the Old World (Europe) and the New World (the Americas) are transferred between hemispheres.

1493   Sweet oranges from East Asia are cultivated in Europe by this time, and Columbus introduces both oranges and lemons to the Americas on his second voyage; three years later he presents a pineapple from Guadeloupe to King Ferdinand of Spain.

1497   The Portuguese navigator Vasco da Gama sails around the Cape of Good Hope, opening a sea route to the Indian Ocean and the Spice Islands of what is now Indonesia.

Portuguese explorers discover Brazil, which is named after its plentiful – and commercially valuable – brazilwood trees.

c.1500   Millefleurs tapestries portraying complex designs of hundreds of flowers are woven in Flanders and northern France for an aristocratic clientele in England and elsewhere. ↑ 07, see p.156

The value of eating citrus fruit to prevent or cure scurvy has been established.

1502   Portuguese traders introduce peanuts from Argentina, Brazil and Peru to Africa.

c.1503   Albrecht Dürer paints a full-size image of an iris; in the same year he paints his celebrated *Great Piece of Turf*. ↑ 08, see p.263

1505   The Portuguese exploit wild cinnamon growing in Ceylon (now Sri Lanka), establishing a monopoly on the trade.

1506   Spanish colonists in the West Indies begin growing sugar cane from Southeast Asia.

1508   The first use of woodcut printing with coloured blocks in Germany; the growing accuracy of printing techniques allows the dissemination of knowledge about plant reproduction and structure.

c.1510   Leonardo da Vinci makes a study of the star of Bethlehem, one of his few surviving sketches of flowers; among the others is a nature print of a sage leaf.

1511   Afonso de Albuquerque conquers the city of Malacca (which dominates sea trade between China and India) for Portugal, which has a monopoly over the early maritime spice trade between the Moluccas or Spice Islands (now Maluku) and Europe.

1515–19   Coffee from Arabia appears in Europe.

1516   The first processed sugar is shipped from the Caribbean to Spain; soon afterwards Portugal begins to import sugar from Brazil.

Spanish colonists introduce the banana to the New World (Hispaniola) from Africa.

1520   Under Suleiman the Magnificent, Ottoman nobles grow hyacinths, tulips and other bulbs in Turkey.

Chocolate, a luxury drink among the Aztec in Mexico, is introduced to Spain.

1520s   Ginger arrives in Mexico, probably from East Asia; from there it is transported to Europe.

1527   The Spanish conquest of the Aztec is complete; the conquistadors bring back to Spain plants including tomato, avocado, papaya and vanilla.

1529   Maize from America, grown in Turkey, is introduced to England as 'turkey corn'.

c.1530   Wheat is introduced to China, where it becomes a staple crop in areas where rice is not grown.

Laudanum processed from opium is introduced as a pain reliever.

1530–36   The modern age of botanical illustration begins with the publication of the *Herbarum Vivae Eicones* (*Living Pictures of Plants*) by Otto Brunfels, with illustrations by Hans Weiditz.

1533   In Italy, the University of Padua establishes a professorship in botany, separating plant study from medicine for the first time.

1535   The herbalist Leonhart Fuchs founds a Hortus Medicus (medicinal garden) at Tübingen in Germany.

Gonzalo Fernández de Oviedo y Valdés draws the first illustration of a pineapple.

1537   The potato is introduced to Europe from South America, but is only slowly accepted.

1538   The name 'carnation' makes its first appearance; the flower's ancient Greek name was *dianthus* (still used today), 'flower of Zeus'.

1541   The French explorer Jacques Cartier introduces the cabbage to Canada.

1542   Leonhart Fuchs publishes his *De Historia Stirpium*, the first modern herbal, illustrated by Albrecht Meyer.

1543   One of the first physic gardens is established by Luca Ghini at the University of Pisa. He creates Europe's first herbarium in 1551.

A Tuscan physician named Pietro Andrea Mattioli suggests the tomato, recently introduced from the Americas, might be edible.

1545   Orto Botanico di Padova, the second botanic garden in Europe, is founded by the Venetian Republic in Padua, Italy.

1546   Hieronymus Bock (also known as Tragus) commissions David Kandel to illustrate his herbal *Kreuter Buch*, one of the first to include plant descriptions from first-hand observation, rather than copying the work of Dioscorides.

1554   Tulips are sent to Europe from Turkey.

1556   The cultivation of tobacco begins in Europe.

1559   Conrad Gessner records the earliest known instance of a cultivated tulip flowering in Europe, in the garden of Johann Heinrich Herwart in Augsburg, Germany.

09

10

11

12

13

1562 William Cecil builds the first conservatory in England, at Burghley House in Lincolnshire, to protect his subtropical plants and trees.

1565 The French botanist Carolus Clusius becomes interested in growing bulbs.

1568 Ulisse Aldrovandi founds one of the earliest botanic gardens, at Bologna University, where he is a professor of natural sciences and a noted plant collector and illustrator.

1569 The Spanish physician Nicolás Monardes publishes *The Joyful News*, which lists many new plants, including tobacco and the first mention of a sunflower.

1570 Potatoes can be purchased in markets in Seville.

1573 The botanist and physician Leonhard Rauwolf begins three years of plant-collecting in Asia Minor and the Middle East; this leads to the creation of Germany's first herbarium of dried plants.

The peanut is introduced into China from the Americas, probably by Portuguese sailors who had docked in Brazil.

1576 The crown imperial (*Fritillaria imperialis*) is introduced into Europe via Constantinople (now Istanbul).

Carolus Clusius publishes a flora of Spain and Portugal, the first national flora in Europe.

1580 The Spanish *Florentine Codex* records the assets of South America, and cites the agave as an important source of food for the local population.

1583 *De Plantis Libri*, the first modern classification of plants, is published by Andrea Cesalpino. It is claimed by some experts to be the first general botanical work to supersede ancient writings.

c.1585 The artist and adventurer Jacques le Moyne de Morgues produces the flower illustrations that distinguish his later career.

1588 Tabernaemontanus (Jacob Theodor) publishes a herbal, the *Neuw Kreuterbuch*. The woodcuts are reused to illustrate John Gerard's *Herball*.

c.1590 The invention of the microscope encourages the detailed study of plant anatomy and sexual reproduction, and the first experiments in plant physiology.

1590s The white potato is known as the bastard potato because it is considered inferior to the sweet potato.

c.1591 The Flemish artist Joris Hoefnagel is commissioned to illustrate the spectacular *Mira Calligraphiae Monumenta* (*Miraculous Moments of Calligraphy*). ↑ 09, see p.101

1592 *De Plantis Aegypti* by Prosper Alpini includes the first known picture of a coffee plant.

1593 Carolus Clusius establishes the Hortus Academicus in Leiden, the first botanic garden in the Netherlands, and begins to grow tulips in earnest.

The French botanist Pierre Richer de Belleval founds the first botanic garden in France, at Montpellier.

1595 The death of Sultan Murad III in Turkey is marked by the planting of 500,000 hyacinths.

1596 Publication of *Pen Ts'ao Kang Mu*, the best-known of early Chinese herbals.

1597 John Gerard publishes his *Herball*, using old Flemish and German woodcuts from Christophe Plantin's collection, and creating a demand in England for such publications.

c.1599 The first known cabinet of curiosities is created, containing unusual plants, minerals and animals.

c.1600 Engraving and etching are introduced as means for printing botanical illustrations.

Jan Brueghel the Elder earns the nickname 'Flower' for his skill with floral still lifes.

King Christian IV of Denmark founds the Copenhagen Botanic Garden.

1603 The Flemish physician Adriaan van den Spiegel publishes instructions for drying herbarium specimens.

1606 Thousands of black mulberry trees are imported to England by James I in an unsuccessful attempt to start a silk industry, which requires the white mulberry tree in order to succeed.

1607 Francisco Hernández de Toledo, court physician to the king of Spain, publishes the *Index Medicamentorum* in Mexico City, the first herbal of Spanish America, after seven years of cataloguing.

1608 Pierre Valet publishes *Le jardin du roy très chrestien Henry IV* (1608). ↑ 10, see p.68

1609 John Tradescant the Elder is appointed gardener to Robert Cecil, first Earl of Salisbury, at Hatfield House in Hertfordshire; Tradescant is sent abroad to visit famous gardens and nurseries and bring back exotic plants. ↑ 11, see p.264

1610 Tea is first imported to Europe by the Dutch East India Company.

1611 The renowned map engraver Theodore de Bry and his son-in-law Matthew Merian publish *Florilegium Novum*.

1612 English colonists in Virginia begin growing tobacco for export.

Emanuel Sweert, Dutch florist and prefect of gardens for Emperor Rudolf II, publishes *Florilegium* as a guide to his stock for the Frankfurt Fair of 1612. ↑ 12, see p.228

1613 The first double hyacinth is illustrated in *Hortus Eystettensis* by Basilius Besler, one of the most important florilegia of the seventeenth century.

1614 The Dutch Van de Passe brothers begin publication of their *Hortus Floridus* at a time when such florilegia are becoming more popular. ↑ 13, see p.138

1619 The passion flower, a South American native seen as symbolic of Christ's Crucifixion, blooms for the first time in Italy.

1620s The compound microscope is invented in the Netherlands, although its specific inventor is uncertain; in Italy, Galileo Galilei makes a microscope in 1625.

1621 The first potatoes, native to the Andes, are planted in Germany.

The University of Oxford Botanic Garden is founded.

1622 *Theatrum Florae* by Daniel Rabel is published.

1629 The English botanist John Parkinson publishes *Paradisi in Sole Paradisus Terrestris*, possibly the most famous English gardening book of the seventeenth century; his descriptions of 100 species of daffodil help to ensure the plant's popularity.

1632 Work begins on the Taj Mahal, later renowned both for its gardens and for the carved flowers decorating its walls.

c.1633 Mohammad Khan illustrates the *Dara Shikoh Album* for the Mughal prince of the same name.

1634 The paying of inflated prices for tulip cultivars in The Netherlands leads to the development of so-called Tulipomania. At its height over the next few years, single bulbs change hands for many times the average annual income.

1635 The Jardin du Roi (now Jardin des Plantes), a garden of medicinal herbs, is established in Paris by King Louis XIII.

1636 Jacques-Philippe Cornut publishes the first herbal of French territory in New France (Canada), illustrated by Pierre Valet.

1637 An outbreak of bubonic plague in Haarlem helps to end the tulip boom in The Netherlands.

John Tradescant the Younger makes his first trip to Virginia; he returns to England with specimens of bald cypress (*Taxodium distichum*) and American sycamore (*Platanus occidentalis*). In subsequent years he also brings back the tulip tree and red maple, among other species.

1638 The Hortus Medicus (later Hortus Botanicus) opens in Amsterdam as a garden of medicinal herbs. Rare plants imported by the Dutch East India Company make it a centre for research.

1640 John Parkinson publishes the *Theatrum Botanicum*, a compendium of more than 4,000 plants.

1645 Nicolas Robert begins painting the plants at the Château de Blois in the Loire for Gaston d'Orléans, younger brother of Louis XIII; his works become the foundation of the *Vélins du Roi* (depictions on vellum of plants from the royal gardens).

The first coffee house in Europe opens in Venice.

1646 Vincenzo Leonardi illustrates the *Hesperides sive de Malorum Aureorum Culture et Usi Libri Quatuor* by Giovanni Battista Ferrari, about citrus fruit, for the collector Cassiano dal Pozzo.

1647 Rice from Asia is first grown in Virginia.

14

15

16

17

1650 The London gentleman gardener Alexander Marshal begins working on his *Florilegium*; the project will take him about thirty years. ↑14, see p.303

1651 *Rerum Medicarum Novae Hispaniae …* records an early exploration of the natural history of the New World in 1570 by Francisco Hernández de Toledo.

1652 Pasqua Rosée, a Greek immigrant from Sicily, opens the first coffee house in London.

The Dutch East India Company sets up a permanent base at the Cape in South Africa, causing a rapid spread of African flora to Amsterdam and Leiden, transported by traders.

The English apothecary Nicholas Culpeper publishes *The English Physician*. *The Complete Herbal* is published the following year.

1656 The Jesuit priest Michał Boym publishes *Flora sinensis*, which includes depictions of plants he has observed in China and India in a book on the Jesuit mission in China. ↑15, see p.194

1658 Oliver Cromwell, ruler of the English Commonwealth, dies from malaria; it is said that he refused to take quinine – from the cinchona tree – because it was introduced to Europe from South America by Catholic Jesuits.

The first advertisement for tea appears in England.

1661 The Dutch increasingly take control of the lucrative spice trade with the Spice Islands in the East Indies.

The first mention occurs of a pineapple grown in England.

1662 The Royal Society of London for Improving Natural Knowledge (more commonly known as the Royal Society) is formed.

1664 First mention of the calla lily (*Zantedeschia aethiopica*), an import from South Africa, occurs in the Royal Garden in Paris.

1665 The English natural philosopher Robert Hooke publishes *Micrographia*, the first book to feature illustrations of plants and animals beneath the microscope.

1668 Jacob van Meurs provides engravings for *New Description of Africa* by Olfert Dapper, despite the fact that neither of them has ever visited Africa.

1669 Robert Morison becomes Professor of Botany at Magdalen College, Oxford; this represents the first recognition of botany as an academic discipline in England. Three years later he draws up the first classification of umbellifers.

1673 Foundation of London's Chelsea Physic Garden by the Society of Apothecaries. It soon becomes the foremost botanic garden in Europe.

1675–77 German botanical illustrator Maria Sibylla Merian publishes *Blumenbuch*.

1676 British troops at Jamestown in North America are drugged after eating *Datura stramonium*, which becomes known as Jimson weed.

1678 Hendrik van Reede tot Drakestein, the Dutch governor of Malabar, brings together teams of artists and local Brahmins to draw plants accurately in Cochin, eventually published in the *Hortus Malabaricus*. ↑16, see p.313

The English clergyman and naturalist John Banister sends plants from North America to his patron Bishop Henry Compton at Fulham Palace in London, including *Magnolia virginiana* and *Rhododendron viscosum*.

1680 Paul Hermann becomes the first professional botanist to visit the Cape in South Africa, on his way to Ceylon (now Sri Lanka).

1682 The first botanic garden in Japan is founded as the Koishikawa Medicinal Herb Garden; it is now the Botanical Garden of the University of Tokyo.

In his book *The Anatomy of Plants*, English plant anatomist and physiologist Nehemiah Grew suggests that plants reproduce sexually.

1686 The English botanist John Ray begins publication of the *Historia Plantarum*, a three-volume systematic record of the natural world and a precursor to the Swedish botanist Carl Linnaeus's taxonomy in its use of species for classification.

1689 William of Orange and Queen Mary ascend to the English throne. As keen plant collectors, they help to elevate botany to royal status. The collection of specimens enters a new era, in which botanists make use of state-sponsored expeditions to bring back plants for the Glass Case Garden at Hampton Court Palace, and further private collections.

1690s The British East India Company begins to import cheap cotton and calico fabric from India.

1693 Hans Sloane records the first grapefruit in Jamaica; it probably originated there as a result of accidental hybridization between other cultivated citrus.

1694 Joseph Pitton de Tournefort publishes *Elemens de botanique*, illustrated by Claude Aubriet.

1697 Father Francisco Cupani publishes the first scientific description of the Sicilian plant *Lathyrus odoratus*, the wild ancestor of today's sweet pea.

1699 The English sailor William Dampier explores the western coast of Australia with an artist who makes drawings of previously unknown plants.

Maria Sibylla Merian moves to the Dutch colony of Suriname to document and paint its insects and plants.

c.1705 Ogata Kōrin paints irises on a folding screen covered in gold foil; the painting is now one of Japan's national treasures. ↑17, see p.296

1705 Maria Sibylla Merian publishes *Metamorphosis Insectorum Surinamensium*, a survey of insects and plants in Suriname.

1709 Giovanni Maria Farina opens a perfumery in Cologne; he will produce the renowned *eau de cologne* using scent from the bergamot bitter orange.

The Chinese imperial garden Yuan Ming Yuan (Garden of Perfect Brightness) is constructed near Beijing during the reign of the Kangxi Emperor.

1712 Engelbert Kaempfer publishes *Amoenitates Exoticae*, an illustrated account of his travels in Asia.

1714 Czar Peter I of Russia founds a herb garden in St Petersburg as the basis of a botanical institution. It later becomes the St Petersburg Botanical Garden.

Amédée-François Frézier, a French spy, introduces the Chilean strawberry to Europe. Later crossed with the Virginian strawberry, it creates the garden strawberry we know today (identified in 1765).

1716 The English gardener Thomas Fairchild produces the first artificial hybrid by brushing pollen from a sweet william on to the stigma of a carnation, using a feather.

1720 The Japanese shogun Tokugawa Yoshimune plants the famous cherry trees in Asukayama Park in Edo (now Tokyo).

The Dutch botanist Henry Telende puts a mixture of tanner's bark (oak bark) and horse manure into glass frames to produce heat and create 'bark stoves', in which exotics such as pineapples can be grown.

1721 The final Calico Act bans the import of cheap Indian cotton and calico to Britain.

1723 Gabriel de Clieu, a French naval officer, carries a single coffee tree from Paris to Martinique; within fifty years it yields thousands of trees.

1728 The American horticulturalist John Bartram founds the oldest surviving botanic garden in North America, Bartram's Garden in Philadelphia.

1730 The Dutch pharmacist Albertus Seba discovers a method of preserving botanical specimens by accelerating the rotting process to reveal the internal skeleton of the leaves.

The first illustrated nursery catalogue is produced, for the London nurseryman Robert Furber by Pieter Casteels.

1731 Philip Miller writes the first comprehensive *Gardener's Dictionary* in London.

The English naturalist Mark Catesby begins publishing his *Natural History of Carolina, Florida and the Bahama Islands*, the first published natural history of North America.

1732 The German botanist Johann Jacob Dillenius publishes *Hortus Elthamensis*, with 417 drawings of plants in the garden of James Sherard at Eltham, near London.

The first seed of Levant cotton (*Gossypium herbaceum*) is sent from the Chelsea Physic Garden (founded 1673) in London to Georgia in North America.

1733 Georg Dionysius Ehret meets the Nuremberg physician Christoph Jacob Trew, who becomes his lifelong patron. Trew later publishes *Hortus Nitidissimis...* (1750–92), a huge work that extends over forty years and features the work of many leading illustrators of the time, including Ehret, Barbara Regina Dietzsch and August Wilhelm Sievert.

1735 Carl Linnaeus publishes *Systema Naturae*, laying out a new system for classifying plants according to the way they reproduce.

1736 Georg Dionysius Ehret publishes the first illustration of the sexual system of plant classification devised by Carl Linnaeus.

18

19

20

21

22

1737 In North America, Benjamin Franklin experiments with nature printing, using real leaves on banknotes to deter counterfeiters.

Elizabeth Blackwell starts illustrating and publishing her *Curious Herbal* in London to pay off debts incurred by her husband, who is in debtors' prison. ↑ 18, see p.64

A southern magnolia (*Magnolia grandiflora*) introduced from southeastern North America flowers in London.

Swedish botanist Carl Linnaeus publishes *Hortus Cliffortianus*, a catalogue of the garden of the Dutch banker and plant-collector George Clifford.

1742 Madeleine Basseporte becomes Royal Painter to King Louis XV in France.

1745 The ambitious eight-volume *Phytanthoza Iconographia* by the German botanist and apothecary Johann Weinmann is completed, with 1,025 copper engravings depicting more than 4,000 plants.

1746 Christopher Tärnström becomes the first of Carl Linnaeus's seventeen 'apostles' when he leaves Sweden for China to collect plants for the great botanist. He dies of fever before he has sent back a single specimen, leaving a young family, and after that Linnaeus recruits only single men as plant collectors.

c.1750 Florist societies begin to appear in northern England, bringing together growers of particular genera; tulips, pinks, hyacinths, auriculas and ranunculus are among the most popular types.

1752 Albertus Seba's vast collection of natural specimens is auctioned for high prices. Objects remain in natural history museums and zoological institutes around the world today.

1753 In *Species Plantarum*, Linnaeus develops a workable classification system (still in use today) that can be applied to all plants, and creates a modern system of naming plants by genus and species rather than with long phrases. This enables the many new species being discovered around the globe to be classified and named consistently.

1755 The Dutch botanist Nikolaus Joseph von Jacquin is appointed head of imperial gardens at Schönbrunn in Vienna and sent to the West Indies to collect plants.

King Ferdinand VI founds the Real Jardín Botánico de Madrid for the study of plants from the Spanish empire.

1758 Church of England rector Edward Stone first investigates willow bark as a herbal medicine. Salicin, its active ingredient, later becomes known as aspirin.

Swedish botanist Anton Rolandsson Martin, one of Linnaeus's 'apostles', brings lichens and mosses back to Sweden after a brief visit to the island of Spitsbergen in the Arctic Ocean.

1759 Madame de Pompadour, mistress of King Louis XV, has 200 types of hyacinth grown under glass at Versailles; such fashionability helps the flower's popularity to spread in Europe.

Scottish botanist William Aiton is recruited from the Chelsea Physic Garden to run a new botanic garden at Kew created by Princess Augusta of Saxe-Gotha, the Dowager Princess of Wales; it is the forerunner of the Royal Botanic Gardens, Kew.

1760 Kew receives one of its first tropical orchids, *Epidendrum rigidum*.

1761 The German botanist Joseph Gottlieb Kölreuter is the first scientist to report making hybrids between plants, and to observe the role of insects in pollination.

Work begins on the *Flora Danica*, a national flora of Denmark. ↑ 19, see p.238

1762 A ginkgo tree is brought from Asia and planted in Kew Gardens. Still alive today, it is the oldest surviving example in England.

1763 Carl Linnaeus receives the first plates from Johannes Gessner showing 'group portraits' of plants in Linnaean families. ↑ 20, see p.29

The first botanic garden at Cambridge University is founded by Dr Richard Walker, Vice-Master of Trinity College

Governor Arthur Dobbs of North Carolina discovers the carnivorous plant now known as the Venus flytrap. In 1770 the first picture of the plant in Britain is made by John Ellis.

1765 American botanist, horticulturalist and explorer John Bartram and his son William discover a rare tree in Georgia. In 1785 it is named *Franklinia alatamaha* after Benjamin Franklin.

c.1765 The Japanese colour woodblock printing technique called *nishiki-e* is perfected.

1768 The Ancient Society of York Florists is founded, the world's oldest horticultural association.

Philip Miller finally accepts Carl Linnaeus's binomial nomenclature in the eighth edition of his *Gardener's Dictionary*.

1770 The Dutch East India Company destroys an entire year's supply of nutmeg and cloves with the goal of maintaining high prices for spices in Europe.

John Ellis writes *Directions for Bringing Over Plants and Seeds from the East Indies and Other Distant Countries ...*, in which he details the difficulty of transporting botanical specimens.

Joseph Priestley coins the name 'rubber' for the natural latex of the South American tree *Hevea brasiliensis*.

Lieutenant James Cook lands at Botany Bay in Australia on the *Endeavour*, with the naturalists Joseph Banks and Daniel Solander on board, together with the artist Sydney Parkinson. ↑ 21, see p.311

1770s Kew sends the Scottish plant hunter Francis Masson to the Cape in South Africa to gather its remarkable indigenous plants, including *Stapelia*.

1771 William Curtis founds his own botanic garden in London; in 1779 he opens it to the public.

Mary Delany begins making découpage paper flowers at the age of seventy-one; she will make more than 1,000.

Joseph Priestley discovers that plants convert carbon dioxide into oxygen.

1772 George III appoints Joseph Banks as scientific advisor for Britain's royal gardens, including Kew.

1773 The French explorer Pierre Poivre steals propagation material for clove, nutmeg, cinnamon and black pepper from the Dutch-controlled Molucca Islands and takes them to Mauritius and Réunion, thus breaking the Dutch monopoly on the spice trade.

William Curtis becomes director of the Chelsea Physic Garden for five years.

1776 The Declaration of Independence asserts North America's intention to become independent from British rule.

1777 The first illustration is produced (in England) of the South African bird of paradise plant, *Strelitzia reginae*.

A French botanist smuggles cacti and cochineal insects out of Mexico to try to break the Spanish monopoly on the purple dye cochineal, but the plants fail to thrive in the French Caribbean colonies.

1780 The Dombey Affair, a diplomatic incident, is caused when the French botanist Joseph Dombey sends part of his herbarium of Peruvian flora home and it is seized by a British ship and sent instead to the British Museum in London.

1783 Spanish botanists led by José Mutis begin the Royal Botanical Expedition to New Granada on behalf of the Crown; it lasts until 1816. The illustrators include Francisco Javier Matís. ↑ 22, see p.242

1784 Carl Peter Thunberg, one of Carl Linnaeus's 'apostles', publishes *Flora Japonica*, a record of fifteen months spent cataloguing the plants of Japan.

The first seed business in North America is established in Philadelphia.

1785 The botanist and physician William Witherington publishes the first scientific explanation of the effects of digitalis from the foxglove.

1786 Pierre-Joseph Redouté, one of the most famous of all botanical artists, starts work cataloguing specimens at the Jardin du Roi (now the Jardin des Plantes) in Paris.

The Austrian botanical illustrator Ferdinand Bauer produces 1,500 sketches of eastern Mediterranean plants observed on his journey with Oxford professor John Sibthorp in Greece and Turkey.

1787 *Curtis's Botanical Magazine* is first published by William Curtis; today it is the world's oldest continuously published colour-illustrated periodical.

Kew botanists coax the tropical orchid *Prosthechea cochleata*, or cockleshell orchid, to bloom for the first time in Britain. Their success leads many botanical enthusiasts to try cultivating these mysterious plants.

Sydenham Edwards becomes the main artist for *Curtis's Botanical Magazine*; over the next twenty-eight years he contributes hundreds of illustrations to the journal.

A team of Spanish botanists, including the Mexican artist Atanasio Echeverría y Godoy and Juan Vicente de la Cerda, begin a twelve-year expedition in Mexico and the Caribbean, seeking plants that will benefit Spain economically.

Colonel Robert Kyd of the British East India Company sets up a botanic garden at Sibpur outside Calcutta to grow plants of economic benefit; it is now the Acharya Jagadish Chandra Bose Indian Botanic Garden. Among its accomplishments is the introduction of the tea plant to India from China.

23

24

25

26

27

1787   *HMS Bounty*, under the command of Lieutenant Bligh, collects breadfruit trees from Tahiti to export to Britain's Caribbean colonies; the ship's crew mutinies on the journey in 1789.

1788   Joseph Jacob Plenck begins publishing the immense *Icones Plantarum Medicinalium ...*, an eight-volume survey of 758 common medicinal plants from Europe.

The Linnean Society is founded in Britain under the direction of James Edward Smith, who has purchased the herbarium of the late Carl Linnaeus with the help of Joseph Banks.

1789   US Secretary of State Thomas Jefferson begins a career of introducing plants to North America, including vanilla, tea and the tomato.

1790   The Scottish surgeon and naturalist Archibald Menzies travels with the English naval officer Captain George Vancouver on his expedition to the Pacific Northwest, collecting herbarium specimens.

The German poet Johann Wolfgang van Goethe suggests that the organs of flowering plants are all modifications of the basic leaf form.

James Sowerby begins a collaboration with James Edward Smith that will produce thirty-six volumes of *English Botany*.

Joseph Banks appoints the Austrian Franz Bauer the first botanical artist in residence at the Royal Botanic Gardens at Kew.

Crown Prince Frederik of Denmark orders a dinner service decorated with illustrations from *Flora Danica*, which began publication in 1761. The service is intended as a gift for Catherine the Great of Russia, who dies before its completion.

Chrysanthemums are introduced into England from China.

1791   William Bartram publishes *Bartram's Travels*, a record of his plant expeditions in the southern United States.

1793   Christian Conrad Sprengel publishes the landmark work *The Secret of Nature Revealed*, using his own illustrations to show how instrumental insects are to plant fertilization. The information is later used by Charles Darwin.

The Vélins du Roi are moved to the new Muséum Nationale d'Histoire Naturelle during the French Revolution.

The American inventor Eli Whitney patents the cotton gin, dramatically increasing the growth of the cotton industry in the southern United States.

1799   The polymath Alexander von Humboldt and botanist Aimé Bonpland begin a five-year collecting and exploring trip to North, Central and South America.

A Collection of Roses from Nature is published by the British botanical artist Mary Lawrance.

The Englishman John Lyon begins collecting North American plants; he may have contributed to the extinction of the Franklin tree by his aggressive collecting.

1799–   *The Temple of Flora* is published; the
1807   ambitious tribute to the work of Carl Linnaeus by various artists and the botanist Robert John Thornton is a commercial disaster. ↑ 23, see p.94

1801   Gérard van Spaendonck completes the second volume of *Fleurs dessinées d'après nature*; his illustrations are frequently hailed as the best flower engravings of all time.

Japanese gardeners develop gardens at Horikiri on the edge of Edo (now Tokyo) for growing irises.

Ferdinand Bauer sails with Matthew Flinders on his two-year voyage around the Australian coast.

1802   The first seeds to be sold in packages in America are marketed by a Shaker community in Enfield, Connecticut.

1803   Étienne-Pierre Ventenat publishes *Jardin de la Malmaison*, describing the exotic plants in the garden of the French empress Joséphine.

Morphine is extracted from the resin of the opium poppy; it becomes a popular painkiller.

The first garden dahlia is grown in Britain.

1804   Meriwether Lewis and William Clark set off to cross North America and reach the Pacific; they discover dozens of plants unknown to science, including bitterroot (*Lewisia rediviva*), blue flax (*Linum lewisii*) and the California rhododendron (*R. macrophyllum*).

The first shipload of bananas arrives in New York, but the fruit does not become popular in North America until after the Civil War.

The Horticultural Society of London (now the Royal Horticultural Society) is founded.

The Japanese devil lily (*Lilium lancifolium*) is cultivated at Kew; today it is known as tiger lily.

1805   Alexander von Humboldt publishes his *Essai sur la géographie des plantes*, often identified as the beginning of the science of ecology.

Pierre-Joseph Redouté is appointed official flower painter to Empress Joséphine, and records the flowers in her garden at Malmaison near Paris.

1806   Publication begins of the *Flora Graeca* by John Sibthorp and Ferdinand Bauer; this flora of Greece is one of the world's botanical masterworks. ↑ 24, see p.10

1807   William Wordsworth publishes 'Daffodils', a renowned poem of the Romantic movement.

1809   The Botanischer Garten München is founded in Munich, Bavaria.

1810   Robert Brown publishes *Prodromus Florae Novae Hollandiae et Insulae Van Diemen*, his first publication on the flora of Australia.

1812   George Brookshaw publishes *Pomona Britannica*, featuring 256 kinds of British fruit. ↑ 25, see p.147

The English tea inspector John Reeves travels to China and begins collecting scientific botanical and zoological paintings by Chinese artists through the British East India Company.

The Norwegian people are spared starvation by using elm bark to make bread.

1813   The French government publishes a botanical and agricultural survey of the country, undertaken over six years by the Swiss botanist Augustin Pyramus de Candolle. Candolle coins the word 'taxonomy' to describe his new system of plant classification. His theory that plant species compete with one another is influential on Charles Darwin's theory of evolution. Today, scientists refer to the Darwin-Wallace theory of evolution.

1815   Sydenham Edwards founds his magazine, the *Botanical Register*.

1816   The Sydney Botanical Garden is founded in Australia.

John Reeves introduces *Wisteria sinensis* to Europe from China.

1817   The first Bourbon rose, a chance hybrid, is discovered growing on the French Isle de Bourbon (now Réunion) in the Indian Ocean.

Jacob Bigelow publishes the first volume of *American Medical Botany ...*, the first such book in America to be printed in colour. ↑ 26, see p.176

1817   Franz Bauer produces *Strelitzia depicta*, containing what are regarded as the first botanical illustrations to be produced using the new technique of lithography. ↑ 27, see p.15

1820s   The botanist Carl Friedrich Philipp von Martius and the zoologist Johann Baptist Ritter von Spix visit Brazil; the result is the much later *Flora Brasiliensis*.

The glasshouse becomes a popular garden feature for the wealthy.

1820   The United States Botanic Garden is created in the grounds of the Capitol in Washington, DC.

French chemists isolate quinine from the bark of the cinchona tree, making possible the production of a chemically synthesized treatment for malaria.

1822   Sir Stamford Raffles, the founder of modern Singapore, develops a botanic and experimental garden at Fort Canning.

1823   The British East India Company employees Charles Alexander and Robert Bruce discover a previously unknown tea in Assam, in northern India.

1824   The Scottish botanist David Douglas begins the second of three plant collecting expeditions to North America on behalf of the The Horticultural Society of London (later the Royal Horticultural Society), from which he introduces to Britain the Douglas fir and other timber trees, as well as garden plants. In all, he introduces about 240 species to Britain.

Pierre-Joseph Redouté completes his masterpiece, *Les Roses*.

1826   An act of the US Congress sets off a short-lived mania for planting mulberry trees for silkworms.

William Jackson Hooker becomes editor of *Curtis's Botanical Magazine*, a position he occupies until his death in 1865.

1827   The National Horticultural Society of France is founded.

John James Audubon publishes the first part of *Birds of America*, a huge ornithological survey, in which plants play a prominent part as backgrounds to the birds.

1828   Publication begins of *Honzo zufu*, one of the most important Japanese botanical works.

1829   Two banana plants are shipped from Mauritius to England. One of the plants is purchased by the Duke of Devonshire's gardener Joseph Paxton, who successfully propagates it.

28

29

30

31

32

1830s Rhododendrons are introduced to Western Europe from India.

Lithography comes to replace copperplate engraving as the most up-to-date method of printing illustrations.

1831–6 During his long voyage around the world on the *Beagle*, Charles Darwin becomes increasingly convinced that species could, and did, evolve.

1832 Some 137 different European weeds are noted as being naturalized in the flora of New York.

c.1834 The Japanese artist Katsushika Hokusai paints his series of woodblocks known as *Large Flowers*, which strongly influence later Impressionist art in Europe.

1834 Walter Hood Fitch publishes his first plate in *Curtis's Botanical Magazine*, after being sought out as an artist by William Jackson Hooker. This is his first of more than 10,000 published illustrations, including 500 for Hooker's *Icones Plantarum*.

1836 The Wakefield and North of England Tulip Society is established; today, it is the last remaining of numerous tulip societies that were formed in the north of England in the eighteenth and nineteenth centuries.

1838 The German botanist Matthias Schleiden discovers that all living plant tissue is composed of cells.

The United States Exploring Expedition sets out to survey the Pacific Ocean and its surrounding lands. It collects more than 60,000 plant and animal specimens from the Pacific islands.

The first recorded shipment of tropical orchids arrives in the United States.

1839 China goes to war with Britain to prevent the British importing opium to China from their colony in India.

The prickly pear cactus is introduced to Australia for use as a hedging plant; it later becomes a serious pest.

1840 Kew becomes Britain's national botanic garden.

1841 *The Gardener's Chronicle* begins publication, with John Lindley as its horticultural editor.

1843 The Scottish botanist and plant-hunter Robert Fortune makes the first of four journeys to China, and brings many specimens back to England. He becomes best known for introducing tea plants from China to India in 1848.

1844 William Henry Fox Talbot begins publishing the first photographic book, *The Pencil of Nature*. ↑ 28, see p.221

1845 After the abolition of 'window' tax, the falling price of glass allows more people to have a glasshouse in which to grow exotic plants.

A potato blight begins in Ireland that devastates the country's principal crop, leaving millions of people starving and forcing many to emigrate to North America, England, Scotland, Wales and Australia.

While plant-hunting for The Horticultural Society of London (now the Royal Horticultural Society), Robert Fortune discovers winter jasmine (*Jasminum nudiflorum*) near Shanghai.

1847 The English botanist Joseph Dalton Hooker (son of William Jackson Hooker) begins a three-year expedition to the Himalayas. He introduces 43 rhododendron species to England, which were used to breed hardy hybrid rhododendrons. ↑ 29, see p.248

1848 The National Herbarium in the United States is founded, with specimens collected by the US Exploring Expedition in the Pacific.

Alfred Russel Wallace sets off with Henry Bates to South America in an attempt to discover the mechanism driving evolution. He remained in South America until 1852.

1849 The British botanist Richard Spruce begins a fifteen-year exploration of the Amazon basin and the Andes, where he collects more than 30,000 specimens.

English gardener and architect Joseph Paxton manages to get the *Victoria amazonica* to flower for the first time in the UK, in a specially constructed glasshouse at Chatsworth in Derbyshire. ↑ 30, see p.267

1850 The Parisian seed firm Vilmorin-Andrieux begins to publish large posters of vegetables and fruit to accompany its annual seed catalogues. ↑ 31, see p.107

1851 Joseph Paxton's Crystal Palace is designed and constructed for the Great Exhibition. It is modelled on the structure of the glasshouse he built at Chatsworth to house the *Victoria amazonica*.

The London nurseryman Hugh Low discovers the giant pitcher plant (*Nepenthes rajah*) in Borneo.

1852 The first edition of *The Orchid Grower's Manual* is published in Britain, where collecting and growing orchids reaches a remarkable level, dubbed 'Orchidelerium'. The author Benjamin S. Williams later becomes the proprietor of the Victoria & Paradise Nurseries in Holloway, London.

1853 The giant waterlily blooms outside its natural habitat for the first time in America under the care of Caleb Cope, president of the Pennsylvania Horticultural Society.

A herbarium is begun at the Royal Botanic Garden in Sydney, Australia, with 1,800 specimens assembled by its director of gardens, Charles Moore.

Austrian Alois Auer publishes *The Discovery of the Natural Printing Process: An Invention*, instructing readers in nature printing. ↑ 32, see p.145

A herbarium is founded at Hunter House, Kew Gardens. Today it houses more than seven million specimens.

1854 Commodore Matthew Perry arrives in Japan, forcing it to open its borders to trade with the West; early Japanese exports include irises and maples.

Alfred Russel Wallace begins an eight-year exploration of the East Indies. He discovers the 'Wallace Line' of evolution between the Australian and Asian flora and fauna.

1855 The writer Charles Kingsley (known for *The Water Babies*) coins the term 'pteridomania' to describe the Victorian passion for ferns, which began in the late 1830s but reaches its height between 1850 and 1890.

1856 The British horticulturalist and plant hybridiser John Dominy obtains blooms from the first artificial orchid hybrid, *Calanthe × dominii*.

1858 During his expedition to Southeast Asia, Alfred Russel Wallace sends an article to Charles Darwin outlining a theory of evolution. The article is published along with a description of Darwin's theory the same year.

1859 Charles Darwin's groundbreaking work, *On the Origin of Species*, is published.

After a false start in the 1820s, a botanic garden is founded in Singapore.

The influential Missouri Botanic Garden is founded by businessman Henry Shaw.

1860 The English creator of 'nature prints', Henry Bradbury, commits suicide after the Austrian pioneer of the process, Alois Auer, accuses him of plagiarism.

1861 The Horticultural Society of London receives its Royal Charter and becomes the Royal Horticultural Society.

1862 Charles Darwin publishes the first thorough study of orchid pollination.

William Morris designs his first flower-inspired wallpaper. 'Trellis' is issued two years later.

Specimens obtained by Jean Pierre Armand David from China form the basis of *Plantae Davidianae*, in which Adrien René Franchet of the museum at the Jardin des Plantes describes nearly 1,500 new species.

1863–4 Berthe Hoola van Nooten publishes her survey of plants in Java, using the new technique of chromolithography.

1864 The American diplomat and philologist George Perkins Marsh publishes *Man and Nature*, an early work of ecology in which he argues that deforestation could lead to desertification.

The first International Botanical Congress is held in Brussels.

1866 Gregor Mendel, considered to be the father of modern genetics, publishes *Experiments in Plant Hybridisation*, which establishes the laws of inheritance; he has spent years studying the genetic traits of *Pisum sativum*, the pea plant.

La Société botanique de France organizes the fourth International Congress in Paris, with the express aim of establishing laws of botanical nomenclature.

1867 The French breeder Jean-Baptiste Guillot introduces the first hybrid tea rose, 'La France'.

1869 The US businessman James Arnold leaves $100,000 in his will to advance agriculture and horticulture. His executors award the money to Harvard University to establish the arboretum that now bears his name; its first director is Charles Sprague Sargent.

33

34

35

36

37

1872 Farmers in Florida begin growing sweet oranges, having obtained seed from New Orleans.

The current trend among Western artists to copy Japanese art, fashion and aesthetics is dubbed 'Le Japonisme' in France.

1875 The British colonial government takes control of Singapore Botanic Gardens. Over the following decades, Kew-trained botanists develop the gardens into an important botanical institute.

1877 Frederick William Burbidge travels to Borneo on behalf of London nurserymen James Veitch & Sons to collect orchids and other exotic plants.

British traders send seed of the rubber tree (*Hevea brasiliensis*) from Brazil to establish plantations in Malaya.

1878 Harry Veitch of James Veitch & Sons sends the botanist Charles Curtis to Mauritius and Madagascar to collect exotic plants. Curtis returns with many specimens, including *Angraecum sesquipedale* (Darwin's orchid).

Matilda Smith begins her forty-five-year association with *Curtis's Botanical Magazine*, supplying the publication with some 2,300 botanical illustrations.

1880 Prompted by Charles Darwin and Alfred Russel Wallace's wife Annie, Marianne North travels to Australia and New Zealand and spends more than a year there painting exotic flora. ↑ 33, see p.154

1881 Frederick Sander, the 'Orchid King', buys a 1.6-hectare (4-acre) plot in St Albans, Hertfordshire, for his glasshouses; he does more to encourage England's orchid craze than any other individual.

1882 A German nurseryman, Louis Boehmer, begins exporting Japanese plants from Yokohama to the West; the trade is soon taken over by Japanese merchants.

The Marianne North Gallery opens at Kew Gardens to display the artist's work.

Ogawa Kazumasa becomes the first Japanese person to study photography in the West when he moves to Boston, Massachusetts. After returning to Japan he opens his own collotype business and produces exquisite images of flowers.

1883 The first greenhouse is built in Japan by Viscount Itsujin Fukuba, who imports a collection of tropical orchids from England and France.

1884 The English publisher George Routledge brings out *The Language of Flowers*, illustrated by Kate Greenaway.

1885 Sponsored by the Royal Horticultural Society, the first Orchid Conference takes place in London, with plants supplied by Kew Gardens.

1889 Husband-and-wife team of illustrator Sarah Ann Featon and writer Edward Featon publish New Zealand's first full-colour art book, *The Art Album of New Zealand Flora*, to dispel the myth that the country has no flowers.

A gigantic aroid from Sumatra (*Amorphophallus titanum*) flowers for the first time in cultivation at Kew Gardens. It is more commonly known as the corpse flower because of its smell. ↑ 34, see p.276

1890s The writer and artist Beatrix Potter develops an interest in mycology, the study of fungi, and produces exquisite illustrations of various specimens.

c.1890 Claude Monet buys the house he has been renting in Giverny and starts creating the garden featured in so many of his paintings.

1890 Leopold Blaschka and his son Rudolf sign an exclusive ten-year contract to make glass flowers for Harvard University. The association lasts until Rudolf retires, in 1938. ↑ 35, see p.285

1891 The New York Botanical Garden is founded with help from the Torrey Botanical Club, for botanists wishing to identify plants brought back from expeditions.

1893 The American Fern Society is established.

The American botanist and horticulturalist Luther Burbank publishes *New Creations in Fruits and Flowers*, detailing some of the hundreds of new varieties he has created through cross-breeding on his estate in Santa Rosa, California; they include the russet Burbank potato, today the most widely cultivated potato in the United States.

1896 The busy Lizzie (*Impatiens walleriana*) is introduced to North America from the island of Zanzibar.

1897 The first orchid-growing society is founded in Manchester, England.

1898 The German biologist and vocal supporter of Darwin's theories, Ernst Haeckel, begins publishing *Art Forms in Nature*. Printed in part form, ten plates at a time, it is finally complete in 1904. ↑ 36, see p.12

1899 A pathogen, *Fusarium oxysporum*, spreads through banana plantations in many countries, devastating crops.

The LuEsther Mertz Library is founded at the New York Botanical Garden to provide a research base for the growing field of botany as an academic discipline.

c.1900 Morphine adiction becomes so prevalent in the United States that the St James Society offers to post heroin, gratis, to anyone wishing to give up the habit.

1902 Barbara McClintock is born in Hartford, Conneticut. She becomes one of the world's greatest experts in cytology, the study of cell structure, function and chemistry.

1903 Henry E. Huntington buys the San Marino Ranch in California, a working ranch with orchards, citrus groves, crops and livestock. The ranch has become the Huntington Botanical Gardens, with more than a dozen gardens housed in 120 acres.

1904 Nurseryman Frederick Sander offers a £10,000 reward (about £110,000 in today's money) to the first person to send him a particular Asian slipper orchid (*Paphiopedilum fairrieanum*) and for exclusive intelligence of its location.

Chestnut blight (*Cryphonectria parasitica*) is unintentionally introduced into the USA from Japanese nursery stock. First discovered in New York's Zoological Garden, by 1940 most of the country's mature chestnut trees have been wiped out.

1906 In Olton, Warwickshire, Edith Holden begins to write and illustrate a diary. Seventy-one years later, the diary was published under the title *The Country Diary of an Edwardian Lady*.

Famed photographer Edward Steichen starts breeding delphiniums. In 1913 the French Horticultural Society awarded him a gold medal, and several of his hybrids were used in Monet's garden in Giverny.

1907 The potato cultivar 'Irish Cobbler' is introduced to Japan, where it becomes the most popular type of potato. White potatoes are now one of the five major crops in Japan.

1908 The first commercially grown avocados in the United States are planted in California for Henry E. Huntington at his San Marino ranch (now the Huntington Botanical Gardens).

English botanist Arthur Harry Church publishes the first part of *Types of Floral Mechanism*, with his own illustrations. The book explores floral morphology. ↑ 37, see p.60

Olive cultivation begins on Shodo Island. Japan is now considered one of the centres of world olive production.

The white carnation becomes the symbol of Mother's Day in America when the founder of the holiday, Ann Jarvis, turns up at the first official celebration with 500 blooms.

1910 Foundation of the Brooklyn Botanic Garden, a 52-acre garden in the borough of Brooklyn, New York City.

1912 Tokyo mayor Yukio Ozaki sends Japanese cherry trees to the city of Washington. Since 1935 a Cherry Blossom Festival has been held annually.

1913 Foundation of Kirstenbosch National Botanical Garden in South Africa, at the base of Table Mountain in Cape Town.

Artist Maud H. Purdy joins the new Brooklyn Botanical Garden, where she works as an illustrator for thirty-two years.

1914 Renowned British horticulturalist, plantsman and garden writer Edward August Bowles publishes his first book, *My Garden in Spring*.

1915 Richard Willstätter earns a Nobel Prize in chemistry 'for his researches on plant pigments, especially chlorophyll'.

The famous poppy fields of WWI begin to bloom in the war-ravaged soils of France and Belgium.

1916 Elizabeth White – daughter of a New Jersey cranberry grower – and botanist Frederick Coville harvest and sell the first crop of blueberries in Whitesbog, New Jersey.

1918 Maryland votes the black-eyed Susan (*Rudbeckia hirta*) its state flower.

1919 American botanists Nathaniel Lord Briton and Joseph Nelson Rose begin publishing *The Cactaceae*, illustrated by English artist Mary Emily Eaton.

38

39

40

41

42

1920 American botanist and inventor George Washington Carver, a former slave in Missouri, addresses the Peanut Growers Association at a national conference supporting a tariff on imported peanuts. His reputation was founded on his research into and promotion of crops such as peanuts and sweet potatoes as an alternative to cotton.

1921 The American Orchid Society is founded. The society now boasts a worldwide membership.

1922 The American Horticultural Society and the National Horticultural Society are founded concurrently. The organisations are merged in 1926 and the name 'The American Horticultural Society' retained.

Cornell University scientist Dr Lewis Knudson discovers that orchid seeds placed in a mixture of water, sugar and agar (a viscous substance derived from seaweed) successfully germinate.

1923 Foundation of the Japanese Society for Horticultural Science.

1924 Plant collector Frank Kingdon-Ward collects seeds of the famed blue poppy (*Meconopsis betonicifolia*) in an area of Tibet he described as 'the wooded hills east of sacred Lhasa'.

1925 Imogen Cunningham, a photographer renowned for her botanical images, completes a two-year in-depth study of the magnolia flower.

1927 British artist John Nash publishes *Poisonous Plants: Deadly, Dangerous and Suspect*, a book he both writes and illustrates. ↑38, see p.50

1928 Karl Blossfeldt, German photographer, sculptor, teacher and artist, publishes the seminal *Urformen der Kunst,* using close-up photographs of plants and animals to reveal the architectural nature of their structures. The book made Blossfeldt internationally famous at the age of 63. ↑39, see p.86

1929 Foundation of the Cactus and Succulent Society of America in Pasadena, California. The society is now affiliated with over 80 clubs and has thousands of members across the globe.

1930 Man Ray and Lee Miller develop the technique of solarization, a phenomenon in photography in which the image recorded on a negative or on a photographic print is wholly or partially reversed in tone.

1931 Foundation of the Jardin Botanique Montréal in Canada. A year later the mayor of Montréal, Camilien Houde, hires for the project unemployed workers affected by the Great Depression.

1934 The jasmine (*Jasminum sambac*) becomes the official flower of the Philippines.

English-born American plant physiologist Kenneth V. Thimann isolates pure auxin, a key plant growth hormone.

1935 Founding of the Liberty Hyde Bailey Hortorium, part of Cornell University, the premier institute in the United States for horticultural science.

1936 Blooms created by photographer and delphinium breeder Edward Steichen are displayed for a week at the Museum of Modern Art in New York. As yet this is the only dedicated flower show presented by MoMA. The flowers were of varying hues, and some of the 'Steichen Strain' delphiniums were 2 metres (6 feet) tall.

With a programme entitled 'Autumn Pruning by C.H. Middleton', Cecil Middleton becomes the first gardening presenter on television. The BBC had created a garden in the grounds of their studios in Alexandra Palace, north London.

1937 The Nobel Prize is awarded to Albert Szent-Györgyi in the field of physiology or medicine with 'special reference to vitamin C and the catalysis of fumaric acid'.

George Russell, a renowned lupin breeder, is awarded the highest award bestowed by the Royal Horticultural Society for developing a strain of fabulous lupins. This 'jobbing Yorkshire gardener' has finally agreed to sell his creations commercially a year later.

1942 The Horticultural Society of India is founded in Lyallpur (now Punjab province in Pakistan) with the aim of promoting the science and practice of horticulture.

1943 Russian scientist Nikolai Vavilov dies during the siege of Leningrad. Credited with collecting over 220,000 seeds and tubers from 64 countries, he suffered terribly at the hands of Stalin in the Great Purge of the 1930s. When the Nazis cut off food to Leningrad, Vavilov and his team protected his seed collection from the starving residents of the city. Many of the scientists, including Vavilov, died of starvation.

1945 In the USA, the Conrad-Pyle Company introduces the hybrid tea rose 'Peace', which was developed by French horti-culturalist Francis Meilland before the war. Coincidentally, the rose is announced the same day Berlin falls and the war is declared over.

1948 *Curtis's Botanical Magazine* introduces colour printing to replace lithographs, ending the tradition of hand-colouring that had been used in this publication for years.

1949 A group of twenty flower bulb exporters come up with a plan to turn the Keukenhof (kitchen garden) in Lisse, Netherlands into a permanent spring garden. More than seven million flowers (daffodils, tulips, hyacinths) cover an area of 32 hectares.

Research by British scientist Kathleen Drew-Baker leads to the development of the nori (edible seaweed) industry in Japan.

1950 Foundation of the US National Science Foundation.

Publication of *Variation and Evolution in Plants* by the US botanist George Ledyard Stebbins, combining Darwinian natural selection and modern genetics to produce a modern evolutionary synthesis.

1950s American biologist, humanitarian and Nobel laureate Norman Borlaug creates new varieties of disease-resistant dwarf wheat, which produce high yields and are credited with saving millions of lives around the world.

1952 British illustrator Margaret Mee moves to Brazil to teach art in the British school of São Paulo. She becomes a botanical artist for São Paulo's Instituto e Botânico in 1958. ↑40, see p.41

1956 Trials begin of the human contraceptive pill in the USA. Scientists M.C. Chang of China and American Gregory G. Pincus settled on three active ingredients derived from the wild Mexican yam, having experimented with more than 200 substances.

1958 Extracts from the [common] Madagascar periwinkle (*Catharanthus roseus*) – vincristine and vinblastine – are found to have powerful anti-cancer properties. The compounds have been used in chemotherapy drugs since the early 1960s.

The National Seed Storage Laboratory, the main US seedbank, is established in Fort Collins, Colorado. Its long-term aim is to preserve seeds of crops vital to US agriculture.

Founding of the Hunt Institute for Botanical Documentation within Carnegie Mellon University.

1959 Foundation of the International Society for Horticultural Science, to promote horticultural co-operation between nations.

1960 Robert Burns Woodward, an American organic chemist, synthesises chlorophyll for the first time.

1962 The Flower Association of Japan is founded.

American marine biologist and conservationist Rachel Carson publishes *Silent Spring*, an indictment of the indiscriminate use of pesticides in agriculture. The book and her subsequent writings become major works in the birth of the modern environmental movement.

1964 Andy Warhol produces *1964 Flowers* based on a photograph of hibiscus blooms.

The celebrated Scottish musician and leading light in the post-war folksong revival Rory McEwen gives up music to devote himself to botanical painting. ↑41, see p.271

1965 The Reverend William Keble Martin, British priest, botanist and botanical illustrator, publishes *The Concise British Flora*. The book contains over 1,400 paintings in colour and myriad black and white drawings. ↑42, see p.318

1968 William S. Gaud, former United States Agency for International Development (USAID) director, coins the phrase 'Green Revolution' in response to increased agricultural production worldwide, particularly in the developing world.

1970 American biologist and humanitarian Norman Borlaug is awarded the Nobel Peace Prize in recognition of his contribution to world peace. His development of high-yielding dwarf wheat strains is seen as a world-stabilising influence by increasing food supply.

The first list of endangered plants suggests that 20,000 species need some form of protection to ensure they survive.

1972 Fresh from Virginia Commonwealth University, Alice Tangerini is employed as illustrator in the Botanical Department of the Smithsonian National Museum of Natural History. She goes on to illustrate more than 1,000 plants, many of them new to science.

1977 *Wild Flowers of Britain*, by Roger Phillips, is one of the first guidebooks to use photographs for flower identification. It sells over 400,000 copies within five years.

Tulips and Tulipomania, by Wilfrid Blunt, is published with illustrations by musician-turned-botanical-artist Rory McEwen. Blunt was an art teacher, author and artist and had taught McEwen at Eton College.

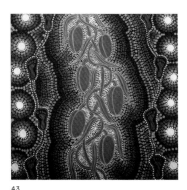

43

44

45

46

1980 American scientists join Chinese colleagues for the first Sino-American Botanical Expedition since 1949. One of the key destinations is the Metasequoia valley in Luchaun Xian, where a tree found in the fossil record (*Metasequoia glyptostroboides*) was found living in the 1940s.

1981 Publication begins of the three-volume work *The Banksias* by Celia Rosser. It is the first time such a large genus has been illustrated in its entirety by a single botanical artist.

1983 The American scientist Barbara McClintock is awarded the Nobel Prize for her discovery of genetic transposition. She demonstrates that genes are responsible for activating and deactivating physical traits.

1984 The New York Botanical Garden introduces a certificate programme in botanical art.

The Hawaii Tropical Botanical Garden is opened to the public. It was the brainchild of Dan Lutkenhouse, a man with no botanical training, who had been creating the site in the Onomea Valley since 1977.

1988 World-renowned botanical artist Auriol Batten publishes *Flowers of Southern Africa*.

A posthumous exhibition of the flower paintings of musician-turned-botanical-artist Rory McEwen is held at London's Serpentine Gallery.

Artist Margaret Mee makes her fourteenth expedition to the Amazon to paint the midnight flowering of the nocturnal cactus *Selenicereus wittii*. She is tragically killed in a car crash in England later that year.

1989 Foundation of the South African Society for Horticultural Sciences. Its mission is to promote horticultural science in South Africa and neighbouring countries.

c.1990 The Aboriginal artist Marie Ryder begins painting her *Bush Tucker Dreamings*. ↑ 43, see p.83

1992 The United Nations Conference on Environment and Development, the first international Earth Summit, establishes the Convention on Biological Diversity, and there is agreement on the Climate Change Convention.

1993 Anne-Marie Evans, botanical illustrator and teacher, publishes her influential *An Approach to Botanical Painting*, laying out a five-step approach that she puts into practice as a teacher of botanical illustration at the Chelsea Physic Garden in London.

1994 *Australian Rainforest Fruits: A Field Guide* is published by author Wendy Cooper and artist William T. Cooper.

Science Press (Beijing) and Missouri Botanical Garden (St Louis, USA), begin joint publication of *Flora of China*, the first modern English-language account of China's 31,000 vascular plants.

Christabel King becomes chief botanical artist at Kew Gardens. ↑ 44, see p.108

The Flavr-Savr tomato is the first genetically modified crop approved for human consumption and commercial marketing.

Foundation of the American Society of Botanical Artists.

1995 The Chelsea Physic Garden Florilegium Society is founded by the first graduates of the garden's diploma course in botanical illustration. The Society's primary aim is to record in paintings and drawings the plants present in the Physic Garden.

1997 The *Vienna Dioscorides*, a sixth-century Greek manuscript of *De Materia Medica* by Dioscorides is inscribed in UNESCO's Memory of the World programme. The manuscript contains over 400 images of animals and plants.

1999 Vera Scarth-Johnson, renowned botanist and botanical illustrator, dies. From the 1960s she collected native plants from the Endeavor River Valley of Queensland, Australia, completing 160 illustrations before her death.

2000 Thale cress (*Arabidopsis thaliana*) is the first plant to have its genome completely sequenced by the Arabidopsis Genome Initiative.

The Brooklyn Botanic Garden begins its Florilegium Project, in which the garden's living collection is recorded by accomplished artists in watercolour, pen and ink and other media.

2001 The Minnesota School of Botanical Art is founded in Minneapolis, with the intention of serving both science and art.

2004 The Japanese Association of Botanical Illustration publishes *Endangered Plants of Japan: A Florilegium*. The book contains several illustrations by renowned botanical artist Mariko Imai.

2005 The Ashmolean Museum in Oxford stages the exhibition 'A New Flowering: 1,000 Years of Botanical Art'. The exhibition is curated by the acclaimed collector of botanical art, Shirley Sherwood.

Hawaiian ethnobiologist Isabella Abbott is named a Living Treasure of Hawaii. She was the first native Hawaiian woman to receive a PhD in science and became a leading expert on Pacific algae.

2007 After thirty years of work Dr. Somsri, Thailand's leading durian expert, announces the creation of a durian fruit with an odour no more offensive than a banana. Durians are renowned for their foul smell.

Construction begins on the Oman Botanic Garden in Muscat. When finished it will cover 423 hectares and will be the largest botanic garden on the Arabian Peninsula.

2008 Opening of the Shirley Sherwood Gallery at Kew, dedicated to botanical illustration.

The Svalbard Global Seed Vault is established to preserve seeds of the world's edible plants.

The first volume is published of the *Highgrove Florilegium*, a study of Prince Charles's garden in Gloucestershire, with illustrations by various botanical artists; a second volume follows in 2009.

2009 After an extensive restoration project, the Marianne North Gallery reopens at Kew. A key part of the venture involves the restoration and conservation of 833 paintings produced by North.

The first All-African Horticultural Congress, entitled 'Grown Under the Sun', takes place in Nairobi, Kenya.

2010–12 The Yemini-born artist Zadok Ben-David produces *Blackflowers*, an installation of flower silhouettes made from painted hand-cut aluminium. ↑ 45, see p.325

The New York artist E. V. Day is awarded the Munn Artists Residency by the Versailles Foundation to live and work on Monet's estate in Giverny.

2011 The Japanese artist Yayoi Kusama makes the pointillist painting *Heart Flowers* as a reaction to the Japanese earthquake and tsunami that killed more than 15,000 people.

The British artist Mat Collishaw creates *Whispering Weeds*, a moving version of Albrecht Dürer's *Great Piece of Turf* (1503), in which the grass appears to be buffeted by the wind.

2013 British photographer Hannah Collins begins picturing Amazonian rainforest plants used by indigenous peoples in rituals and medicines.

c.2013 Magdalena Turzánska, a biologist from the Institute of Experimental Biology at the University of Wroclaw, Poland, wins photography awards for her work with a fluorescence microscope. ↑ 46, see p.301

2014 Georgia O'Keeffe's painting Jimson *Weed/White Flower No.1* (1932) is sold for more than $44 million, making it the most expensive work ever by a female artist.

Greek-born artist Spiros Hadjidjanos uses computer technology to create 3D versions of photographs from Karl Blossfeldt's classic work, *Art Forms in Nature (Urformen der Kunst)* (1928).

2015 Kew's botanical illustrator Christabel King publishes *The Kew Book of Botanical Illustration*.

The Arnold Arboretum at Harvard University launches a ten-year project, the Campaign for Living Collections, to boost plant exploration and collection. The aim of the campaign is to acquire approximately 400 species of plants from their natural habitats.

Singapore Botanic Gardens is inscribed as a UNESCO World Heritage Site at the 39th session of the World Heritage Committee in Bonn, Germany.

2016 It is announced that one in five of the world's plant species is at risk of extinction, although 2,000 new species are still being discovered every year. Loss of habitat caused by increased farming is considered the main threat.

Phony peach (*Xylella fastidiosa*), a disease of trees and plants, has wrought havoc in the United States and Europe, and scientists declare that it could dwarf the effects of ash dieback in the United Kingdom.

A new tally of 390,900 plant species known to science is announced by the Royal Botanic Gardens, Kew.

UNDERSTANDING PLANT TAXONOMY

Taxonomy is a branch of science concerned with systematically organizing living organisms into groups based on their similarities. All organisms, including plants, are divided into kingdom, division, class, order, family, genus and species (see glossary). A key part of botanical science – and therefore a key purpose of botanical illustration – is to identify individual plants and classify them into groups in order to learn more about the evolution of the plant kingdom.

The most basic taxonomic division for many years was between plants and animals, but this has since expanded into six groups of organisms: Protista, Fungi, Plantae, Animalia, Eubacteria and Archeobacteria. After this first level of taxonomic division – the 'kingdoms' – further divisions specify more and more variation, in accordance with the way that plants have evolved to suit different environments and functions. An organism is placed into the kingdom Plantae if it possesses several key characteristics, such as being multicellular, using photosynthesis to generate energy and possessing the correct anatomy for this process – chloroplasts containing the chemical chlorophyll, a green pigment, which animals and members of the other kingdoms do not have.

Within the plant kingdom, the systems used to classify plants have evolved from simple observation of a plant's obvious characteristics (leaf size and shape, whether the plant has flowers, what type of root system it has and so forth) to more technical differentiation based on molecular structure. The formal scientific name of a plant follows on from its taxonomic grouping, and is made up of the plant's genus and species. The meadow buttercup *Ranunculus acris*, for example, is grouped in the genus *Ranunculus*, which identifies it as a buttercup, and given the species name *acris*, which denotes this particular variation of meadow buttercup. To distinguish between *Ranunculus acris* ('meadow buttercup'), which has a running root system and yellow flowers, and *Ranunculus aconitifolius* ('Fair Maids of France'), which does not have a running root system and has white flowers, is to recognize two different species.

In the eighteenth century the Swedish botanist Carl Linnaeus first theorized the pivotal system of naming and grouping plants in accordance with their sexual systems (the organs in their flowers, as well as their fruit and seeds); he divided them into groups based on similarities in the structure of the male and female parts. The analysis of gene sequences in DNA has further refined the taxonomic system, helping to map the evolution of families and genera. Remarkably, most of the DNA analyses undertaken in recent times have confirmed what Linnaeus's system predicted in 1735.

'Nomenclature' is the process of giving plants names that are descriptive of the plant itself and that give an indication of its position within the map of plant evolution.

Plants have both common names, which are easy to remember but vary from place to place, and scientific names, which are written in Latin and are often italicized (this is a convention rather than a rule set out by the International Code for Nomenclature). The scientific names – which combine the plant's genus and species, the system introduced in 1753 – enable botanists to describe and identify plants by their characteristics; they also indicate a plant's place within the plant kingdom, thereby helping to trace the evolution of the botanical world. Latin is used partly because it was the traditional language of scholarship and partly because it is not spoken today, so its meanings are fixed. This allows plant types and names to be standardized around the world to avoid confusion, and also allows easy identification with older sources.

Further rules that govern how plants are named have been set down to avoid confusion or mis-identification. These rules are officially laid down by an international group of experts who review problems that arise in nomenclature every five years. One key rule is that the earliest published botanical name is the correct one. There have been numerous cases of two names existing simultaneously for the same species before the error is realized and the original name established as the standard.

GLOSSARY OF BOTANICAL TERMS AND TECHNIQUES

ANNUAL
A plant that grows, produces seed and dies within a year, or occasionally within a few months. Annuals can be sown in late winter under glass (tender annuals) or directly into the ground in spring (hardy annuals).

ANGIOSPERM
A seed-producing flowering plant; angiosperms are one of the most diverse groups of plants, containing about 350,000 species.

BIENNIAL
A plant that complete its life cycle in two years, germinating and growing in the first year, and flowering and producing seed in the second.

BINOMIAL SYSTEM
The universal system of naming living organisms, including plants, with two names: a capitalized genus name plus a species name, for example *Cyclamen* (genus) and *coum* (species).

BOTANIC(AL) GARDEN
A garden used for research into the relationships between plants – often associated with a university or professional botanical organization, and they are usually open to the public. The plants in botanic gardens are arranged either taxonomically, by geographical area or by habitat.

CABINET OF CURIOSITIES
A collection of natural and other notable objects, often kept in a display case.

CODEX (pl. CODICES)
An ancient manuscript in the form of a book.

CULTIVAR
A plant produced in cultivation by selective breeding and differing genetically from the wild species by possessing a desirable attribute, such as differently coloured flowers, extra petals or variegated leaves.

CYANOTYPE
A type of photographic printing that produces a blue image, or a white image on a blue background.

DECIDUOUS
Describes a plant that loses its leaves each year in order to survive the harsh conditions of winter (some tropical plants are deciduous in the dry season in order to conserve water).

DOUBLE
In a flower, describes the genetic production of double or multiple flower petals in plants that normally produce flowers with three, four or five petals. Doubling often makes a plant sterile, because its male and female organs turn into petals.

ENGRAVING
Cutting a design into a hard surface, such as stone or metal; also, a print reproduced from such a design.

ETCHING
A method of printing in which an artist incises a design on a metal plate with a needle and then burns the metal with acid.

EVERGREEN
Describes plants that retain their leaves all year round. Evergreen leaves are often darker, thicker and tougher than deciduous ones. In hot and dry countries evergreen leaves can be densely covered in hair, making them appear grey or silver.

EVOLUTION
The process by which living organisms adapt and change over generations.

FAMILY
A higher botanical classification group than GENUS. A family contains genera (pl. of genus) that are related to one another because they share certain fundamental characters. For example, the sage genus *Salvia* is related to the mint genus *Mentha* because both have square stems and hooded, tubular flowers; both genera belong to the family *Lamiaceae*.

FERTILE
Describes a plant that possesses the capacity to reproduce, meaning that it is capable of producing fruit, seed-producing flowers or anthers containing pollen. Often HYBRIDS are not fertile and thus unable to reproduce.

FLORA
The collective name for flowering plants, or for plant life found in a specific region. Also denotes a publication describing the collective plants of a specific region.

FLORILEGIUM
A term that originally described a collection of plants gathered into a single bouquet, planter or urn, or a painting presenting such an arrangement of plants. Today it most commonly describes a treatise on flowers that concentrates on their ornamental rather than medical or botanical value.

FRUIT
A seed-bearing structure that forms from the ripened ovary in flowering plants. Its purpose is to enclose the seeds in order to aid their dispersal, for example by being eaten or carried on the wind

GENUS (pl. GENERA)
A subdivision of a botanical family that contains one or more species according

to similar characteristics that show their close relationships. For example, the genus *Cyclamen* contains twenty-two species including the species *Cyclamen coum*, which has small, round leaves and short, squat flowers in spring; *Cyclamen hederifolium*, with ivy-like leaves and narrower flowers in autumn; and *Cyclamen repandum*, with ivy-like leaves and narrow flowers in spring. These all belong to the *Primula* family, Primulaceae. The name of a genus is always written with a capital letter.

GERMINATION
The first stage of a seed's growth, from embryo to the formation of its first root and then leaves.

GOUACHE
A type of opaque watercolour paint.

HERBACEOUS
Describes plants whose stems are not woody; herbaceous plants grow from an underground root system, produce flowers and seed, then die back to the ground each year, surviving the winter in their dormant root system below ground.

HERBAL
A book or manuscript created to communicate the medical properties of plants.

HERBARIUM
A systematically arranged collection of dried and pressed plant specimens preserved for scientific study.

HORTICULTURE
The science and art of growing plants.

HYBRID
A genetic cross between two different species (usually but not always in the same genus). For example, *Primula x polyantha* is a cross between the cowslip, *Primula veris*, and the primrose, *Primula vulgaris*; the 'x' denotes that it is a hybrid with its own binomial name.

INFLORESCENCE
A collective term for the complete flower head arranged in a particular structure on one stem or shoot of a plant. There are different types of inflorescence: most members of the carrot family, *Apiaceae*, for example, produce their small flowers in an umbrella-shaped inflorescence called an umbel, whereas plants in the genus *Wisteria* produce flowers along one long axis in a raceme.

INTAGLIO
A design that is engraved or incised into a hard surface and used to create an image in relief.

INVASIVE
Describes plants that encroach on and invade the territory of other plants, often pushing them out of their chosen habitat.

INVOLUCRUM
A sheath or membrane that surrounds or covers a seed.

LITHOGRAPH
An image that is prepared on a flat stone surface using grease or oils and then used to create an ink print.

LOBE
In a leaf, one of two or more projections or divisions (the leaf blade remains joined as one leaf, rather than being divided into leaflets). A maple leaf, for example, usually has three or five major lobes.

MATERIA MEDICA
A Latin medical term for the body of collected knowledge about the therapeutic properties of any substance used for healing (i.e. medicine).

MICROGRAPH
A magnified digital image taken through a microscope. Micrographs are used to study elements of a plant that are invisible to the naked eye.

MIDRIB
In a leaf, the central supporting vein or axis of the leaf blade or lamina.

NATIVE
A plant that occurs naturally in a particular country or region. Native plants may occur in a number of places within a country or region (indigenous) or be restricted to just one place (endemic).

NATURAL PHILOSOPHY
The philosophical study of nature and the natural world as the precursor of modern science from the time of Aristotle until the separation of biology, physics and chemistry in the nineteenth century.

NATURALIZE
To introduce a plant successfully to a new region. In some cases naturalization can be overwhelmingly invasive, as with the introduction of gorse into New Zealand.

NATURE PRINTING
A technique of recording the appearance of a plant or leaf either by applying ink to its surface and pressing it on to paper or by making an impression of the object in a soft lead plate and using the impression for printing.

NECTAR
A sugary substance produced in many flowers to attract pollinating insects.

ORNAMENTAL
A plant grown for its attractive appearance. rather than for its medicinal or other uses.

PERENNIAL
A plant that lives for many years; the term is frequently used in association with herbaceous plants that die back to a rootstock every winter.

PINNATE
Describes a leaf consisting of several smaller leaflets arranged along a central midrib or

leaf stalk. The leaflets are either opposite or alternate to one another along the midrib.

PISTIL
The female organ of a flower, consisting of the ovary, style (ovary stalk) and stigma (the pollen receptacle at the tip of the style).

PLANT-HUNTER
Someone who acquires or collects plant specimens for the purposes of research or cultivation, or as a hobby. Plant specimens may be kept alive, but are more commonly dried and pressed to preserve their quality.

POLLEN
Fine, powdery microscopic grains that are released by flowers' male organs and can fertilize other flowers' female organs.

POLLINATION
The means by which fertilization occurs in flowers. Pollen is carried by the wind or transported from flower to flower by insects (and, more rarely, birds and animals), which deposit it on the receptive stigmas (see PISTIL).

PROPAGATE
To reproduce a plant either from seed (sexual reproduction) or by taking cuttings, pegging down branches as layers, dividing plants or making grafts (asexual).

RADIOGRAPH
An image produced on a sensitive plate by X-rays or other similar radiation.

RESIN
A sticky organic substance secreted by some plants, notably pine and fir trees. Resin deters foragers and lowers the freezing point of water in the plant, thereby maintaining life in extremely cold conditions. Resin also acts to reduce water loss in hot and dry conditions.

SAP
A life-maintaining fluid in a plant's stem and leaves, consisting of water, minerals and sugar.

SEM MICROGRAPH
A digital image from a scanning electron microscope, which scans the object using a beam of electrons.

SHRUB
A woody plant that is shorter than a tree, such as a bush.

SPECIES
The basic unit of plant and animal classification within a genus. It is written in binomial classification with a lowercase letter, as in *Cyclamen libanoticum*. Species share close genetic relationships, but those that encompass a large geographic range may be further divided based on very minor characters such as size, leaf shape or flower colour. Such changes can be called subspecies (abbreviated to subsp., usually occurring in geographically isolated populations), varieties (var., usually within

one population) or formae (f., very minor variation within a population).

SPORE
A reproductive cell that enables primitive plants to reproduce. In some ways equivalent to pollen, spores are usually carried by wind and occasionally by water.

STAMEN
The male organ of a flower, consisting of the filament stalk, anther (pollen-bearing structure) and pollen.

STIPPLE ENGRAVING
A type of engraving in which tone is created by dots of different sizes and densities.

SUBSPECIES
A group of plants that genetically belong within a species but have characteristics that make them distinct from it in small ways. Subspecies are usually found as geographically isolated variants. For example, all primroses, *Primula vulgaris*, in western Europe have yellow or white flowers, but in Turkey all *Primula vulgaris* subsp. *sibthorpii* have pink or lilac flowers.

SUCCULENT
A plant with swollen water-bearing stems and/or leaves that occurs naturally in desert regions in order to conserve water, such as the cactus, *Pachypodium* or many euphorbias.

SUCKER
To produce running underground stems from which a plant can reproduce by sending up new shoots that produce roots as they extend. The term is also used for the shoots themselves.

TAXONOMY
The scientific study of classifying and naming plants.

TUBER
An underground part of a plant's stem or swollen root that acts as a storage organ for sugars and water.

VARIETY
A wild minor variant within a species, for example *Primula denticulata*, which has lilac flowers, and *Primula denticulata* var. *alba*, which has white flowers. The term usually refers to plants within a population that differ in one or two small ways from the typical species.

VELLUM
A smooth material for writing on, made from animal skin.

WOODBLOCK
A block of wood engraved in relief and used for printing an image.

X-RAY
A photographic or digital image of the internal composition of something produced by X-rays being passed through it and being absorbed to different degrees by different materials.

SELECTED BIOGRAPHIES

ANNA ATKINS
(Britain, 1799–1871)

Anna Atkins was trained in botany by her father and became a skilled illustrator and plant collector. She used the cyanotype process invented by her mentor the astronomer Sir John Herschel – in which sunlight was used to create a photogram on chemically treated paper – to record the images printed in 1843–53 in *Photographs of British Algae: Cyanotype Impressions*. With her friend Anne Dixon she went on to create cyanotypes of ferns and flowering plants.

JOHN JAMES AUDUBON
(United States, 1785–1851)

Born in Haiti and brought up in France, Audubon moved to the United States in 1803. He tried various business ventures before combining his skill as an artist with his lifelong interest in ornithology in a project to find, identify and draw the birds of North America. The project took some fourteen years as Audubon travelled the country. Each bird was placed against a background of plants, depicted either by Audubon or by his assistant, Joseph Wilson. The resulting book, *Birds of America* (1827–38), with its huge lithographs of nearly 500 bird species, is considered a landmark of natural-history illustration.

WILLIAM P.C. BARTON
(United States, 1786–1856)

William Barton's interest in botany began while he was studying medicine under his uncle Benjamin Smith Barton, author of the first American textbook on botanical science. William joined the US Navy as a surgeon in 1809 and became a leading organizer of naval health practice and hospitals. In 1815 he became professor of botany at the University of Pennsylvania, and in 1817 he published an illustrated herbal, *Vegetable Materia Medica of the United States*. He published floras of Philadelphia (1817) and North America (1821), illustrated with hand-coloured engravings.

WILLIAM BARTRAM
(United States, 1739–1823)

From a young age, William Bartram accompanied his father, John, founder of the first American botanic garden, on plant-collecting expeditions throughout eastern North America, during which he developed a skill for botanical drawing. In the 1770s he made his own four-year journey through the South and Florida, where he collected many new species; he published an illustrated account of his travels in 1791. From the late 1770s Bartram ran his father's garden, but he also illustrated *Elements of Botany* (1803–4) by his friend Benjamin Smith Barton.

MADELEINE FRANÇOISE BASSEPORTE
(France, 1701–1780)

After receiving early training as a history painter from a wealthy friend, Madeleine Basseporte became an apprentice to the flower painter Claude Aubriet. On Aubriet's death in 1742 she replaced him as official painter at the Jardin du Roi in Paris, where she worked until her own death. As well as recording the plants in the gardens of King Louis XV, she taught his daughters botanical art and mixed with leading botanists of the time, including Carl Linnaeus.

FERDINAND BAUER
(Austria, 1760–1826)

Orphaned as an infant, Ferdinand Bauer was brought up with his brother Franz by the monk Norbert Boccius, who taught them natural history and illustration. The brothers worked at the Royal Botanical Garden at Schönbrunn Palace in Vienna before Ferdinand accompanied Professor John Sibthorp of Oxford University to Greece and Turkey, illustrating *Flora Graeca* (1806–40). Bauer later became botanical artist on Matthew Flinders's expedition to Australia. His album of drawings, *Illustrationes Flora Novae Hollandiae* (1806–13), was a commercial failure, and Bauer ended his life in relative obscurity.

FRANZ BAUER
(Austria, 1758–1840)

Like his brother Ferdinand, Franz Bauer was trained in plant illustration by his guardian, Norbert Boccius, and worked at the Royal Botanical Garden at Schönbrunn Palace, Vienna. He moved to London, where the naturalist Sir Joseph Banks helped him to become the first botanical artist at Kew. Bauer held the position for the rest of his life, producing highly detailed anatomical illustrations and instructing pupils including Queen Charlotte. He became a member of the Royal Society and was appointed official botanical painter to George III.

BASILIUS BESLER
(Germany, 1561–1629)

An apothecary from Nuremberg, Besler was employed by Johann von Gemmingen, prince bishop of Eichstätt in Bavaria, to maintain and catalogue his renowned botanic garden. The sixteen-year task resulted in *Hortus Eystettensis* (1613), in which Besler showed species at near life-size with an unprecedented level of realistic detail. The 1,084 illustrations included not only medicinal and culinary plants, but also garden flowers and exotic plants such as arum lilies.

ELIZABETH BLACKWELL
(Britain, 1707–1758)

Trained as an artist in her native Scotland, Elizabeth Blachrie moved to London after secretly marrying her cousin Alexander Blackwell. When Alexander's poor business decisions led to his confinement in debtors' prison, Elizabeth sought to support her young family by illustrating a herbal of European plants, including many British wild flowers, which she found in the Chelsea Physic Garden. The first edition of *A Curious Herbal* (1737–9) included 500 plants in two volumes and raised enough money to release her husband from prison. He travelled to Sweden, where he became court physician to Frederick I but was later accused of treason and executed. Little is known of the later life of Elizabeth, who remained in London.

LEOPOLD BLASCHKA
(Bohemia, 1822–1895)

Trained as a goldsmith and gem-cutter, Leopold Blaschka joined the family glass business, and developed a technique of 'glass-spinning' that allowed him to create intricate and detailed models. After moving to Dresden, Blaschka began to make glass models, including 100 orchids for a local noble, and marine invertebrates, which were bought by museums and universities. Blaschka, who was joined in his work by his son Rudolf in about 1880, was approached by the Harvard professor George Goodale to provide glass models of flowers for teaching purposes. The Blaschkas eventually made some 4,400 glass flowers and details for Harvard. Rudolf continued working alone after his father's death in 1895.

KARL BLOSSFELDT
(Germany, 1865–1932)

Untrained in photography, the German artist Karl Blossfeldt made striking abstract close-ups of plants and other organisms. A professor of fine arts in Berlin, he designed cameras that allowed him to magnify his subject up to thirty times, revealing patterns and structure in plants. He made his reputation with *Art Forms in Nature* in 1928. Hailed as a landmark in the history of photography, the book appealed particularly to followers of contemporary abstract and surrealist art movements.

PIETER VAN DER BORCHT
(Flanders, c.1540–1608)

Pieter van der Borcht trained as an artist in Mechelen before moving to Antwerp in 1572 during the Dutch Revolt. He had already worked for the Antwerp publisher Christophe Plantin and now became his assistant, illustrating many of Plantin's books with religious and comical scenes. Van der Borcht came to specialize in botanical illustration, and provided more than 3,180 watercolours to illustrate books by such naturalists as Rembert Dodoens and Carolus Clusius.

HENRY BRADBURY
(Britain, 1831–1860)

In 1855 Henry Bradbury created illustrations for *The Ferns of Great Britain and Ireland* using a technique known as nature printing, in which a specimen was pressed into a soft lead plate to leave an impression that could be used for printing. Bradbury patented the process without acknowledging that he had learned the technique from its creator, the Austrian printer Alois Auer. After a bitter controversy, Bradbury became depressed and eventually committed suicide while a second book, *Nature-printed British Seaweeds* (1859–60), was still being printed. Frequent exposure to the lead used in the printing process may have contributed to his depression.

MARK CATESBY
(Britain, 1682/3–1749)

Born into a well-off family in Essex, Mark Catesby studied natural history in London before moving to Virginia. He supplied seeds to London nurseries, and in 1722 the Royal Society sponsored him to collect plant and animal specimens in Carolina and the West Indies. Back in London, Catesby spent more than twenty years preparing his *Natural History of Carolina, Florida and the Bahama Islands* (1731), including learning how to etch. The early plates showed only animals, but Catesby later included plants, both as backgrounds and as subjects in themselves.

ARTHUR HARRY CHURCH
(Britain, 1865–1937)

One of the leading academic botanists of his lifetime, Arthur Church taught at the University of Oxford, where he specialized in the development and structure of plants. Partly as an aid to his students, he produced accurate illustrations of the internal structures of flowering plants, although his academic ideas about botany were not greatly influential. A great admirer of floral beauty, Church set out to illustrate the hundred best flowers by season. His work was published in *Botanical Memoirs* (1919–25).

NICHOLAS CULPEPER
(Britain, 1616–1654)

The son of a clergyman, Culpeper was apprenticed to an apothecary and later became a herbalist. Under the influence of radical Christian preachers, he pioneered diagnostic medicine, treating his patients with a combination of herbs and astrology. He spent his time translating Latin medical texts into English and collecting medicinal herbs around London, identifying them for his highly influential *English Physitian and Complete Herbal* (1652). Alienated by his contemporaries for his radical views and cheap remedies, Culpeper later served as a battlefield surgeon in the Civil War.

IMOGEN CUNNINGHAM
(United States, 1883–1976)

After studying chemistry at the University of Seattle, Imogen Cunningham became an apprentice in the studio of the photographer Edward Curtis and studied platinum printing in Germany before opening her own portrait studio in Seattle. She turned to plant photography after closing her studio to concentrate on raising her children, and maintained her interest after returning to her career. A member of the influential photography group f64, based in San Francisco, she became one of the leading American photographers of the mid-twentieth century.

LEONARDO DA VINCI
(Italy, 1452–1519)

One of the greatest artists of any age, Leonardo was a polymath for whom the term 'Renaissance man' was coined. Born in Tuscany, he showed artistic talent at a young age and was apprenticed to the artist Verrocchio in Florence. He worked for seventeen years in Milan for Duke Ludovico Sforza, before moving to Venice and then back to Florence, where he worked for Cesare Borgia; later he worked in Rome for Pope Leo X before moving to France at the invitation of King Francis I. Leonardo completed few paintings, but they include such masterpieces as *The Last Supper*, *Mona Lisa* and *The Virgin and the Rocks*. He is renowned for his closely observed sketches of plant and human anatomy, as well as his military and mechanical designs.

WILLIAM DAMPIER
(Britain, 1651–1715)

William Dampier was an English seaman and privateer. A voyage to raid Spanish vessels in the East Indies took him to New Holland (Australia), and his journals of that trip drew a commission from King William III to return to New Holland. Landing in western Australia in August 1699, Dampier sailed north along the coast, recording the flora and fauna (his botanical drawings may have been made by his clerk, James Brand). After his ship sank on the homeward journey, the surviving drawings were published as *A Voyage to New Holland ...* in 1703.

CHARLES DARWIN
(Britain, 1809–1882)

Charles Darwin was possibly the most influential naturalist who has ever lived. Born to a family of scientists, he studied natural history at Cambridge University before in 1831 becoming naturalist on board HMS *Beagle*, then setting out on a five-year voyage around the world. Darwin's observations of specialist adaptations in plants, birds and animals prompted years of further research before he published *On the Origin of Species* (1859), which outlined a theory of evolution caused by natural selection. Hugely controversial at the time, the idea of evolution quickly became accepted as historical truth by the vast majority of scientists.

MARY DELANY
(Britain, 1700–1788)

Born into a well-connected English family, Mary Granville received a varied education before an unhappy marriage to the MP Alexander Pendarves. After his death, she married an Irish clergyman, Patrick Delany, with whom she lived for nearly twenty-five years in Dublin. Her lifelong interest in botany was encouraged by her friend the Dowager Duchess of Portland, who introduced her to such botanists as Sir Joseph Banks. After being widowed again in 1771, Mary began to create découpage flowers from cut paper, amassing a large collection that came to the attention of the royal family and is now in the British Museum.

BARBARA REGINA DIETZSCH
(Germany, 1706–1783)

Daughter of the Nuremberg artist Johann Israel Dietzsch, Barbara was trained in her father's workshop. Her

reputation soon spread to the Netherlands and England, but she rarely left the city of her birth. She also declined invitations to become a court artist, preferring to work on depictions of birds, insects and flowers, as well as popular genre scenes and landscapes. Her work combined the traditions of Dutch and French still-life painting with a high degree of detail.

DIOSCORIDES
(Rome, c. AD 40–90)

Born in what is now Turkey, Dioscorides was a surgeon in the Roman army, a position in which he travelled widely through the Roman Empire, collecting information about medicinal plants and minerals. He compiled his knowledge in *De Materia Medica*, a Greek herbal that became one of the most enduring herbals of the next 1,500 years in the West. It remains our major source of information about medicine in the classical world, and was reproduced frequently in illustrated manuscripts in both Europe and the Islamic world.

REMBERT DODOENS
(Flanders, 1517–1585)

The physician and botanist Rembert Dodoens left his native Flanders to become physician to the Austrian court of Emperor Rudolph II, but returned in 1582 as professor of medicine at the University of Leiden. His reputation rests on his *Cruydeboeck* (1554), a herbal that divided flora into six kingdoms, with detailed text and more than 700 illustrations. It was translated many times, and was a standard reference work in Europe for more than 200 years.

ALBRECHT DÜRER
(Germany, 1471–1528)

Albrecht Dürer was one of the most celebrated German artists of the Renaissance, best known for highly skilled woodcuts and engravings, although he was also a pioneer of landscape painting. He worked mainly in his native Nuremberg, although he travelled as far as Italy to study art and corresponded with such contemporary artists as Leonardo da Vinci. Dürer was renowned for his printmaking, through which his influence spread across Europe.

ATANASIO ECHEVERRÍA Y GODOY
(Mexico, 18th century)

Little is known of the life of the Mexican botanist Atanasio Echeverría y Godoy, who in 1787 joined the Royal Botanical Expedition to New Spain, led by Martín de Sessé y Lacasta and José Mariano Mociño. Echeverría was one of three Mexican artists employed by the Spaniards to document the flora of Spanish America, and he produced the majority of the expedition's illustrations. The succulent genus *Echeveria* is named after him.

SYDENHAM EDWARDS
(Britain, 1768–1819)

The son of a schoolmaster in Wales, Sydenham Edwards showed great artistic talent as a child, copying from a book of botanical plates. A visitor who saw his drawings recommended him to William Curtis, founder of *Curtis's Botanical Magazine*, who oversaw the boy's artistic training. Edwards produced more than 1,700 watercolours for the magazine from 1787, in addition to illustrating other books; in 1815, after falling out with the new editor at *Curtis's*, he founded *The Botanical Register*.

GEORG DIONYSIUS EHRET
(Germany, 1708–1770)

Georg Ehret became one of the most influential European botanical illustrators for his pioneering work, first with the Anglo-Dutch collector George Clifford at his estate near Haarlem, where Ehret worked with the young Carl Linnaeus, and later in London. Trained originally as an apprentice gardener, Ehret was able to study many of the new species that were brought to the Netherlands and Britain as Europeans explored the Pacific, Asia and the

Americas. In 1737 Ehret, Clifford and Linnaeus published the renowned *Hortus Cliffortanius*. Ehret was also an outstanding illustrator of butterflies.

JOHN ELLIS
(Britain, c.1710–1776)

John Ellis made his money as a linen merchant but was also an enthusiastic natural philosopher, becoming a member of the Royal Society in 1754 and publishing a 'natural history' of corals in 1755. As the royal agent for West Florida and later for Dominica, Ellis imported many American seeds and plants into Britain for the first time. He described his methods for transporting plant specimens in his book *Directions for Bringing over Plants and Seeds from the East Indies and Other Distant Countries* (1770).

WALTER HOOD FITCH
(Britain, 1817–1892)

The Glasgow-born artist Walter Hood Fitch was one of the most prolific botanical illustrators of the nineteenth century – he drew up to 200 plates a year – and one of the most popular. An apprentice textile designer, he was recruited by William Jackson Hooker, the editor of *Curtis's Botanical Magazine*, to produce botanical lithographs. Fitch's first plate appeared in the magazine in 1834, and he soon became its sole artist. When Hooker became director of Kew in 1841, Fitch became the sole artist for all Kew publications. Even after leaving Kew in a dispute over pay in 1877, he remained active as a botanical illustrator for another decade.

WILLIAM HENRY FOX TALBOT
(Britain, 1800–1877)

The British aristocrat Henry Fox Talbot was famed for his discoveries during the early development of photography. Four years before the Frenchman Louis Daguerre announced his invention of the daguerreotype in 1839, Talbot used paper treated with salt and silver nitrate to capture images using a camera lens. Talbot's subsequent development of the calotype process shortened the length of exposure required to produce an image. His contribution to plant illustration came by placing leaves on photosensitive paper and exposing them to sunlight to produce 'photogenic drawings', one of which was included in the first photographic book, Talbot's *Pencil of Nature* (1844–6).

JOHN GERARD
(Britain, c.1545–1612)

The London herbalist John Gerard grew many rare plants in his garden, including newly introduced exotics from the Americas. He described these plants in his extensive *Herball* of 1597, in which he also reused text from the herbal of Rembert Dodoens. One of the most influential works of the seventeenth century, Gerard's book was illustrated mainly by woodcuts from Dodoens's publication.

NEHEMIAH GREW
(Britain, 1641–1712)

Sometimes called the 'father of plant anatomy', Nehemiah Grew studied at Cambridge and Leiden, Holland, where he used an early microscope to study the structure of plants. Returning to London, his growing reputation for botany earned him election as a fellow of the Royal Society. Grew's major work, *The Anatomy of Plants*, was published in 1682 with eighty-two plates that reveal the inner structure of plants. Grew was the first to identify the fact that plants have organs with different functions, as do animals.

ERNST HAECKEL
(Germany, 1834–1919)

The German zoologist Ernst Haeckel was an enthusiastic supporter of Charles Darwin's theory of evolution, and his research led him to coin many important biological terms, including 'ecology', the study of how organisms relate to their environment. Many of Haeckel's evolutionary claims turned out to be wrong, however, and he was accused of faking his research into embryology. He nevertheless remained a major scientific figure of his day. A talented artist, he made hundreds of sketches and watercolours of plants and animals to reveal their structure and symmetry; a selection of 100 plates were published in 1899 as *Kunstformen der Natur* (*Art Forms in Nature*).

KATSUSHIKA HOKUSAI
(Japan, 1760–1849)

Katsushika Hokusai was one of the most influential Japanese artists of the late Edo period, specializing in *ukiyo-e* ('depictions of the floating world'). His long career encompassed portraits, book illustration and erotica, but he is best known for the woodcut landscapes he produced late in his life, such as *Thirty-Six Views of Mount Fuji*. His work was an important influence on the development of Japonisme in Europe, where his prints appealed particularly to the Impressionists.

ROBERT HOOKE
(Britain, 1635–1703)

Hooke's reputation rests on his pioneering use of the microscope to investigate the structure of living organisms, but his scientific curiosity extended to investigating the nature of light and of gravity, suggesting an early theory of evolution, and building vacuum pumps, clocks, telescopes and microscopes. He was also an accomplished architect and surveyor and an early and influential town-planner. In 1665 he published *Micrographia*, which contained detailed drawings of the structure of objects, plants, mites and fleas as revealed under the microscope. Hooke's close observation of plants led him to suggest the word 'cell' for their fundamental units, based on their resemblance to closed prison cells.

JOSEPH DALTON HOOKER
(Britain, 1817–1911)

Joseph Hooker was the director of Kew Gardens for twenty years from 1865, and one of the most influential botanists of the nineteenth century. The son of Kew's first director, William Jackson Hooker, Joseph developed an early passion for botany, and qualified as a surgeon in order to join the Royal Navy and travel. His first voyage, to the Antarctic in 1839–43, brought him the chance to study plants in the Southern Ocean, particularly New Zealand. In 1847 he began a five-year expedition to India, and the new species of *Rhododendron* he collected sparked a gardening craze at home. Later trips took him to the Holy Land and to the western frontier of the United States. Many of the drawings Hooker made on his travels were turned into finished illustrations by Walter Hood Fitch.

WILLIAM JACKSON HOOKER
(Britain, 1785–1865)

The first official director of Kew Gardens, Hooker developed an interest in natural history during his childhood in Norfolk. With independent means and the sponsorship of the naturalist Sir Joseph Banks, Hooker made botanical expeditions to Iceland, France, Switzerland and Italy before settling in Suffolk, where he created a renowned herbarium that received plants from around the world. He became an influential figure, and was responsible for persuading the government to appoint botanists to all its official expeditions. After lecturing in Glasgow from 1820, he was appointed director of the new Royal Botanic Gardens at Kew in 1841, and oversaw its expansion. Hooker wrote and edited many books, illustrated by himself and others. His son Joseph followed him as director of Kew.

ALEXANDER VON HUMBOLDT
(Prussia, 1769–1859)

The Prussian naturalist and explorer Alexander von Humboldt trained as a mining engineer before the death of his mother in 1796 left him financially independent.

He began planning an overseas expedition, accompanied by the French botanist Aimé Bonpland. With permission from the Spanish government the pair travelled to New Spain, where they spent five years exploring and observing the natural history. Their travels took them up the Orinoco, into Venezuela, south to the Andes, and to Mexico and Cuba. Among Humboldt's many discoveries, the most significant was his development of the idea of plant geography: that organic life is distributed on Earth according to physical conditions, such as altitude and elevation.

NIKOLAUS JOSEPH VON JACQUIN
(Netherlands, 1727–1817)

After studying medicine in Leiden and Paris, Jacquin began to specialize in botany before moving to Vienna. There he was commissioned to join a royal expedition to the West Indies, where he was the first botanist to record many local plants. An early adopter of the binomial system, he earned the praise of its inventor, Carl Linnaeus, for two books recording American plants, published in 1760 and 1763. Jacquin's renown earned him professorships in Hungary and later in Vienna, where he continued to publish beautiful folios of plants illustrated with engravings of his own drawings. He was knighted for his services to botany in 1774 and ennobled in 1806.

GERTRUDE JEKYLL
(Britain, 1843–1932)

Gertrude Jekyll, with her painterly approach to colourful plantings, was one of the most influential garden designers and horticulturalists of the late nineteenth and early twentieth century. A lifelong enthusiasm for plants and plant-collecting led her to design a garden for her mother in 1885, after which she went on to design some 400 more, as well as writing prolifically. Her partnership with the architect Edwin Lutyens played a prominent role in the Arts and Crafts movement in Europe and North America from about 1890 to 1910.

TED KINSMAN
(United States)

Educated in New York state, Ted Kinsman studied optical engineering and physics before working for the research laboratories of the US Navy. In 1992, Kinsman began his own company to explore his interest in combining physics with photography, notably through time-lapse films of blooming flowers. Kinsman went on to specialize in educational science photography, particularly scanning electron micrographs, X-rays, and ultra-high-speed photography that uses exposures of less than a millionth of a second. He is an assistant professor at Rochester Institute of Technology in New York.

KAWAHARA KEIGA
(Japan, 1786–c.1860)

The son of a painter in Nagasaki, Kawahara Keiga studied painting before obtaining permission from the Japanese government to work in Dejima, the 'factory' or trading post to which Dutch traders were confined as part of Japanese efforts to limit Western interference and influence. He painted many images of life in Japan for his Dutch patrons, including prints of Japanese flora and fauna commissioned by the botanist Philipp Franz von Siebold. Instructed by visiting European artists, Kawahara was responsible for introducing Western artistic techniques to traditional Japanese painting.

ROB KESSELER
(Britain, born 1951)

The British artist Rob Kesseler has celebrated plants throughout his career, originally in the form of sculpture but more recently in microscopic photography. He has worked for many years with scientists from Kew and the Gulbenkian Science Institute in Portugal to explore the creative potential of the microscopic world.

OGATA KŌRIN
(Japan, 1658–1712)

The son of a wealthy merchant, Ogata Kōrin was taught by leading Japanese artists of his time, but became noteworthy for his development of an impressionistic style of painting based on idealized rather than naturalistic forms. A member of the renowned Rimpa School, he is best known for painting on folding screens covered in gold foil.

JACOPO LIGOZZI
(Italy, 1547–1627)

Born in Verona to a family of artists, Jacopo Ligozzi was a painter for the Habsburg court in Vienna before returning to Italy to work for the Medici family in Florence, where he replaced Giorgio Vasari as head of the artists' guild. Although Ligozzi was an accomplished painter of frescoes and altarpieces, he is best known for his studies of plants and animals. In addition to working for the Medici, he recorded plants from the botanic garden created in Bologna by the naturalist Ulisse Aldrovandi.

CARL LINNAEUS
(Sweden, 1707–1778)

Carl Linnaeus was possibly the most influential botanist in history, partly because he formalized the modern binomial – 'two-named' – system of classifying living organisms. Having trained in botany in Sweden and the Netherlands, he was fascinated by taxonomy, the relationship between families of organisms. He proposed classifying plants based on their sexual organs and method of reproduction. Linnaeus also initiated much eighteenth-century plant-hunting, sending botanists known as the 'apostles' around the globe to collect specimens.

RORY McEWEN
(Britain, 1932–1982)

Born into an aristocratic Scottish family and educated at Eton, Rory McEwen initially became a musician; he was a leading figure in the rising popularity of folk and blues music in the 1960s. At the same time, he was a talented flower artist (influenced by his maternal great-grandfather, the botanist and artist John Lindley). In 1964 McEwen gave up music and devoted himself to floral art, painting large minimalist watercolours on vellum. Diagnosed with terminal cancer at the age of fifty, he committed suicide.

MARCELLO MALPIGHI
(Italy, 1628–1694)

Educated at the University of Bologna, Marcello Malpighi earned doctorates in both philosophy and medicine before carrying out extensive research into the anatomy of plants and animals. One of the first generation of microscopic researchers, Malpighi discovered the structure of the lungs, for example, and the link between arteries and veins in organisms; in plants, he made drawings of individual organs for the first time, and drew the stages of development of legumes. His research was published in *Anatome Plantarum* (1679), with engravings by the Englishman Robert White.

ROBERT MAPPLETHORPE
(United States, 1946–1989)

The American photographer Robert Mapplethorpe studied graphic art in New York City. From the mid-1970s he became known for large-scale black-and-white portraits, male and female nudes, many of which are erotic in nature. His subjects included many of his friends, including fellow artists and composers, and he also produced numerous self-portraits. He also photographed still lifes of flowers throughout his career, and published *Flowers* in 1990.

ALEXANDER MARSHAL
(Britain, c.1620–1682)

Self-taught as an artist, Alexander Marshal is notable for having painted flowers simply in order to portray their beauty. His informal paintings featured imperfect, 'real' plants, complete with fallen petals, discoloured leaves and occasional feeding insects. Marshal showed his works only to his friends, but they were later collected in his extensive *Florilegium*, the only such surviving publication from seventeenth-century England.

FRANCIS MASSON
(Britain, 1741–1805)

The Scottish gardener Francis Masson began working at Kew in the 1760s, where he became the garden's first plant-hunter. The director, Sir Joseph Banks, sent him on a mission to South Africa that yielded 500 new species, then to the Antilles, Portugal, South Africa (again) and North America. Masson faced various difficulties – including being imprisoned by the French and captured by pirates – that made his trips less successful than they might have been.

MARGARET MEE
(Britain, 1909–1988)

Margaret Mee studied art in London with the British painter Victor Pasmore. His emphasis on observation, mass, shape and space influenced the flower paintings Mee produced after moving in 1952 to São Paulo, Brazil, where she dedicated herself to painting plants. From 1956 she made a series of expeditions into the Amazonian rainforest, during which she painted many species previously unknown to science. Her book *Flowers of the Brazilian Rainforests* was published in 1968. In 1976 she was awarded the MBE for services to Brazilian botany.

MARIA SIBYLLA MERIAN
(Germany, 1647–1717)

Maria Sibylla Merian learned to paint when her stepfather introduced her to miniature flower painting. In 1680 she published *The New Book of Flowers* in Nuremberg, intended as a model book for artists and embroiderers; it was followed by *The Caterpillar Book*, showing butterflies and moths. Merian later moved to Amsterdam, where her daughters Johanna Helena and Dorothea Maria also became noted natural-history artists; the latter accompanied her mother in 1699 to Suriname, where they collected specimens for *Metamorphosis Insectorum Surinamensium* (1705), a work that ensured Merian's reputation as a pioneering entomologist.

JACOB VAN MEURS
(Netherlands, c.1619–1680)

The Dutch bookseller and engraver Jacob van Meurs published as many as seventy-five books between 1650 and 1680 reflecting expanding Dutch contacts around the world. He brought out a range of works by various authors and engravers reporting the latest botanical discoveries from China, Africa and the Americas.

MARIA MONINCKX
(Netherlands, 1673–1757)

Maria Moninckx was the daughter of the artist Jan Moninckx, with whom she collaborated from 1686 to 1709 on recording plants in the recently founded Hortus Medicus, Amsterdam's botanic garden. She contributed several very accomplished plates to the nine-volume *Moninckx Atlas* (1686–1709); her father painted most, and other illustrators made lesser contributions.

MARIANNE NORTH
(Britain, 1830–1890)

Although not formally trained, the talented painter Marianne North enjoyed two great advantages for a female artist in the nineteenth century: money and political connections (her father was the MP Frederick North). From 1871 she travelled widely, painting botanical species in North America, the Caribbean, Brazil, Japan, Australia, New Zealand, and Southeast and South Asia. Her 833 paintings, many of which depict plants in wider scenes, are today housed at Kew in the Marianne North Gallery, which was built in 1882.

GEORGIA O'KEEFFE
(United States, 1887–1986)

One of the leading American artists of the twentieth century, Georgia O'Keeffe had a conventional training before turning her back on realism in her twenties to experiment with abstraction. Her work was first exhibited in 1916 by the photographer and gallery owner Alfred Stieglitz, whom she married in 1924. Among her favourite subjects were flowers, of which she made huge, close-up paintings into which some critics read a sexual significance. From 1929 O'Keeffe spent much of her time painting landscapes and animal bones in New Mexico, where she moved permanently in 1946.

JOHN PARKINSON
(Britain, 1567–1650)

The London apothecary and herbalist John Parkinson became royal botanist to King Charles I, but his reputation was largely overshadowed by the defeat of the Royalists in the English Civil War (1642–51). Parkinson was a leading gardener of his day, importing new plants from the Eastern Mediterranean and the new colonies in North America. His *Paradisi in sole paradisus terrestris* (1629) – written to introduce Charles's young French queen, Henrietta Maria, to English gardens – described the organization of flower, kitchen and orchard gardens. In 1640 Parkinson published *Theatrum Botanicum*, a catalogue of some 3,800 English plants – some never recorded before – intended as a guide for his fellow apothecaries.

SYDNEY PARKINSON
(Britain, 1745–1771)

Scottish-born Sydney Parkinson was the first British artist in Australia, where he drew both native plants and Aboriginal peoples. An apprentice draper, he had a skill at botanical illustration that earned him a position with Sir Joseph Banks, one of the leading naturalists of the day. Parkinson accompanied Banks as botanical artist on the expedition to the Pacific led by Lieutenant James Cook in 1768, reaching Tahiti and New Zealand, as well as Australia. He made hundreds of drawings in difficult conditions on board ship, but he died of dysentery on the voyage home, and his work was later prepared for publication by others.

RACHEL PEDDER-SMITH
(Britain, born 1975)

Trained at the Royal College of Art in London, the contemporary botanical artist Rachel Pedder-Smith undertook a PhD project using dried plant specimens from the Herbarium at Kew. This led to more than a decade's work at the Herbarium that established Pedder-Smith's reputation. Widely collected, she has won the Royal Horticultural Society gold medal four times.

PIERRE-JOSEPH REDOUTÉ
(Belgium, 1759–1840)

Born into a family of decorative artists, Pierre-Joseph Redouté learned the family business before moving to Paris to paint theatre sets. Spotted sketching flowers by the botanist Charles Louis L'Héritier, Redouté contributed illustrations to L'Héritier's works; his images drew the attention of the flower artist Gérard van Spaendonck, who recruited Redouté to paint 500 flower pictures for the collection known as the *Vélins du Roi*. Redouté became official court painter to Marie Antoinette and, after the French Revolution, to Napoleon's empress, Joséphine; he later worked for the restored Bourbon royal family. His most famous work, *Les Roses* (1817–24), confirmed his position as one of the most popular flower artists of all time

STELLA ROSS-CRAIG
(Britain, 1906–2006)

Of Scottish heritage, Stella Ross-Craig was brought up in southern England. After attending art school, her talent as an illustrator and a long interest in botany got her a job at

Kew, where she drew illustrations for *Curtis's Botanical Magazine*. In 1948, Ross-Craig published the first volume – there would eventually be thirty-one – of *Drawings of British Plants*, an innovative set of cheap paperbacks illustrated by a total of more than 1,300 lithographs of black-and-white drawings, many made from dried specimens in the Kew Herbarium. Ross-Craig completed the project in 1973. In 1999 she became the sixth recipient of the Kew Award medal.

LILIAN SNELLING
(Britain, 1879–1972)

Raised in Kent, Lilian Snelling became a botanical artist after being invited to paint a flower collector in the early years of World War I. She worked at the Royal Botanic Garden in Edinburgh before moving in 1921 to Kew, where she became the main artist and lithographer on *Curtis's Botanical Magazine*; she illustrated it until her retirement in 1952. Her prominence as one of the outstanding flower artists of her generation was recognized by a special edition of the magazine, the MBE in 1954 and the Royal Horticultural Society's Victoria Medal in 1955.

JAMES SOWERBY
(Britain, 1757–1822)

James Sowerby studied art at the Royal Academy in London before establishing a reputation as a flower artist, drawing plates for the French botanist Charles Louis L'Héritier in the late 1780s and being recruited by William Curtis to draw for his new journal, *Curtis's Botanical Magazine*. Sowerby published widely in his own right, including vast illustrated surveys of British fossils and minerals, but his most significant creation was as a plant illustrator was *English Botany*. Published in thirty-six volumes over twenty-four years from its inception in 1790, *Sowerby's Botany*, as it became known, contained 2,592 hand-coloured engravings and marked a new level of scientific detail in botanical illustration.

GÉRARD VAN SPAENDONCK
(Netherlands, 1746–1822)

Gérard van Spaendonck trained as a decorative painter in Antwerp before moving to Paris, where in 1774 he became miniature painter in the court of Louis XVI. In 1780 he became professor of flower painting at the Jardin du Roi (he taught Pierre-Joseph Redouté), where he contributed botanical paintings to the collection known as the *Vélins du Roi*. Spaendonck was noted particularly for a transparent watercolour technique and stipple engraving that allowed delicate gradations of colour, as displayed in his seminal work *Fleurs dessinées d'après nature* (*Flowers Drawn from Life*; 1799–1801). He received the Légion d'honneur in 1804 and was ennobled by Napoleon in 1805.

EDWARD STEICHEN
(United States, 1879–1973)

Born in Luxembourg, Edward Steichen emigrated to the United States with his family as a baby. After apprenticing as a lithographer, he began to take photographs, influenced by his friendship with the photographer Alfred Stieglitz. Steichen was an early adopter of colour photography, and in 1911 he took the first modern fashion photographs, for the magazine *Art et Décoration*, laying the foundations for a career as a leading fashion photographer. He served as a military photographer in both world wars, and was later an influential director of photography at the Museum of Modern Art in New York.

ALICE TANGERINI
(United States, born 1949)

Born in Maryland, Alice Tangerini studied at Virginia Commonwealth University before joining the National Museum of Natural History at the Smithsonian Institution in 1972 as staff illustrator in the botany department. In that position, she made illustrations of more than

1,000 plants in pen, brush and ink, working mainly from dried and pressed specimens. Tangerini's scientifically precise drawings have appeared in dozens of periodicals and books.

JOHN TRADESCANT THE ELDER
(Britain, c.1570s–1638)

The English naturalist and collector John Tradescant was head gardener for Robert Cecil, 1st Earl of Salisbury, and later for the 1st Duke of Buckingham and King Charles I. Travelling widely throughout Europe on his employers' behalf, he collected bulbs, seeds and natural curiosities that he later displayed in an early example of a public museum in Lambeth, south London, where he and his son John Tradescant the Younger maintained a botanic garden.

IWASAKI TSUNEMASA (also called KAN-EN)
(Japan, 1786–1842)

Born into the samurai warrior class, Iwasaki Tsunemasa served the Tokugawa shogunate as superintendent of the shogun's botanic garden in Edo (Tokyo). He wrote a natural history of the Edo region and a guide to the cultivation of flowering plants, but his masterpiece was the *Honzō Zufu* (*Illustrated Manual of Medical Plants*; 1828–54), a collection of botanical woodcuts that ran to ninety-six volumes.

PIERRE-JEAN-FRANÇOIS TURPIN
(France, 1775–1840)

Pierre-Jean-François Turpin was a French soldier and amateur artist when he met the botanist Pierre Antoine Poiteau in Haiti in 1794. With Poiteau's encouragement, Turpin learned the basics of botany, and the two men collaborated throughout their careers. Turpin's skill made him the leading botanical illustrator of the early nineteenth century in France, and he illustrated numerous works by important botanists, including Augustin Saint-Hilaire, Alexander von Humboldt and Aimé Bonpland.

BERTHE HOOLA VAN NOOTEN
(Netherlands, 1817–1892)

Berthe Hoola van Nooten moved to the colony of Suriname with her preacher husband in 1838, from where she sent plant cuttings back to the Netherlands. The family then moved to Louisiana, where her husband died, then to Texas, and then to Java, where Berthe's brother was a successful businessman. There she attempted to take advantage of European interest in exotic plants by drawing forty plates of Javanese flora. With the patronage of Queen Sophia Mathilde of the Netherlands, her drawings were published in 1863–4 and went through a number of editions – although Van Nooten herself died in poverty in the Dutch colony of Batavia.

HENDRIK VAN REEDE TOT DRAKENSTEIN
(Netherlands, 1636–1691)

Hendrik van Reede tot Drakenstein joined the Dutch East India Company as a soldier in 1656, serving mainly in Cochin and the Malabar region of India's southwest coast, and becoming the commander of Dutch Malabar in 1670. Later service in the Company took him to the Cape Colony – now South Africa – Sri Lanka and Bengal in northeastern India. Encouraged by the Company's enthusiasm for scientific information about its colonies, he employed a huge team of botanists and illustrators to catalogue plants in Malabar in the 1670s, concentrating on those that might have medical or economic value. The first of the eventual twelve volumes of *Hortus Malabaricus* appeared in 1678.

ALFRED RUSSEL WALLACE
(Britain 1823-1913)

The co-discoverer with Charles Darwin of natural selection, Alfred Russel Wallace independently conceived the theory of evolution. Born in Monmouthshire, then part of England, Wallace studied as a surveyor, but having read works by Alexander von Humboldt and William Henry Edwards he began travelling with entomologist Henry Bates to Brazil from 1848 to 1852 in order to gather evidence of the transmutation of species. His specimens were lost in a fire in which he and the ship's crew had to abandon ship. Undeterred Wallace set off again to explore the Malay Archipelago (Malaysia and Indonesia) from 1854 to 1862, where from Borneo in 1855 he wrote the essay 'On the Law which has Regulated the Introduction of New Species' – it was published in *Annals of Natural History* later that year. In 1858 he wrote 'On the Tendencies of Varieties to Depart Indefinitely from the Original type' concepts, which prompted Darwin to publish 'On the Origin of Species' the following year.

HANS WEIDITZ
(Germany, 1495–c.1537)

The son of a Strasbourg sculptor, the Renaissance artist Hans Weiditz spent his career largely in Augsburg and Strasbourg producing illustrations for books, and is known as the Petrarch Master for the caricatures of everyday life he produced to accompany Petrarch's maxims. Weiditz revolutionized botanical illustration with his woodcuts for *Herbarum vivae eicones* by Otto Brunfels, employing a far higher degree of realism than comparable works.

FURTHER READING

Wilfrid Blunt and William T. Stern
The Art of Botanical Illustration. London: Collins, 2015

Helen Bynum and William Bynum
Remarkable Plants That Shape Our World. London:
Thames & Hudson, 2014

Roderick Cave
Impressions of Nature: A History of Nature Printing. London
and New York: The British Library and Mark Batty, 2010

Brent Elliott and Simon Hornby
Flora: An Illustrated History of the Garden Flower. London:
Scriptum Editions/RHS, 2001

William A. Ewing
Flora Photographica: Masterpieces of Flower Photography.
London: Thames & Hudson, 1991

Celia Fisher
The Golden Age of Flowers. London: The British Library, 2011

Celia Fisher
The Medieval Flower Book. London: The British Library, 2007

Susan M. Fraser and Vanessa Bezemer Sellers (eds.)
*Flora Illustrata: Great Works from the LuEsther T. Mertz
Library of the New York Botanical Garden.* New York: The
New York Botanical Garden and Yale University Press, 2014

Carolyn Fry and Kathy Willis
Plants: From Roots to Riches. London: John Murray Press, 2015

Geoff Hodge
*RHS Botany for Gardeners: The Art and Science of Gardening
Explained & Explored.* London: Mitchell Beazley, 2013

Paul Hulton and Lawrence Smith
Flowers in Art from East to West. London: British Museum
Publications, 1979

Sandra Knapp
Flora: An Artistic Voyage Through the World of Plants.
London: Scriptum Editions/Natural History Museum,
2003

John W. Kress and Shirley Sherwood
The Art of Plant Evolution. London: Royal Botanic Gardens,
Kew, 2009

Laird, Mark
A *Natural History of English Gardening.* New Haven
and London: Yale University Press, 2015

Michael Largo
*The Big, Bad Book of Botany: The World's Most
Fascinating Flora.* New York: William Morrow, 2014

Judith Magee
Chinese Art and the Reeves Collection. London: Natural
History Museum, 2011

Hans Walter Lack
*The Bauers Joseph, Franz & Ferdinand: An Illustrated
Biography.* London: Prestel, 2015

Martyn Rix
The Golden Age of Botanical Art. London: Andre Deutsch,
2012

Martyn Rix and Shirley Sherwood
Treasures of Botanical Art. London: Royal Botanic Gardens,
Kew, 2008

Sacheverell Sitwell
Great Flower Books 1700–1900. London: H. F. & G. Witherby,
1990

Shirley Sherwood
A New Flowering: 1000 Years of Botanical Art. Oxford:
Ashmolean Museum, 2005

ACKNOWLEDGEMENTS

PUBLISHER'S ACKNOWLEDGEMENTS

A project of this size requires the commitment, advice and expertise of many people. We are particularly indebted to our consultant editor Dr James Compton for his vital contribution to the shaping of this book and his exhaustive botanical knowledge.

Special thanks are also due to our international advisory panel for their knowledge, passion and advice in the selection of works of art for inclusion: Rosie Atkins, Gillian Barlow, Brent Elliott, Celia Fisher, Patrica Jonas, Rob Kesseler, Hans Walter Lack, Gren Lucas, Henry Noltie, Mikinori Ogisu, Pia Östlund, Lynn Parker, Martyn Rix, Charlotte Tancin, Alice Tangerini and Anita Walsmit Sachs.

We are also grateful to Sarah Bell and Jenny Faithfull for their tenacious picture research, and to Tim Cooke, Daniel Goode, Rosie Lewis, Gillian Northcott Liles, Matilda Slight and Tjoa Shze Hui for their invaluable editorial assistance.

Finally we would like to thank all the artists, illustrators, collectors, libraries and museums who have given us permission to include their images.

TEXT CREDITS

The publisher is grateful to the following writers for their texts:

Rosie Atkins: 21, 50, 96, 114, 118, 227, 230, 236, 294, 317; **Helen Bynum**: 16, 67, 133, 182, 265; **Ruth Chivers**: 47, 49, 65, 79, 83, 143, 105, 189, 213, 217, 122, 231, 254, 255, 275, 284, 296, 301, 306, 307, 323, 225; **James Compton**: 24, 25, 26, 35, 36, 48, 52, 54, 55, 58, 62, 66, 70, 76, 77, 85, 92, 94, 107, 110, 116, 127, 128, 140, 144, 145, 153, 164, 169, 170, 171, 175, 181, 188, 190, 191, 196, 207, 216, 221, 234, 237, 240, 248, 250, 256, 267, 272, 273, 283, 285, 286, 287, 292, 295, 298, 312, 314; **Tim Cooke**: 23, 27, 33, 39, 42, 53, 61, 69, 72, 100, 113, 115, 117, 123, 129, 130, 139, 141, 142, 148, 159, 167, 177, 193, 197, 198, 204, 218, 229, 235, 241, 260, 279, 289, 309, 321, 325; **Brent Elliott**: 12, 13, 29, 32, 37, 90, 99, 119, 160, 172, 173, 183, 186, 187, 202, 214, 246, 258, 259, 277, 322; **Celia Fisher**: 20, 46, 80, 104, 132, 151, 152, 157, 166, 180, 206, 226, 264, 288, 297; **Carolyn Fry**: 30, 38, 45, 162, 163, 179, 205, 224; **Patricia Jonas**: 17, 43, 73, 88, 93, 195, 233, 245, 271, 278, 311; **Rob Kesseler**: 11, 215, 223, 320; **Hans Walter Lack**: 10, 14, 15, 34, 78, 101, 106, 126, 146, 158, 165, 194, 232, 242, 261, 263; **Paula McWaters**: 125, 293, 305, 319; **Pia Östlund**: 121, 150, 290; **Lynn Parker**: 31, 41, 149, 276; **Martyn Rix**: 18, 82, 86, 97, 108, 154, 211, 253, 280, 300; **Julian Shaw**: 40, 60, 91, 124, 137, 147, 161, 282, 316; **Charlotte Tancin**: 28, 44, 63, 64, 68, 95, 134, 136, 138, 156, 174, 185, 200, 228, 212, 247, 268, 269, 302, 308, 313; **Alice Tangerini**, Smithsonian Institution: 131, 244, 281; **Guy Tindale**: 51, 57, 89, 201, 209, 243; **Jacek Wajer**: 56, 257 and **Martin Walters**: 19, 59, 71, 74, 75, 81, 84, 87, 98, 103, 109, 111, 112, 120, 135, 155, 168, 176, 178, 184, 192, 199, 203, 208, 210, 219, 222, 238, 239, 249, 266, 270, 274, 299, 303, 304, 310, 315, 318.

PICTURE CREDITS

Every reasonable effort has been made to identify owners of copyright. Errors and omissions will be corrected in subsequent editions.

DEA / CHOMON / agefotostock: 106; akg-images / De Agostini Picture Lib. / G. Nimatallah: 186, 326ll, akg-images/Gilles Mermet: 114, akg-images/The British Library: 80, 327l; bilwissedition Ltd & Co. KG / Alamy Stock Photo: 86, 336cl, © Chronicle / Alamy Stock Photo: 94, 331l, © Fine Art / Alamy Stock Photo: 12, 333cr, © imageBROKER / Alamy Stock Photo: 102–103; The Baltimore Museum of Art: Thomas E. Benesch Memorial Collection, BMA 1970.4.20: 209; Bobbi Angell, Marlboro, VT: 73; The Antiquarian Antique Print and Map Gallery, Houston, Texas: 62; Image courtesy of Antiquariat Reinhold Berg eK: 104; The Archives of Rudolf and Leopold Blaschka and the Ware Collection of Blaschka Glass Models of Plants: 285, 333c; The Art Archive / Eileen Tweedy: 10, 331cl, The Art Archive / Kharbine Tapabour / Collection Grob: 64, 330l; © Castello del Buonconsiglio, Trento, Italy / The Art Archive /DeA Picture Library: 46; Alberto Baraya & Galeria Nara Roseler, São Paulo: 243; Photograph by Ian Bavington-Jones: 127, 128. 318, 334r; General Collection, Beinecke Rare Book and Manuscript Library, Yale University: 151; Zadok Ben David: 324–325, 335cr; Biblioteca Nazionale Napoli: 261; Biblioteca Real Jardín Botánico, CSIC, Madrid: 68, 121, 134, 165, 242, 328cl, 330r; Bibliothèque nationale de France: 218, 272; Images courtesy Blain Southern / Mat Collishaw: 235; © BM Archives: 76; Biodiversity Heritage Library: 56, 204; The Bodleian Library, MS. Ashmole 1461 (69r): 264, 328c; Bodleian Libraries, Shelfmark: MS. Ashmole 1431: 132; bpk / Staatliche Kunstsammlungen Dresden / Herbert Boswank: 126; Bridgeman Images: 265, British Library, London, UK / © British Library Board. All Rights Reserved / Bridgeman Images: 157, Photo © Christie's Images / Bridgeman Images: 66, 222, 228, 328r, Hamburger Kunsthalle, Hamburg, Germany / Bridgeman Images: 37, Minneapolis Institute of Arts, MN, USA / Gift of Mrs Carl W. Jones in Memory of Her Husband / Bridgeman Images: 120, Minneapolis Institute of Arts, MN, USA / The Ethel Morrison Van Derlip Fund / Bridgeman Images: 170, Museum of Fine Arts, Boston, Massachusetts, USA / Bridgeman Images: 310, Museum of Fine Arts, Boston, Massachusetts, USA / Bequest of the Estate of George P. Dike / Elita R. Dike Collection / Bridgeman Images: 188, Museum of New Zealand Te Papa Tongarewa, Wellington, New Zealand / Gift of Rex Nan Kivell, 1951 / Bridgeman Images: 50, 334l, National Geographic Creative / Bridgeman Images: 13, Natural History Museum, London, UK / Bridgeman Images: 206, 295, 333fl, Private Collection / Bridgeman Images: 85, Private Collection / Prismatic Images / Bridgeman Images: 210, Royal Collection Trust © Her Majesty Queen Elizabeth II, 2016 / Bridgeman Images: 223, 303, 329l, Société Nationale d'Horticulture, Paris, France / Archives Charmet / Bridgeman Images: 107, 332cr, Victoria and Albert Museum, London, UK / Bridgeman Images: 298, Werner Forman Archive / Bridgeman Images: 45, 326cl; © The Trustees of the British Museum: 36, 92; Courtesy of Brooklyn Botanic Garden: 88; Plate 6 from The Highgrove Florilegium. Magnolia Sieboldii painted by Mayumi Hashi. © A. G. Carrick 2008: 199; Alice Cazenave, Photographer in Alternative Processes: 259; Courtesy of the Artist and Chambers Fine Art: 89; Courtesy Cheim & Read, New York: 129; Photograph courtesy Robert Clark: 59; Image courtesy Hannah Collins: 177; © W. T. Cooper from Fruits of the Australian Tropical Rainforest, 2005: 217; © Lisa Creagh, 2016: 185; © 1925, 2016 Imogen Cunningham Trust: 198; Curtis Botanical Magazine/ Martyn Rix: 305; Courtesy of M. Reza Dadpour: 255; Courtesy of Regula Dettwiler: 231; herman de vries, Eschenau: 307; © Monika E de Vries Gohlke: 93; © Dumbarton Oaks Research Library and Collection, Rare Book Collection, Washington, D.C.: 124; © Jean Emmons 125; M. C. Escher's "Flowers" © 2016 The M. C. Escher Company-The Netherlands. All rights reserved. www.mcescher.com: 148; By Courtesy of Claudia Fährenkemper: 53; Courtesy Frantic Gallery: 11; Image courtesy Frederick Warne & Co. & The Victoria and Albert Museum. Reproduced by kind permission of Frederick Warne & Co.: 74; © Inez and Vinoodh. Courtesy Gagosian Gallery: 141; Image courtesy of the artist and Gagosian Gallery, © DACS 2016: 19; George Eastman Museum, Bequest of Edward Steichen under the direction of Joanna T. Steichen 1979.2474.0002 / © The Estate of Edward Steichen / ARS, NY and DACS, London, 2016: 105; Courtesy George Glazer Gallery, New York: 273, 314; Cultura RM Exclusive/Albert Lleal Moya/Getty Images: 119, DEA / G. Dagli Orti / Getty Images: 315, Photo by Florilegius/SSPL/Getty Images: 55, Science & Society Picture Library / Getty Images: 221, 332l; The J. Paul Getty Museum, Los Angeles: 101, 328l; Ghent University Library, BHSL. HS.0092: 20, 326r; Spiros Hadjidjanos/Private Collection: 321; Agathe Haevermans: 275; Alexander Hamilton: 139; Lightweeds, Location sensitive light projection, Simon Heijdens 2005: 225; By Courtesy of Asuka Hishiki: 43; Copyright © 2013 O. Holovachov (www.holovachov.com): 167; MS Am 1118.111. Houghton Library, Harvard University: 115; Louisa Howard, Dartmouth College Electron Microscope Facility: 161; Huang Xu: 173; Courtesy Hunt Institute for Botanical Documentation, Carnegie Mellon University, Pittsburgh, PA: 317; Mieko Konishi. Courtesy Hunt Institute for Botanical Documentation, Carnegie Mellon University, Pittsburgh, PA: 135; © The Hunterian, University of Glasgow 2016: 208; Single Oriental Poppy ©, New York, 1968. © The Irving Penn Foundation: 201; © Mieko Ishikawa 131; Courtesy of the Artist and Jablonka Maruani Mercier Gallery: 65; Collection Jonathan Cooper Gallery, Image Scanned by Giclée UK Ltd: 249; Joseph Bellows Gallery: 258; Collection of Rob Kesseler: 247; © Christabel King: 108, 335cl; Ted Kinsman / Science Source: 323; Albrecht Dürer Blau blühende Schwertlilie – Iris Germanica, 1501–1505, Inv.-No. 1851-25. Kunsthalle Bremen - Der Kunstverein in Bremen Department of Prints and Drawings. Photo: Lars Lohrisch: 263, 327r; Courtesy KUSAMA Enterprise, Ota Fine Arts, Tokyo / Singapore and Victoria Miro, London. © Yayoi Kusama: 33; Aude Le Barbey: 239; © Lee Kwang Ho / Johyun Gallery: 57; Photo Les Arts Décoratifs, Paris / Jean Tholance. All Rights Reserved: 230; Library of Congress: 150, 219, 327cl; Courtesy, The Lilly Library, Indiana University, Bloomington, Indiana: 52; © The Linnaean Collection of The Linnaean Society of London, www.linnaean.org: 140; The LuEsther T. Mertz Library of The New York Botanical Garden: 187, 294; Margaret Stones, Flora of Louisiana: Watercolor Drawings, E. A. McIlhenny Collection, LSU Libraries, Baton Rouge, LA: 97; © Werner Bischof/Magnum Photos: 246; Katinka Matson: 197; © Masumi Yamanaka: 293; Copyright The Estate of Rory McEwen all rights reserved: 271, 334cr; Gift of George E. Schoellkopf, 2013, © 2000–2016 The Metropolitan Museum of Art. All rights reserved.: 69; © Steven N. Meyers: 49; © Garry Fabian Miller / Courtesy HackelBury Fine Art: 122; Courtesy of Missouri Botanical Garden, St Louis, USA: 292, 313, 329cr; Monash University Collection. Donated by the Botany Department, Monash University 1989. Copyright Monash University. Image courtesy of Monash University Museum of Art: 281; Scott A. Mori: 169; Collection Muséum d'Histoire Naturelle de Grenoble: 234; Nationaal Archief/Spaarnestad Collection/ Leendert Blok: 172; Courtesy the National Diet Library, Japan: 32, 84; The Collection of National Palace Museum: 196, 260; Naturalis Biodiversity Center, Leiden: 63; NATURE – Eucalyptus © 1997 Jean-Baptiste Huynh: 99; From The New York Public Library: 110; Nezu Museum, Tokyo: 296, 329r; © Nobuyoshi Araki / Courtesy of Taka Ishii Gallery, Tokyo: 289; ÖNB, Vienna, Cod. med.gr.1, fol.83: 146, 326cr; Reproduced by permission of the Osler Library of the History of Medicine, McGill University: 269; Pia Östlund: 21; Panteek Antique Prints: 144, 192, 283; Courtesy of Heiti Paves: 205; By Courtesy of Rachel Pedder-Smith: 252–253; Peter H. Raven Library / Missouri Botanical Garden: 25, 40, 136, 155, 202, 257, 300, 302, 308, 322; Private Collection: 195; public domain / British Library: 262; © RHS, Lindley Library: 29, 75, 118, 227, 256, 286, 287, 330c; Hideo Horikoshi / RHS, Lindley Library: 203; Photo © Centre Pompidou, MNAM-CCI, Dist. RMN-Grand Palais / Adam Rzepka 183, Photo © Centre Pompidou, MNAM-CCI, Dist. RMN-Grand Palais / Adam Rzepka. © Estate Brassaï – RMN-Grand Palais: 113, Photo © Muséum national d'Histoire naturelle, Dist. RMN-Grand Palais / image du MNHN, bibliothèque central: 116, 171, Photo © RMN-Grand Palais (Institut de France) / Gérard Blot: 284, 316; Calla Lily, 1988. © Robert Mapplethorpe Foundation. Used by permission.: 270; Reproduced from the Collections of the Royal Botanic Garden, Edinburgh: 18, 191, 251; © The Board of Trustees - Royal Botanic Gardens: 16, 31, 41, 58, 78, 149, 154, 168, 175, 178, 182, 232, 248, 267, 274, 276, 288, 332cl, 332c, 333l, 333cl, 334c; Royal Collection Trust/© Her Majesty Queen Elizabeth II 2016: 207; The Royal Library of Denmark and Copenhagen: 238, 330cl;